On the Outside Looking Out

# On the Outside Looking Out

*John Ashbery's Poetry*

John Shoptaw

Harvard University Press
Cambridge, Massachusetts
London, England
1994

Copyright © 1994 by the President and Fellows of Harvard College
All rights reserved
Printed in the United States of America

*Library of Congress Cataloging-in-Publication Data*
Shoptaw, John, date.
On the outside looking out: John Ashbery's poetry / John Shoptaw.
p.   cm.
Includes index.
ISBN 0-674-63612-0 (cloth). — ISBN 0-674-63613-9 (paper)
1. Ashbery, John—Criticism and interpretation. I. Title.
PS3501.S475Z86 1994
811'.54—dc20
94-25956
CIP

# Acknowledgments

I could have gone on indefinitely perhaps, but I never could have finished without a lot of help. I am grateful first of all to Helen Vendler, who generously and consistently encouraged my efforts. At an early stage, Joel Porte and Barbara Johnson contributed their suggestions and enthusiasm. Over the years my many students of contemporary poetry, in particular Jane Avrich, Steve Monte, Kathryn Koo, Eric Marler, and Andrew Foote, have delighted and challenged me with their conversation and their readings. Charles Bernstein, Stephen Yenser, Stephen Fredman, Marjorie Perloff, and Ellen Oliensis read the manuscript and carried me onward with their valuable comments and encouragement. At Harvard University Press, Margaretta Fulton kept the end in view and made me believe I could reach it, and Anita Safran read and edited the manuscript with scrupulous intelligence.

I am particularly indebted to John Ashbery, who gave me access to his unpublished papers, patiently answered innumerable questions over the years, and read and checked the accuracy of the manuscript; the interpretations here are mine, not his, but they wouldn't have been the same without his generous assistance. At Houghton Library, Rodney Dennis and Elizabeth Falsey very kindly gave me access to Ashbery's uncatalogued papers, and Bonnie Salt let me rummage around in the boxes for missing links; the present Curator of Manuscripts, Leslie A. Morris, granted me permission to quote from and reproduce Ashbery's unpublished material. Facsimiles are reproduced by permission of the Houghton Library, Harvard University.

An early version of Chapter 2 appeared in *Verse* 8.1, guest-edited by Susan M. Schultz; of Chapter 11 in *Temblor* 7, edited by Leland Hickman; and of Chapter 12 in *New American Writing* 10, edited by Maxine Chernoff and Paul Hoover.

# Contents

On the Outside Looking Out

# Abbreviations

# Introduction: Ashbery's Misrepresentative Poetics

In a 1982 interview John Ashbery offered this statement of poetics by way of advice: "you should try to make your poem as representative as possible."[1] "Representative" here is implicitly opposed to "personal." In another interview Ashbery cautioned against looking for the "personal core" of his poems: "These are not autobiographical poems, they're not confessional poems. . . . What I am trying to get at is a general, all-purpose experience—like those stretch socks that fit all sizes."[2] This "all-purpose" poetic representativeness is akin to political representation in which a candidate is selected to fill a position, stand for a segment of society, and represent its interests.[3] For writers in the United States, at least since Ralph Waldo Emerson, the analogy of political with poetic representation has been especially significant; as Walt Whitman famously asserted, "the United States themselves are essentially the greatest poem."[4] Ashbery associates his democratic representativeness with postmodern eclecticism: "My idea is to democratize all forms of expression, an idea which comes to me from afar, perhaps from Whitman's *Democratic Vistas*—the idea that both the most demotic and the most elegant forms of expression deserve equally to be taken into account. It seems to me that there is something of this in postmodernism."[5] All forms of expression are afforded equal access to Ashbery's representative chambers.

Ashbery has also likened his representative poetics to the abstract argumentation of music: "What I like about music is its ability of being convincing, of carrying an argument through successfully to the finish, though the terms of this argument remain unknown quantities. What remains is the structure, the architecture of the argument, scene or story. I would like to do this in poetry."[6] This indeterminate poetics echoes Wallace Stevens's hypothesis in "The Creations of Sound": "If the poetry of X was music," then "X" would equal anybody, "a different poet, / An accretion from ourselves."[7] Yet while Stevens's poetry tends to represent anybody's thoughts and feelings in an intoned, interior language, Ashbery's poetry renders anybody's expressions in what Stevens called their own "flawed words and stubborn sounds" (158). Ashbery's architectural argument recalls Cleanth Brooks's formulation in "The Heresy of Paraphrase": "The essential structure of a poem . . . resembles that of architecture or painting: it is a pattern of resolved stresses. Or, to move closer still . . . , [poetic structure] resembles that of a ballet or musical composition."[8] Ashbery's structural poetics may also be traced to France, where the word "structure" was buzzing in the late 1950s and early 1960s (Ashbery was living in Paris in 1958 when Claude Lévi-Strauss's *Structural Anthropology* appeared). While they cannot be resolved into stable unities or bipolar oppositions, Ashbery's poetic designs do not negate but misrepresent critical precepts.

As one of his representative American speakers puts it: "Heck, it's anybody's story" (W 16). But if Ashbery's poetry tells "anybody's story" in general, it sounds like nobody's story in particular: "This is / No one's story!" (W 34). Ashbery may represent life as strange or confusing or "difficult" as it seems to us during those times when we try to make sense of it, but no one else represents life the way he does. The thesis of this book is that Ashbery's poetry is not so much representative as "misrepresentative." We may think of an Ashbery poem as an assembly of unruly, irresponsible, factional, long-winded, strange, and outspoken members. Its particulars (details of time and place, objects, selected words) are often vague, unexpected, abstracted, conflicting, misplaced, or missing; its argument or narrative is insufficiently supported, inconsistent, incomplete, and fragmented; its discourses, genres, and forms are strangely mixed or misapplied; its grammar and syntax are twisted, disconnected, or elongated; and its autobiographical subject is withheld or covertly generalized, resulting in an abstract expressionism which unsettles and contorts all other subject matters by removing their frame of reference. While Ashbery's poetry is as representative and inclusive as Whitman's, it is also as misrepresentative, exclusive, and restrained as Emily Dickinson's. In her own statement of misrepresentative poetics, "Tell all the Truth but tell it slant— / Success in Circuit lies" (#1129),[9] Dickinson misrepresents the judicial oath to "tell the truth, the whole truth, and nothing but the truth," a distortion compounded by a pun on "lies," a variation on the idiom "to slant the truth," and even a circumferential play on "Circuit court." I mean misrepresentation as an alternative to various interpretative strategies that treat Ashbery's poetry as purely nonrepresentational, self-referential, nonsensical, parodic, or deconstructive.

Ashbery's poetry is all these things, but his misrepresentations do not as a consequence rule out meaning, expression, and representation; they renovate them.

Ashbery developed his misrepresentative poetics with the aid of the modernists. His earliest formulation of this poetics arose from his reading of W. H. Auden. In his 1949 undergraduate thesis at Harvard on the poet, he isolated Auden's "technique derived directly from the Icelandic poetry—that of giving one unusual and often uncharacteristic particular about an object, which, in a strange way, serves to characterize it."[10] He cited as illustration a choral speech from Auden's early play *Paid on Both Sides:* "The Spring unsettles sleeping partnerships, / Foundries improve their casting process, shops / Open a further wing on credit till / The Winter."[11] The young Ashbery was also fascinated by Auden's tendency to allegorize abstractions with wayward, overly specified particulars, a tendency he illustrated with a passage from "The Sea and the Mirror," in which Prospero tells Ariel that "historic deeds / Drop their hauteur and speak of shabby childhoods / When all they longed for was to join in the gang of doubts / Who so tormented them."[12] Thirty years later, Ashbery noted "a similar way of personifying and of making ideas concrete" in his own poetry, though he confessed that "not many people see this in my work and I don't think Auden did either."[13] In 1950, in his master's thesis at Columbia University on Henry Green, he remarked the British novelist's practice of rehiring the same cast of stock characters for each novel, an anti-psychological technique which reveals "his interest in milieus rather than in the individual characters who compose them." In Ashbery's structuralist view, Green's characters are determined by the relations in which they are involved (or from which they abstain). Ashbery connected Green's relational constructs with his having worked for several years in a factory as "a manufacturer in the literal sense of the word" before turning to literary fabrications.[14] A few years later, living in France, Ashbery was drawn to Gertrude Stein's narrative abstraction. In a 1957 review of her long poem *Stanzas in Meditation* he argued that "it is usually not events which interest Miss Stein, rather it is their 'way of happening', and the story of *Stanzas in Meditation* is a general, all-purpose model which each reader can adapt to fit his own set of particulars."[15] Like Stein, Ashbery is interested not in events "themselves" (a truly abstract concept) but in the way they happen to us, the way we experience them. By making his poetry the stream of everybody's or anybody's consciousness, he creates an all-purpose subjectivity which is neither egotistical nor solipsistic: "Most of my poems are about the experience of experience. . . . The particular occasion is of lesser interest to me than the way a happening or experience filters through to me. I believe this is the way in which it happens with most people. I'm trying to set down a generalized transcript of what's really going on in our minds all day long."[16]

This "generalized transcript" inevitably omits many particulars of the transcriber's own experience. Chief among Ashbery's misrepresentations is his avoidance of homosexuality as a subject matter; "I do not think of myself as a gay poet."[17] The word "homosexual" appears only once in his poetry, in the prose poem "Haibun": "I'm hoping that homosexuals not yet born get to inquire about it, inspect the whole random collection as though it were a sphere" (W 39). And although Ashbery, like Whitman before him, imagines homosexuals always among his readers, his poetry provides no secret passage to a coterie of gay readers who "catch" its specially encoded, hidden meaning. Frank O'Hara, for example, was as enthusiastically bewildered as straight readers by Ashbery's disjunctive serial poem "Europe." In making his poems "as representative as possible," Ashbery disorients all readers equally.

But although, or rather because, Ashbery leaves himself and his homosexuality out of his poetry, his poems misrepresent in a particular way which I will call "homotextual." Rather than simply hiding or revealing some homosexual content, these poems represent and "behave" differently, no matter what their subject. With their distortions, evasions, omissions, obscurities, and discontinuities, Ashbery's poems always have a homotextual dimension.[18] This homotextuality is historically conditioned. Ashbery's poetics evolved during the late 1940s and early 1950s, a particularly repressive and paranoid period of American history marked by the investigation and harassment of homosexuals and Communists by Senator McCarthy, the House Un-American Activities Committee, the FBI, the Selective Service System, and the police. In 1950, for example, a Senate Report declared "sexual perverts" a security risk, alleging their greater susceptibility to persuasion and blackmail by foreign agents. Like Communists and spies, homosexuals could pass undetected, and thereby threatened the moral fiber of the federal bureaucracy and the military.[19] The influence of the national paranoia on Ashbery's writing may be gauged from an unpublished notebook entry, dated June 15, 1947, under the heading of "Dreams": "I was at a meeting in what was apparently the living room of a certain brick house on Memorial Drive, Cambridge. It was run by the communists and apparently the meeting was about the [my math] professor. Someone was trying to win me over to the communist side, I being neutral. Suddenly policemen with machine guns entered, and I was looking at the front of a house. People in the house thrust long poles through the windows and with them lifted up a facsimile of the housefront against the house; as a protection, I guess. Machine guns were fired and the person who had been trying to win me over shouted 'Go

4

home!' I escaped through the French windows and ran over the bridge. . . . This dream was partly suggested by an article I had been reading on the beating of Jews by their fellow students in Roumania in 1938." The homotext of this interpretative transcript is clearly legible: the sudden intrusion of police on a private meeting, the association of the situation of Jews and Communists with the dreamer's, the further association of the violent police with "fellow students," the protection offered by the misrepresentative façade or "facsimile," and even the escape through "French windows" (Ashbery "escaped" through French surrealism and, in 1955, to France itself, where he would live for a decade). For the time being, the best escape seemed a false front. In a 1976 interview, Ashbery recalled that "in the early 50's, I went through a period of intense depression and doubt. I couldn't write for a couple of years. I don't know why. It did coincide with the beginnings of the Korean War, the Rosenberg case and McCarthyism. Though I was not an intensely political person, it was impossible to be happy in that kind of climate. It was a nadir."[20] Ashbery himself was exempted from service in the Korean War only after he went on government record as a homosexual. The consequences of this act in a time of what Ashbery called "anti-homosexual campaigns" were uncertain: "Of course this was recorded and I was afraid that we'd all be sent to concentration camps if McCarthy had his own way. It was a very dangerous and scary period."[21] During these volatile years, misrepresentation was not only an aesthetic principle but a survival tactic.

Ashbery's poems behave privately in publication, mounting their own form of "Token Resistance" (ATS 3) to mainstream culture. Though his poetry is not often political in the sense of taking up controversial public subjects or sides, it nevertheless takes a homotextual stand: "My politics shouldn't matter," as he puts it in *Flow Chart*. "It's my finger / that should— it's here I'll take my stand" (FC 155). Ashbery's evasive maneuvers against the enemy within are evident in "A Boy," a tense encounter in which both patriarchal and national pressures are deflected. Written in 1952 or 1953 after Ashbery first saw John Huston's *The Red Badge of Courage,* "A Boy" opens with a supple son seeming to comply with his father's wishes, while noting that "the tide pushes an awful lot of monsters / And I think it's my true fate" (ST 20).[22] By the poem's end, the father demands from his deserting son not only obedience but a confession: "*My boy.* Isn't there something I asked you once? / What happened?" (ST 20). "A Boy" finally raises the white badge of cowardice: "They're throwing up behind the lines. / Dry fields of lightning rise to receive / The observer, the mincing flag. *An unendurable age*" (ST 21). The author behind these strange lines never completely surrenders them to understanding.

One of the most important misrepresentative features of Ashbery's poetry is illustrated by the homophonic, homophobic stereotype audible in the last line of "A Boy," beneath the surreal "mincing flag": "mincing fag." Ashbery has called attention to this technique of sonic revision. When asked about "marginal places" in his poems, he provided a verbal instance: "I just wrote a poem this morning in which I used the word 'borders' but changed it to 'boarders.' The original word literally had a marginal existence and isn't spoken, is perhaps what you might call a crypt word."[23] Building on Ashbery's nonce word, I will use the terms "crypt word" and "crypt phrase" for words displaced by, but still recoverable in, the final poetic text, "marker" for the resulting misrepresentation, and "cryptography" for the process itself. I mean the term "crypt word" to suggest both a puzzle, something encoded, and a burial plot, something hidden, forgotten, or simply covered over. Neither wholly in nor out of the poem, neither purely signifiers nor signifieds, neither vehicles nor tenors, neither poetic phrases nor paraphrases, crypt words break down trade barriers in Ashbery's lyric economy. Cryptography is the missing center of his method of composition: "I always begin at zero and discover my thought by writing. Words, pieces of phrases suddenly take on an interest which they didn't have before. I link these fragments without regard to construction, and finally, I throw out the elements which got me under way."[24] The residual power of these rejected fragments is acknowledged in "The System": "the word that everything hinged on is buried back there. . . . It is doing the organizing, the guidelines radiate from its control" (TP 95).

The revision of "boarders" for "borders" occurs in an unpublished poem, "Games in the Sun" (dated July 22, 1981). The poem itself concerns cryptic agency (cancellations are struck through, and handwritten revisions are italicized):

The cryptogram forgotten, somehow,
In some unspeakable way
Under the spray of bachelor's buttons.
~~It~~ Looks very much like the day
We came, and had to leave.
Now, there are only overnight voyages--
Long ones--and we shall all be
Seeing *now* the end of so many things
It feels like life on an exalted plane
Because that's what it is.

No need to interrogate
Anything—
The ~~borders~~ *boarders* have taken care of that.
And life is soft, exudes a sweet juice
In time that lingers.

The poem begins by visiting the site of what Ashbery would later call "Forgotten Sex" (AG 17). The opening spermal spray germinates into bachelor's buttons, which exude a "sweet juice" or essence "that lingers" in the memory well beyond the act itself. This cryptographic process is "unspeakable," both indescribable and "objectionable," like the initial act. The cryptic revision of "borders" to "boarders" changes scenes from an "exalted plane" (also a stygian "airplane" taking its "boarders" on "overnight voyages" across "borders") to the sweeter hereafter of a great good place where one's encrypted, unspoken wishes are granted. National, behavioral "borders," with their guarded interrogations, have been erased, though the Dickinsonian dashes mark their disappearance.

In fact, Ashbery rarely revises by crypt words on paper; his few penned revisions are usually synonyms or paraphrases. It is impossible and unnecessary to determine whether, or in what way (soon forgotten, half noticed), these misrepresentations were (un)intended. Since cryptography is based on preexistent forms of spoken and written discourse, it is more accurate to say that ordinary language collaborates in their production. Nor is it either possible or particularly helpful to give a detailed taxonomy of crypt words; their forms are delightfully unpredictable. But a broad survey does reveal a few basic cryptographic practices. In general, Ashbery's lyric markers are the products of sonic, visual, or associational misrepresentation. Sometimes a strange marker will (distantly) echo a more familiar word or phrase (throughout this book I will suggest crypt words and phrases parenthetically): "it all came / gushing down on me" (FC 170; "crashing"); "the pen's screech" (FC 108; "scratch"); "emotions, / The crushed paper heaps" (TCO 32; "crushed hopes"); "your blurred version" (TP 36; "vision"). Sometimes a "blurred version" results from added, dropped, or substituted letters: "signs of metal fatigue" (FC 199; "mental"); "screwed into palace" (TCO 39; "into place"); "Time stepped" (TCO 66; "stopped"); "heart bees" (TCO 88; "beats"); "long piers of silence" (RM 16; "periods"). At other times the marker is generated by a process of association: "behind in my solicitations" (FC 176; "payments"); "blown out of context" (FC 157; "taken out of context," "blown out of proportion"); "But if breath could kill" (DDS 33; "looks"); "a creator returned to the desolate / Scene of this first experiment" (DDS 37; "return to the scene of the crime"); "make this / Jungle and call it space" (SP 10; "make a house a home," "it's not much, but I call it home," "it's a jungle out there"). And sometimes sonic, literal, and associational modes of cryptography appear in combination: "the time-inflicted lesions of the old" (TP 9; "time-honored lessons"); "The lace / Of spoken breathing" (HBD 37; "loss of breath"); "and the future is our table and chairs" (AWK 97; "the future is ours," "furniture"); "A free / Bride on the rails" (HBD 13; "a free ride," "ride the rails"); "His head / Locked into mine" (HBD 45; "his eyes looked into mine"). It is significant that in the last example, as opposed to the cryptographic pair "mincing flag" and "mincing fag," the "strange" (homo)erotic locution displaces its "expected" romantic version. Cryptography cannot simply be equated with concealment; crypt words are paradoxically situated on the outside looking out.

Some crypt words exert their radial influence without specific markers or syntactical locations, as at the end of "More Pleasant Adventures":

In the rash of partings and dyings (the new twist),
There's also room for breaking out of living.
Whatever happens will be quite ingenious.
No acre but will resume being disputed now,
And paintings are one thing we never seem to run out of.
(W 16)

The first four lines of this stanza illustrate various senses of the unheard but exemplary crypt word "plot"—a plot twist, a grave plot, an intrigue, and a plot of land. Like a canvas with borders "we never seem to run out of," the missing word "breaks out in a rash" (an audible crypt phrase) of significations. Yet "plot" doesn't appear in the original typescript, and Ashbery, who had no recollection of this buried word, exclaimed "that's quite ingenious" when I first showed it to him.[25] Perhaps his phrase "the new twist," as in "he gave the old plot a new twist," kept "plot" on the tip of his pen. But however it happened, the final stanza organizes itself around the unwritten word.

One of the unacknowledged precursors of Ashbery's cryptography is the French poet and novelist Raymond Roussel. Ashbery first read the work of this eccentric, secretly homosexual millionaire in 1951, when Kenneth Koch returned from France with a copy of Roussel's *La Vue*. Ashbery himself went to France in 1955 on a Fulbright Fellowship, with the intention (soon abandoned) of writing a doctoral thesis on Roussel. In a 1961 essay, he described Roussel's surreal cryptography: "Sometimes he would take a phrase containing two words, each of which had a double meaning, and use the least likely meanings as the basis of a story. Thus the phrase *maison à espagno-lettes* ('house with window latches') served as the basis for an episode in *Impressions d'Afrique* about a house (a royal family or house) descended from a pair of Spanish twin girls. Elsewhere, he would transform a common phrase, a book title or a line of poetry into a series of words with similar sounds. A line of Victor Hugo [from 'Napoléon II'], '*Un vase tout rempli du vin de l'espérance*' was denatured by Roussel into '*sept houx rampe lit Vesper,*' which he developed into a tale of Handel using seven bunches of holly tied with different colored ribbons to compose, on a banister, the principal theme of his oratorio *Vesper.*"[26] For Ashbery, the resultant puzzling narrative is tantalizingly instructive, operating "like a Chinese box that one turns over and over, certain that there is a concealed spring somewhere, that in a moment the lid will fly open, revealing possibly nothing more than its own emptiness, but proving that reality is only a false bottom."[27] Michel Foucault, whom Ashbery once met in France in the late fifties, was also fascinated by Roussel's cryptographic texts: "it is possible to discern, as if at the bottom of a pool, the white pebble of that similar though imperceptible sentence; but it is only a surface undulation, a legible echo, and from within its silence, since it is never uttered, it sets free the whole brilliant and vibrant surface of words."[28] Crypt words and phrases must be hidden for their misrepresentative power to be released.

I will illustrate the diversity of Ashbery's misrepresentations by considering two quite different works, first a translucent lyric, "At North Farm," and then a work primarily in experimental prose, *The Vermont Notebook.* The introductory poem of *A Wave,* "At North Farm" nicely illustrates Ashbery's all-purpose narration:

Somewhere someone is traveling furiously toward you,
At incredible speed, traveling day and night,
Through blizzards and desert heat, across torrents, through narrow passes.
But will he know where to find you,
Recognize you when he sees you,
Give you the thing he has for you?

Hardly anything grows here,
Yet the granaries are bursting with meal,
The sacks of meal piled to the rafters.
The streams run with sweetness, fattening fish;
Birds darken the sky. Is it enough
That the dish of milk is set out at night,

That we think of him sometimes,
Sometimes and always, with mixed feelings?
(W 1)

This lucid but indeterminate poem exemplifies what Marjorie Perloff has termed the "poetics of indeterminacy." The poem raises a host of questions: Who is traveling toward "you"? Does "you" mean "we" or Ashbery or someone else? Is it singular or plural, specific or general? Where is "Somewhere" and "here"? Is there an allegorical significance to the pastoral details? The poem doesn't provide us with enough consistent information to answer such basic reading questions. As Perloff says of "Rivers and Mountains," "The reader can invent any number of plots and locations that fit this 'all-purpose model.'"[29]

But although we cannot determine any single plot or subject for the poem, we can identify the representational, relational system which produced it, and through which its particulars circulate. This does not mean, however, that Ashbery is a systematic poet. In a 1977 interview Ashbery took pains to argue that there "is no systematic rationale or systematic anything in my poetry. If it is systematic, it's only in its total avoidance of any kind of system or program."[30] His Vietnam-era prose poem "The System" associates his anti-systematic method with the demise of the Establishment: "The system was breaking down" (TP 53). Yet for all Ashbery's resistance to self-conscious, systematic poetic production, it becomes increasingly apparent that his poems are kept afloat by the systems into which their sender unknowingly enters. He puts it paradoxically in his long poem "A Wave": "By so many systems / As we are involved in, by just so many / Are we set free on an ocean of language that comes to be / Part of us, as though we would ever get away" (W 71). In my discussions of Ashbery's poems, I locate their meaning in their mode of production. My readings are thus not "close" but textually specific. Rather than considering poems "as such," I examine how they misrepresent and reformulate the various systems of discourses, texts, and practices within which they are produced.

Ashbery's gradual realization of "At North Farm" is revealed in the typescript (see figure). Though the poem ends up as an unrhymed inverted sonnet, its twelve typewritten lines show that Ashbery didn't begin with this idea in mind (and may not have noticed it at all). Only after drafting the poem on the typewriter did he write in the title (while Ashbery often begins with a title, sometimes recycled from the titles of unpublished poems, he just as often ends with it, as though he discovered the subject of his poem by writing it). He also specified his core narrative of travel and delivery with a handwritten allusion in what is now the poem's third, long-distance line,

At North Farm

incredible

Somewhere someone is traveling furiously toward you,
At breakneck speed, traveling night and day,
But will he know where to find you,
Recognize you when he sees you,
Give you the thing he has for you?

But yet the granaries are bursting with meal,
The streams run with sweetness, fattening the fish,
Birds darken the sky. Is it enough
That the plate of milk is set out at night,
That we think of him sometimes, feeling
Sometimes and always, with mixed emotions?

dish

Through blizzards and desert heat, across torrents, through narrow passes

The sacks of meal piled to the rafters.

12/30/81

"At North Farm"

which misrepresents the postman's motto, translated from Herodotus (*Histories,* VIII, 98), and inscribed on the New York City Post Office: "Neither snow, nor rain, nor heat, nor gloom of night stays these couriers from the swift completion of their appointed rounds." The allusion differs significantly from those we might find in *The Waste Land* or *The Cantos.* It is typically Ashberian in that it refers us to our common knowledge and language: to understand the postman's motto, we need not know its origin in Herodotus, only its popularly recycled version, once on the lips of every American schoolchild. When his allusions are obscure, they tend to misrepresent familiar sources; our understanding of the title "On First Listening to Schreker's *Der Schatzgräber*" (ATS 58), for instance, depends not on our knowing this piece of music but on our hearing the distorted echo of Keats's "On First Looking into Chapman's Homer." The narrative system of "At North Farm," which I will call the postal or communications system, is common in Ashbery poems, especially those featuring the pronoun "you," the destination of four of the poem's first six lines. This relational network requires a messenger (who may also be the sender), a message, and a receiver.[31] The first stanza of "At North Farm" locates itself in the "Somewhere" of the approaching messenger, the second in the "here" of the waiting receiver. We can generate different readings of "At North Farm" depending on what details we select. Taking "you" as Ashbery's readers, and "we" as the autumnal, expectant poet waiting along with us, we may read the poem self-reflexively as the advent of a new poem or of *A Wave* itself. Or we may take "someone . . . traveling" at the speed of light to be God's "incredible" messenger, Christ (or Santa; the poem was written between Christmas and New Year's eve) with his gifts. Or "we may think of him" with "mixed feelings" as Death, whom we perhaps put off with an apotropaic "dish of milk." Or "he" may be a new or returning lover, drawn by the milk like a stray tomcat. Any of these readings is possible, yet none of them accounts for all the particulars in the poem. But if the details change at "incredible speed," the postal system keeps them in circulation.

Ashbery drew both the characteristic syntax and the title of "At North Farm" from *The Kalevala,* a collection of Finnish oral epic poems. Its varied repetitions—"But will he know where to find you, / Recognize you when he sees you," "Yet the granaries are bursting with meal, / The sacks of meal piled to the rafters"—are patterned on the paraphrastic parallelisms characteristic of the Finnish epic.[32] North Farm, as Ashbery has explained, is "a place referred to frequently in that poem, with the epithet 'gloomy and prosperous north farm.' . . . It's situated somewhere near hell."[33] The mainstay of the North Farm economy is a truly indispensable appliance known as the Sampo: "it ground a binful in the dawn,    one binful of things to eat; / it ground a second of things to sell,     a third of household supplies" (p. 60). Ashbery remarked that "the plenty alluded to" in his own poem "has an unnatural origin, some magical reason for being there, since it didn't grow there."[34] "At North Farm" is itself a Sampo, mashing the slack paraphrases of the oral epic and the courtly concision of the sonnet into a typically misrepresentative mixture of poetic kinds.

The mixture is homotextual. In *The Kalevala,* North Farm is the region where heroes travel in search of wives. Ashbery has described his messenger as "a lover, perhaps of a somewhat ominous kind that would remind one of mortality,"[35] thus locating himself, along with us, "here" at North Farm in the wife's receiving position. In this regard "At North Farm" recalls Auden's famous rendition of the Anglo-Saxon lyric "The Wanderer": "But ever that man goes / Through place-keepers, through forest trees, / A stranger to strangers over undried sea, / Houses for fishes, suffocating water" (EA 55). The similarities between the two poems are manifold (both employ the syntax of variant repetition, both adopt an Anglo-Saxon alliterative stress meter, both are well stocked with fish and restless birds), but "The Wanderer" resembles "At North Farm" most crucially in its homotextual displacements. Auden's poem plumbs the unfathomable destiny of sexual orientation, a "Doom . . . dark and deeper than any sea-dingle." In Auden's version, the wanderer, exiled from his wife, dreams of her "Waving from window, spread of welcome," and wakes among sea-birds and "new men making another love" (EA 55). But in the Old English poem, the wanderer's "wife" (never specified by Auden as "she") is his liege-lord, who inexplicably banished him to the wrenching frustration of his dream: "Often, when grief and sleep combined together enchain the wretched solitary man, it seems to him in his imagination that he is embracing and kissing his lord and laying hands and head on his knee. . . . Then the friendless man awakes again and sees before him tawny waves, sea-birds bathing, spreading their wings, rime falling and snow, mingled with hail."[36] As the paranoid exile of Ashbery's "Worsening Situation" confides: "My wife / Thinks I'm in Oslo—Oslo, France, that is" (SP 4). Like "Oslo" and "France," "I" and "my wife" intersect only in the poem. In an unpublished, untitled fragment beginning "Dame Shadows brought me a present," Ashbery considers his homotextual use of his second person: "Difficult to write this: you, of course, is not my wife—I have no wife: / It is a man, presently asleep, whom I have known for some time but not too well." Such moments of determinate attribution are rare in Ashbery's poetry, published or not; his second-person pronouns function most commonly as homotextual variables within his all-purpose systems.

Ashbery employs quite different forms of misrepresentation in one of his least discussed volumes, *The Vermont Notebook* (1975).[37] The title is itself misrepresentative: Ashbery recalls that he wrote the book largely "on buses traveling through New England, though not Vermont. . . . Generally speaking I guess it's a catalogue of a number of things that could be found in the state of Vermont, as well as almost everywhere else—another 'democratic vista.'" "It's a kind of messy grab bag as the word notebook implies,"[38] Ashbery said of his experiment in automated writing: "most of it was written on a bus, which I found to be an interesting experience. Writing on a moving vehicle. Not only did my mind move, the landscape was moving as well. A bus is not the most poetic place either, so this was an experiment in writing in an uninspiring environment." Vermont, however, is not one state among others but the Americanized green world of New England: "Vermont is quite different, for some reason, from the surrounding New England states. The minute you cross the arbitrary border into New Hampshire, it looks slightly scruffy. Vermont seems greener and lusher. But on the other hand, Vermont is full of things like carports and supermarkets and x-rated movie theatres and all the other things that exist everywhere else."[39] Like one of the lands in Elizabeth Bishop's "The Map," Ashbery's Vermont is colored differently from its neighbors. As a child, Ashbery went on a bus trip to Vermont with his maternal grandfather to look for ancestors of his mother's family.[40] But as Vermont has become Americanized, *The Vermont Notebook* contains little or nothing of local or autobiographical color.

With its rambling catalogues and its ungainly prose and verse, this wayside book is typically atypical of Ashbery's poetry. It was published by the relatively small Black Sparrow Press (with sprouting pages justified from the bottom margin rather than the top) the year that Viking Press brought out *Self-Portrait in a Convex Mirror*. In the title poem of that book, Ashbery writes that Parmigianino labored over his convex self-portrait "So as to perfect and rule out the extraneous / Forever" (SP 72); *The Vermont Notebook*, written after "Self-Portrait," looks like a wastebasket for all the extraneous poetic matter ruled out by its famed contemporary. As Ashbery noted, it "contains some passages of very experimental writing. It's one of the few things I've written that seems to have been influenced by Gertrude Stein."[41] Certain stretches of this book would indeed remind many readers of Stein's incremental repetitions:

> I tell the old story of the dump. I work on the story to be the real story of the dump which is never telling. If it ever was telling it would not be the dump which it is. The dump escapes the true scape of the telling and in so doing it is its own scape—the dump dumped and dumping. As I swear the dump is my sweet inner scape self so do I condone the dump for having

nothing left for me only the will to go on dumping creating it out of its evacuation. I will go to the dump. I am to be in the dump. I was permanently the dump and now the dump is me, but I will be permanently me when I am no longer the dump air. The dump air lasts. (VN 31)

With its repeated paralleling of "I" and "dump," this "inscape" (as coined and delineated in Gerard Manley Hopkins's own *Notebooks*) of a Stevensian man taking a dump on the dump is, after all, as faithful a snapshot of poetic "expression" as anything in "Self-Portrait in a Convex Mirror."[42]

Ashbery's waste heap begins simply enough, with twelve pages of catalogues that make and break their own rules of representation and sequence. Rather than composing a one-size-fits-all narrative as in "At North Farm," Ashbery here lets his catalogues combine to represent one class after another, often switching their affiliation in mid-sentence: "Front porches, back porches, side porches, door jambs, window sills, lintels, cornices, gambrel roofs, dormers, front steps, clapboards, trees, magnolia, scenery, McDonald's, Carrol's, Kinney Shoe Stores" (VN 25). What ties this list together and justifies its isolation on a page of Ashbery's book? All these items might loosely represent wooden things, but the membership rules keep changing. At first the choices seem motivated as much by sonic resonance (varying "or") as by the nostalgic enumeration of a class (porches, house borders). The next three items, "trees, magnolia, scenery," hardly equivalent members, at best denominate three ways of indicating the view outside. And the final three names of store (not associative) chains represent the (last and first) names of people who may not exist anymore or anywhere, but who nevertheless want us to "pay a visit." This word-string, then, not only itemizes the standard American small town but capitalizes on nostalgic associations with the "country," where everybody knows everybody's name.

Ashbery's assemblage bears comparison with Whitman's catalogues in "Song of the Broad-Axe," a hymn to manual labor containing the following list of everyday, broad-axed products: "Citadel, ceiling, saloon, academy, organ, exhibition-house, library, / Cornice, trellis, pilaster, balcony, window, turret, porch" (338). The first ill-assorted collection interposes a house part and a musical instrument among buildings, lowers the class of "Citadel" by adding on an unvaulted "ceiling," and places "academy" suspiciously near "saloon." The second catalogue, from which Ashbery seems to have ordered, stretches the definition of architectural ornaments to include "porch," and arranges its sequence more by sound than sense. But unlike Ashbery, Whitman does not question the discursive implications of his catalogues; in "Song of the Broad-Axe," for instance, he sings inadvertently not only labor but advertisement. Ashbery's catalogues disturb not only logical and capitalist but political and legal representation, as in the following list of charges:

> Murder, incest, arson, rape, grand larceny, extortion, forgery, impersonating an officer, resisting arrest, loitering, soliciting, possession of a controlled substance, drunken driving, reckless endangerment, slander, mental cruelty, non-assistance of person in danger, perjury, embezzlement, sodomy, child abuse, cruelty to animals, bootlegging, adultery, bigamy, bearing false witness. (VN 17)

The letter of the law (civil or criminal, felony or misdemeanor) gets fuzzier and its repressive spirit gets clearer as the list progresses. The charge of "sodomy," followed by "child abuse, cruelty to animals," is aimed against under-represented members of society ruled by a legal and political system which places all of these "unnatural practices" in the same "class."

As particulars (mis)represent their classes, so discourses—oral and written language games—register social spheres and situations. Fragments of discourse not only imitate but participate in what they represent, so that the resultant poem is, as Stevens puts it, "Part of the res itself and not about it" (338; cf. "res publica"). *The Vermont Notebook* composts a variety of everyday American discourses: "We are glad that you could come. It is nice that you are here. We are glad to have you with us" (VN 37; a "neighborly," anonymous motel welcome); "This is where we are spending our vacation. A nice restful spot. Real camp life. Hope you are feeling fine" (VN 89; a capsule greeting, which Ashbery copied from a 1949 postcard signed "Em & Edythe"); "the large 'chain' stores with their big friendly ads and so-called 'discount' prices actually charge higher prices so as to force small competitors out of business" (VN 59; a "paranoid" conspiracy theory); "The perils of just aimlessly sitting. Of having continually to go out and fix something. These never endanger us, but they condition us more than we know" (VN 49; a journal reflection). In these samples Ashbery represents American talk and writing with an eerie lack of telltale exaggeration, so that his simulations become indistinguishable from actual American discourses and from his own poetry.

Indeed, sometimes these discursive samples are not simulations but extensive borrowings, cut out and pasted directly onto the democratic page. Near the end of *The Vermont Notebook*, five pages of seemingly parodic discourse, calmly inventorying ecological disasters, are taken verbatim from a newspaper article entitled "Fishing Improves At Marco": "At a location one mile off Marco, 57,000 old automobile tires have been wired together forming an underwater structure. At another location four and one-half miles into the Gulf, some 5,000 tons of construction debris has been piled along the bottom" (VN 81).[43] Ashbery also regularly recycles pieces of his own discarded poems in his published works. The last three pages of *The Vermont Notebook* (VN 97–101), for instance, are lifted from an unpublished, similarly titled poem, "American Notes," its unindented prose blocks now standing alone, one per page, as separate poems. *The Vermont Notebook* is composed almost entirely of assorted collections, but recollecting always involves misrepresenting. As Ashbery wonders in "American Notes," "Isn't it funny the way something can get crowded clean out of your memory, it seems completely new to you when you see it again, although some part of your mind does remember, though not in any clearcut way?" (VN 97). So too Ashbery's poems remember his dismembered leftovers. Each representative usage, idea, feeling, and observation in *The Vermont Notebook,* and in Ashbery's poetry in general, may strike us either as conventionally sincere or parodic. But his misrepresentative poetics cuts across theories of literary intention. Ashbery means always to write good poetry, and he "means" the final version of what he says by letting it stand. Nevertheless, the misrepresentative force of his revisions makes itself felt.

I have arranged my study of Ashbery's poetry chronologically and historically, devoting a chapter to each of his books. Such an organization enables me to trace the development of his poetry. I mean "development" here in a particular sense. The concept of development is often invoked to support evaluations of a poet's work. Thus, Ashbery's career could be described as a reconstruction, from the demolition of the line in *The Tennis Court Oath* to its mature restoration in *Self-Portrait in a Convex Mirror,* or, conversely, as a decline, a gradual capitulation, after an early experimental breakthrough, to academic tastes. While either developmental narrative may be adduced to evaluate one volume over another, neither has any objective validity. But the contrary thesis, that an author's works simply change—one after, but not because of, the other—suffers on its part from an ahistorical and unsubjective absoluteness. I contend that Ashbery does develop his poetry, in a nonlinear, musical fashion, by both consciously and unwittingly misrepresenting his previous work, making each book in some way a departure from the previous one and (by a progressive elimination) from all the others. As his authorial persona in *Flow Chart* laments, "one is doomed, / repeating oneself, never to repeat oneself" (FC 7). But because he tends not to want to leave anything behind, he incorporates earlier musical ideas into later works. Often this means exploring a minor theme, argument, or design sketched in an earlier work: the camp travelogue of "The Instruction

Manual" is elaborated, the possibilities of the manual more "developed," in the long poem "The Skaters," and the all-purpose autobiography of "The Picture of Little J.A." is expanded in *Flow Chart.* Such developments as these, not innately superior but inevitably more complicated, are what my book attempts to chart.

Ashbery professes almost a blind faith in his "destiny," a belief announced in the opening poem of his first book: "Destiny guides the water-pilot, and it is destiny" (ST 9). It seems strange that a poet of improvisation, collage, surrealism, and randomness would subscribe to such a notion, but Ashbery only follows his destiny to the extent that he doesn't know what he is doing. In the most important distinction forged in his poetic career, Ashbery chooses the "latent happiness" of unknown (and perhaps nonexistent) developments over the "frontal happiness" of the event itself: "this second kind of happiness is merely a fleshed-out, realized version of . . . the idealistic concept that got us started along this path" (TP 81). Ashbery's development, his career "path," is influenced by the reception of his poetry. In America's bicentennial year, *Self-Portrait in a Convex Mirror* garnered Ashbery the Pulitzer and other prizes, and converted him from a marginal to a central misrepresentative, "On the outside looking out" (W 13). In his later career, his evolving self-consciousness as a misrepresentative poet intensifies his revisionary impulse and heightens his sense of irresponsibility to the public expecting more "Ashbery" from Ashbery. In an interview published in the English journal *Poetry Review,* he remarked on the unrepresentative character of several representative poets, such as Leopardi, Plath, Lowell, and Ginsberg: "It's rather strange to me, the people who get taken up as spokespersons for everybody living at a certain time . . . . But it seems odd to me and something I wonder about a great deal: why is it that the average Joe when writing poetry doesn't really illuminate the experience of a number of readers the way a very odd, exceptional, damaged sensibility does?"[44] While there may be no such thing as an "average Joe" in or out of the poetry world, Ashbery's own friendly, inscrutable, incomplete silhouette takes its place as an indispensable misrepresentative of his times.

# 1

## "You All Now Know"

### *Some Trees*

*Some Trees* (1956) is as remarkable for what it excludes or slights as for what it represents. There is no detailed description of the natural world nor any identifiable scenes from contemporary life. Though most of the poems were written in New York, where Ashbery moved after he graduated from Harvard in 1949, urban landmarks pass unmentioned.[1] Only "Some Trees" and the last section of "The Picture of Little JA in a Prospect of Flowers" employ something like a "lyric I." Readers of Ashbery's later work will miss here both the rhythms and diction of ordinary speech and the cascading syntax and images of the purportedly generic "Ashbery poem." What we do find in *Some Trees* are still lifes in polished, formal, and sometimes archaic diction, and insular lines of high sonic resonance.

The reverberating formality of the poems collected in *Some Trees* is evident in their titles, nearly half of which indicate the form or mode of their poems ("Pantoum," "Pastoral," "Sonnet") rather than their elusive subject matters. The overt, intricate formality of these poems (three sestinas, a pantoum, and a canzone) tends to obscure whatever contents they may or may not contain. Almost all end-words, the surreal, dead-pan "Canzone" leaves hardly any room for deviation into sense: "Acts of our grass / Transporting chill / Over brazen grass / That retorts as grass / Leave the clay, / The grass, / And that which is grass" (ST 44). We make out only some fractured story of children ("chill") exiled for brazen acts. The formal ingenuity of *Some Trees* must have attracted Auden, who selected it for the Yale Younger Poets' Series. Yet Auden's "Canzone" (1942), from which Ashbery learned the form, hardly resembles Ashbery's: "When shall we learn, what should be clear as day, / We cannot choose what we are free to love? / Although the mouse we banished yesterday / Is an enraged rhinoceros today" (CP

256).[2] Both canzones concern sexual repression, but sense itself lies buried in Ashbery's leaves of grass. The echoing poems of *Some Trees* seem as clear as a cloudless day, and as empty.

The opening poem, "Two Scenes" (ST 9), sets the tone for the volume. This elegant poem pays homage both to Stevens (with its philosophical cast and sonorous vocabulary) and to Auden (with its industrial landscape and military language) but remains a world apart from either. There is no definite relation (such as there and here, then and now) between the numbered scenes. Each nine-line scene with its closing quotation reflects the other; in fact, "Two Scenes" could be read with the stanzas reversed. As the scenes mirror each other, each line echoes itself and creates, for its duration, a distinct sonic environment. The fifth—railway—line fulfills its repetitive destination: "Destiny guides the water-pilot, and it is destiny." The misrepresentative substitution of "water-pilot" for "engineer," which removes the guiding rails, is significant; destiny becomes a matter of faith ("and it *is* destiny"). But as the phonemic slippage in "so much news, such noise" suggests, these lines deliver little more than the ring of truth. The sounds of "Two Scenes" do not so much echo sense as invent it. In the enjambed rhyme of "We see you in your hair, / Air resting around the tips of mountains," "hair" only sounds like the rarefied "Air" it is likened to. And the narrative in the second scene involving "canal machinery," "an old man," "paint cans," and "laughing cadets" is little more than the story of a vowel.

But although every train of thought seems off schedule, if not derailed, "Two Scenes" maintains its communications system. The melodic first line, "We see us as we truly behave," submerges the idiomatic wish to "see ourselves as others see us," which organizes these two scenes of being seen. The news of who or how we are arrives by rail and sea, via new recruits ("Two Scenes" was written in 1953, near the end of the Korean War) or over the wireless. The poem plays out an implicit analogy between the clouded mirrors of life and art which justifies such obscurities. "We" wait for each glass to clear up as we await the day of specular truth, "perhaps a day of general honesty" ("general amnesty"), on which we would see and accept each other as we are. But for now, news of each other remains en route.

The "we" of "Two Scenes" may represent not only all of us but a secret society whose members behave openly among themselves: only "We see us as we truly behave." Often the communications system in *Some Trees* encodes a gay network of friends circulating among enemies and possible informants. These poems show the influence of Auden's early cryptic poems, on guard with "Sentries against inner and outer" (EA 33) and ever vigilant against the "constant whisper and the casual question" (EA 40). In the investigative glare of *Some Trees,* it is difficult to identify the enemy within. The homotextual arbor of "The Grapevine" (ST 19), first published in 1953, begins with an unspecified admission that doubles as a veiled threat: "Of who we and all they are / You all now know. But you know / After they began to find us out we grew / Before they died thinking us the causes / / Of their acts." In this word-of-mouth network of "fruits," not only have the names been withheld but the pronouns have been changed at every opportunity. Who committed, who detected, these fatal acts, "we" or "they" or "you"? To "you" (including the readers), the investigating "they" uncomfortably resembles the uncovered "we." Discovery is costly for the investigators: there is no way of knowing in this homophobic grapevine which behavioral system is "deviant" and which is "straight," which behavior defines and is misrepresented by the other. The revenge of those found out consists of planting seeds of doubt and suspicion among those knowing. They themselves may be subject to investigation.

Written during the McCarthy years, many of the poems in *Some Trees* exhibit both the agility and the power of evasion. But not all of them are aloof or wickedly devious. One sad instance is the slender nursery rhyme, "The Thinnest Shadow" (ST 43; dated January 1953). In his Norton Lectures, Ashbery offered this poem as an example of Laura Riding's influence on his poetry. Riding's nursery rhyming is audible in "The Sad Boy," where John is caught with one shoe off and one shoe on: "Pity the lucky Sad Boy / With but a single happy boot / And an extra foot / With no boot for it."[3] Ashbery's "shadow" seems equally bootless. Even the jaunty nonce word of "The Thinnest Shadow"'s opening lines, "He is sherrier / And sherriest," revises "charier" from the first draft. The mirror's parental injunction, "Be supple, young man, / Since you can't be gay," encodes subtlety as the alternative to openly gay behavior. Without the reinforcing "we," "he" is dogged by his misrepresentations: "His heart is full of lies / And his eyes are full of mold." During this dispiriting and frightening period, Ashbery suffered a bout of writer's block (from December 1950 through December 1951); he recalls being finally "jolted out of this by going with Frank O'Hara—I think it was New Year's Day, 1952—to a concert by David Tudor of John Cage's 'Music of Changes.'"[4] With Cage's changes ringing in his ears, Ashbery's response to the repressive climate of the late 1940s and early 1950s in the United States was most often neither fight nor flight but a resourceful gaiety.

Ashbery had been using "gay" in his poetry for nearly a decade before *Some Trees* appeared.[5] The unpublished "Poem," written in August 1944, begins with an injunction to "Salvage from love the heart's most brilliant hangings, / Snare in the flesh that alien gaiety. / Lovers fall at the limits of your dream. / / My gay glance faltering into fear." An unpublished ballad, "The Party" (dated December 30, 1949), began as a spectacle of gays behaving like "[c]rooks": "Though gaiety was our intent / Our private lusts, assembled there / In all their strangeness, came and went / Like ~~rooks~~ crows upon the clattering air." When Ashbery was chosen class poet of Harvard in 1949, he used his droll poem "A Sermon: Amos 8:11–14" (dated July 1946) for the senior class poem. "A Sermon" urges covert rebellion instead of courtly love: "Break vows as fagots: ignore / Promises, prayers, lusting before the door, / Nor press the sinning Tartar to his knees."[6] "Faggots," that is, are to break vows like kindling. Few such sinners are spared by Amos, as God's prophet warns: "I have overthrown *some* of you, as God overthrew Sodom and Gomorrah, and ye were as a firebrand plucked out of the burning" (Amos 4.11). Though T. S. Eliot prays in *The Waste Land* to be plucked out, other prophets seek the fire.

Even the serene love lyric, "Some Trees" (ST 51), which Ashbery wrote on November 8, 1948, for one of his Harvard classmates, exhibits the caution attendant upon unsanctioned behavior. These enjambed, hesitant couplets, "each / Joining a neighbor, as though speech / Were a still performance," barely foreshadow the later mannered sonorities of Ashbery's New York poems. The couplets of "Some Trees" sound "natural," following their nature being the couple's own defense. Ashbery has since written off "Some Trees" as "a conventional modern poem of that period, my farewell to poetry as we know it—it had a paraphrasable meaning."[7] Nevertheless, the hushed poem never speaks its piece. This story of imminent love and communication (the "day of general honesty" prophesied in "Two Scenes") is "anybody's story." Yet this love is unaccompanied by open gestures even though by mutual agreement the lovers have retreated from the disagreeable world. The joy of the poem consists simply in being surrounded by the nonjudgmental presences of Baudelaire's corresponding trees. Even so, this still life cannot last, and the time of tightly regulated iambs and reticent self-reflection resumes: "Placed in a puzzling light, and moving, / Our days put on such reticence / These accents seem their own defense."

In the first draft (see figure), winter days themselves put on reticence: "~~Season of~~ Fast fixed in puzzling light and fading / Your ~~days~~ shapes put on such reticence, / Our errors seem their own defence." "Season of" suggests a Keatsian ("Season of mists and mellow fruitfulness") apostrophe to the reluctant season. Ashbery read Keats intensively while at Harvard, but he chose well here not to follow Keats, which would have meant turning away from his friend. A more likely model for his ending was Auden's postal lyric (later entitled "The Letter"), written twenty years earlier, when

These are amazing: each
Joining a neighbor, as if speech
Were a still performance.
Arranging ~~quite~~ of by chance

To meet as far, this morning,
From the world as agreeing
With it, you and I
Are suddenly what the trees try

To tell us we are;
That their merely being here
means something, ~~a step~~ *That soon*
That we may touch, ~~can~~ love, explain.

~~What joy~~ *How good* not to have invented
This comeliness! It is what we wanted:
Silence ~~about to be filled~~ with noises,
Canvas on which emerges

a ~~gathering~~ of smiles, a winter morning.
~~Season of~~ puzzling light and fading
Your ~~days~~ put on such patience,
Our errors seem their own defence.

"Some Trees"

Auden himself was twenty. Auden too keeps his meanings to their wintry letter:

I, decent with the seasons, move
Different or with a different love,

23

Nor question overmuch the nod,
The stone smile of this country god
That never was more reticent,
Always afraid to say more than it meant.
(EA 25)

Like Ashbery's reticent "chorus of smiles," Auden's letter says less than it means.

It is illuminating to compare "Some Trees" with an unpublished lyric, "Poem about Autumn," written just a week earlier (handwritten addition italicized):

With eyes full of fear
Of our choosing the right word,
Those in the street conspire
To pass by unheard.
A cold time of your mind
Alters the nature of things
When it alteration finds,
And all that I am saying
With a child's insincerity
Easily becomes too true.
This dance of metamorphoses--
How can we follow it, who
Are but one thing and another?
Yet I think that the year
Loves us, and will weather
All *our* means of making it clear;
In change is a kind of happiness
That is not created by us.

In this elongated Shakespearean sonnet (abab cdcd efef ghgh ii), which borrows from the first quatrain of sonnet 116 ("Love is not love / Which alters when it alteration finds"), the poet seeks to allay his beloved's fear of changing things by speaking of them. "Everything's so perfect," the conversation goes, "why spoil it by saying anything?" Some trees, days, poems apparently come ready-made; one need only transcribe them. Ashbery's Shakespearean response to love's alteration is that change itself is an opportune "happiness." The fear of description in "Poem about Autumn" parallels the fear of communication. The trees in "Some Trees" prophesy that "soon / We may touch, love, explain." Its winter morning is not a found poem after all but a series of inventive metamorphoses: a still performance, a noise-filled silence, and a choral canvas. Whereas the discursive "Poem about Autumn" concludes with a happy optimism that the lovers will "weather" the change of their declarations, the scenic "Some Trees" ends with the lovers' reticence winning out, and the puzzling feelings go unexplained.

Ashbery's poetics are themselves placed in a puzzling light in "The Mythological Poet." Dated May 9, 1950, soon after he arrived in New York City, the two-part poem opened Ashbery's privately printed first collection, *Turandot and Other Poems* (1953).[8] In *Some Trees,* however, it gives way to the more finished "Two Scenes," and it is left out of *Selected Poems* (1985). But its enjambed, prosaic, measured music ("The music brought us what it seemed / We had long desired") lasted in Ashbery's poetry after the sonic and linear introversion of "Two Scenes"—written more than two years later—had been largely abandoned.

"The Mythological Poet" divides its attention between the music and the musician. The unnamed mythological musician is apparently Orpheus, founder in Ovid's *Metamorphoses* both of music and of homosexuality. In fact, "The Mythological Poet" anticipates Ashbery's finest Orphean lyric, "Syringa": the poet is "a kind of lewd / Cloud" (ST 35; "god") in the earlier poem, "a bluish cloud" (HBD 71) in the later. "The Mythological Poet" first bore the Coleridgean title "The Shadow of the Dome of Pleasure," and the dreamy aestheticized reign of the domed "ancient willows" seems threatened by ancestral voices prophesying war (the United States was about to be drawn into the Korean War): "the world / Of things, that rages like a virgin / Next to our silken thoughts" (ST 35). Here the raging world appears innocuous, like a pet: "It can / Be touched, they said. It cannot harm" (ST 34). But then, in this allegory of aestheticism, a sudden ocean breeze shakes the "jousting willows" with "a new / Music, innocent and monstrous / As the ocean's bright display of teeth" (ST 35). Harold Bloom takes this "new music" to be Ashbery's new poetry, displacing "the toothless murmuring / Of ancient willows" (ST 34)—an interpretation that will be borne out in "Syringa," where Orpheus successfully answers a challenge from the elder musician, Apollo.[9] Yet it would be a mistake to concede the clear superiority (or inferiority) of this oceanic, sublime new music over the mannered murmuring of the willows, a "toothless" music Ashbery will have recourse to throughout his career. In the reflecting, second section of the poem, the mythological poet, "merely / An ornament" (ST 35), seems as ineffectual as the willows.

The world and the worldliness of the new Orphean musician become clearer in part II. The scene of the poet "acquiescing / To dust, candy, perverts" at the "zoo" (ST 35) conjures up the homophobic scenario of the "pervert" offering candy to children. In an untitled, handwritten draft of the poem this zoological world itself inspires the new music: "a ~~suppler~~ Tune," "subtler yet more exalted; perhaps / A warning we cannot understand." Whether "inserted" into the "panting forest" (like the "fast thick pants" in "Kubla Khan") or "openly / Walking" in the "square," the "lewd" musician "does not care" (ST 35; cf. "We don't care / / Though," ST 19; "And heaven will not care," ST 66) who watches or listens. The somewhat sinister "pervert" appears elsewhere in *Some Trees.* In "The Pied Piper" the hypnotic child-abductor is awarded an ambiguous epilogue: "his love was strongest / Who never loved them at all" (ST 69). In "He," the entity "hymned" (poet, God, beloved) is also whispered to be a shady character, who "has had his eye on you from the beginning" (ST 60). Frank O'Hara, who called *Some Trees* "the most beautiful first book to appear in America since *Harmonium,*"[10] would later sentimentalize the pederast in "Ave Maria" (1960), both a hymn to the unexperienced "virgin" and a "perverted" Dr. Spock manual. In the final rhetorical question of "The Mythological Poet" Ashbery is equally sentimental: "And oh beside the roaring / Centurion of the lion's hunger / Might not child and pervert / Join hands . . .?" (ST 36). The Edenic simplicity of diction from the poem's beginning now shows its rhetorical force. With its brilliant beginning, "And oh," the question presents prophecy as an afterthought. In Isaiah's paradise regained, all manner of creatures (wolves, lambs, lions) lie together: "and a little child shall lead them" (Isaiah 11:6). Ashbery's polite request has a noncommittal charm. Orpheus's loss of Eurydice dwindles to a loss of appetite: "their hunger / From loss grown merely a gesture?" (ST 36). But the world-weary, aestheticized union of the "child and pervert" in "The Mythological Poet" is all the more compelling in its restraint.

Among the several portraits of the young gay artist in *Some Trees* the best known is "The Picture of Little J. A. in a Prospect of Flowers," which Delmore Schwartz, one of Ashbery's early favorite poets, accepted for *Partisan Review* in 1951. Dated April 15, 1950, about three weeks before "The Mythological Poet," the poem is equally ambitious and far-ranging and also shows the strain of its reach. The poem falls into three parts, the second of which largely duplicates the more compelling third. Still, this lively poem is more indicative of Ashbery's future experiments than many of the more finished lyrics in *Some Trees.* Ashbery had more than enough unpublished poems resembling "Some Trees" from Deerfield and Harvard to fill out the volume, had he wished. "The Picture of Little J. A." shows his dissatisfaction with a style "which" (to cite Ashbery's epigraph from Boris Pasternak) "he mastered rather early and apparently without great difficulty" (ST 27).[11]

In the first, most novel section Ashbery experiments with narrative collage, employed later in the cartoon-like non sequiturs of such poetry comics as "Farm Implements and Rutabagas in a Landscape" (DDS 47) and "Daffy Duck in Hollywood" (HBD 31). From the title (patterned after Andrew Marvell's "The Picture of little T. C. in a Prospect of Flowers"), to the epigraph (from Pasternak), to the Dick-and-Jane primer or Punch-and-Judy show ("Dick gives Genevieve a swift punch / In the pajamas," ST 27), to *Macbeth* ("'Aroint thee, witch!' the rump-fed ronyon cries," I.iii.6), to Defoe's *Roxana* ("He clap'd me first during the eclipse"), Ashbery relates the conception of the hero *ab ovo* through primary narratives, adapting James Joyce's nursery style of the first section of *A Portrait of the Artist as a Young Man.*

"The Picture of Little J. A." is a study in artistic virtue. Watching the imperious little T. C. taming and naming the wild flowers and advising the roses on their most flattering colors and smells, Marvell marvels, "Happy, who can / Appease this virtuous Enemy of Man!"[12] In the third section of Ashbery's poem, the poet reads his own childhood snapshot "among the blazing phlox" (ST 28-29):

I had a hard stare, accepting

Everything, taking nothing,
As though the rolled-up future might stink
As loud as stood the sick moment
The shutter clicked.

This verbal negative, with its hard c's, needs developing. To the little J. A. (in the eyes of the young J. A.), the undeveloped roll of the film of the future might last only as long (and mean only as much) as the moment the shutter clicked. In these surreally synesthetic lines, "loud" displaces "long," and "stink" (like spoilt meat) revises Pasternak's "spoilt from childhood by the future." Pasternak's conclusion to *Safe Conduct* eulogizes the Futurist Vladimir Mayakovsky, who eliminated his future by committing suicide ("shot" not by a camera but a gun), as the epitome of the undeveloped revolutionary State. As Pasternak looks back on the Bolshevik Revolution's spoilt child, so the "revolutionary" poet Ashbery looks back on his "negative" self. What he sees there is a "hard stare" from the phallic "pale and gigantic fungus" which he takes as a sign of virtue surviving an all-consuming "phlox" (ST 28) or flux. Like Pasternak, the young gay poet of the McCarthy era needs stubbornness to survive. The poem itself, with its mismatched sections (12, 13, 17 lines) of quinzains (one willful sestet in part II) and off-rhyming couplets, exhibits a stubborn resistance to form. Though Ashbery realizes that the "virtuous" survival of "recent scenes of badness" is largely a construction of memory ("So fair does each invent his virtue," ST 28), this virtue nevertheless constitutes the trans-historical self: "For as change is horror, / Virtue is really stubbornness" (ST 29). This is surprising moral reasoning from the future "poet of flux." The virtú of this "Dick," who gives Genevieve a punch, Defoe's heroine the clap, and his fraternal opponents a kick, is gendered male. This solid state of mind had been defined in 1914 by Gertrude Stein in *Tender Buttons:* "Callous is something that hardening leaves behind what will be soft if there is a genuine interest in there being present as many girls as men."[13] Ashbery's picture is obviously parodic, but the stubborn affirmation of his first-person ending remains: "I am not wrong / In calling this comic version of myself / The true one" (ST 29).

But why would this more mannered than manly poet define himself in these terms? The argument behind the picture may be that a young male poet may lose his "virtue," his "virginity," even his heterosexuality, without losing his self-fashioning determination. Virtue, so the saying goes, is its own reward. For Ashbery, however, virtue is rewarded only retroactively, in the fame of published poems in which the past is irrevocably lost and recaptured: "And only in the light of lost words / Can we imagine our rewards" (ST 29). As Proust says, in what becomes another encrypted moral for "Picture," "the true paradises are the paradises that we have lost." Ashbery will explore the futures looked forward to and back upon in "Self-Portrait in a Convex Mirror," where the forty-five-year-old complicates the issues of self and history by choosing a sixteenth-century painting of a twenty-year-old artist for reflection. And he will look back on this composite photograph of a stubborn child and a sententious young man in *Flow Chart:* "The eyes are a profound cobalt blue, accepting / of moral dilemmas and sprouting proverbs" (FC 19; "spouting wisdom"). But for now, it is enough that the project of losing words has been recognized.

Another elliptical self-portrait, "The Painter," takes up the poetics of formal perfection.[14] Dated June 17, 1948, five months earlier than "Some Trees," this sestina is the earliest poem collected in the volume. As in "Some Trees," the poem's enjambed tetrameters keep to an effortless syntax and a colorless vocabulary (the end-words are "buildings," "portrait," "prayer," "subject," "brush," and "canvas"). It is remarkable, for instance, that the only color word in "The Painter" is "white." The poem has little of the antic quality of Ashbery's later sestinas ("A Pastoral," ST 72; "Faust," TCO 47), which capitalize on the surrealist potential of their repeated end-words. Critics have traced the blandness of the diction to the influence of Stevens and Elizabeth Bishop.[15] As Ashbery remarks, he "read, reread, studied and absorbed" Bishop's *North and South* (1946), the volume containing her Stevensian sestina, "A Miracle for Breakfast," before writing his own.[16]

The most productive flaw in the poem is the incongruity between its formal perfection and its romantic subject matter: the painter in sublime confrontation with the ocean. Like Prufrock, Ashbery's painter does not think the sea will sit for him. One key model for "The Painter" is Robert Browning's "Andrea del Sarto (called 'The Faultless Painter')." With its source material in Vasari, its long verse paragraphs and extended apostrophe, and especially its exploration of the aesthetics and psychology of perfection, Browning's poem will also be an important model for Ashbery's "Self-Portrait," for which "The Painter" becomes a preliminary sketch. Like Ashbery's "Perfectly white" sestina, the painting by Browning's del Sarto is monochromatic and finished: "All is silver-gray / Placid and perfect with my art." Painstakingly painting his wife, Andrea settles for technical excellence while chafing at the flawed soulful paintings of his rivals Michelangelo and Raphael: "Their works drop groundward, but themselves, I know, / Reach many a time a heaven that's shut to me."[17] Ashbery literalized Browning's metaphor ("Their works drop groundward") in his envoy by having rival painters drop the painter's blank painting seaward: "They tossed him, the portrait, from the tallest of the buildings; / And the sea devoured the canvas and the brush / As though his subject had decided to remain a prayer" (ST 55). This fall is also modeled on the end of Auden's "Musée des Beaux Arts," in which the ship's crew in Pieter Breughel's *Icarus* "must have seen / Something amazing, a boy falling out of the sky" (EA 237).

The most malleable of the end-words in "The Painter" is "subject," meaning topic, self, and subjection. To paint his "self-portrait" the painter masters his ego (as he had his model wife) and dips his brush into the sea, subjecting his conscious perfections to his oceanic "soul," in a parody of the impassioned self-expression of abstract expressionism ("Imagine a painter crucified by his subject!"). "'My soul,'" Ashbery's maritime painter prays, "'when I paint this next portrait / Let it be you who wrecks the canvas'" (ST 54–55; "shipwreck," "sail"). As though drawn on sand, the painting's ambiguous "subject" loses its vital signs: "Finally all indications of a subject / Began to fade, leaving the canvas / Perfectly white" (ST 55). Ashbery may not have "expressed himself" or captured his subjectivity in this perfectly sustained sestina, but he succeeds thereby in drawing the mock-heroic proportions of the subject's submersion in his work.

Like most poems in *Some Trees,* "The Painter" is a narrative. In these early poems Ashbery begins what will be an extensive experimentation with narrative conventions. Such narratives are best read representatively in terms of their genres or modes of discourse rather than traditionally (for plot and character). I will consider three types of lyric narratives in *Some Trees:* narrative collage, the hybrid of narrative and commentary, and generic narration. The narrative collage is illustrated by "A Long Novel" (dated July 5–11, 1952), a 24-line poem which opens in the midst of an oft-told tale: "What will his crimes become, now that her hands / Have gone to sleep? He gathers deeds / / In the pure air, the agent / Of their factual excesses. He laughs as she inhales" (ST 64). The vocabulary ("crimes," "agent," "gathers [evidence]," "factual") places the coupleted couple in a detective novel with romantic designs, while the present tense and the atmospheric *film noir* smoke adapt the novel into a screen play. Ashbery is not yet comfortable with writing verse according to the laws of prose discourse; the exalted lyrical phrase "the pure air" and hymning character sketches ("He stands quieter than the day," "He is the purest air") betray an insecurity of method. These constricted, conventional narratives convey their own message, that the end is written into the beginning: "If it could have ended before / It began—the sorrow, the snow / / Dropping, dropping its fine regrets" (ST 64). Suspenseful line-breaks and drenching repetitions give this epilogue its melodramatic charm. No need, then, to read the last page to discover how it comes out: "So the end / / Was the same: the discharge of spittle / Into frozen air" (ST 64–65). So Proust's well-read Swann discovered with Odette. It is not clear that our "realistic" life-stories, the narrative's moral goes, are any less predictable.

Later in 1952 Ashbery wrote a less studied narrative, "Popular Songs," which also begins in the middle:

He continued to consult her for her beauty
(The host gone to a longing grave).
The story then resumed in day coaches
Both bravely eyed the finer dust on the blue. That summer
("The worst ever") she stayed in the car with the cur.
That was something between her legs.
Alton had been getting letters from his mother
About the payments—half the flood
Over and what about the net rest of the year?
(ST 10)

The involuted consonance ("car with the cur," "gone to a longing") of "Popular Songs" anticipates the willful music of "Two Scenes," while the jarringly disjunctive lines point toward the novel-collages of *The Tennis Court Oath*. Yet "Popular Songs," like "A Long Novel," is discursively legible. In spite of its title and embedded (slightly altered) 1930s song titles ("Blue blue Ridge Mountain," "The Garden of the Moon"), "Popular Songs" mimes the conventions not of song but of romance. We need not know anything about Alton, his mother, or what the payments are for, to know that we are reading about an affair with familial pressures. The delights of reading this kind of poem come from its constant changes, not only of scene but of narrative level and discourse. The first two lines ("beauty," "host," "grave") are redolent of gothic romance; the third, a plot summary, tells the story of the story ("The story then resumed"; "journey") in elevated romantic diction; the fourth is a generic description of an aftermath, with an inevitable adverb of feeling, "bravely" in this case, noting finer sentiments, and the atmospheric adjective "blue" obscuring the object (both the sky and the "car").

"Popular Songs" cuts rapidly from one narrative language to the next in part because there is no single narrative vantage point. There are traces of an oral narration ("The worst ever," "That was something"), but not enough to inhibit the poem's hyper-activity. Ashbery recalls that "Popular Songs" was composed "many years before the word 'pop' was coined [1962]. It was written in an attempt to conjure up the kind of impression you would get from riding in the car, changing the radio stations and at the same time aware of the passing landscape. In other words, a kind of confused, but insistent, impression of the culture going on around us."[18] Like "A Long Novel," "Popular Songs" narrates the end of an affair. Its stock recognition scene, "Some precision, he fumed into his soup" (ST 10), in which one lover's words taste bitterly ironic in the mouth of the other, punctuates it like the earlier poem's "spittle." The "lesson" of "Popular Songs" also involves narrative inevitability: "There is no way to prevent this / Or the expectation of disappointment" (ST 11). But the poem disappoints only those looking for narrative rather than discursive consistency.

A "true confession" in the realist first person leads to the same ending, but without regrets. Ashbery's Proustian "Errors" (ST 47), beginning "Jealousy. Whispered weather reports," narrates a voracious, triangulated desire: "You stupefied me. We waxed, / Carnivores, late and alight." The jealous lover listens in through gothic eaves: "We thought then of your dry portals, / Bright cornices of eavesdropping palaces." The cigarette smoke screen of "Errors" also lends a guilty atmosphere to the tale: "It fumed / Clear air of wars. It desired / Excess of core in all things. From all things sucked / A glossy denial" (ST 47; "moderation in all things"). But the bitter ending is no less clear: "Some violent compunction." Though adopting the first person, these epistolary narratives (cf. "The Way They Took," ST 66) heighten the narrative while defusing the drama of narration. With no narrative accountability, "Errors" tells its steamy story in the heightened colors of romantic intrigue. But "Errors" appears to be true to more life than such naturalistic forerunners as "Some Trees." In the poem's closing words, "Who doubts it is true?"

Several of the poems in *Some Trees* separate into two parts, which function most often as a narrative and its reflective aftermath. The volume's most mysterious narrative is the closing poem "*Le livre est sur la table*" (ST 74–75; dated August 31, 1950), neatly divided into two numbered lessons of four Stevensian tercets each, from which all indications of a narrative subject seem to have faded. Its style resembles the Harvard poems before it ("Some Trees" and "The Painter") more than the New York poems to follow; the surrealist "logic / Of strange [juxta]position," verbal "resonance," and linear "integrity" (ST 74) thematized in the opening tercet have yet to define Ashbery's own style. "*Le livre*" is a tantalizing poem, ending *Some Trees* with a question mark in the sand: "Is the bird mentioned / In the waves' minutes, or did the land advance?" (ST 75). The Stevensian chords are unmistakable;[19] indeed Ashbery concedes that he was "half consciously imitative of Stevens" here.[20] "The Idea of Order at Key West," with "she" as actor, "we" as reflectors, and the "sea" as scene, resonates in Ashbery's alliterative permanent waves, "a world in which a woman / Walks and wears her hair and knows" (ST 74; the Stevensian "know" appears frequently in *Some Trees*). The inaugural act of "Anecdote of the Jar," "I placed a jar in Tennessee" (46), is performed at the beginning of part II, where "The young man places a bird-house / Against the blue sea" (ST 74). What we miss in "*Le livre*" is Ashbery's lively, animating humor. The aesthetic thesis ("All beauty, resonance, integrity") and tragic questions ("But what // Dismal scene is this?") which frame part I are taken straight from the aesthetician's and translator's desk. "*Le livre*" seems to buckle under the weightiness of its submerged subject.

What is, or was, the subject of "*Le livre*"? In the early drafts of part II the "woman" traced in the waves was identified: "the gestures on the shore are those / Of screeching Electra." With this name exhumed, we can recognize the "Dismal scene" in "*Le livre*" as the murder of Clytemnestra, the flown gull (girl) as "screeching Electra," and the "old man" pouting at the gathering Furies as the servant who rescued the "young man," Orestes, from an early slaughter. Ashbery recalls reading Gilbert Murray's "high-flown" translations of Greek drama in the early 1950s.[21] Murray's creaking stage machinery is evident in these lines from Aeschylus' *The Choëphoroe* (the chorus on the approach of Orestes): "But what is this? / A child led to the House from lands / Far off, and blood upon his hands!"[22] Ashbery had more success and fun playing off Murray's archaisms in his Audenesque play *The Heroes,* also written in 1950. Here is Ulysses: "Ai, regret that will fall on the house of Achilles. Foolish he was to invite Theseus, slayer of monsters. A shadow falls over the hero just before he commits a heroic act" (Plays 14). In its final form, "*Le livre*" concerns the traces or secrets of a mysteriously tragic transgression still locked in the scenery of the crime. The representative pattern sentence from a French Grammar, "*Le livre est sur la table,*" badly and wittily translated as "The table supports the book," places the question of gender definition on the table. But all that remains of the subject—the bird, the woman—is the poem: the birdhouse, the book, the painting. The book's days, scrawled on the beach ("la plage," "la page"), are numbered. But even if the "secrets" hadn't vanished, they would still be secret.

Like "*Le livre,*" the two-part poem "Illustration" (dated September 20, 1950) is a meditation on a narrative whose lesson remains undisclosed. The two sections or chapters of "Illustration" are related as stimulus and response, scene and aftermath, and, most importantly, illustrative narrative and moral. With its stable narrative (the poem recounts the suicide of a novice), common vocabulary (with significant exceptions, "roc" and "peplum"), unhurried formal phrasing, and an ironic pathos reminiscent of "The Painter," whose hero (or merely his metonymic "portrait") similarly drops out of sight, "Illustration" is a perfectly sustained poem. It reads like a hagiography, simplified for edification, decorously phrased, and bathed in a sentimental irony: "A mother offered her some nylons / Stripped from her very legs. Others brought / / Little offerings of fruit and candy" (ST 48). The ceremonial simplicity is Stevensian, recalling the devout childlike diction of "Cy Est Pourtraicte, Madame Ste Ursule, et Les Unze Mille Vierges," whose blushing novice "an offering made / Of radishes and flowers" (3). But Ashbery's sheer wit shows through in the gift of the nylons, whose giver clearly regards her own act, rather than suicide, as the supreme sacrifice. Even the novice's death ironizes the subject, who finally sheds her habit in a tenderly exhibitionist fall: "naked / / As a roc's egg, she drifted softly downward / Out of the angels' tenderness and the minds of men" (ST 49; cf. Apollinaire, "Zone": "Roc so celebrated in song and story").[23] The irony relies here on less than devout clichés: "naked as a jaybird," "dropped like a stone" ("roc" or "rock"), and "out of sight out of mind."

Ashbery's novice, who desires Shakespearean "Monuments" and wants like Sir Philip Sidney "to move / / Figuratively" (ST 48), illustrates the immortality of the poet as the inexhaustible poem which outlives its interpretations. As it takes up the question of interpretation, "Illustration" enters the communications system. The novice "in her peplum of bright leaves" (ST 50) is at once the sender, the messenger, and the message, and "we" in the crowd of witnesses to this spectacle, including the poet and the readers, are the receivers. The "meteoric career" (one narrative crypt phrase here) of the poem and poet illustrates no single truth or moral—"There is so much in that moment! / So many attitudes toward that flame"—and thereby appears as the "somber vestment" of "the truth we know" (ST 49). The "roc," metamorphosing in part II into the lustrous "rockets" that "sighed / Elegantly over the city," outdistances any identifications. The novice "burning in effigy" (another operative crypt phrase) is itself "only an effigy / Of indifference, a miracle // Not meant for us" (ST 50) to understand or judge. As such, the "roc" resembles a verbal icon, indifferent to our meanings. As W. K. Wimsatt wrote in "The Intentional Fallacy" (1946), "the poem is not the critic's own and not the author's (it is detached from the author at birth . . .). The poem belongs to the public." [24] Further on in Ashbery's career, in "Syringa," the pyrotechnic poem leaves even the poet in the dark, "a bad / Comet screaming hate and disaster, but so turned inward / That the meaning, good or other, can never / Become known" (HBD 71). In its refusal to illuminate, the comet represents the artist's indifference to his critical reception. As Ashbery put it in a later essay, "The Invisible Avant-Garde" (1968), the artist must assume "an attitude which neither accepts nor rejects acceptance but is independent of it" (RS 394). The flame's own attitude does not depend on ours.

Judgments in "Illustration" go beyond the literary; a moral tracks the tale. Like the novice, the sexually indiscreet community sheds indifferent light: "We twinkle under the weight // Of indiscretions" (ST 49; "buckle"). One of Ashbery's descriptions of these indiscretions, "Moths climb in the flame" ("climb in" misrepresenting "are drawn toward"), recalls Bishop's manmoth, who "climbs fearfully," like his encrypted relative the "human fly," before descending into the subway. Written soon after Bishop's first stay in New York from 1934 to 1935,[25] "The Man-Moth" recalls another famous New York poem of climbing, falling, and subway scuttling, Crane's "To Brooklyn Bridge" in which a "*bedlamite,*" having come "*Out of some subway scuttle,*" climbs to the bridge's parapets: "*Tilting there momently, shrill shirt ballooning, / A jest falls from the speechless caravan.*" [26] These unforgettable lines, with their sadly prophetic Pierrot, surely influenced Bishop's own darkly whimsical poem, which may be read as her elegy for the gay poet who had committed suicide about two years earlier.[27]

"Illustration" is similarly elegiac. Searching for an ending to the poem, Ashbery drew on the now deleted second section of "The Hero" (ST 23), written eleven days earlier. This poem's earlier titles, "Doctor Gradus ad Parnassum" and "Harold in Italy," each paraded the inflated notion that "the avant-garde artist is a kind of hero" (RS 393). In what was to have been part II of "The Hero," the heroic figure with his "high resolve" was labeled "a mere // Gigolo" before "we" realized that "these are only effigies / Of remorse—not ours // As the leaves are not winter's / Because it is the end." As winter leaves, once they fall, are no longer winter's (or the trees'), the elegiac subject lies beyond ridicule and the poet's remorseful effigies themselves become anonymous "lost words." There was, however, a recent gay suicide for Ashbery to commemorate, if only in "hidden syllables" (HBD 71). Four months earlier, one of Ashbery's teachers at Harvard, F. O. Matthiessen ("Moths"), committed suicide by jumping from the twelfth story of a Boston hotel. The homosexual Matthiessen died shortly before he was to testify before the House Un-American Activities Committee. Ashbery first read Stevens closely with Matthiessen and wrote a paper on Stevens's "Chocorua to Its Neighbor" for him. Stevens himself, when he heard that his friend "Matty" had died, wrote Norman Holmes Pearson that "the evil thing, for him, was that he was a man of ideas who found himself being crawled over by a lot of people from a quite different sort of world and I suppose that he had reached the point where the almost total lack of understanding and sympathy was too much for him."[28] Adapting the sentimental figure of falling leaves ("peplum of bright leaves") from "The Hero," Ashbery presumed neither understanding nor sympathy. "Illustration" succeeds by virtue of its restraint. Its indifference to our wanting to understand something "not meant for us," coupled with its tenderness, is precisely what gives the poem its evasively moving power.

Auden's reading of "Illustration" is intriguing. For someone who clearly valued *Some Trees* enough to select it for the Yale Younger Poets Series, Auden is surprisingly grudging in his "Foreword," which amounts to a refutation of surrealism and a lesson for the younger poet. Auden argues that the surrealists from "Rimbaud down to Mr. Ashbery" seek to return to a "golden age" when all myths and rituals were held in common, via the magical routes of childhood and of dreams:

> There is, however, a vast difference between these psychic worlds and the world of antiquity. The mythology of each of the former is unique—there are as many mythologies as there are individuals—and their origin [lies] . . . in the unique particulars of the individual's personal history. . . . The subject of Mr. Ashbery's "Illustration" is a woman who acts out her private mythology and denies the reality of anything outside herself; that is to say, she is insane. As a ritual sacrificial act she jumps off a high building. . . . She is mad, but is the kind of public sanity which regards nothing as sacred or even personal, the unauthentic life of the crowd watching her fall, not equally insane? Her action, crazy as it is, arouses a feeling of envy at her capacity so heroically to reject.[29]

How do we read Auden's reading? His rejection of the "private" poetics of surrealism doesn't keep him from identifying strongly with the novice rather than with the "sane" public he earlier endorses. Auden's emphasis on the right to privacy suggests that another argument is quietly taking place beneath the distinction between public and private symbolism. The voyeuristic crowd has no business regarding the writer's private life. Yet the "unique particulars" of Ashbery's mythology are never simply private. "Illustration" concerns the way poems survive by outdistancing the subjects (and authors) they commemorate. If Ashbery's particulars weren't (mis)representative, his myths wouldn't attract us to their flames.

Generic narrations, a third kind of narrative poem in *Some Trees,* focus on the narrator rather than the narrative. The (stock) narrator tends to flatten events and styles, but this very lack of emphasis and significance produces a mysteriously pointless story-board. Two such poems, "The Instruction Manual" and "And You Know," both written in 1955, were the last poems to be included in *Some Trees* (neither poem appears in an early table of contents). Both poems employ long lines that fill up their pages like prose. "The Instruction Manual" (dated September 12, 1955), the more successful of the two, in some ways reaches back to an earlier style.[30] With its evenness, its transparency, and its sentimental ironies, "The Instruction Manual" resembles "Illustration" (1950) more than the disjunctive narrative collage "Popular Songs" (1952). But Ashbery's manual aims at pure description or narration, dispensing with evaluative commentary or symbolic heightening. Marjorie Perloff sees the poem as uncharacteristic of Ashbery's work because its "reality-dream-reality structure" follows the pattern of what M. H. Abrams has labeled the "Greater Romantic Lyric."[31] While "The Instruction Manual" is indeed atypical in foregrounding its dreamy narrator, it turns out to be one of the most productive poems in *Some Trees,* prefiguring the narrative voyages and narrating personae of "The Skaters."

Ashbery recalls that he wrote "The Instruction Manual" when he

was working for a publisher, writing and editing college textbooks. I never actually wrote an instruction manual, but I wrote the poem in an office of McGraw-Hill in New York. There wasn't any window in the room so that was an invention. To me, it is more "confessional" than it appears to be on the surface. The poem really ends with me returning to the boring task I have to do, where the poem began. It leads back into me, and is probably about the dissatisfactions with the work I was doing at the time. And my lack of success in seeing the city I wanted most to see, when I was in Mexico. The name held so much promise: Guadalajara.[32]

If anything, Ashbery's noncommittal poem is "counter-confessional" in that it tells what didn't happen. Ashbery had vacationed in Mexico with Jane Freilicher, Joe Hazan, and Grace Hartigan in the summer of 1955, but didn't visit the promising city. When he returned to New York, he learned that a candidate for the Fulbright Fellowship had canceled and as first runner-up he was about to leave for France, probably another dream informing "The Instruction Manual."

Yet the pseudo-romantic lyric never completely departs from its frame—neither wakes nor sleeps—to arrive at its story. There is no shift in style or added richness of detail, for instance, between the framing reality and the dream, only the two-dimensional vividness of "local color." More important, despite the autobiographical origins of the poem, the colorless narrator is no more "real" than the stereotypical colorful "characters" he describes (a pun on "Manuel" may have suggested the title). He is merely a personification of the travelogue discourse in which "The Instruction Manual" is written. This discourse, typified by James Fitzpatrick's famous travel shorts (silent films with voice-over narration), was already delightfully parodied in several Warner Brothers cartoons, Tex Avery's *The Isle of Pingo Pongo,* for example. Avery's parody of Fitzpatrick's formulaic close, "And so, as the sun sinks slowly in the west, we sadly say goodbye to the beautiful isle of Pingo Pongo," is reflected in Ashbery's tender farewell: "And as a last breeze freshens the top of the weathered old tower, I turn my gaze / Back to the instruction manual . . ." (ST 18). A travel guidebook is itself a peculiar kind of instruction manual in which the absent narrator speaks to the implied readers of a scene appearing before their eyes as their walking tour unfolds. In "The Instruction Manual" the confusion of narrative levels and times continues to remind us that we are "dreaming." While the band takes an intermission (story time doubling for narrative duration), the narrator takes the implied reader "into one of the side streets. / Here you may see one of those white houses with green trim / That are so popular here. Look—I told you!" One of the proprietors offers these narrative tourists "a cooling drink" (ST 16–17). These droll conflations predate postmodernism. They may be found in Laurence Sterne's *Tristram Shandy* and Keats's witty "Ode on a Grecian Urn," which never leaves its urn for its vision (otherwise the depicted lovers would be moving). But time in "The Instruction Manual" doesn't stand still. The narrator has only as much time on hand to narrate as he can spare from his manual: "Yet soon all this will cease" (ST 15). Guadalajara is no eternal city; even the band's schmaltzy selection, "*Scheherazade* by Rimsky-Korsakov" (ST 14), reminds one of a former narrator, whose head was on the line.

Nevertheless, the narrator seems perfectly unruffled. The descriptions of "The Instruction Manual" are so stereotypical as to be offensive were it not that our focus is the touring gaze rather than the deliberately simplified scene:

> First, leading the parade, is a dapper fellow
> Clothed in deep blue. On his head sits a white hat
> And he wears a mustache, which has been trimmed for the occasion.
> His dear one, his wife, is young and pretty; her shawl is rose, pink, and
>     white.
> Her slippers are patent leather, in the American fashion
> (ST 15)

The wit of the incongruously neutral phrasing "in the American fashion" is lost on the narrator, no cultural relativist. He intends no parody in his sentimental depiction of the husband and "His dear one, his wife." Near the end of our stay, the tour guide congratulates himself: "How limited, but how complete withal, has been our experience of Guadalajara! / We have seen young love, married love, and the love of an aged mother for her son" (ST 18). Though invisible to the tour guide, the omission of gay love is conspicuous. With this omission Ashbery's disaffected travelogue reads like an anthropological manual of heterosexual mating rituals.

Ashbery's "new metal" (ST 14) may best be analyzed by isolating the various works from which it is alloyed. In Ashbery's words, "The Instruction Manual" "describes in a paint-by-numbers way what is going on but it doesn't draw any conclusions. It aims at pure description."[33] One model here was probably Roussel's long poem "La vue" (1903). There Roussel studies a small photograph of a seaside prospect on a penholder, "fixed inside a ball of glass" which magnifies it. Roussel likewise "magnifies" his description into two thousand impossibly detailed lines, focusing at one point, for example, on a passenger of a distant yacht: "one side of his moustache, / Which is stiff and twirled to a point, stands out against / The horizon of the sea, and quite by chance / Exactly at the crest of a small wave."[34] Roussel's monotonous alexandrines collapse the distance between here and there, frame and dream. Yet his objective, infinitely patient narrator is refined out of his narrative's existence.

Ashbery was also instructed by Max Jacob, another deadpan surrealist. Jacob, who entered the monastery of St. Benoît in 1927, doubtless informed the surreal couplet "In a far recess of summer / Monks are playing soccer" (ST 27) in "The Picture of Little J. A." In 1953 Ashbery was reading and translating the prose poems of *Le cornet à dés* (1917), compact narrations which outlined new methods for incorporating novelistic discourse in poetry. One of these pieces, "Literature and Poetry," begins in a resort which is about to be erased by a flood. A boy accosts the unnamed vacationers: "I have been in Naples; . . . in the streets you can be quite alone, without anyone seeing you; not that there aren't many people in Naples, but there are so many little streets that there is never more than a single person on them!" The boy's father protests that his son has never been to Naples, whereupon the narrator declares the boy to be a poet. The narration closes with an observation, the winding "paths left dry by the sea had made him dream of the streets of Naples," which leads eventually into the framing close of "The Instruction Manual," "I turn my gaze / Back to the instruction manual which has made me dream of Guadalajara" (ST 18).[35] In "The Instruction Manual" the stylized innocence of Jacob's child is ironically reduced to the bored naiveté of the technical writer, and the romance of the place name is produced by the winding paths of a manual. We are left to declare whether or not the functionary is a poet.

There are American veins in Ashbery's metal: the "long lines in the poem were suggested by Whitman, whom I was reading very much at the time, admiring his easygoing lines and their celebratory character."[36] Ashbery's distance from his panoramic catalogues is also a characteristic of Whitman's representative spectator in "Song of Myself": "Looking with side-curved head curious what will come next / Both in and out of the game and watching and wondering at it" (191). Yet if Whitman's Americans are typical, they are also real; Ashbery's self-effacing guide celebrates (Latin) America in only two dimensions. The exotic local colors of "The Instruction Manual" remind one of Stevens's "An Ordinary Evening in New Haven" (published in 1950), which sweeps us away to "longed-for lands": "In the land of the lemon trees, yellow and yellow were / Yellow-blue, yellow-green, pungent with citron-sap, / Dangling and spangling, the mic-mac of mocking birds" (349). Ashbery surely dipped his brush into Stevens's paint cans: "Around stand the flower girls, handing out rose- and lemon-colored flowers" (ST 14). But in Stevens's voyage the narrator collapses into the poet, a conjunction which (as in "La vue") tends to reduce narration to description.

Here as often, however, Bishop is a more immediate source than Stevens. In his 1969 review of Bishop's *The Complete Poems* Ashbery admired "Arrival at Santos" for "its prosy, travel-diary style, its form so perfectly adapted to its content that there isn't a bulge or a wrinkle."[37] Bishop's poem, which first appeared in *A Cold Spring* (1955), is a clear forerunner to Ashbery's travelogue: "Here is a coast; here is a harbor; / here, after a meager diet of horizon, is some scenery: / impractically shaped and—who knows?—self-pitying mountains" (89). Yet after the initial travelogue simplifications, the viewer's witty insights are worlds beyond the narrator's bland reflections in "The Instruction Manual."

All modern imaginary voyages follow in the wake of Baudelaire; his "Le voyage" informs both "The Instruction Manual" and "The Skaters": "The child enthralled by lithographs and maps / can satisfy his hunger for the world: / how limitless it is beneath the lamp, / and how it shrinks in the eyes of memory!"[38] Bishop would agree: "More delicate than the historians' are the map-makers' colors" (3). Yet Baudelaire's "Voyage," unlike Ashbery's manual, is a meditation on the voyager ("only those who leave for leaving's sake") rather than a dramatization of the narrator. The narrator of "The Instruction Manual," of course, knows Guadalajara only by name. While a junior at Harvard in September of 1947, Ashbery wrote a poem of three quatrains entitled "Embarkation for Cythera," after Baudelaire's "Un voyage à Cythère," in which the music of the name fuels the performance: "Now the bow dragged over mournful strings / / Expands and breathes the tints of Cythera / Into the fever's beat." The "cithera," stroked by a ship's musical "bow," launches us toward its namesake.

Proust, whom Ashbery read at Harvard, dedicated an entire section of *Swann's Way* to the nominal romance: "Even in spring, to come upon the name Balbec in a book sufficed to awaken in me the desire for storms at sea and for Norman Gothic."[39] In a less successful generic narration, "And You Know," Ashbery plays out the schoolchild's romance with place names: "Goodbye, old teacher, we must travel on, not to a better land, perhaps, / But to the England of the sonnets, Paris, Colombia, and Switzerland / And all the places with names, that we wish to visit—Strasbourg, Albania" (ST 57–58), and so on around the classroom globe. But this parody of Sam Woods's film *Good-bye, Mr. Chipps* unfortunately turns sour, since the condescension of the pupils, in contrast to that of the gently patronizing voyager of "The Instruction Manual," is not itself held up for scrutiny. Ashbery's friend James Schuyler mastered the homeroom narration in "Current Events," also dating from the 1950s, where the class historian records the class outing to the state capital: "All present and accounted for except the above mentioned at 7:45 sharp Mr. Olson shut the pneumatic door and set his powerful bus in motion. It was off on another never to be forgotten excursion for the Eighth Grade Classmates of School Thirty-Six."[40] As in "The Instruction Manual," such ironies as "another" are lost on the intrepid class reporter. (Ashbery entered this report into the record at a memorial reading for Schuyler at M.I.T. in April 1991, to the uproarious pleasure of all attending.) While Ashbery's own strangely weathered school poem "And You Know" doesn't wear as well as Schuyler's "Current Events," "The Instruction Manual" is for many what "Over 2000 Illustrations" is for Ashbery, "a substance that is undescribable and a continuing joy, and one returns to it again and again, ravished and unsatisfied."[41]

Like Eliot's *Prufrock,* Stevens's *Harmonium,* or Auden's *Poems,* Ashbery's *Some Trees* makes an auspicious debut, with its unmistakable, if composite, collection of styles. But the very perfection of its achievement meant that the highly polished book was definitive. To continue writing a "new music," it was necessary for Ashbery to cease writing poetry as he knew it. This break out of the mannered conformity of *Some Trees* resulted in his next and revolutionary book, *The Tennis Court Oath.*

# 2

## Private Investigations

## *The Tennis Court Oath*

We must risk ourselves in opaque weather
—Ashbery, "April Fool's Day" (1959)

For many readers Ashbery's second book, a collection of largely fragmentary, apparently nonrepresentational poems, is itself unrepresentative: either a temporary loss of bearings or a breakthrough in experimentation, but in any case a problematic exception. *The Tennis Court Oath* angered one of Ashbery's most faithful and influential readers, Harold Bloom: "How could Ashbery collapse into such a bog ... just six years after *Some Trees,* and how did he climb out of it again to write *Rivers and Mountains*?"[1] Several poets, however, notably the Language poets (like the New York school, an ill-fitting but adhesive label), singled the book out for praise. Bruce Andrews, who co-edited L=A=N=G=U=A=G=E with Charles Bernstein, lauded *The Tennis Court Oath* as a "critique of clarity and transparency."[2] The poet Susan Howe acknowledged the impact the book made on her when it first appeared.[3] In his long poem *What* Ron Silliman singles out this volume as Ashbery's "one book / that's not too much in love with beauty."[4] The concerted experiments of the Language poets in the 1980s have to some extent acclimated current readers to *The Tennis Court Oath*. But in 1962 few readers were prepared for the shock of a poem such as "Leaving the Atocha Station":

The arctic honey blabbed over the report causing darkness
And pulling us out of there experiencing it
he meanwhile ... And the fried bats they sell there
dropping from sticks, so that the menace of your prayer folds ...
Other people ...           flash
the garden are you boning

and defunct covering . . . Blind dog expressed royalties . . .
comfort of your perfect tar grams nuclear world bank tulip
Favorable to          near the night pin
loading formaldehyde.    the table torn from you
Suddenly      and we are close
Mouthing the root        when you think
generator        homes enjoy leered
(TCO 33; ellipses are Ashbery's)

Ashbery has provided some background to this poem which amounts to
a compact explanation of his representative poetics:

> That poem was written after my first trip to Spain; the Atocha Station is a
> railway station in Madrid. . . . It strikes me that the dislocated, incoherent
> fragments of images which make up the movement of the poem are proba-
> bly like the experience you get from a train pulling out of a station of no
> particular significance. The dirt, the noises, the sliding away seem to be a
> movement in the poem. The poem was probably trying to express that,
> not for itself but as an epitome of something experienced; I think that is
> what my poems are about.[5]

Traditionally, poets have been said to represent the universal through the
particular, so that readers might participate in the poet's representative personal experiences. Ashbery's misrepresentative poetics operate differently;
the poem represents no experience in particular. Though Ashbery had first
left Atocha Station in 1960 with Frank O'Hara, who had come to Madrid
to select some contemporary Spanish art for an exhibit, it is doubtful that
either of them ate (or shunned) "arctic honey" or "fried bats" or saw workers "loading formaldehyde." These surreal particulars represent the experience of the overwhelming impenetrability of a foreign culture. They misrepresent "local color," like the "rose- and lemon-colored flowers" of "The
Instruction Manual." The obvious difference, of course, is that many of the
particulars of "Leaving the Atocha Station" are repulsive. In a long tribute
to Antonin Artaud written around a year earlier, Ashbery praised Artaud's
call for an "all-important horror" in the theater. For Ashbery, even an extreme, Poe-like passage from Artaud's letters from the asylum at Rodez—
"a rat, who lodged himself in a piece of bread I had near me on a table and
ate out the inside of it, covered my books with rat dung"—is representative
in that it can "translate the feeling of anguish and cosmic hatred that all of
us have felt at one time." As Ashbery puts it, "horror inspires creation."[6]

But the horrors and oddities of "Leaving the Atocha Station" are linguistically contrived. The first line splits the difference between two novelistic sentences, say "The golden sun passed over the horizon causing darkness" and "Honey [or Tea] spilled over the newspaper's weather report," creating a confusion of levels, familiar from "The Instruction Manual," in which blotting a weather map precipitates darkness. I agree with Perloff that the opening of "Leaving the Atocha Station" "reads rather like a Dada collage or *cadavre exquis* made by jumbling and cutting up the lines from *The Waste Land:* 'Oh keep the Dog far hence, that's friend to men, / Or with his nails he'll dig it up again!'"[7] As Eliot's "hypocrite lecteur" is warned against desecrating the boneyard of the poem, the reader of "Leaving Atocha Station" is frightened away from exhuming a buried narrative (as one irresistibly tries to do): While reading the newspaper ["nuclear world bank"] and smoking ["tar grams"], we watched the seeing-eye dog dig up a tulip garden for a buried bone. With its symbolist horror and artifactitious appearances, *The Waste Land* indeed looms large over "Atocha." Then again, the homotextuality of "Suddenly and we are close / Mouthing the root" partially uncovers practices alien to some heterosexual tourists.

Yet, first impressions notwithstanding, *The Tennis Court Oath* is not the unqualified exception it appears to be. Ashbery's experiments are neither entirely unprecedented nor entirely opaque. Once the initial horror (or exhilaration) of reading *The Tennis Court Oath* passes, many readers will find the volume as diverse and challenging as any Ashbery has written. Only a third of the volume's poems aggressively disrupt grammar, syntax, punctuation, and physical layout. The rest are mostly written in an "intermediate" style, and some (ten or so) would not be out of place in *Some Trees.* Conversely, some of the darker passages from the earlier volume would be at home in *The Tennis Court Oath:* "At last twilight that will not protect the leaves / Death that will not try to scream / Black beaches / That is why I sent you the black postcard that will never deafen" (ST 38). But in *Some Trees,* Artaud's horror could be overlooked.

In the more disjunctive poems of *The Tennis Court Oath* Ashbery paid homage to his counterparts in painting. The composite traces of the abstract expressionists (Franz Kline, Jackson Pollock, Willem de Kooning, Joan Mitchell), collagists and assemblage artists (Robert Rauschenberg, Jasper Johns), and gestural realists (Larry Rivers, Jane Freilicher) are discernible in the book. Even the renderings of classical paintings in *The Tennis Court Oath* have a contemporary finish. The title of the volume comes from Jacques-Louis David's famous painting of the Fathers of the French Revolution, *The Oath of the Tennis Court* (1791).[8] One study for the painting depicts a few painted heads of revolutionaries atop nude bodies. In the artistic ambiance of the late 1950s, David's unfinished painting resembled the erased and purposely unfinished canvases of de Kooning and Rivers. Juxtaposed with "unfinished" paintings such as these, the revolutionary undress of Ashbery's title shows through.

In the "statement of intent" which appeared on the dust jacket of *The Tennis Court Oath* without his consent (and was later suppressed), Ashbery announced: "I attempt to use words abstractly, as an abstract painter would use paint. (I have perhaps been more influenced by modern painting and music than by poetry.) . . . As with the abstract painters, my abstraction is an attempt to get a greater, more complete kind of realism." Ashbery's associations with abstract painters date from his first years in New York. Though he was never the fixture Frank O'Hara was, he frequented the Cedar Street Tavern for various symposia and events of The Club, organized by some of the leading painters of the New York school. In May 1952, for instance, an evening with "New Poets" (moderated by Larry Rivers) featured Barbara Guest, O'Hara, Schuyler, and Ashbery.[9] In Paris in 1959 Ashbery translated instructions to workmen installing a now legendary exhibition of works from the Museum of Modern Art, *The New American Painting,* set up by O'Hara and Porter McCray. In a 1968 talk, Ashbery located the "influence" of the abstract expressionists on the New York school poets not in the product but in the process: "The artists liked us and bought us drinks and we, on the other hand, felt that they—and I am speaking of artists like de Kooning, Franz Kline, Motherwell, Pollock—were free to be free in their painting in a way that most people felt was impossible for poetry. So I think we learned a lot from them at that time, and also from composers like John Cage and Morton Feldman, but the lessons were merely an abstract truth—something like Be yourself—rather than a practical one—in other words nobody ever thought he would scatter words over a page the way Pollock scattered his drips, but the reason for doing so might have been the same in both cases."[10] In a lecture given at the Yale Art School in 1968, "The Invisible Avant-Garde," Ashbery characterized Pollock of the late 1940s and early 1950s as a high-stakes gambler who "was gambling everything on the fact that he *was* the greatest painter in America, for if he wasn't he was nothing, and the drips would turn out to be random splashes from the brush of a careless housepainter" (RS 390). Pollock's wager probably encouraged Ashbery to discard his award-winning (though not popular) first style to write what might not even be considered poetry.

Particular poems from his early years in France call Pollock's all-over painting to mind. Here is the beginning (or top) of "Winter," published in 1961:

<pre>
      There is a
            I like                however
   He didn't want to get that
                                responsibility?

       to worry about      made
       new cars came out          the      the day

          all we've got     don't try to build[11]
</pre>

This poem-painting quickly upsets the conventions of sequential reading by breaking through both right and left margins, and by preceding a question-marked word ("responsibility?" demands an author) with three capital-lettered words ("There," "I," "He"); it is better looked at, or read around in, than read through. Alternately, taking the title "Winter" and the vacant opening assertion ("There is a") as clues, we may imagine that the intervening words necessary for syntactical sense have been buried or erased in the snow, as in the whited-out canvases of de Kooning or Rivers. But the "new cars," the used American ("came out," "all we've got"), and the general status of "Winter" as a documentary object also bring the collagists and pop artists, or new realists, to mind. In late February of 1961 Ashbery finished a poem called "The New Realism" (TCO 59) and in September of 1962 (*The Tennis Court Oath* was published in February 1962) wrote a catalogue essay, "The New Realism," for the important exhibit at the Janis Gallery in New York that put pop art on the map. The exhibit displayed both French *nouveaux réalistes* (including two favorites of Ashbery, Yves Klein and Niki de Saint-Phalle) and American pop artists (including Tom Wesselmann, Eric Segal, Andy Warhol, Robert Indiana, Roy Lichtenstein, and Claes Oldenburg). In his essay, Ashbery found the common ground of these artists in their obsession with the object:

> The "New Realism" is the European term for the art of today which in one way or another makes use of the qualities of manufactured objects. As the name indicates, it is (like Surrealism) another kind of Realism—the movement which began in the nineteenth century at the same time that machines and machine-made objects began to play such an important part in daily life. . . . One could point to other examples in the arts today (elsewhere for instance the "objective" novels of Robbe-Grillet and Sarraute, or the importance of objects, especially artifacts, in the recent films of Resnais or Antonioni) of this continuing effort to come to grips with the emptiness of industrialized modern life. The most successful way of doing this seems to be to accord it its due. (RS 81)

Ashbery would probably include Roussel with his "objective" long poems and his mechanically produced stories and novels among the surrealist precursors of this movement.

From this description, we would expect Ashbery's poem "The New Realism" to exhibit modernity, as the poem says, by "some utterly crass sign" (TCO 61) or other. We get something of the sort in the suddenly lucid conclusion of the poem, as "she" finds temporary solace at the ends of the earth: "This was as far as she would go— / A tavern with plants" (TCO 62). Finding a narrative equivalent to the mechanically reproduced object in the discourse of the mass-produced popular romance, Ashbery records the retreat of Nature from the Machine: "Dynamite out over the horizon / And a sequel, and a racket" (TCO 62). The most pressing threat to human nature in "The New Realism" is not the noise but the grim wheels of economic justice: "if the returning merchants in the morning hitched the rim of the van / In the evening one must be very quick to give them the slip. / The judge knocked" (TCO 62). Ashbery's objection against the advance of modern objects gives "The New Realism" a critical force lacking in some pop art from the sixties.

In 1960 some of the poems eventually collected in *The Tennis Court Oath* appeared in a limited-edition volume, *The Poems,* with original silk-screen prints by Joan Mitchell. The book was part of a boxed set, which included poetry by Koch (prints by Alfred Leslie), O'Hara (prints by Michael Goldberg), and Schuyler (prints by Grace Hartigan). Also in 1960 Donald Allen's influential anthology, *The New American Poetry: 1945–1960,* grouped the New York Poets (as Allen called them): Ashbery, Koch, O'Hara, Schuyler, Guest, and Edward Field. A year later Ashbery and Harry Mathews, a novelist whom he had met in France, enlisted Koch and Schuyler as co-editors and founded the experimental literary journal *Locus Solus* (named for one of Roussel's novels and emulating the early surrealist review, *Nord-Sud,* edited by Pierre Reverdy), published five times during that year and the next. It was also in 1961 that John Myers, who ran the influential Tibor de Nagy gallery and published *Turandot and Other Poems* in 1953, coined the term the New York School of Poetry (on analogy with the New York School of Painting). Ashbery thinks of the New York school of the 1950s as establishing "a geographical reality and an intellectual opposition with the Black Mountain poets, implanted in North Carolina." In a 1968 talk, Ashbery described the city itself as an action painting: "New York is really an antiplace, an abstract climate, and I am not prepared to take up the cudgels to defend such a place especially when I would much rather be living in San Francisco."[12] Schuyler, who was editing the premier issue of *Locus Solus,* wrote to Ashbery that "part of its unstated objective is a riposte at THE

NEW AMERICAN POETRY, which has so thoroughly misrepresented so many of us—not completely, but the implications of context [with Olson opening the anthology] are rather overwhelming."[13] Though Olson's and Pound's experiments with lineation and discourse leave their mark on Ashbery's "Europe," the New York school poet is not on familiar terms with the objectivist tradition: Ashbery admits that "I have never liked Pound, except for his early works. I met him once at the Spoleto Festival, in 1965 I believe; he read his poems in a thin, almost inaudible voice. Charles Olson introduced us: Pound looked at me in a ferocious manner and didn't say a word to me."[14] Unlike the Black Mountain school, the New York school had no campus or lessons or poetics, other than the absence of a poetics, the very rules by which group discipline might be maintained. None of these founding members wrote anything like the manifestoes coming from Black Mountain. The misnomer notwithstanding, Ashbery remains a New York school poet to the degree that his work is antithetical to critical knowledge and to the project of knowing itself.

The best documentary evidence we have of the existence of the New York school is the wealth of their collaborations. Ashbery's longest collaboration is *A Nest of Ninnies,* a witty conversation-novel (modeled after those of Ronald Firbank, Ivy Compton-Burnett, and Henry James)[15] written with Schuyler, begun in 1952 and finished, after a hiatus, in 1969. Ashbery recalls its genesis: "We were being driven into New York from the Hamptons. . . . We were in the back seat trying to think of something to amuse us, and Jimmy suggested we write a novel. I said how could we do that, and he said, 'Oh it's very simple.' He pulled out a pad and said, 'Think of a first line.' So I did, and he thought of the second line. We proceeded along that way, gathering inspiration from the suburban countryside we were going through."[16] Like *The Vermont Notebook, A Nest of Ninnies* began on the road: "Alice was tired. Languid, fretful, she turned to stare into her own eyes in the mirror above the mantelpiece before she spoke. 'I dislike being fifty miles from a great city. I don't know how many cars pass every day and it makes me wonder.'"[17] This well-furnished novel was fueled by friendly competition; as Schuyler recalled: "writing it, John and I were always trying to cap each other as it went along."[18] In the winter of 1957 Ashbery, Koch, and O'Hara wrote a mystery play (unpublished) featuring themselves and their friends, *The Coronation Murder Mystery* (for Schuyler), with the following cast: "Mike (Mike Goldberg); Psychiatrist (Kenneth Koch); Jimmy Schuyler (John Ashbery); The Body (Frank O'Hara); John Myers (Hal Fondren); Jane (Jane Freilicher); Larry (Larry Rivers)."[19] In 1961 Koch devoted the second issue of *Locus Solus* to collaborations past and present, including "Six Collaborations" by Koch and Ashbery. In a fascinating essay on collaboration, Koch detailed the backbreakingly arbitrary rules for his and Ashbery's sestina, "Crone Rhapsody": "every line contain[s] the name of a flower, a tree, a fruit, a game, and a famous old lady, as well as the word *bathtub;* furthermore, . . . all the end-words are pieces of office furniture." The result was a zany, pop-surrealist monstrosity: "'Pin the tail on the donkey,' gurgled Julia Ward Howe. A larch shaded the bathtub. From the scabiosa on the desk / The maple gladioli watch Emily Post playing May I? in the persimmon bathtub with the fan."[20] As these overgrown lines make clear, Ashbery and Koch used the strict form of the sestina less to align themselves with a formalist tradition than to escape conventional patterns of association. Even more than in a traditional sestina, in this ink-draining game each line keeps its own linear integrity. Further, Koch's rules meant that each selection was a member of an unlikely class, a surrealist variation on Ashbery's own misrepresentational poetics.

The collaborations in *Locus Solus* included selections from *The Immaculate Conception* (c.1935) by André Breton and Paul Eluard and two poems (1937) by Eluard and René Char, all translated by Ashbery. These translations give one measure of the influence of French poetry on *The Tennis Court Oath.* Consider the following dicta from Breton and Eluard's "The Original Judgment": "Don't read. Look at the designs created by the spaces between the words of several lines in a book and draw inspiration from them. . . . Rob sound of its sense; even light-colored dresses hide muffled drums. . . . Damn what is pure, purity is damned in you."[21] With his visual designs, abstract sonorities, and impure mixtures of lyric and pop dictions, Ashbery keeps their commandments. His translation of "New" (1937) by Char and Eluard resembles some of his own poems in its linear integrity, erotic melancholy, and "automatic" conjunctions of images: "The mouth that determines festivals / Untiring is rung by the great clock / Turning tress uselessly drowned."[22] The French surrealist tongue helped Ashbery ring in the new.

Ashbery has taken exception, however, to "automatic writing," the mainspring of the surrealist mechanism. In "A Note on Pierre Reverdy" (unpublished; c.1957–58), Ashbery claims that "Reverdy's poetry avoids the extremes of Surrealist poetry, and is the richer for it":

> Though all rules were seemingly abolished, the poets were careful to observe the rules of grammar and syntax: "Take care," wrote Breton. "I know the meaning of each of my words and I observe syntax *naturally:* syntax is not a discipline, as certain oafs believe." But does one always observe these rules when one is writing automatically? And what, in fact, is automatic writing? Isn't all writing automatic? If one corrects a poem after writing

it, doesn't one happen automatically on the correction? The discipline as it was practiced by the surrealists seems arbitrary and sterile.

Ashbery's quarrel with Breton extended beyond poetics. In a 1968 review of an exhibition of surrealist painting at the Museum of Modern Art, Ashbery pointed out that Breton's banner of *liberté totale* included "every conceivable kind of sexual act except for homosexuality.... This exception may seem unimportant, since homosexuality affects a relatively small fraction of humanity, but to restrict something proclaimed as 'total' is to turn it into its limited opposite." After the movement was attacked by Ilya Ehrenburg as "pederastic," the homosexual surrealist writer René Crevel committed suicide. Ashbery inevitably regards surrealism with mixed feelings: "what is one to think of a vanguard literary movement that found it necessary to excoriate Antonin Artaud?" (RS 6).

Ashbery also uses Reverdy to distance himself from Dada and Modernism. Reverdy, Ashbery argues, was not in the business of demolishing art and beauty, as the Dada theoreticians claimed to be. In any case, as Ashbery notes, history soon turned the anti-art works of Ernst, Picabia, and Duchamp into things of beauty. Ashbery speculates that the Dada artists would perhaps have "agreed with Reverdy when he says, in 'Self-Defense': 'The beautiful does not come out of the artist's hands, but what comes out of the artist's hands *becomes* the beautiful.'" Unlike the French surrealists, and modernists such as Eliot, Reverdy aimed for the beauty of the literal: "Reverdy succeeds in restoring to things their real name, in abolishing the eternal dead weight of symbolism and allegory.... In Eliot's *The Waste Land,* the real world appears ... always artificially bound to an allegorical meaning—the gas-works and the 'dull canal,' for example."[23] While it might be argued that the "real name" of a particular thing itself represents the specificity of reality, producing what Roland Barthes called "the reality-effect,"[24] there is no doubt that Reverdy's immediacy offered the intellectually inclined Ashbery an alternative to Eliot's early poetry.

Ashbery's translations of Reverdy, though not as disjunctive or nonsyntactical as some poems in *The Tennis Court Oath,* exhibit equally moving dislocations, as in "The Invasion": "The young student goes back up to his family / And the other in life / Having climbed over the iron gates / Without knowing where he is going / And the boat arrives bringing the sheep"[25] The lack of punctuation makes the logical relation between the lines, and between the possibly amorous desertion and the ritual invasion, impossible to determine. This kind of indeterminate, emotionally charged narrative, which Ashbery likened to "novels compressed into a tiny space by some superhuman force,"[26] structures the narrative collages and lyric assemblages of *The Tennis Court Oath*.

A double issue of *Locus Solus* (III-IV, Winter 1962) contained a selection from "Three French Poets," Denis Roche, Marcelin Pleynet, and Pierre Martory, translated by Ashbery. These poets, all friends of Ashbery's, experimented along parallel and abstract lines. Martory's "Les Soirées de Rochefort," for example, is an extravaganza modeled on Roussel's parenthetically embedded poem "Nouvelles Impressions d'Afrique," here encircling sailors on leave: "NOW THAT THOSE HOUSES HAVE BEEN CLOSED BY LAW / ((A former marine could think himself in China / (in the orange light that falls from unwatched lanterns / —at twenty, far from Rochefort, the heart breaks . . ." (122; ellipsis is Martory's). In "Black" ("Noir") the art critic and poet Pleynet (an editor of *Tel Quel*) breaks the laws of grammar to loosen the grip of song. It begins with an ostensive definition of its title:

to know how not to hang on any more song

In truth
incredible irritation
the towels still graze his nose
in a time
when the early risers leave themselves
in no more see
look at
and caress the fathers
(120)

The infinitives in "où les matinaux se laissent / dans ne plus voir / regarder / et caresser les pères" (121) are rendered ungrammatically by Ashbery, breaking the syntactical tie between "early risers" and "fathers." Roche, who in 1965 translated three poems from *The Tennis Court Oath* into French, is now the best known poet of the group. In the untitled poem Ashbery translates, Roche stops his unpunctuated lines only to catch his breath: "As a matter of fact that bird how many / Chances didn't I have to know its identity / However it lets its spoor die and / The effluvium underneath lost with perfection" (110). The haphazardness with which these otherwise classical alexandrines close gives each line an elegiac imperfection.

Probably the most urgent of the incitements to *The Tennis Court Oath* was the poetry of Gertrude Stein. In a 1957 review of Stein's *Stanzas in*

*Meditation* Ashbery singled out the syntagmatic, relational character of the 1932 title poem,

> made up almost entirely of colorless connecting words such as "where," "which," "these," "of," ... though now and then Miss Stein throws in an orange, a lilac, or an Albert to remind us that it really is the world, our world, that she has been talking about. The result is like certain mono-chrome de Kooning paintings in which isolated strokes of color take on a deliciousness they never could have had out of context, or a piece of music by Webern in which a single note on the celesta suddenly irrigates a whole desert of dry, scratchy sounds in the strings.[27]

Ashbery will later describe his own poem "Europe" in similar terms. Stein's poem, whose protagonist and subject is the pronoun "they," is an all-purpose narrative: "In its profound originality, its original profundity, this poem that is always threatening to become a novel reminds us of the late novels of James, especially *The Golden Bowl* and *The Sacred Fount,* which seem to strain with a superhuman force toward 'the condition of music,' of poetry" (253). Ashbery quotes one of Stein's Jamesian stanzas, which bears a family resemblance to the stanzas of *The Tennis Court Oath:*

> Be not only without in any of their sense
> Careful
> Or should they grow careless with remonstrance
> Or be careful just as easily not at all
> As when they felt.
> They could or would would they grow always
> By which not only as more as they like.
> They cannot please conceal
> Nor need they find need they a wish [Stanza XVI][28]

To Ashbery, these lines strive to represent "a completely new picture of real-ity, of that *real* reality of the poet which Antonin Artaud called '*une réalité dangereuse et typique.*'" Ashbery here yokes Stein, Stevens ("A Completely New Set of Objects")[29] and Artaud by violence together to drive his own misrepresentative poetics, where one must proceed with the utmost aban-don. Stein's meditations, more than those of the French precursors, provide an analogy for the difficult necessity of reading and of living, which sets a precedent for the harrowingly difficult experience of reading *The Tennis Court Oath.*

Three Steinian narrative poems in this collection—"Idaho," "Europe," and "'They Dream Only of America'"—extend the experiments of *Some*

*Trees* by incorporating actual written and oral documents. The funniest is "Idaho" (dated September 1956), the poem that closes *The Tennis Court Oath*. Soon after the book was published in 1962, O'Hara reported to Ashbery: "Yesterday I went up to Yale to read poetry, and you will be pleased to know that my rendition of Idaho made quite a hit. I had read it out of *Locus Solus* [where 'Idaho' first appeared, in 1961], but we were certainly right about the necessity of its being in the book."[30] The poem is assembled almost entirely from *Soundings* (1925), a popular novel by A. Hamilton Gibbs, which Ashbery found in his parents' home in Sodus. The story of an independent-minded young English girl, in the quiet days before the Great War, who shuns conventions to explore life, love, and art in Paris, must have delighted Ashbery as a middle-brow rendition of his own expatriate experience.

In constructing "Idaho" Ashbery scrambled the narrative sequence of passages from *Soundings* and erased their connective links and determinate contexts. He also recomposed elements within a passage, using the open pages of *Soundings* as a palette. Here is a passage from the original, followed by Ashbery's product:

"Yes," said Nancy, "but I didn't understand—I'm not sure that I do now.—Do you mean—? That isn't marriage." She shivered. "It's—it's death!"

### III

The door of the studio slammed.

"Hullo, honey!" said Cornelia. "You're back early."

. . . . .

"What've you got hold of?"

"Wells' latest, 'Tono Bungay.'"

"Extraordinary title!" said Cornelia. She repeated it twice.

"What does it mean?"

Nancy laughed. "Among other things, it means that I shan't do any work till I've finished it. It's the reason of my being back so early. I dropped into Brentano's just to have a prowl round and get some of the Christmas numbers, and caught sight of a pile of these. I just grabbed one and came straight home.—Oh, by the way, there's a telegram for you. See?" She pointed to the table.

> Cornelia unfolded the piece of crude blue paper that is a
> French telegram.

(line breaks as in original; ellipsis is mine)[31]

> "What does it mean??????????????"
>
> Carol laughed. Among other things,
> till I've finished it. It's the reason of
> dropped into Brentano's.
> get some of the
> a pile of these. I just grabbed one . . . . .
> —Oh, by the way, there's a tele-
> "See?" She pointed to the table.
> Cornelia unfolded the piece of crude paper that is a French telegra.
> ###################
> The mouth of weeds
>
> "marriage." She shivered. "It's—it's a death!"
> II.
> The door of the studio slammed.
> "Hullo, honey!" Cornelia said.

(TCO 92)

Although "Idaho" stands in perfect incompleteness on its own, juxtaposition with Gibbs's prose emphasizes the detailed intricacy, as well as the radicalness, of Ashbery's deconstruction. With the subject matter of this literary chat sheared away, the exasperated "What does it mean??????????????" becomes self-reflexive, Cornelia's shuddering exclamation ("It's—it's a death!") homotextual. It is worth noting that Gibbs too lets Cornelia's inquiry go unanswered, leaving H. G. Wells's emblematically telegraphic title untranslated; even middle-brow novels employ representative poetics. Self-referential details pile up in this segment from "Idaho": the bookstore; the surrealist random selection and elision ("I just grabbed one . . ."); the economically abbreviated ("telegra.") imagist ("The mouth of weeds") style; and the erased, unfinished latency ("till I've finished it") of the fragmentary page on the point of revelation.

"Idaho" stands alone in *The Tennis Court Oath* in containing too much rather than too little punctuation. The decorative curlicues punctuating "What does it mean??????????????" trademark the collage as high-pitched romance, while snapping Gibbs's strings with far too many turns of the screw. The roman numeral II (not III) merely simulates a structural division ("Idaho" has no part I). The curtain-dropping "death!" is preserved from

Gibbs. So too is the cinematic, final punctuation of "Idaho" (and thus of the volume): "A whistle blew shrilly" (TCO 94; *Soundings* 193).[32] The ornamental proofreader's crosshatches suggest galley proofs preceding the final poem ("Idaho" was written on the typewriter). (In *Locus Solus* "Idaho" uses virgules or lyric "slashes" instead of crosshatches—did the printers in Majorca lack the # type?—but crosshatches look better on the page.[33]) Several of the line breaks (notably the printerly hyphenation of "tele-") reproduce the layout of the Little, Brown edition of Gibbs's novel, as though it were a found poem. Ashbery's procedure derives both from Cage's chance operations and from New York school collages, in which the printed page is taken as a piece of material, a corner of which may be torn out and stitched into the poem, and then submitted to the further abstraction of erasures. The writer's question marks and section heading, the proofreader's crosshatches, the printer's hyphen: each marks a separate stage of literary production, and thus layers the textual space of "Idaho." As in the less premeditated action painting, "Idaho" records (or mimes) its own process of construction.

Ashbery's longest narrative collage is "Europe," cut up arbitrarily into 111 sections of telegraphic lines. The very number is daunting, as "when you open a foreign grammar and see how many lessons are ahead."[34] But these lessons lay the groundwork for no known language. Parallels with painting come to mind, especially Rauschenberg's junk collages and erasures, which Ashbery appreciated and alluded to in section 16: "when canvas the must spread / to new junk" (TCO 66–67).[35] Ashbery recalls that Rauschenberg's notorious "erased de Kooning" got him "to wondering; suppose he did erase it? Wouldn't there be enough left so that it would be some *thing?* If so, how much? Or if not, how much could be erased and still have the 'sense' of the original left?"[36] Ashbery's "de Kooning" was *Some Trees;* "Europe" "was a way of trying to obliterate the poetry that at the time was coming naturally to me, and which I didn't like. It was an attempt to shuffle the cards before dealing them again."[37] In his fracturing of "Europe" into grammatical vertebrae, Ashbery also took the cue of Anton Webern (to whom he had compared Stein). Ashbery recalls his enthusiasm on hearing Webern's collected works, which he bought soon after they appeared: "I was tremendously moved by these isolated notes, I mean you often hear a note plucked on a violin and it seems as though you're hearing that note for the first time."[38]

Koch thought "Europe" was "quite brilliant."[39] O'Hara was equally enthusiastic about the poem when it appeared. In a letter to Ashbery, he called it "the most striking thing since The Wasteland, and so far I understand it about as well as Harriet Monroe understood TW. But I'm coming along and it is a great pleasure to find something again which is so intriguing, compelling and attention-demanding, and mysterious."[40] O'Hara's generous response also took the form of writing a new style of poems which "should be collected under the title *Little Verses for the Admirers of Ashbery's Europe.*"[41] He sent Ashbery one of these (as yet uncollected) in a letter written on Bastille Day of 1960, a few months after "Europe" had appeared. With a characteristically joyous hyperbole, O'Hara remarked in the letter that "*Europe* is carrying all before it, it is on everyone's lips and in their hearts":

### POEM

"We'll probably pay for it in August" the radio says
these beautiful steel days of loneliness, I won't pay

       Grieg's country dances
       Stravinsky's *Norwegian Moods*

I don't think of them as lice, I think of them as crabs
it's my zodiacal sign -O-, all part of the strange slump of summer[42]

Though the disjunctiveness here is relatively unobtrusive, the suspension of punctuation and the linear integrity move toward Ashbery's poetics. O'Hara advanced further toward "Europe" by the end of 1960:

### WHAT APPEARS TO BE YOURS

The root           an acceptable connection
ochre       except meaning-dream partly
where the will falters        a screw polished
a whole pair of shutters       you saw it
I went in the door      the umbrella
apart from the hole you see a slide      up
two blue      yes the wind mutters
it slides and gulps      it is the snow[43]

The intimacy of this I-Thou lyric is rendered in two intermingling columns, which stretch and snap syntactical and semantic links at various points beyond any "acceptable connection" between phrases and lovers, much as Ashbery will do, on a much larger scale, in "Litany."

O'Hara's experiment bears comparison with the opening section of Ashbery's monumental ruin "Europe":

To employ her
construction ball

Morning fed on the
light blue wood
of the mouth
                    cannot understand
feels deeply)
(TCO 64)

O'Hara's poem is more spatially and discursively diversified. The excitement of Ashbery's opening lies in its liberated punctuation and grammar. These fragments keep reformulating the sphere, from the ball to the "light blue" "Morning" sky to the wooden "roof" of the mouth to the Rousselian parenthesis, which closes nothing (the unpaired parenthesis and spacious indentation also recall Olson's *The Maximus Poems,* an unacknowledged forerunner). Still close to the lyric phrase of *Some Trees,* the lines cannot be extended beyond a few words without bogging down in modifiers: "filthy or into backward drenched flung heaviness / lemons asleep pattern crying" (TCO 64). The reflexive "construction ball" and the uncontracted marginal "cannot understand" maintain a lyric formality and resonance. Among O'Hara's equally brief phrases, the hemistich "an acceptable connection" is rhythmic and resonant, but the doggedly Freudian qualifier "except meaning-dream partly" shatters the painterly decorum of "ochre." With this technical language (rather than simply mechanical imagery, such as "construction ball"), O'Hara seems further along the road toward the discursive vitality of Language poetry. But Ashbery sustained his discontinuities for 111 sections.

Ashbery constructed "Europe" in the fall of 1958 at the Paris home of Harry Mathews, experimental novelist, publisher and editor of *Locus Solus,* and in 1960 one of the founding members of the French experimental writing group, Oulipo. Like "Idaho," "Europe" was scaffolded on a forgotten novel, by William Le Queux, "a child's story for girls about a mysterious aviatrix in World War I, called *Beryl of the By-plane;* I found it on the *quais.*"[44] Nearly a century earlier, Robert Browning had used the plot of a murder story, which he found in a secondhand book stall, for his own experimental masterpiece, *The Ring and the Book,* but Ashbery made the fractured, scrambled narrative of *Beryl* itself part of the mystery. Just enough of the generic struts of *Beryl* remain in "Europe" to sustain Ashbery's misrepresentative torsion.

With its host of violently executed spies, William Le Queux's World War I novel would surely have been a disturbing "child's story." Set almost entirely in England (not in "Europe"), the novel concerns the exploits of the ace pilots Ronald Pryor and Beryl (cf. "Ash*bery*") Gaselee, who fly "The

Hornet," an experimental flying machine equipped with a top-secret "silencer," which allows the pilots to fly up to their prey undetected. The deadly couple fly for the English secret service, to protect England from the "enemy within." The book is filled with detective story mechanisms: Morse and other codes, disguises, double agents, and newspaper accounts of mysterious fatal "accidents," which only Ronald, Beryl, and the reader properly understand. The self-reflexive possibilities of detective fiction were mined in France in the 1950s by the "objective" or "new novelists" Marguerite Duras, Michel Butor, and Alain Robbe-Grillet, the last two of whom acknowledged Roussel as an important influence. In France in 1955 Ashbery had investigated Roussel and discovered several photographs and even the explanatory first chapter, "In Havana," suppressed from his posthumously published work, *Documents to Serve as an Outline,* which Ashbery later translated.[45] As Ashbery confessed: "It got to be a fascinating hobby, doing detective work on his career."[46] During the fall of 1958 Ashbery (under the pen name "Jonas Berry") was at work translating a popular mystery, *Murder in Montmartre* by one Noël Vexin, into French. His detective reading, translating, and scholarship spilled over into his investigative poetry.

As in Roussel's or Robbe-Grillet's novels, nothing is what it seems in *Beryl;* farmhouses can be munitions factories or airplane hangars, German warplanes carry English insignias, and German spies speak with English or American accents. These doublings, in which the enemy looks and acts "just like you and me," produce a paranoid atmosphere most immediately resembling the McCarthyism of the early 1950s. As one would-be informant complains, "nowadays you dare not say anything about anybody you suspect, for fear of being had up for libel. The law somehow seems to protect the Germans in our midst" (*Beryl,* 97).[47] To gauge the representativeness of this repressive paranoia, we need only substitute "Communists," "homosexuals," or "Jews" for "Germans." By 1958, of course, both McCarthy and Ashbery had left the American scene. But Ashbery doubtless saw the continuing possibilities in Le Queux's grim little novel.

Juxtaposing a few of the 111 stanzas of "Europe" (TCO 82–83) with *Beryl* will give us an idea of Ashbery's procedures:

> The engine had stopped, for, half the propeller
> being broken, the other half had embedded
> itself deeply into the ground. Collins came
> running up, half frantic with fear, but was soon
> reassured by the pair of intrepid aviators, who
> unstrapped themselves and quickly climbed out
> of the wreckage. Ere long a flare was lit and the

broken wing carefully examined; it was soon
discovered that "The Hornet" had been tampered with, one of the steel bolts having been
replaced by a painted one of wood!

"This is the work of the enemy!" remarked
Ronnie thoughtfully. "They cannot obtain sight
of the silencer, therefore there has been a dastardly
plot to kill both of us. We must be a little more
wary in future, dear."
(61; line breaks as in *Beryl*)

104.

| blaze | | | aviators | |
|---|---|---|---|---|
| | out | | dastardly | |

105.
We must be a little more wary in
future, dear

106.
she was trying to make sense of
what was quick laugh
hotel—cheap for them
caverns the bed
box of cereal

Ere long a flare was lit
I don't understand wreckage

107.
blue smoke?                    The steel bolts
It was as though        having been replaced
She had        by a painting of
the river        one of wood!
above the water        Ronnie, thoughtfully

of the silencer

plot to kill both of us, dear.

pet

oh
it that she was there

59

Amid this wreckage we may first pick up the discourse of pulp romance, as in Ronnie's hilariously understated caution to Beryl in #105. Even the dismembered "pet" and "oh" retain a stereotypical sentimental eroticism. The conventions of detective fiction also dot these pages. Whether or not we know their contextual significance, we know that "steel bolts" and the "box of cereal" are clues, that "a flare" and "blue smoke" are signs. In their new context, statements such as "she was trying to make sense of" and "I don't understand wreckage" may be read self-reflexively. In "Europe" we positively identify reader figures ("she studied her map, took her bearings," TCO 73), author figures ("Mr. Bean remained indoors / at the small boats / of our defences, our intentions," TCO 81), and reflexive descriptions ("Is not a 'images' / to 'arrange'" TCO 77). Even the notoriously undecoded ending of "Europe" is readable (TCO 85):

> Once more the light opened out and commenced
> to signal the Morse flashes and flares
> "N.F.", "N.F."
> followed by a long beam of
> light skyward, slowly sweeping in a circle
>
> the breath

In the corresponding passage from *Beryl* (70–71), the signal "N.F., N.F." is a coded message to the German spies, which remains opaque to Ronnie, Beryl, and the reader. Le Queux left this mysterious code unexplained.

Like "Winter," "Europe" is to be pored over. The debris of "The Hornet" is scattered over the postwar waste land of Ashbery's "Europe." In #104, the generically descriptive "aviators," "blaze," and "dastardly," along with the colorless, obliterating "out," litter the open field of the poem, which calls to mind the gridded field of Jasper Johns's stenciled canvases (Ashbery first saw these in New York the summer before he began "Europe").[48] In #107, which anticipates Ashbery's double-columned "Litany," we stumble upon the wreck itself. On the right wing, we note that Ashbery has slightly altered Le Queux's prose for the sake of a Dada joke: the steel bolt is replaced by "a painting of" (rather than a "painted") one in wood. And in the final strewn words of #107, Ronnie and Beryl narrowly escape being "rubbed out" along with their "silencer." As in "Idaho," Ashbery takes his cue from the printed page, this time sheering off a left end—"Ronnie thoughtfully." "of the silencer," "plot to kill both of us"—and pasting it on the right wing of his text. The fragment "it that she was there"—an isolated, mounted specimen of ungrammaticality—represents for Ashbery an ad-

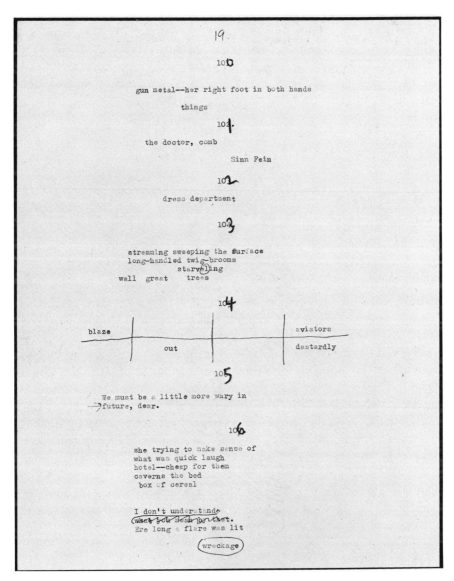

19.

100

gun metal--her right foot in both hands

things

101.

the doctor, comb

Sinn Fein

102

dress department

103

streaming sweeping the surface
long-handled twig-brooms
starveling
wall great trees

104

blaze | | aviators
out | | dastardly

105

We must be a little more wary in
future, dear.

106

she trying to make sense of
what was quick laugh
hotel--chesp for them
caverns the bed
box of cereal

I don't understand
what you mean by that.
Ere long a flare was lit
wreckage

"Europe"

vance over "French surrealist poetry," where "you can always expect the
subject to be followed by the predicate."[49]

There are indications that "Europe" resists not only the forays of traditional sequential reading but also the xenophobic paranoia of Le Queux.
Early on, we witness a homotextual panic regarding an "absolute,

unthinking / menace to our way of life" (TCO 64). The undercover heroine Beryl suspects that "He is probably one of the gang" (TCO 74), a suspicion which leads to renunciation: "The son is not ours" (TCO 74). Then, in the middle of Ashbery's fragmented stanzas, we arrive at a resonantly lucid, Audenesque sonnet, in which an exact embrace cannot cancel the geopolitical grip (TCO 74):

> Precise mechanisms
> Love us.
>
> He came over the hill
> He held me in his arms—it was marvelous,
>
> But the map of Europe
> shrinks around naked couples

Auden's influence on "Europe" is not confined to these couplets. The embattled, watchful, homophobic atmosphere of "Europe" resembles the climate of Auden's boldest experiment in collaged verse and prose, "The Orators." In its opening address, we are put on guard against undercover "perverted lovers": "Have a good look at the people you know; at the boy sitting next to you at this moment, at that chum of yours in the Lower School. Think of the holidays, your father, the girl you met at that dance. Is he one? Was she one?" (EA 63). Auden's Beryl ("There is something peculiarly horrible about the idea of women pilots," EA 88), besieged by "Enemy messages to be decoded" (EA 89), surveys inner and outer irregularities: "Dawn 13,000 ft. Shadows of struts falling across the cockpit. Perfect calm, light, strength. Yesterday positively the last time" (EA 84). Rarely in "The Orators" are the agents, outer and internalized, given the slip. In "Europe" we glimpse the erotic innocence of a closeted world beyond the police and the censors:

> The police
> Had been forgotten
> Scarlet, blue, and canary
> Heads tossing on the page
>     grunting to the coatroom
> there was another ocean, ballads and legends, the children
>     returning to the past—head
> (TCO 71)

But gay sex "on the page" is something the thought police never could abide: "The editor realized / its gradual abandonment / a kind of block where other men come down" (TCO 65). It should be clear by now why "Europe" is a biplane of lyricism on the one wing, and a network of detections, judgments, and executions on the other. In "Europe" Ashbery keeps *Beryl of the Biplane* within quotation marks not only to exploit its self-reflexive possibilities but also to mimic and "pervert" the repressive character of its relentless detections. Le Queux's work is put through the shredder in "Europe" not merely in Ashbery's defense against being read, but in his own resistance to what he reads.

The most widely reproduced short poem in *The Tennis Court Oath* is the detective lyric "'They Dream Only of America'" (TCO 13). This quatrained poem, with which Ashbery wisely chose to conclude *The Poems* (1960), was anthologized both in America and France and translated into French (by Denis Roche), Italian, Danish, and Swedish within a decade of its appearance. For Ashbery this poem belongs in a pivotal new group in which he "achieved a kind of intermediate style, say between the poems in *Some Trees* and the poem 'Europe.'"[50] It is significant that it was first published in 1959 in *Partisan Review*. While most of the poems from this period (1957–1961) were published in narrowly distributed avant-garde magazines—including Diane di Prima and Amiri Baraka's (then LeRoi Jones) *The Floating Bear,* Paul Carroll's *Big Table,* and *Locus Solus*—Ashbery continued to publish poems of "intermediate" difficulty in mainstream journals where he had already placed poems from the early 1950s. *Poetry,* for instance, published the free-verse sonnet "The Idiot" (TCO 20), the purportedly nostalgic quatrained poem "Our Youth" (TCO 41), and the lyrical etching "To Redouté," which was reprinted from an exhibition catalogue of Redouté's flowers: "To true roses uplifted on the bilious tide of evening / And morning-glories dotting the crescent day" (TCO 21). The publishing divide between "intermediate" and "advanced" poems is not completely clear, however. Ashbery's most ambitious attempt in his longer-lined compromise style, "A Last World," appeared first in *Big Table.*

Perloff has accurately labeled "'They Dream Only of America'" a "detective poem" and likened reading it to "overhearing a conversation in which one can make out individual words or phrases but has no clear idea what the speakers are talking about."[51] The appeal of the poem consists less in its surreal juxtapositions than in its slightly dislocating misrepresentations:

They dream only of America
To be lost among the thirteen million pillars of grass:

"This honey is delicious
*Though it burns the throat.*"

And hiding from darkness in barns
They can be grownups now
And the murderer's ash tray is more easily—
The lake a lilac cube.

He holds a key in his right hand.
"Please," he asked willingly.
He is thirty years old.
That was before

We could drive hundreds of miles
At night through dandelions.
When his headache grew worse we
Stopped at a wire filling station.

Now he cared only about signs.
Was the cigar a sign?
And what about the key?
He went slowly into the bedroom.

"I would not have broken my leg if I had not fallen
Against the living room table. What is it to be back
Beside the bed? There is nothing to do
For our liberation, except wait in the horror of it.

And I am lost without you."

The elevated, romantic "dream" of the opening lines relies (as evidenced by the article "the") on the encrypted idiom "to be lost in the crowd." Yet Ashbery's representation of "the crowd" as "the thirteen million pillars of grass" (rather than, say, "millions of blades of grass" or "miles of dandelions"), the definite article notwithstanding, refers to nothing; American guidebooks list no such monumental colonnade. Similarly, the ill-fated lovers' treasured dream of anonymity activates familiar fugitive narratives: hiding in barns, driving at night, and waiting for the liberation. Yet again we would expect more representative substitutions: "And hiding from darkness [in the dark, from the police, from their parents] in barns / They can be grownups [together, free, children] now." Ashbery's pleasant variations make sense only when we recall that "grownups" is a child's word for adults, and that love on the run recaptures childhood pursuits. The third quatrain alternates perversely between present and past tenses, and hence between dramatic (the first and third lines read like stage directions) and novelistic discourses. But though "'Please,' he asked willingly" sounds sufficiently pulpy, the generically tell-tale adverb should follow a response (as in "Of course," he agreed willingly) rather than a plea.

These accumulating acts of misrepresentation point toward a cover-up. Take the suspiciously uncooperative lines "And the murderer's ash tray is more easily— / The lake a lilac cube." Though the first line ends with a blank, we know just what kind of thing is missing: some verbal phrase like "disposed of," which has itself been done away with. The echolalic, bilingual ("lilac cube"; "le lac," "ice cube"), innocent-looking scenic description thus holds the place of buried evidence and significance. The cliff-hanger "That was before" is also discursively elliptical. What passes unsaid is some momentous, unspeakable change, but the chronology of this critical event cannot be ascertained. Either the preceding appeal, when "He" was thirty, or the "following" romantic night drive, could be "before" this unspecified but implied crisis. Likewise, the threadbare suspense of "He went slowly into the bedroom" anticipates the usual shocker: a body, dead or surprised. Instead, we get an epistolary quote, complete with sappy postscript, filling in for a suicide note and a (retrospective) farewell. Although several pieces of the story are missing, enough remain for us to piece together the outlines of a nostalgic narrative situation: (the remembrance of) fugitive love in a dangerous time.

But if "'They Dream Only of America'" is only an assemblage of all-purpose stories (perhaps merely linguistic), what can it mean to its maker? How does the poet fit himself into his one-size-fits-all poem? The way Ashbery in particular figures in the poem may be deduced from certain biographical details.[52] The poem was written in Paris in the summer of 1957, probably on his thirtieth birthday (July 28). That day Pierre Martory, to whom *The Tennis Court Oath* is dedicated, made the luminous remark, "This honey is delicious / *Though it burns the throat.*" In the summer of 1957 Ashbery was preparing for, and doubtless dreaming of, revisiting America; he did so from the fall of 1957 to the spring of 1958. Martory himself made a first, unplanned visit to America that spring. Though they traveled separately, the little poem looks forward to a fantastic voyage and an Edenic destination.

The misrepresentations of "'They Dream Only of America'" are insistently homotextual. The "thirteen million pillars of grass" suggest not only Whitman's *Leaves of Grass,* but the "pillar of salt" to which Lot's wife, no pillar of the community, was reduced for looking back on the destruction of Sodom. "Was the cigar a sign? / And what about the key?" In this cluttered poem, in which every personal pronoun except "she" is represented, the spermal "honey" and phallic props ("pillars," "key," "cigar," "leg") take on a parodic significance. The dismembered names of the perpetrators, "Ashbery" and "Martory," may be partially reconstructed from the line "And the *murder*er's *ash tray* is *more* easily—". The romantic secrecy of the fugitive gay lovers is parallel here to the French Resistance (Martory fought in its ranks, after his escape to Algeria) waiting for America's liberation. Though the term "gay liberation" had not yet been coined, this poem seems to wait for its minting. The utopian "American dream" here fantasizes a time and a place where gay lovers could come out of their lilac cubes.

But the homotextual orientation of Ashbery's misrepresentations, even with biographical particulars smoked out, does not finally crack or unlock "'They Dream Only of America.'" Ashbery's poetry contains no secret to which only an inner circle of readers has access. The compound of inside and outside in this poem is highly unstable. For one thing, the outside is displaced into the imagined future or the remembered past, or even into the present—once looked forward to or some day to be looked back upon. When and where is (or was or will be) the liberation? Was it when the American Ashbery arrived in Paris? Will it be when "they" arrive in America? (But Ashbery had left the United States partly for relief from its repressive political climate.) In the barns of Ashbery's childhood in rural upstate New York? In the dandified countryside of Martory's prewar France? It is always elsewhere, a state better dreamt-of than reached. "They" do not wait in "hope" but in "horror" of the "liberation." Remaining in romantic seclusion, creating the illusion of hidden meanings, may in fact be preferable to the "horror" of exposure, where love and poetry may be impossible. But is "he" or are "they" even in "there" while "we" readers investigate out here? In the fifth stanza, "He" himself is elected to investigate, peering inside with us, uncovering not the literal truth, or a body, but a letter. Yet if liberation is forever out of reach, pleasure is not. "'They Dream Only of America'" continually intrigues with its narrow escapes and new disguises. The ceaseless activity of its tenses, discourses, and roles presents ample evidence that the fugitives' love is there to stay.

Many of Ashbery's poems in his "intermediate style" are close to his New York poems of the early 1950s. One of his favorites is "Thoughts of a Young Girl" (TCO 14), the first poem he wrote after arriving in France in 1955. The story of "Thoughts" seems drawn from the tale of Rapunzel, imprisoned in the tower, though the signature of her dictated letter, "Signed, The Dwarf," suggests she has confused herself with Rumpelstiltskin. The poem consists of two disjointed sestets, and mirrors the narrative-and-commentary structure of several poems in *Some Trees*. With ages separating its documentary stanza from its afterthought stanza, "Thoughts" most closely resembles "*Le livre est sur la table*" (ST 74). But it differs from "*Le livre*" in shifting the point of origin from the physical scene to the document, left in quotes. "*Le livre*" places us at the scene of the crime, looking for traces in the sand; in "Thoughts" (as in "'They Dream Only of America'") only a reflexive letter is given as evidence. The first sestet is a patchwork of epistolary conventions. Between the opening impulse and afterthought, "It is such a beautiful day I had to write you a letter / From the tower, and to show I'm not mad" ("dead"), to the salutatory speech act, "And now I let you go," the poem waxes poetic with a metaphysical doggerel—"I only slipped on the cake of soap of the air / And drowned in the bathtub of the world"— that will continue to fascinate Ashbery. Thirty years later, in *Flow Chart,* he will ferret out "an osselet of meaning in the lizard's tail / of eternity" (FC 32). Here, the mad princess's far-flung possessives are matched by the beloved's ardent apostrophe in the second sestet, in which the mixture of sentimental and prosaically precise epithets ("daughter of my late employer"; cf. Apollinaire, "Zone": "Who is the daughter of a policeman on the Isle of Jersey," 13) deflates the high-flown rhetoric. Next to "Thoughts," "*Le livre*" comes to seem too weighty. The same may be said for the sentimental thoughts of Ezra Pound's Shakespearean young girl in "The River-Merchant's Wife: A Letter": "At fifteen I stopped scowling, / I desired my dust to be mingled with yours / Forever and forever and forever. / Why should I climb the look out?"[53] Ashbery makes it new by keeping the conventional sentiments in quotes.

In 1957 Ashbery wrote a pair of poems in an intermediate style much closer to "Europe" than to *Some Trees,* on lost youth and found sexuality: "Our Youth" and "'How Much Longer Will I Be Able to Inhabit the Divine Sepulcher . . .'" (hereafter "Sepulcher"). The seemingly formal quatrains of "Our Youth" open with ellipses (frequent in this elliptical book), questions, sensuous nights, and Cummings-vintage, sentimental imagery of childhood: "Of bricks . . . Who built it? Like some crazy balloon / When love leans on us / Its nights . . . The velvety pavement sticks to our feet. / The dead puppies turn us back on love" (TCO 41). Despite the nostalgic regard promised by the essayistic title, the poem affords us neither retrospection nor immediacy. While the dramatic question and the rapid changes of scene place "us" readers *in medias res,* the documentary ellipses, Audenesque allegory ("When love leans on us"), and surreal sentimentality (encrypting "when love turns its back on us") all remove us to our own age. Moreover, it seems that "our" youth is in fact the joint property of the writer and some addressee. We are left with the worst of both worlds, neither the sensuous immediacy of innocence nor the conceptual surety of experience.

The all-purpose remembrance of "Our Youth" employs lists of misrepresentative romantic particulars: "The Arabs took us. We knew / The dead horses. We were discovering coffee, / How it is to be drunk hot, with bare feet / In Canada" (TCO 41). The romantic associative chain of Arabian kidnappers, horses, (Turkish) coffee, and manners is strained by "Canada," and snapped by the poem's refrain, "Our youth is dead," which puts an end to sexual adventures. There is an uneasy syntax of innocent and guilty interrogations: "Do you know it? Hasn't she / Observed you too? Haven't you been observed to her? / My, haven't the flowers been?" (TCO 41; "introduced to," "grown"). In the repressive aftermath of the "wonder of hands" (TCO 41), "Our Youth" reduces to a haunted minimalism, reminiscent of Reverdy: "That boy with the monocle / Could have been your father / He is passing by. No, that other one, / Upstairs. He is the one who wanted to see you" (TCO 41). In these inert lines, we join the author inside the narrative window frame. The closing quatrains return us to the animated, elliptical listing of the beginning, "Blue hampers ... Explosions, / Ice ..." (TCO 42), but the ring composition belies the fact that there is no route back nor present consolation. As the end admits, escapism is at best a temporary solution: "We escape / Down the cloud ladder, but the problem has not been solved" (TCO 42). The problem of "our destiny" (TCO 42), sexual and textual, will be solved to Ashbery's satisfaction in "The System" and reformulated in *Flow Chart.* For now "we" exit, like Jack down the bean stalk, with a useless fortune, "All that our youth / Can't use, that it was created for" (TCO 42).

"Sepulcher" (TCO 25–27) covers much the same territory as "Our Youth," but bears little resemblance to the earlier meditation. Whereas "Our Youth," despite its representative disjunctions, generally maintains its elegiac mood, "Sepulcher," despite its fixed quatrains and framed narrative, amounts to a rambling anthology of all the styles currently at Ashbery's command. Written in June 1957, the poem first appeared in a 1959 issue of *Big Table,* along with works of Beat and Black Mountain writers (Allen Ginsberg, Peter Orlovsky, Lawrence Ferlinghetti; Robert Duncan, Ed Dorn, Paul Blackburn, Robert Creeley). The next issue of *Big Table* featured Ashbery among other New American Poets. The next year "Sepulcher" capped the selection of Ashbery's poems in Donald Allen's *The New American Poetry.* "Sepulcher" grafts a sexual initiation ("I'll trade / One red sucker for two blue ones. I'm / Named Tom," TCO 25) onto what reads like a short-lived affair with an older man. Ashbery energizes his pallid romantic subject matter by passing it through a rapid succession of styles. Beginning with an overblown metaphor ("the divine sepulcher / Of life"), he switches to balladic lament ("In pilgrim times he wounded me"), novelistic realism ("the smell of sperm flushed down toilets"), pop surrealism ("The boy took out his own forehead"), practical philosophy ("he has figured out a way to be a religious animal"), cinematic sincerity ("Shaking hands in front of the crashing of the waves"), collagist disjunctions ("Stars / Painted the garage roof crimson and black," TCO 26; "Stars" was first published with a line of asterisks), and a proverbial ("you led me to water / And bade me drink") pastoral narrative ("Bringing me books bound in wild thyme," TCO 27). "Sepulcher" changes not only styles but scenes, while preserving the relational system of surface and depth, the "buried past." The first four quatrains, for instance, shift from "sepulcher" to sea bottom ("Do dolphins plunge bottomward") to "rock / Which encases me" to "a furnace" to "under the house" (TCO 25). In "Our Youth" the relation between outside and inside is similarly employed ("The brick arches led to a room like a bubble, that broke when you entered it," TCO 41). This articulation of the parallel spaces of public and private life will underpin much of Ashbery's later poetry, "Self-Portrait in a Convex Mirror" in particular. It brings the elements of his stylistic montage roughly into congruence.

Ashbery's most far-reaching exploration of youth in *The Tennis Court Oath* is the ambitious "A Last World," written in the spring of 1957 on an Adriatic cruise to Yugoslavia and Greece with Martory. An exasperated but perceptive Bloom singled it out as the "one good poem" of *The Tennis Court Oath*.[54] "A Last World" (TCO 56) initiates arguments which will be musically developed and varied in longer poems. For the first time on this scale, Ashbery makes the story of a homosexual awakening and subsequent evasions representative of the world history of alternative sexuality. This conjunction marks a new phase in his homotextual poetics, a shift from writing misrepresentative details and conventions to considering the history of misrepresentativeness as such: the way things have become. The new look of the way things are is a central topic of Stevens's later poetry, as is the emergence of an encompassing "round mind" (TCO 56), the representative Major Man. But there are crucial differences between the two conceptions. While Stevens's Major Man is meant to be truly representative of the desires of a homogeneous humanity, Ashbery's minor man stands for, or with, all other misrepresentatives.

In its coordination of personal with historical change, "A Last World" serves as an outline for "The Skaters" and ultimately "A Wave." In the opening of "A Wave," for instance, the bad "luck of speaking out / A little too late," of sending a last word after a "car door slamming in the night," precipitates not a morning after but the dawn of civilization as we now know it: "And our landscape came to be as it is today" (W 68). In the beginning of "A Last World" the repressive, homophobic past, in which "one could say nothing hear nothing" and all "borders between men were closed," results in today's global consciousness: "These wonderful things / Were planted on the surface of a round mind that was to become our present time" (TCO 56). Both poems conceive of historical change as a Heraclitean passage: "As though one were to pass through the same street at different times" (TCO 56), "To pass through pain and not know it" (W 68). The avenue of "A Last World" becomes a tidal wave in "A Wave," which alters our present time so thoroughly that we "cannot even know / We have changed, so massive in our difference / We are" (W 81). Writing history, even autobiography, is not simply a matter of looking back. In the tidal paradigm shift, not only the terms of knowing but the knower has changed.

"A Last World" also resembles "A Wave" in its lengthy, erotically exploratory lines. Unlike most poems in the book, "A Last World" measures itself in sentences. The psycho-historical argument stringing together the first twenty-five lines (TCO 56–57) runs roughly as follows: These things were to become our home ["present time"], but, if "he" had been "wise," everything might have been "different." "Still it is not too late" to change. "Yet having once played" with fire (the crypt word for "tawny truth"), he "wished to go far away from himself" and forget. In its desire for "what might have been," and its doubts about the necessity of history, this argument follows another late modernist theory of history, Eliot's "Burnt Norton." Ashbery's structurally central, sexually divided "he" likewise resembles Eliot's Tiresias.[55] In "Burnt Norton" what might have been, and cannot be desired, apparently included Eliot's marriage to Emily Hale. In "A Last World" the choice is more fundamental than choosing (or being chosen by) one spouse instead of another. The opening stanzas of "A Last World" disclose what might have been different, had "all borders between men" remained definitively closed or open. Consider the faint hope of renewal: "Still it is not too late for these things to die / Provided that an anemone will grab them and rush them to the wildest heaven" (TCO 56; "live," "ambulance," "someone," "hospital"). Remembering that blood drops of the dying Adonis, lover of Venus, turned into red-blooming anemones, we know what can make the boy "die" if he is rushed to the "hospital" of his "wildest dreams." An interesting parallel poem to this road to the sexually contagious hospital is Schuyler's "'The Elizabethans Called It Dying'" (1958; also in Allen's anthology): "in the huge glare of the electric sign on Doctors' Hospital / that says HOSPITAL / what are they trying to do, solicit trade in Queens?"[56] In these lines Schuyler follows the Elizabethan pun on "dying" with a modern one on "queens." Ashbery's excited narration is also sparked by David Schubert, the subject of one of Ashbery's Norton Lectures, whose poetry Ashbery describes as "both wildly disjunct and secretly cohesive." In "Kind Valentine" Schubert walks the line of erotic and parodic sentimentality: "And over tight breath, tighter eyes, / The mirror ebbs, it ebbs and flows. / And the intern, the driver, speed / To gangrene! But—who knows—suppose / He was beside her! Please, star-bright," and so on to "a palm coast from afar."[57]

Ashbery's "A Last World" is less buoyantly oppositional than Schuyler's "Elizabethans": "Yet having once played with tawny truth," the story goes, "He wished to go far away from himself" (TCO 56). The evasion is not "dishonesty," but a representative instance of the history of the repressive evasions of society. The "far away" which the frame promises is the "Guadalajara" of stereotypical heterosexuality. Here Adam is Tarzan and Eve is Jane, who "climbs a tree to see if he is coming": "Man is never without woman, the neuter sex / Casting up her equations, looks to her lord for loving kindness / For man smiles never at woman" (TCO 56; "casting down her eyes"). In this Edenic world, where the cast up sum yields man + woman = godly man, the neutered woman counts for nothing, freely choosing to be slave to the Jovian male "power he forces down at her like a storm of lightning" (TCO 57). The New York poet Barbara Guest, who has since combined her own painterly abstractions with those of Language poetry, forecast an equally "primitive" weather in "His Jungle": "Torrents replace the usual seasons / conquest by variety / A handsome thunder, a thaw / Out of earth comes another air / smoky as animal."[58] But unlike Guest's, Ashbery's primitivism preserves its popular origins; "A Last World" draws on Lloyd Hughes's silent thriller *The Last World* (with dinosaurs simulated by Willis O'Brien of *King Kong* fame), in turn based on the story by Arthur Conan Doyle from which Ashbery derived his own indefinitely relative title.

But in "A Last World" primitive subjugations do not guarantee sexual security. Ashbery follows this mythological stanza with a passage concerning the Tiresian "he," "Once a happy old man": "but in the evening in the severe lamplight doubts come / From many scattered distances, and do not come too near" (TCO 57). The cadences of Stevens's "To the One of Fictive Music" ("yet not so like to be / Too near, too clear," 83)[59] are dominant in this passage, yet the story comes out differently. The gathering dark clouds here move in upon the complacent old man like desiderata, or the memory of desires (cf. "Terrific units are on an old man," ST 9), represented by "six boys in black" who rot with age. In spite of himself, the old man offers his "treasure" (fortune, destiny, genitalia, passions) and is summarily rejected: "the darkness will have none of you." An erotically charged apostrophe ("You who were always in the way / Flower") results in the politely policing interrogation: "What have you got there in your hand?" Private desires become public displacements: "Passions are locked away, and states of creation are used instead, that is to say synonyms are used" (TCO 57). In *The History of Sexuality* Foucault describes this metamorphosis as "the great process of transforming sex into discourse."[60] The conclusion one might draw from the mytho-historical argument of "A Last World" is that if one knew better about personal and societal repression ("if that somebody was wise," TCO 56), things might be different, and sexual desires might be expressed openly without the evasion of synonyms. But for Ashbery the world of "synonyms" is, among other things, the world of poetry.

"A Last World" must continue, then, with an initiatory rite, a myth of the Fall to complement the falling darkness that besets the old man: "A firebrand is made. Woman carries it," "Naked men pray the ground and chew it with their hands / The fire lives / Men are nabbed" (TCO 57, 58). Euripides in *The Trojan Women* tells us that Hecuba dreamed of giving birth to a firebrand, which was interpreted as a "synonym" for her son Paris, whose desire ultimately caused the fall of Troy (while Paris, France, meant the liberation of Ashbery). Ashbery had been reading Gilbert Murray's translations of Greek tragedies while writing *The Compromise,* and was approaching Greece as he wrote "A Last World," so he surely knew this myth of the fall into history. The exotically violent rite of the poem, reminiscent of the surreal rites in Roussel's *Impressions of Africa,* is interrupted by the police. But with its mythological scaffolding, its diagnosis of the sexual disorders of the Western world, and its sexually anomalous old man at the center, "A Last World" more than "Europe" rivals *The Waste Land.*

After the war, and a blessing for the dead, Ashbery, narrating sketchily, continues his *Odyssey* with the prodigal veteran's return: "We thought the sky would melt to see us / But to tell the truth the air turned to smoke, / We were forced back onto a foul pillow that was another place" (TCO 58). In "A Wave" too the prodigal is "welcomed / Without enthusiasm" (W 85). On the sexually inert shriveled middle earth of "A Last World," the only salvation is the Whitmanian memory of "our comrades": "But we can remember them and so we are saved" (TCO 58).

Rather than conclude with this achieved happy ending, Ashbery appends an enigmatic coda, where the "sky is a giant rocking horse": "Everything is being blown away; / A little horse trots up with a letter in its mouth, which is read with eagerness / As we gallop into the flame" (TCO 58). The particular quality of this epilogue springs from its discursive sources. The encrypted last word, "sunset," ushers in a lost world of childhood fantasy reading, a past time when rocking horses were poised for proto-sexual adventures, unlike the urban present where "death is a new office building filled with modern furniture" (TCO 58). On the following page, the poem "The New Realism" recalls these early reading pleasures: "The child skipped happily over / The western pages." But, ever vigilant, the "Police formed a boundary to the works / Where we played / A torn page with a passionate oasis" (TCO 59). In "A Last World," as in such later poems as "Grand Galop" and "Pyrography" and parts of *Flow Chart,* the Western doubles as the story of Western civilization, and the pony with the letter is the Pony Express bearing a resonating variation of the title, "a last word." But the "giant rocking horse" in the sky reins in the Trojan Horse, which arrives as a consequence of the firebrand's surviving the Indian massacre. The arrival of the "letter" spells the end of the "synonyms" of poetry, as it does in "At North Farm." But the sentimental apocalypse with which "A Last World" concludes is not simply "the end," since the "flame" into which the cowboys disappear is also the "tawny truth" of desire. These apocalypses, as "A Wave" will amply demonstrate, are really costume changes, for natives of western New York state as for Western civilization.

Though probably not a "necessary development" in his career (such determinations are always made after the fact), Ashbery's later poetry would not be the same without the fractured imperfections of *The Tennis Court Oath.* Not only his so-called "intermediate" poems but those in an advanced state of decomposition opened up new possibilities and recharged old ones. *The Tennis Court Oath* thus destabilizes Ashbery's poetry. So too the all-over prose of *Three Poems* will dissolve the dense, formal meditations of *The Double Dream of Spring,* and the offhandedly personal recollections of *Flow Chart* will loosen up the stylized retrievals of *April Galleons.* Ashbery's next book, *Rivers and Mountains,* begins reassembling the missing pieces of its problematic predecessor.

# 3

## "Taurus, Leo, Gemini"

### Rivers and Mountains

In *Rivers and Mountains* Ashbery reconnects the syntactical fragments of *The Tennis Court Oath* and joins a newly discovered authorial persona with his implied readers. This slim volume, dominated by "Clepsydra" and "The Skaters," draws less on quoted writing than on used speech. Its poetic styles are diversified by a public address system largely neglected by its predecessor. Though grammatically disjunctive, *The Tennis Court Oath* is discursively unified by its literary languages, ranging from popular fiction to surreal lyric. Within such a universe, the poet has difficulty addressing his readers in their own language. In one elongated, clarified aside in "Measles," for instance, an authorial persona enters to apologize to his importunate readers: "Pennies, these I can give you. I have nothing else, and the air . . . I ought to, but I cannot, feeling the air and you there. I cannot set you free, whispering only to be there" (TCO 45; Ashbery's ellipsis). With his starched diction and sonorous rhymes, Ashbery here only offers his readers more of *Some Trees*. In "The Skaters" he gives more than he refuses: "But calling attention / Isn't the same thing as explaining, and as I said I am not ready / To line phrases with the costly stuff of explanation, and shall not, / Will not do so for the moment" (RM 39). With his hyperbolical insistence (as though it were a matter of life and death, not poetics), this speaker is characterized as well as versified. *The Tennis Court Oath* attracts readers by largely ignoring their existence; *Rivers and Mountains* calls them in by their pronoun "you" and speaks a language they will recognize, if never wholly understand.

But the two volumes are less disjunctive than they appear. Some of the most coherent-looking poems in *Rivers and Mountains* are produced by procedures dating from *The Tennis Court Oath*. The most obviously unified poem in *Rivers and Mountains,* "Into the Dusk-Charged Air," was assembled according to earlier Dada compositional procedures. Written in December 1961 and published in *Locus Solus* the following summer, this stately nonsense poem would have fit perfectly into *The Tennis Court Oath.* The 152-line catalogue of rivers, surpassed only by Joyce's 600 rivers from the "Anna Livia" chapter of *Finnegans Wake,* resembles no poem in *Rivers and Mountains* ("Clepsydra" is its fluid, single-stanza successor) so much as the contemporary collaborations of Ashbery and Koch—for instance, their "New Year's Eve," which begins calmly: "Water flowed slowly over the bridge in Danbury / On New Year's Eve, while a Chicago of chocolate milk / Formed in Zurich. The root beer went floating by. / You could see the coke on the dazzling mountaintops of Trieste."[1] In this contemporary variation on Japanese linked verse, Ashbery wrote the odd and Koch the even lines, each of which contains a place name and a drink. Part of the fun of reading "New Year's Eve" comes from replaying the poets' game— watching what Ashbery will do with the "Chicago of *choc*olate milk" ("Koch," "coke") unloaded on him. Ashbery's lines tend (with notable exceptions) to be more drab, or less gaudy, than Koch's. "Formed in Zurich," for instance, dissipates Koch's build-up by slowing the action ("Formed") and damming the flow with another "ch." The jaunty poem lurches forward with one foot on the brake.

Ashbery's own river poem lulls us with its sluggish, impervious, colorless monotony, reminiscent of "The Painter." Though "flow" is its most common verb, "Into the Dusk-Charged Air" doesn't, or rather its current is so slow as to be barely perceptible. The poem opens with a sublime global perspective:

Far from the Rappahannock, the silent
Danube moves along toward the sea.
The brown and green Nile rolls slowly
Like the Niagara's welling descent.
(RM 17)

After fording several of these lines, we grow used to their strange conjunctions. In Ashbery's recombinant geography, any river may occur in any order, next to any other. The "Danube," for instance, is only one of many rivers "Far from the Rappahannock," and its narrative focus in the main clause doesn't prevent it from going underground for the remainder of the poem. And the Niagara is "like" the Nile primarily because it lies near it in geographical dictionaries. This "nature poem" (Ashbery once found *Rivers and Mountains* in the travel section of a bookstore) is marked by a pseudoscientific, Rousselian objectivity. But several of its descriptions merely reverberate their rivers' names: "Near where it joined the Cher" and "The Rubicon is merely a brook" (RM 17). Lines merge like rivers through enjambments, many of which ("black stones / And mud," "The Nelson is in Canada, / Flowing.") imply that rivers are among the most prosaic of Nature's wonders. Like the catalogues in *The Vermont Notebook,* "Into the Dusk-Charged Air" occasionally breaks its own procedural rules. The clogged lines "Stammered. The Zambezi chimed. The Oxus" (RM 18) and "Through dreaming night. You cannot stop" (RM 19), for instance, contain two and no rivers respectively. Other lines depart from the present, descriptive tense and lapse into the past tense and conditional aspect; and a few exclamation points and question marks dislodge the periods. Two stanza breaks disconnect this river poem. One of them—"The Afton has flowed. / / If the Rio Negro / Could abandon its song" (RM 18)—indicates how difficult it is to conclude this indefinitely extendable, monochromatic poem—a problem Ashbery will encounter again in his mighty *Flow Chart.* "New Year's Eve" ended by inscribing the duration of composition: "It was New Year's Day!" In a surrealist version of James Thomson's "The Seasons," Ashbery stops "Into the Dusk-Charged Air" with a freeze: "The / Thwaite, cold, is choked with sandy ice; / The Ardèche glistens feebly through the freezing rain" (RM 20). In the original long-hand draft, "Into The Dusk-Charged Air" ended one line earlier, on "ice." But the final, unenjambed alexandrine (a closural departure in length) more aptly catches his poem in transition between states.

Ashbery charts a more sinister and American world in "Rivers and Mountains" (RM 10). The title refers to a school of Chinese landscape painting in which the perspective is often so collapsed, with an immense mountain dwarfing riverside travelers, that the landscape looks something like a relief map.[2] But the confusion between the map and its terrain, both in the poem and in the paintings, is instructive. The nearest antecedent for "Rivers and Mountains" is Bishop's "The Map" (1935). Praising Bishop reflexively as a "writer's writer's writer," the writer's writer singled out "The Map" for its textured materiality: "the very materials—ink and paper—seemed to enlarge the horizons of the poem as they simultaneously called it back to the constricting dimensions of the page, much as a collage by Schwitters or Robert Motherwell."[3] Another map of "Rivers and Mountains" is provided by Auden's "The Orators," perhaps the single most productive poem behind Ashbery's own poetry: "We have brought you, they said, a map of the country; / Here is the line that runs to the vats, / This patch of green on the left is the wood, / We've pencilled an arrow to point out the bay" (EA 77).

As in "Rivers and Mountains," the map is provided not as an aid to reflection but as a guide to infiltration.

Like Bishop and Auden, Ashbery questions the seeming naturalness of political geography. Ashbery's poem begins in tortuous secrecy:

> On the secret map the assassins
> Cloistered, the Moon River was marked
> Near the eighteen peaks and the city
> Of humiliation and defeat—wan ending
> Of the trail among dry, papery leaves
> Gray-brown quills like thoughts
> In the melodious but vast mass of today's
> Writing through fields and swamps
> Marked, on the map, with little bunches of weeds.
> (RM 10)

Crawling along this sentence, we draw out the troubling analogy between ourselves and the map-reading assassins. The syntax is treacherous. The opening phrase dead-ends in a reading that the assassins themselves are cloistered on the map. But the comma (in place of a period) forces us to retrace our steps until we uncover the hidden relative pronoun ("map [which] the assassins / Cloistered"): the assassins have spirited away the map of Moon River and environs. Further, the mapped region keeps shifting before our eyes. Unlike the rivers of "Into the Dusk-Charged Air," "Moon River" is mapped on the 1961 pop charts as the Academy-Award winning Johnny Mercer song (music by Henry Mancini) in Hollywood's whimsical guide to Greenwich Village, *Breakfast at Tiffany's*. The "paper trail" (one generative crypt phrase) then doubles back on itself, ending up with "papery leaves" and "quills," as Ashbery surveys the contemporary literary landscape in his own version of Charles Olson's "field composition" (another crypt phrase). These "rioters" (RM 10; "writers") are strategically positioned to take "the city / Of humiliation and defeat."

The suspense thriller of "Rivers and Mountains" is folded into three stanzas: the first surveys the territory; the second infiltrates it; and the third summarizes tactics, warfare, and the mop-up operation. The ground covered in the second stanza is recognizable as the Eastern seaboard of the United States. After driving the business-looped interstate highway system ("So going around cities / To get to other places," RM 10), an undercover "you" arrives in the New England coastal suburbs with "Fisheries and oyster beds," turn-of-the-century B&Bs, and polite, "formal traffic" (RM

11). Ashbery also maps the capitalist topography, "public / Places for electric light / And the major tax assessment area" (RM 11), thereby diversifying his own lyric economy.

In the sketchy conclusion of "Rivers and Mountains," sixteen unpunctuated lines falling to a final period, news arrives of "the great drama that was being won" (RM 11). Homotextual spies "in the observatory" will infiltrate and "quietly move among the rustic landscape" ("natives"), whose coursing "love" has wetted its river-bed, while having "Slowly risen in the night to overflow / Wetting pillow and petal" (RM 11–12). These nocturnal spies remain "determined to place the letter / On the unassassinated president's desk" (RM 12; President Kennedy was killed two years later). The prototype for this scene came from Fritz Lang's silent movie *Spies* (1928; Ashbery saw it in Paris in 1956), in which three agents are assassinated while attempting to deliver their letters (each blood-stained missive is placed on the desk of their sinister president). In "Rivers and Mountains" the "enemy" may be either the revolutionary assassins or the insurgents. The double-agent poem, a complex of industrial ("paper processed," "turn off the machinery") and military ("Your plan was to separate the enemy into two groups") discourses, may be grouped with several poems from the 1950s and 1960s by American poets as diverse as Olson, Theodore Roethke, and Robert Bly, who were trying to understand and undermine the spreading suburban America.[4] But by incorporating these enemy tactics into his poem, Ashbery affords his readers no disaffected vantage point safely away from America's "afflictions." Like many readers, Ashbery remains alienated but charted.

One of Ashbery's favorite maps of the American scene in *Rivers and Mountains* is "The Ecclesiast" (RM 21), which he published individually three times in the sixties and has included in both his 1967 and his 1985 *Selected Poems*. When he wrote the poem, in October 1962, he had lived in Paris continuously for four years. Yet the poem is textured in the American idiomatic grain. There is something terribly new under the sun in "The Ecclesiast": "'Worse than the sunflower'" (RM 21), which swamps the daily life of the poem's female protagonist. Ashbery will explore this rupture in the historical, cultural, and personal systems of self-representation in "The Skaters," "The System," and, most expansively, in "A Wave." In "The Ecclesiast" its effects are registered on that institutionally, heterosexually defined American woman, the "housewife," a.k.a. "honey," in her marital doll's house: "You see how honey crumbles your universe / Which seems like an institution—how many walls? / / Then everything, in her belief, was to be submerged / And soon" (RM 21). This structurally unsound poem (with stanzas of 10, 9, 9, 8, and 4 lines) marks the destruction of one institutional site. In "The Skaters" a disaffected woman, having lost the Penelopean patience of Pound's Cathay poems, declares: "Seventeen years in the capital of [Egg] Foo-Yung province! / Surely woman was born for something / Besides continual fornication, retarded only by menstrual cramps" (RM 62). In the "wake" of, or "waking" from, the overwhelming demolition (divorce) of the American dream in "The Ecclesiast," "You wake up forgetting" (RM 21), for in the Biblical prophet's words, "There is no remembrance of former things" (Eccl. 1.11).

From the standpoint of Ashbery's continuing articulation of "the system" of modern life, the poem's third stanza is the most interesting:

> For the shoe pinches, even though it fits perfectly.
> Apples were made to be gathered, also the whole host of the world's
>     ailments and troubles.
> There is no time like the present for giving in to this temptation.
> Tomorrow you'll weep—what of it? There is time enough
> Once the harvest is in and the animals put away for the winter
> To stand at the uncomprehending window cultivating the desert
> With salt tears which will never do anyone any good.
> My dearest I am as a galleon on salt billows.
> Perfume my head with forgetting all about me.
> (RM 21)

This well-worn sampler draws on misrepresented proverbs, idiomatic phrases, and literary constructions. The first line combines the proverb "If the shoe fits, wear it" with the idiomatic noun phrase "where the shoe pinches." The proverb "Apples were made to be gathered" grafts "Rules were made to be broken" onto Herrick's "Gather ye rosebuds" ("Apples" recalls Ashbery's childhood orchards). The third line reverses the Lord's Prayer ("lead us not into temptation") and rephrases it with an all-American optimism. The next sentence fills out a pastoral homily with stateside idioms, "what of it" and "time enough," and expands the sentimental narrative of the housewife weeping lyric tears ("sowing salt seeds") at the window with a pragmatic injunction against uselessness. The final high-flown epistolary couplet elevates itself upon Wyatt's Petrarchan sentiments ("My galley charged with forgetfulness"). This patchwork exhibits the "small piece of truth" (RM 21) of each threadbare, misshapen idiom. In "Idaho" and "Europe" Ashbery made collages out of popular novels; in "The Ecclesiast" he pastes in turns of phrase and figures of speech. The limitation of this procedure, as with his earlier collages, is that the various phrases and idioms are less used or incorporated into his poetic system than mentioned or quoted.

Not until his prosaic masterpiece *Three Poems* will Ashbery weave idioms and devalued discourses directly into his textual fabric.

One major feature of Ashbery's later styles, emerging in several of the shorter poems in *Rivers and Mountains,* is his use of that most personal and most multiple pronoun, "you." Whitman patented this freely gendered and numbered pronoun for future poets, straight and gay. In 1970, having nearly finished *Three Poems,* Ashbery explained that "you" in his poems "can be myself or it can be another person, someone whom I'm addressing"[5]—a lover, God, the reader, the poem, and so on. That is, "you" functions not only pronominally (indicating different individuals) but systemically (indicating different types of "you"). In *Rivers and Mountains* this multidirectional "you" is still under construction.

One lesson Ashbery learned from Whitman's second person is that it provides a way for "you" and "I" to meet in publication. Following the straggling line-ups of *The Tennis Court Oath,* Ashbery's second person acquires a fugitive's resourcefulness. The distance Ashbery's "you" has covered since the lover's retreat of "Some Trees" may be measured in "If the Birds Knew" (RM 16; written in 1961). "Devot[ed] to immaculate danger," these lovers meet under an atmospheric cover ("So I was glad of the fog's / Taking me to you") which conspires in their hazardous pleasure. As the unruly "Clouds that rocks smote newly" are "disbanded," the lovers find themselves exposed. Ashbery indicts his own "second person" as "The person or persons involved / Parading slowly through the sunlit fields / Not only as though the danger did not exist / But as though the birds were in on the secret" (RM 16). This vantage point affords readers the punitive bird's-eye view of the law, with "you" and "I" identified in the criminal justice system as the "person or persons involved." But instead of running for cover, the suspects parade their open secret.

Another amorous tale told to "you," "Civilization and Its Discontents" (written in 1961), singles out the lovers with the Freudian "oceanic feeling" of its spacious, unpunctuated opening stanzas:

A people chained to aurora
I alone disarming you

Millions of facts of distributed light
(RM 14)

In these isolated lines the captivating icon of the Stevensian aurora borealis ("The wreath of the north pole," RM 14) provides a mere backdrop for the discontented lovers, whose unproductive love civilization has prohibited.[6]

The third line demonstrates the lyric economy of Ashbery's unchained "you," representing both the rapt civilized crowd of spectators and the multifaceted aurora. A later poem, "The New Spirit," will raise the spectacle of human particulars as an object of veneration: "He thought he had never seen anything quite so beautiful as that crystallization into a mountain of statistics" (TP 48). In "Civilization and Its Discontents" the cosmic vision is meant to aggrandize the affair: "Somewhere in outer ether I glimpsed you / Coming at me, the solo barrier did it this time" (RM 14; "sound barrier"). In the wake of the apparition the poem slips into a too revealing second person: "I miss the human truth of your smile" (RM 14). "I" can only address "You" after civilization is shut out: "there was clear water and the sound of a lock" (RM 14). The poem pulls out of its nose-dive into sincerity at the last moment by temporalizing the aurora as the growing future prospect, "Like a coat that has grown too big, moving far away, / Cutting swamps for men like lapdogs, holding its own, / Performing once again, for you and for me" (RM 15; "a son," "too small"). This vista of independence, projecting a silent picture of a prodigal son's departure, suffers rhetorically by chaining the lover's coat of many colors to "you." In "Clepsydra," which begins and ends likewise with the auroral future, the apostrophizing poet will realize he is only talking to himself.

In the building-block quatrains of "These Lacustrine Cities" (RM 9; written in 1963),[7] which opens *Rivers and Mountains,* a naturalized civilization is itself both the spectacle and the speaker. The poem begins with long prosaic lines, broken into melodic phrases, in the discourse of an urban sociology lecture with Freudian overtones: "These lacustrine cities grew out of loathing / Into something forgetful, although angry with history. / They are the product of an idea: that man is horrible, for instance, / Though this is only one example" (RM 9; "out of nothing"). In the 1960s, lakeside cities such as Ashbery's Rochester were forgetting their anger with the help of nature. For their urban renewal, these corporate deities enlist artists in creating a fantastic, pastoral cityscape, which "with artifice dipped back / Into the past for swans and tapering branches" (like swanboats in the Boston Public Garden). The lyric, potentially dissident first person is usurped by the deities, who contact their artist from their panoptic control tower ("a tower / Controlled the sky"): "Much of your time has been occupied by creative games / Until now, but we have all-inclusive plans for you. / We had thought, for instance, of sending you to the middle of the desert." In this contemporary urban jeremiad, the chosen poet-prophet destined for greatness becomes the company man singled out for promotion. This unnervingly funny, still small voice of the system is the major artifice of "These Lacustrine Cities"; it will speak again in the New York poems of the 1970s and 1980s. But the systemic focus softens in the final couplet with an abstracted sentimental image of a housewife weeping over her ironing: "this single monument, / Whose wind is desire starching a petal, / Whose disappointment broke into a rainbow of tears." In the final spectacle of the artist's "single monument," the ironic city planners have been ironed out.

Ashbery's first poem addressed primarily to the reader is "A Blessing in Disguise" (RM 26), the most elaborated second-person poem in *Rivers and Mountains*. Dated January 1962, "A Blessing in Disguise" recalls the Harvard poems, the effortless "Some Trees" in particular. But its impishness benefits from Paris experiments. The balladic quatrains begin by separating "you" and "I" from the dreary commercial world: "Yes, they are alive and can have those colors, / But I, in my soul, am alive too." The opening "Yes," less an affirmation than a concession, includes an otherwise silent "you" in its disenchantment. But this apparent privilege vanishes at the end as "you" the reader becomes indistinguishable from "you" the consumer: "I prefer 'you' in the plural, I want 'you.'" In this hilarious erotic confession, the intimately close reader is multiplied into the purchasing readership. Ashbery, after all, wants as many of "you" as he can get. This "you" is also multiply employed, as when a talking page declares, "You see, / You hold me up to the light in a way / / I should never have expected." Here, the second person represents the lover, the reader, and even the poem itself (with "I" its adoring creator), and each "you" stands for the other. With lines like these, Ashbery's manifold "you" enters the system. A century earlier, Whitman coyly embraced his readers in the clearest precursor to this poem, "Whoever You Are Holding Me Now in Hand" (270–271). Whitman is a jealous poet ("You would have to give up all else, I alone would expect to be your sole and exclusive standard"), who promises intimacies ("Or if you will, thrusting me beneath your clothing, / Where I may feel the throbs of your heart or rest upon your hip") but not possession ("Even while you should think you had unquestionably caught me, behold! / Already you see I have escaped from you"). Ashbery's own love song to his readership is governed by a lover's discourse. But by misrepresenting romantic clichés, he keeps both them and his reader at a distance: "you always tell me I am you, / And right" (you're always right), "I cannot ever think of me" (you never think of me), "Whom I cannot ever stop remembering" (I will never forget you). No reader has a monopoly on the poem: "Remember to pass beyond you into the day / On the wings of the secret you will never know." Since full disclosure leads to boredom, Ashbery's readers wouldn't have it any other way.

Ashbery's hapless reader is tormented in "The Recent Past":

You were my quintuplets when I decided to leave you
Opening a picture book the pictures were all of grass
Slowly the book was on fire, you the reader
Sitting with specs full of smoke exclaimed
How it was a rhyme for "brick" or "redder."
The next chapter told all about a brook.
(RM 23)

"You" and "you," paired at the bookends of the first line, embrace a warped heart-rending tale ("only a baby," cf. the 1930s Dionne quintuplets) in which "quintuplets" (or "pentameters") number the dwindling "you" among Ashbery's fit audience. Bonnie Costello makes the intriguing suggestion that this "you" includes the unsuspecting readers of *The Tennis Court Oath*.[8] While time has told that many readers (especially younger poets) have felt emboldened rather than abandoned by the book, there is no doubt that the bespectacled reader in "The Recent Past" is a bit harassed. I admit I prefer the animated antics of "The Recent Past" to the elegant humor of "A Blessing in Disguise," even though the joke is at my expense. The poem is full of funny and intriguing ideas, such as the leaves-of-grass fire and the buried rhymes of "book" and "reader" for "brick" and "redder." But more happens all around the reader than to him; "you" remains his imperturbably befuddled self. In "Paradoxes and Oxymorons," the brilliant descendant of "A Blessing in Disguise," the "poet" explains that a "plain level" is "that and other things, / Bringing a system of them into play" (Sh 3). In the long run, Ashbery's best poetry depends on how well he brings his reader into his systems.

The latest poem in *Rivers and Mountains* is "Clepsydra," one of the last poems Ashbery wrote while he was in France. The poem was composed in the spring of 1965, roughly a year after "The Skaters" and also after "Fragment," the long poem Ashbery chose to conclude his next volume, *The Double Dream of Spring*. Ashbery himself considers "Clepsydra" a pivotal poem. When interviewed in 1976 by Richard Kostelanetz for *The New York Times*, he reconstructed his writing life according to the seductive narrative of a "career," patterning his own stylistic phases after Picasso's. The newly prominent author of *Self-Portrait in a Convex Mirror* looked back to "Clepsydra" as a completed puzzle, in which he had reassembled the fragments of "Europe" and the more regular pieces of "Fragment":

After my analytic period, I wanted to get into a synthetic period. I wanted to write a new kind of poetry after my dismembering of language.

Wouldn't it be nice, I said to myself, to do a long poem that would be a long extended argument, but would have the beauty of a single word? "Clepsydra" is really a meditation on how time feels as it is passing. The title means a water clock as used in ancient Greece and China. There are a lot of images of water in that poem. It's all of a piece, like a stream.[9]

Ashbery's new poetics of verbal continuity echoes Hart Crane's ambitions: "It is as though a poem gave the reader as he left it a single, new *word,* never before spoken and impossible to actually enunciate, but self-evident as an active principle in the reader's consciousness henceforward" (Crane's italics).[10]

Ashbery related his own new "clepsydra," a word he had learned recently while reading Maurice Scève's *Délie,* to "argument" (RM 27). As a water clock, the clepsydra was used to time lawyers' arguments in court, providing, as Ashbery puts it in "Pyrography," "a strict sense / Of time running out" (HBD 9). After "Europe" and "The Skaters," Ashbery discovered a new way of "carrying an argument through successfully to the finish, though the terms of this argument remain unknown quantities."[11] "Clepsydra" is itself a "long extended argument": a plot summary, a philosopher's system, a lover's quarrel, and a lawyer's presentation. The case argued is a divorce: that of the past from the present, the poem from the poet, and one lover from another. In its faulty romantic logic, conclusions break with their "premises / Undertaken before any formal agreement had been reached" (RM 30). These unwritten laws are what drained the life from the long-term relationship: "And it was in vain that tears blotted the contract now, because / It had been freely drawn up and consented to as insurance / Against the very condition it was now so efficiently / Seeking to establish" (RM 30). This romance had been insured at the price of its hazardous spontaneity, with the result that "any signs of feeling were cut short by / The comfort and security, a certain elegance even" (RM 30). Love had become a "writ," an empty, formal gesture. All that is left is the dispirited letter of the law.

Grounds for divorce, however, are strenuously denied by the indivisible form of "Clepsydra," a single 253-line stanza. This unbroken verse paragraph resembles the contemporary mountainous stanzas of the late books of Louis Zukofsky's *A.* But whereas Zukofsky divided his lines objectively into five words apiece, Ashbery counterbalanced his own roughly pentameter lines with the cadences of the periodic sentence. The longest of these, occurring early on in "Clepsydra," showcases Ashbery's new liquid measure and several dimensions of his argument:

Each moment
Of utterance is the true one; likewise none are true,
Only is the bounding from air to air, a serpentine
Gesture which hides the truth behind a congruent
Message, the way air hides the sky, is, in fact,
Tearing it limb from limb this very moment: but
The sky has pleaded already and this is about
As graceful a kind of non-absence as either
Has a right to expect: whether it's the form of
Some creator who has momentarily turned away,
Marrying detachment with respect, so that the pieces
Are seen as parts of a spectrum, independent
Yet symbolic of their spaced-out times of arrival;
Whether on the other hand all of it is to be
Seen as no luck.
(RM 27)

For the first time in Ashbery's verses, the serpentine sentence, descending from Wordsworth's "Intimations of Immortality" and "Tintern Abbey" ("all the mighty world / Of eye, and ear,—both what they half create, / And what perceive"),[12] from Stevens's "Auroras of Autumn" ("This is form gulping after formlessness, / Skin flashing to wished-for disappearances / And the serpent body flashing without the skin," 307), and from Proust and James, has taken full precedence over the integral line.[13] If we read "Clepsydra" after *Some Trees,* for instance, we would expect line breaks at the end of sonic and syntactical units (after "one," "true," "air," "truth," "Message," and so on). But here the enjambments seem more Wordsworthian "half-meant, half-perceived" (RM 27) pauses along the way. Only upon reflection do the end-words sound their momentous ideas (time, truth, indirection, likeness). In the all-over writing of "Clepsydra" we find prosaic "lines contracting into a plane" (RM 28). Across this plane, commas, colons, and semicolons function less as logical connectives than as musical rests. In "The Skaters" the lines are longer but the sentences are shorter, and they tend to stand on their own. The sentences of "Clepsydra," whether fragmented, joined, or independent, are driven by an overlapping, multilayered argumentation.

The arguments of "Clepsydra" are polyphonic, sounding in the text "the way a waterfall / Drums at different levels" (RM 27). The long philosophical sentence quoted above questions the meaning of atmospheric nature: "whether" it is an existentialist "gesture" of an overcast solar god or "whether" there has been, unfortunately, "no luck" in communicating a "message." The conjunction's crypt word "weather," itself rendering the French "le temps" and reinforced by variations on "moment," recasts this inquiry as "a meditation on how time feels as it is passing," from invisible, possible cause to serpentine effect. Linguistic ("utterance," "Message") and lyric ("from air to air") vocabulary adds a self-reflexive dimension to the argument; we readers search out possible meanings hidden by the poet, bounding from poem to poem. In the legal discourse of "pleaded" and "Marrying," along with the troubling personification of air and sky respectively as bounding predator and dismembered prey, lie traces of the divorce (a painful separation "limb from limb") in which "either" lover utters a share of the truth, though "none are true" or faithful. One has "momentarily turned away" from the other, "Marrying detachment with respect," while the other questions his "non-absence." The poem itself may be "Nothing more, really, than surprise at your absence" (RM 28). Embedded within clauses and figures, and shorn of its principles and facts, the romantic argument of "Clepsydra" furtively proceeds.

"Clepsydra" is a wake, which may be divided into three parts or tenses: the lover wakes up alone, remembers his dream of love ("that first meeting," RM 29), and returns to wakefulness ("It seemed he had been repeating the same stupid phrase," RM 32). The poem begins at dawn with the confusing first moments of a solitary consciousness:

Hasn't the sky? Returned from moving the other
Authority recently dropped, wrested as much of
That severe sunshine as you need now on the way
You go.
(RM 27)

Unlike the lectures of "The Skaters" or the stately discussion of "Fragment," "Clepsydra" is largely an interior dialogue.[14] Even the opening question is repunctuated (we expect a question mark after "dropped" or "go" rather than "sky") so that it answers itself. The pronouns operate musically, signaling new movements or "keys," from the interiorized "you" and identified "we" of the opening frame to the generic "you" ("Long may you prosper," RM 31) and performative "I" of the dream ("I mean now") to the narrative "he" ("It seemed he had been repeating") and specular "you" ("until / You wake up alone") of the close. Even "she" makes a cameo appearance in the reminiscence: "And yet her hair had never been so long" (RM 31). But rarely is there anything approaching even a Jamesian dialogue with another like-minded person or reader. In "Clepsydra" the persona thinks out loud.

In this new sentence-measured verse, grammatical choices are especially significant. Consider the fragmentary rhetorical question, "Hasn't the sky?", which verges on Chicken Little's anxiety about the sky falling. "Hasn't" is in the present perfect tense, announcing a key argument in "Clepsydra," that the present perfects and justifies the past; it is a negation, marking the "non-absence" of the corroborating interlocutor; and it is a contraction, introducing perhaps the unwritten "contract" of love (other contracted negations will follow). Most significant, the initial elliptical sentence is a question. In "Clepsydra"—and elsewhere—Ashbery explores the analogy between question and answer and stimulus and response. In "Intimations of Immortality" Wordsworth gave thanks not for present liberties "But for those obstinate questionings / Of sense and outward things" (528). Ashbery tends to identify romanticism not only with skeptical, idealist questioning but with subjective, erotic response: "Response being, by its very nature, romantic, / The very urge to romanticism. The precise itch" (AG 72).

The proper sequence of question and reply, stimulus and response, premise and conclusion, and cause and effect guarantees a temporal, logical, and epistemological order. But true love is in the eyes of the assured lovers, an "assurance / Which, you might say, goes a long way toward conditioning / Whatever result?" (RM 29). In this inverted syntax, the response precedes its stimulus, the reply its waking question, and the narrative is framed within the mirror of a simile: "It is we, our taking it into account rather, that are / The reply that prompted the question, and / That the latter, like a person waking on a pillow / Has the sensation of having dreamt the whole thing" (RM 28). So the opening question, "Hasn't the sky?", and subsequent meditations, asked by just such a waking person, may be prompted not by a cataclysmic loss but by a mere dream. In these doubts about the authenticity of his response Ashbery employs the discourse of behavioralism. (Though Ivan Pavlov conditioned responses by the turn of the century, B. F. Skinner and others institutionalized behavioral psychology and therapy in the late 1950s.) His interest in the expansive, neo-romantic conditioning of everyday life is more than theoretical. The doubting, familiar questions of "Clepsydra" may be framed in romantic terms: "If our love has failed, have we lived in vain?" and "If our romance has ended, was it ever real?"

Harold Bloom has judged "Clepsydra" a "beautiful failure" and an "apparent dead end" because "its solipsism . . . is too perfect."[15] I am arguing, on the contrary, that "Clepsydra" is one of the most productive poems of Ashbery's career, stimulating in turn *Three Poems,* "Self-Portrait," "Syringa," and "A Wave," and that it succeeds to the extent that it overcomes the solipsistic temptation of universal self-knowledge. But the subtly and densely woven argumentation of "Clepsydra" does appear solipsistic and self-enclosed, like facing mirrors. The solipsism in "Clepsydra" is unusual in that it is jointly and temporally conceived; the lovers assured themselves of their future on the basis of their blissful present, now past. Having returned "to participate in that dream" (RM 28), the waking lover claims that their first "moments of utterance" meant something not because they were revelatory but because they were "blind," like the introverted lovers themselves. As he asks rhetorically (with a contracted negation): "But / Wasn't it their blindness, instead, and wasn't this / The fact of being so turned in on each other that / Neither would ever see his way clear again?" (RM 28). These modernist "moments of timeless elasticity and blindness" (RM 29), marked by their "Emptiness," recall the echoing, meaningless, indistinguishable moments of E. M. Forster's Marabar caves in *A Passage to India* (Ashbery wrote a paper on Forster's novels while at Harvard). Ashbery's oddly paradoxical name for these blind moments, "previsions," recalls another conditioning narrative, "The Beast in the Jungle," whose protagonist bases his life on a self-emptying prophecy. In his preface, James describes Marcher as "condemned to keep counting with the unreasoned prevision of some extraordinary fate."[16] Upon inspection, Ashbery's dream of love and fame may in fact be an empty "Gesture finally dissolving in the weather" (RM 29), created out of nothing by no animating spirit or performative "fiat lux": "But there was no statement / At the beginning. There was only a breathless waste, / A dumb cry shaping everything in projected / Aftereffects" (RM 29). Properly speaking, "Clepsydra" is not solipsistic since its speaker claims to know neither himself nor his elapsing world.

In this first full profession of his agnostic faith, Ashbery anchors the universal hollow shell of aftereffects to an invisible, unknowable center. The past, without our knowing it, expands into a future that never quite materializes, yet never disappears. With a nuclear energy, "An invisible fountain continually destroys and refreshes the previsions" (RM 29); these moments are empty only in that they are unfulfilled. "Clepsydra" concludes with the narcissistic claim that "this / Wooden and external representation / Returns the full echo of what you meant / With nothing left over" (RM 33). This conclusion revises the perspective of its premises: where the waking exile had wondered about the existence of the authorial solar point behind the sky, now he lies at the center of the echoing hemisphere of his universal poem. This reverberating image is a "prevision" of the serpentine hand and central head of "Self-Portrait in a Convex Mirror," though by then the poet is no longer so sure that the hand responds to the stimuli of the head. In our deconstructive world we too may find it difficult to believe in this world-poem without supplement. But there is no permanent alternative to a blind faith in the weather.

"Clepsydra" stands as a skeptically informed act of faith in progression. Along with "Self-Portrait in a Convex Mirror," "Clepsydra" anticipates *Three Poems,* in the blind faith that "any direction taken was the right one" (RM 32); "Syringa," in the spectacle of the blind and blinding moments of the comet-poem which consumes its origins, "raging and burning the design of / Its intentions into the house of your brain" (RM 33); and "A Wave," in the exploration of blind moments. The final weather report of "Clepsydra," "while morning is still and before the body / Is changed by the faces of evening" (RM 33), comes from a travel notebook Ashbery kept in Rome in 1956, years before "Clepsydra" had been "begun."[17] His sense of fate or destiny—that unforeseeable ends are somehow written into forgotten beginnings—pacifies his solipsism (the sense that responses create stimuli) and motivates what he comes increasingly to imagine as his career.

Ashbery's much better known long poem, "The Skaters," is at once a kind of farewell to the poetics of the New York school and, after a long dormant period, a foundation for the talking poetics of *Flow Chart.* The poem was written on the typewriter[18] in Paris between the fall of 1963 and the spring of 1964, and first appeared in the fall of 1964 in *Art and Literature,* an international magazine Ashbery helped edit after *Locus Solus* had ended its run. With its Whitmanian run-over lines and rapid succession of speakers and topics, "The Skaters" never gives the reader a moment's rest. The poem is divided into four parts (of 7, 11, 8, and 4 pages): the first is composed entirely of free-verse paragraphs; the second encloses within its paragraphs an exodus of forty quatrains; like a critical essay, the paragraphs of the third "quote" indented lyrics (including an unrhymed sonnet); and the last condenses its free verses into little isolated stanzas. In these four chapters, corresponding roughly to the four seasons of childhood, youth, maturity, and old age, we can trace a faint autobiographical design—Ashbery's snowbound childhood in upstate New York, his "voyage" to Cambridge and New York City, his coming of age in Paris, and an imagined, Prufrockian old age—but "The Skaters," appearing after Robert Lowell's *Life Studies,* isn't "confessional." Few of its childhood memories, for instance, are Ashbery's: "I didn't want them to be specific ones that applied to me but only ones that anybody would use if they were thinking autobiographically; they were just to be forms of autobiography."[19] Ashbery will employ misrepresentative autobiography most extensively in *Flow Chart.* In "The Skaters," he brings this essentially personal form of discourse into his poetic system.

One of the most engaging features of the poem is its host of voluble, disarmingly direct first-person speakers. But as one "Ashbery" gives way to the next, we realize that the author can only enter his poem by subjecting himself to its mysterious rules.

Yet it would be naive simply to discount the "phony explanations" (RM 40) delivered in the poet's own mask. In the most quoted passage from "The Skaters," near the end of part I, the implied author interrupts his dense, free-standing description of one "Helga" in her "Jersey City" apartment: "It is time now for a general understanding of / The meaning of all this. The meaning of Helga, importance of the setting, etc." (RM 38). The intrusion of the author is a common device in surrealist theater, as in Luigi Pirandello's *Six Characters in Search of an Author* (1921). Near the conclusion of Ashbery's play *The Compromise* (1956), the dramatist enters only to confess he can't think of an ending: "Whenever I tried to imagine this play I could always get just this far and no further" (Plays 117). The secret formula of "The Skaters" has to do with the principle of selection, "Which I am not ready to discuss, am not at all ready to, / This leaving-out business. On it hinges the very importance of what's novel / Or autocratic, or dense or silly." The author vouchsafes only that "the carnivorous / Way of these lines is to devour their own nature, leaving / Nothing but a bitter impression of absence, which as we know involves presence, but still" (RM 39). This vaguely existentialist formulation is illustrated with the familiar experience of watching snow falling, as we focus alternately on individual flakes and on the storm: "Hence, neither the importance of the individual flake, / Nor the importance of the whole impression of the storm, if it has any, is what it is, / But the rhythm of the series of repeated jumps, from abstract into positive and back to a slightly less diluted abstract" (RM 39). This wonderful analogy stands as Ashbery's first provisional explanation in his poetry of his misrepresentative poetics. The passage illustrates partly by example. The explanation pairs "positive" with "abstract," for instance, thereby bringing the left-out, expected opposites "negative" and "concrete" into the storm-system, along with the metaphor of photographic development from negative to positive (and back again). Sometimes Ashbery jumps from one flurry to a different storm entirely, so that the particulars float in two systems at once. Early in part I, for instance, Ashbery drenches us with a concert of Cagean particulars: "ruptures of xylophone, violins, limpets, grace-notes, the musical instrument called serpent, viola da gambas, aeolian harps, clavicles, pinball machines, electric drills, que sais-je encore!" (RM 35; "raptures"). He follows this performance with mixed reviews: "The passage sustains, does not give. And you have come far indeed" (RM 35). This kind of jump from the spectacle to the spectator encourages us in the audience to "reread" or resituate the difficult musical movement as the "passage" of a life or career, which "sustains" without yielding its significance. At other times, we are not sure to what storm the flakes belong. When our author asks "Who, actually, is going to be fooled one instant by these phony explanations" (RM 40), we too wonder: is Ashbery explaining or isn't he? If not, how do we read these explanations? My reading of this passage is that while "I" is delightfully "phony" his explanation is real, though the abstract overwhelms the positive. *Three Poems* (1972) begins with a less defensive first person pondering the same problem: "I thought that if I could put it all down, that would be one way. And next the thought came to me that to leave all out would be another, and truer, way" (TP 3). If "The Skaters" gives the impression of putting it all down, its secrets lie with what has been put away.

Ashbery's oscillatory "rhythm substituting for 'meaning'" (RM 47) recalls Stevens's oscillations between imagination and reality. In Stevens's best known explanation, "Notes Toward a Supreme Fiction," the poles are the unnamed sun (reality) and its doubling moon (imagination): "We move between these points: / From that every-early candor to its late plural" (209). His "The Comedian as the Letter C," vacillating between the romantic South and a real North, is certainly a model for "The Skaters." And "Of Modern Poetry" may have given "The Skaters" its oscillatory cue: "a man skating, a woman dancing, a woman / Combing" (175). In fact, "The Skaters" resembles Stevens's poems more in its stylistic and tonal rhythms than in any verbal echoes. But Ashbery's oscillations are different partly because his poles of "imagination" and "reality" cannot be gendered male and female respectively, as they often are in Stevens's poetry. We should heed the "devilish" wish of the authorial persona in part II of "The Skaters," one of Ashbery's few instances of hostility toward a markedly straight "you": "I'd like to bugger you all up. / Deliberately falsify all your old suck-ass notions / Of how chivalry is being lived. What goes on in beehives" (RM 41–42). Reality is not exclusively heterosexual.

"The Skaters" swings between its own congruent poles: presence and absence, parts and whole, proximity and distance, the present and the past, concrete and abstract, collecting (putting in) and selecting (leaving out, canceling), homosexual attraction and retreat, reality and dream, and public and private. The order of the last two pairs is reversible, because "the real reality" dreamt by "truer imaginings" (RM 54) in "The Skaters" does and does not lie beyond public realities. These reversals show how reductive it would be to label "The Skaters" and such oscillatory poems as "Self-Portrait" and "A Wave" "logocentric." The emphasis in Ashbery's work is always upon the movement or rhythm between poles rather than upon the bipolar opposites themselves.

The beginning of "The Skaters," though stylistically anomalous, adumbrates much of the poem:

> These decibels
> Are a kind of flagellation, an entity of sound
> Into which being enters, and is apart.
> Their colors on a warm February day
> Make for masses of inertia, and hips
> Prod out of the violet-seeming into a new kind
> Of demand that stumps the absolute because not new
> In the sense of the next one in an infinite series
> But, as it were, pre-existing or pre-seeming in
> Such a way as to contrast funnily with the unexpectedness
> And somehow push us all into perdition.
> (RM 34)

This abstract, labored opening, more storm than flakes, with its philosophical and scientific vocabularies, awkward phrasing ("contrast funnily with the unexpectedness"), and logical lapses ("And somehow"), provides a singularly bumpy and sketchy description of presumably graceful skaters. Ashbery titled "The Skaters" after "Les Patineurs," a medley by Constant Lambert of the skaters' ballet from Giacomo Meyerbeer's opera, *Le Prophète.* As he later commented on the piece, "what probably interested me was a discrepancy between what the music was originally written for—it's made up of extracts from serious operas rearranged and a kind of superficial, supposedly comic ballet. This seemed like the kind of credibility I like to investigate."[20] Compare the opening of "The Skaters" with some lines from Wordsworth's *The Prelude:* "All shod with steel, / We hissed along the polished ice in games / Confederate" (I, 460–62).[21] The sibilant din in this clear forerunner echoes in Ashbery's first line, "These decibels," yet Wordsworth presents a perfectly credible scene which transports us and him into his boyhood. In Ashbery's opening, the skaters are barely glimpsed above the piercing "decibels." The unnatural yet intriguing discrepancy between abstract language and nostalgic subject matter, which attracted Ashbery to Lambert's collaged ballet score, provides two more poles between which "The Skaters" hovers.

But the abstract opening is not disembodied. The impressionistic description "hips / Prod out of the violet-seeming into a new kind / Of demand" ("violent sea"), cadenced after Whitman's "Out of the Cradle" and Hopkins's "Hurrahing in Harvest" ("very violet-sweet"), reveals the eros latent in "flagellation." The word "demand" includes in its bilingual system the French meanings "question" and "desire," which "somehow push us all into perdition" ("lead us not into temptation") as if through a hole in the ice. The Wordsworthian "pre-existing or pre-seeming" nature of this "new" demand, where the male prods out in response to an indwelling stimulating question, will be called "frontal happiness" in "The System" (TP 71ff.). The climactic moment of sexual initiation cannot be re-inhabited in narration, "I shall never return to the past, that attic" (RM 43). It is "heavily canceled" (RM 42) like the stamps Ashbery collected as a child. Yet the demand remains in "The Skaters" as the impulse to motion, the skater's "sawing motion of desire" (RM 53).

The most prominent allegory of desire, in part II of "The Skaters," is the voyage. Amid forty surging, run-over quatrains the voyager renounces his mundane citizenship: "But once more, office desks, radiators—No! That is behind me. / No more dullness, only movies and love and laughter, sex and fun. / The ticket seller is blowing his little horn—hurry before the window slams down. / The train we are getting onto is a boat train, and the boats are really boats this time" (RM 44). This epic partygoer was last seen in the prose "Argument" of Auden's "The Orators": "Going abroad to-night? The face lit up by the booking clerk's window. Poetry of the waiting-room. Is it wise, the short adventure on the narrow ship? The boat-train dives accomplished for the hoop of the tunnel" (EA 66). But where Auden's voyager lets his consciousness flow, Ashbery's proclaims his threadbare excitement to the world. Yet in the final dissolving quatrain, the demand remains unsatisfied,

A concert of dissatisfaction whereby      gutter and dust seep
To engross the mirrored image and its landscape:

As when
              through darkness and mist
                              the pole-bringer
                                    demandingly watches
I am convinced these things are of some importance.
(RM 47)


This split-level stanza, with its interior three-step line, reveals that the plain-speaking, informally shaped poetry of Williams's *Paterson* encouraged Ashbery's casual peregrinations.

Among the most inviting travelogues in "The Skaters" is the "Crusoe" episode. Atop his cliff, the lay meteorologist, who concludes "The glass is low; no doubt we are in for a storm," descries a Turneresque view, both beautiful and sublime: "Sure enough: in the pale gray and orange distances to the left, a / Waterspout is becoming distinctly visible. / Beautiful, but terrifying; / Delicate, transparent, like a watercolor by that nineteenth-century Englishman whose name I forget" (RM 55). This painterly writing, marred by a memory lapse, suggests Bishop's "Crusoe in England" with its "waterspouts," looking like "Glass chimneys, flexible, attenuated, / sacerdotal beings of glass." Her islander's memory is similarly full of holes: "'They flash upon that inward eye, / which is the bliss . . .' The bliss of what?" (163, 164; ellipsis is Bishop's). Poetic influence has now come full circle; "Crusoe in England," which was probably finished around 1965, after *Rivers and Mountains* had appeared, is directly indebted to "The Skaters." By this time, Bishop had seen both Ashbery's admiring essay on her first two books and the weightier tribute of *Some Trees*. In a postcard dated April 27, 1976, Bishop invited Ashbery to breakfast with her and thanked him for the gift of a book: "The geography book is *wonderful*. I can't quite believe it's real, it is so apt. I may use some of its questions & answers as a POEM, or a foreword, to my book."[22] In the end the book, Monteith's *First Lessons in Geography* (1884), provided the epigraph for her last volume, *Geography III* (1976). It seems likely that Ashbery selected this present for Bishop because it was both a geography book and an instruction manual.

Nearly a decade after experimenting with collage in "Europe" and "Idaho," Ashbery pasted passages from an actual instruction manual into "The Skaters," from

> a book called *Three Hundred Things a Bright Boy Can Do.* . . . It's a book for children, about the things they can do to amuse themselves. In fact, as a child I had a similar book, an old set of *The Book of Knowledge,* published around the same time in England, and I was fascinated especially by the chapter "Things to Make and Do," although I don't think I ever did any of them. There's a lot of that in "The Skaters"—like peering at stamps through a magnifying glass. My boredom and a rather lonely childhood on our farm was something, I think, that came back rather strongly to me. We also lived in a sort of snow belt, so there was a lot of trying desperately to amuse oneself in the snow. . . . What I originally intended to do in "The Skaters" was to use the titles of the section[s] from that book as titles—at the head of each section. I began it that way actually, with a list of titles rather like the sort of table of contents at the beginning of a Milton canto. I began this way, but then I found that the poem was a lot more mysterious if I removed the scaffolding of titles.[23]

Though this early version has disappeared, the substitution of a randomly selected instruction manual for Milton's guide book, the Bible, is fascinating and typical of Ashbery's misrepresentative poetics.

Ashbery's procedures in "The Skaters" differ from those of *The Tennis Court Oath*. First, he collages *Three Hundred Things* sparingly; only around twenty-five lines from this manual appear in the thirty-page poem. Many "childhood" selections are either omitted or drawn from elsewhere; there are no passages of stamp collecting in *Three Hundred Things,* for instance, and no passages in the poem from the book's skating chapter, "On the Ice." More significantly, passages selected are, following Wittgenstein's distinction, not so much mentioned as used. The preservation of published line-endings and random word-clusters gave "Europe" and "Idaho" an explicitly textual appearance; the quoted material remained more or less "in quotes." But in "The Skaters" the passages from *Three Hundred Things,* while retaining a citational quality, introduce new topics and discourses. Compare this passage from *Three Hundred Things* with its collaged version from part II of "The Skaters":

> *Fire Designs.*—This is very simple, amusing, and effective. Make a saturated solution of nitrate of potash (common nitre or saltpetre), by dissolving the substance in warm water, until no more will dissolve; then draw with a smooth stick of wood any design or wording on sheets of white tissue paper, let it thoroughly dry, and the drawing will become invisible. By means of a spark from a smouldering match ignite the potassium nitrate at any part of the drawing, first laying the paper on a plate or tray in a darkened room. The fire will smoulder along the line of the invisible drawing until the design is complete.[24]

> In my day we used to make "fire designs," using a saturated solution of
> nitrate of potash.
> Then we used to take a smooth stick, and using the solution as ink, draw
> with it on sheets of white tissue paper.
> Once it was thoroughly dry, the writing would be invisible.
> By means of a spark from a smoldering match ignite the potassium nitrate
> at any part of the drawing,
> First laying the paper on a plate or tray in a darkened room.
> The fire will smolder along the line of the invisible drawing until the design
> is complete.
> (RM 50)

Ashbery does not mount or preserve this passage as a ruin of language or (pop) culture. Rather, he allows his lines "to devour their own nature" (RM 39) as a protean artifact. This temporal more than spatial "leaving-out business" produces here the jump from oral autobiography ("In my day") to manual instructions ("ignite the potassium nitrate"). Before this passage of fire writing, Ashbery collaged in another long section from *Three Hundred Things* on how to make a "flame fountain" (RM 49),[25] a self-reflexive figure that quickly doubles as the ardent expression of desire: "But how luminous the fountain! Its sparks seem to aspire to reach the sky!" (RM 49). Together, the passages illustrate a poetics of writing as the consummation of desire. As the instructor warns, "any intense physical activity like that implies danger for the unwary and the uneducated. Great balls of fire!" (RM 50).

Ashbery's most interesting and far-reaching variation on a collaged theme from *Three Hundred Things* concerns the rules of perspective in painting—the vanishing point in particular. Ashbery had practiced the rules himself at age eleven while studying painting in Rochester. Though his extracts from *Three Hundred Things* on perspective amount only to a few scattered lines, their periodic appearances allow Ashbery to figure perspective both as an escape from self-consciousness and as a narrative vantage point. Ashbery's instructor teaches us, for example, that the activity of skating offers the perfect "enjoyment / Of motion—hips free of embarrassment etc.":

> The figure 8 is a perfect symbol
> Of the freedom to be gained in this kind of activity
> The perspective lines of the barn are another and different kind of example
> (Viz. "Rigg's Farm, near Aysgarth, Wensleydale," or the "Sketch at Norton")
> In which we escape ourselves—putrefying mass of prevarications, etc.—
> In remaining close to the limitations imposed.
> . . . . .
>
> The lines that draw nearer together are said to "vanish."
> The point where they meet is their vanishing point.
>
> Spaces, as they recede, become smaller.
> (RM 47–48; my ellipsis)

The last three lines here are lifted from *Three Hundred Things,* where the illustrations mentioned in parentheses appear. The boundaries of perspective (within the bound infinity of the figure 8) allow for a skating rhythm away from and back to the "masses" of other sexual "planets." What vanishes when two parallel lines appear to meet (like the elongated lines of "The Skaters"), within the self-imposed limitations of time and place, is embarrassment ("We children are ashamed of our bodies," RM 34). Escape in "The Skaters" is found not in the bliss of solitude but in mutual forgetfulness.

But when one of the homotextual parallel lines reappears closeted (*"close to* the limitations") in public life, a hyperbolically severe perspective on one-self as a "putrefying mass of prevarications" (RM 47) dominates. A periodic movement from a speaking freedom to a narrating self-consciousness may be traced throughout "The Skaters." After his balloon-enclosed question ("Where was I?"), the analogizing lecturer of part I ("As balloons are to the poet, so to the ground / Its varied assortment of trees") speeds toward the vanishing point, safety-"belted" (RM 40) into his "vehicle," only to be halted by the working world's suspicion that he is only "half a man," a loafing gay poet with no place in the system of bourgeois life:

> We are a part of some system, thinks he, just as the sun is part of
> The solar system. Trees brake his approach. And he seems to be wearing but
> Half a coat, viewed from one side. A "half-man" look inspiring the disgust
>    of honest folk
> Returning from chores
> (RM 40)

With its internalized disgust, this passage looks back to "The Thinnest Shadow" (ST 43). In its to and fro motion "The Skaters" describes the primary rhythm of Ashbery's poetic career: the ceaseless oscillation between the reflected self and the systems of life as he knows them.

The pole of solitary existence, which dominates the last two sections of the poem, marks the body's secret. Part III of "The Skaters" opens with a "shield of a greeting" (SP 82) familiar to readers of "Self-Portrait," in which the art of poetry is an art of self-defense: "Now you must shield with your body if necessary / . . . the secret your body is. / Yes, you are a secret and you must NEVER tell it" (RM 51). In a protectively indented passage Ashbery's self-protective poem is imagined as a beast from Marianne Moore's armored menagerie (apparently a large jellyfish):

> Its oval armor
> Protects it then, and the poisonous filaments hanging down
> Are armor as well, or are they the creature itself, screaming
> To protect itself? An aggressive weapon, as well as a plan of defense?
> (RM 53)

In "The Skaters" this armor is ultimately the dream, the poet's aggressively solitary gesture against a sexually repressive reality. As he prepares to leave his inset lyric, the poet reminds himself: "back to dreaming, / Your most important activity" (RM 53).

In the Crusoe episode of part III, the cliff-dweller maintains his exalted viewpoint until he is drenched: "I really am starting down now. Good-bye, Storm-fiend" (RM 56).[26] Then, after a stanza break, he snaps us awake: "In reality of course the middle-class apartment I live in is nothing like a desert island. / Cozy and warm it is, with a good library and record collection" (RM 56). The island-dweller is not himself away from home: "Yet I feel cut off from the life in the streets. / Automobiles and trucks plow by, spattering me with filthy slush. / The man in the street turns his face away. Another island-dweller, no doubt" (RM 56). His wandering isolation recalls the promenade of Apollinaire's "Zone" (1912): "Now you stride alone through the Paris crowds / Busses in bellowing herds roll by / Anguish clutches your throat / As if you would never again be loved."[27] With its long lines and wearily enthusiastic speaker, "Zone" is a clear forerunner to "The Skaters." But whereas Apollinaire's *flaneur,* telling his ominous story to himself, is cut off from the streets, Ashbery is cut off from his first-person pedestrian, whom he spatters with self-pity. Though avoided by the "man in the street," a statistical cliché, Ashbery's walker accepts his solitude philosophically rather than anxiously, as though he and his fellow man existed merely to prove the existence of solitude rather than to mourn its fact. Away from home Ashbery's others take refuge "In a store or crowded café," where they dream about the real world: "A revolution in Argentina! Think of it! Bullets flying through the air, men on the move; / Great passions inciting to massive expenditures of energy, changing the lives of many individuals. / Yet it is all offered as 'today's news,' as if we somehow had a right to it, as though it were a part of our lives" (RM 57; an anti-Peronist military uprising in Argentina was smashed in April 1963). This vicarious reality is as easily consumed as coffee: "Here, have another—crime or revolution? Take your pick" (RM 57; "cream or sugar"). This editorializing will have a bitter aftertaste for some readers. But it is important to locate Ashbery's point of view. The Parisian persona is not parodying authentic political involvement, only the romanticized excitement of comfortable café-dwellers: "None of this makes any difference to professional exiles like me, and that includes everybody in the place. / We go on sipping our coffee" (RM 57; "exile" or "ex-isle" is the generative crypt word).

Nevertheless, worldly upheavals do make a difference, even to Byronic dreamers. In a counter-rhythm Ashbery joins the representative café-dwellers: "We step out into the street, not realizing that the street is different, / And so it shall be all our lives; only, from this moment on, nothing will ever be the same again" (RM 57). History can make differences too big to comprehend. In "A Wave" Ashbery will focus on the sort of storm, or revolution, which changes the system so profoundly that we have no way of taking it in. The United States' own contemporary crisis, perhaps contributing to the change of rulers in "The Skaters," was Kennedy's assassination and Johnson's sudden inauguration: "Thus a great wind cleanses, as a new ruler / Edits new laws, sweeping the very breath of the streets / Into posterior trash" (RM 37). In this mythology of history, a crisis is a purgative storm. But it is not only during historical cataclysms that the parallel lines of private and public life are brought together. As Ashbery well understands, the relation between one's private and public manners intimately depends on the state of political permission: "The wind and treason are partners, turning secrets over to the military police" (RM 37). Under these circumstances, "the history of costume is no less fascinating than the history of great migrations" (RM 41). For Ashbery, as later for Foucault, the history of sexual "customs" (encrypted here) is as important as that of great migratory waves.

With the diminished stanzas of part IV, "The Skaters" breaks up into haiku-like autobiographical fragments. One single-lined stanza lodges a complaint, "The tiresome old man is telling us his life story" (RM 63), yet no narrative vantage point unifies the stanzas. Each seems to have its own first-person narrator: "This is my fourteenth year as governor of C province" (RM 60), "I have spent the afternoon blowing soap bubbles" (RM 61), "'At thirty-two I came up to take my examination at the university'" (RM 62). What these autobiographers share is that they have reached an age where there is nothing left to tell. Some lines function as stereotypically "poetic" journal entries: "The wind thrashes the maple seed-pods, / The whole brilliant mass comes spattering down" (RM 60); "The birch-pods come clattering down on the weed-grown marble pavement" (RM 61–62). Others identify places and times arbitrarily by an algebraic ideogram: "There are a few travelers on Z high road" (RM 61); "the first full moon of X month" (RM 62). The solitary stanzas assume the meditative economy of haiku: "Heads in hands, waterfall of simplicity. / The delta of living into everything" (RM 63). These post-narrative illuminations are themselves interchangeable. Though spring is mentioned most often as its season, part IV of "The Skaters" is a timeless world devoid of narrative sequence: "The constellations are rising / In perfect order: Taurus, Leo, Gemini" (RM 63). Ashbery's own birth sign, Leo, has been inserted out of order, before the self-conscious male twins, and it is here "The Skaters" comes to rest, not with its author but with a sign for double lives.

# 4

## "Soonest Mended"

### *The Double Dream of Spring*

Winter under cultivation
Is as arable as Spring.
—Emily Dickinson (#1707)

The formal variety of *The Double Dream of Spring* (the title of a painting by Giorgio de Chirico) matches that of *Some Trees* and *The Tennis Court Oath* and exceeds that of any of Ashbery's more recent books. These poems, written largely in the United States, include a sestina, a collage in verse and prose, an interpolation of one poem into the margins of another ("The Hod Carrier"; cf. Stevens's "Hermitage at the Center"), an Audenesque ballad, a prose poem, translations from Arthur Cravan's and from Ashbery's own French "originals" (an experiment tried earlier by Laura Riding), nearly Virgilian hexameters, and the dizains of "Fragment." Their diversity notwithstanding, many of these poems exhibit an intensified abstraction. In *The Tennis Court Oath* Ashbery's "leaving-out business" (RM 39) consisted of omitting portions of sentences so as to leave them visibly unfinished; in "The Skaters" it meant juxtaposing abruptly different discursive and formal areas of verse. In *The Double Dream of Spring* Ashbery's abstract expressionism involves minimizing or erasing the markers of everyday spoken language, producing a compacted, somber, abstract lyric discourse.

In the heavily reworked quatrains of "Rural Objects," for instance, "you" and "I" meet finally in an awkward syntactical setting: "And now you are this thing that is outside me, / And how I in token of it am like you is / In place" (DDS 43). The skewed parallelism here leaves these twins separated at birth. In a tiny late stroke of abstraction, Ashbery changed the first "And how" to "And now," as though erasing a fragment of the letter "h." The seventh stanza of his highly praised "Fragment" begins with this fragmentary sentence: "Although beyond more reacting / To this cut-and-dried symposium way of seeing things / To outflank next mediocre condition / Of storms" (DDS 80; "beyond merely"). Omitting the definite article before "next" keeps the weather forever inclement, outflanking tense and time itself. Neither of these sentences, both addressed to "you," leaves much in the way of spoken or written communication. As Ashbery puts it in "Sunrise in Suburbia," a poem from which all suburban landmarks (pets, garage, sprinklers, and so on) have been removed, "The inflection is suspended" (DDS 49).

Depriving language of the context of social discourse results in dislocation; it makes for poetry which takes place in space, as "Plainness in Diversity" ("sameness") acknowledges: "Silly girls your heads full of boys / There is a last sample of talk on the outer side / Your stand at last lifts to dumb evening / It is reflected in the steep blue sides of the crater" (DDS 16). In this underpunctuated, displaced opening Ashbery abstracts a "sample" of American "talk," but the surrounding language can't communicate with it, and the "silly girls" are subsequently lost in a painterly space. Any effort against the current of mainstream representational American poetry must have gratified a number of poets and readers excited by the New American Painting. But in the mid-1960s, in the midst of the relentlessly pervasive streamlined stereotypes of consumer culture, the decorous painterly abstraction of some of these poems may have also seemed outmoded.

There are signs in *The Double Dream of Spring* that Ashbery, returning to live in the United States after a decade abroad, was somewhat at a loss for words to address his countrymen and women—except as private individuals. Several of the poems in this volume were written in a period of personal loss and public turmoil. Within two years Ashbery's father and his fellow poet Frank O'Hara had died, the latter only a few months after Ashbery had returned to live in the United States in November 1965. By then, the Vietnam War was rapidly escalating. Ashbery wrote a commemorative article on O'Hara's career, "Frank O'Hara's Question," in *Book Week* (25 September 1966) in which he remarked that O'Hara's irreverent poetry incited participation in all causes rather than in a particular program or movement. The piece angered the poet Louis Simpson, an editor of the 1957 formalist anthology *The New Poets of England and America*. Writing in a special issue of *The Nation,* Simpson badly misinterpreted Ashbery's tribute to his friend as an insult to "anti-war" poets: "John Ashbery . . . complimented [O'Hara] on not having written poetry about the war. This struck me as a new concept of merit—praising a man for things he has not written. But it was not amusing to see a poet sneering at the conscience of other poets."[1] Ashbery wrote an angry letter to *The Nation* in which he quoted his *Book Week* article:

Frank O'Hara's poetry has no program and therefore it cannot be joined. It does not advocate sex and dope as a panacea for the ills of modern society; it does not speak out against the war in Vietnam or in favor of civil rights; it does not paint gothic vignettes of the post-atomic age; in a word, it does not attack the establishment. It merely ignores its right to exist, and is thus a source of annoyance to partisans of every stripe. . . . It is not surprising that critics have found him self-indulgent: his *culte du moi* is overpowering; the poems are all about him and the people and images who wheel through his consciousness, and they seek no further justification: "This is me and I'm poetry, Baby," seems to be their message, and *unlike the message of committed poetry, it incites one to all the programs of commitment as well as to every other form of self-realization: interpersonal, dionysian, occult or abstract.* (italics and ellipsis are Ashbery's)

Ashbery also pointed out, lest his protest against Simpson's attack be likewise misunderstood, that he had "signed and contributed money to the petition protesting the war circulated by the Committee of the Professions and published in the *Times* last June 5; was a sponsor of the anti-war fast and poetry read-in at St. Mark's Church last January; and participated in the April 15 [1966] Spring Mobilization march."[2] In his abstractly committed poems from the later 1960s Ashbery engages political subjects through their discourses of subjection.

The more engaging lyric abstractions in *The Double Dream of Spring* are composed from public discourses. In "Definition of Blue," for instance, the romantic "individual" is inextricable from the "establishment" he opposes:

The rise of capitalism parallels the advance of romanticism
And the individual is dominant until the close of the nineteenth century.
In our own time, mass practices have sought to submerge the personality
By ignoring it, which has caused it instead to branch out in all directions
Far from the permanent tug that used to be its notion of "home."
(DDS 53)

This kind of poem, neither overt protest nor parody, in which the lyric "I" only appears off-handedly as "I suppose" (DDS 53), is "committed" in its own way. Far from its home of personal lyric discourse, "Definition" hacks away at the establishment by subjecting the impersonal academic discourses of history and sociology to its own uses.

Another strenuous exercise in discursive subversion is "Decoy." Ten years earlier, the poet in exile praised Gertrude Stein's omission of the inclusive personal pronoun: "What a pleasant change from the eternal 'we' with which so many modern poets automatically begin each sentence, and which gives the impression that the author is sharing his every sensation with some invisible Kim Novak."[3] "Decoy" (1967) signals the repatriated poet's new interest in writing (rather than collaging or simply sampling) common American language and public discourses. The poem opens with the words of the Declaration of Independence, but with a grim new list of unquestioned propositions:

We hold these truths to be self-evident:
That ostracism, both political and moral, has
Its place in the twentieth-century scheme of things;
That urban chaos is the problem we have been seeing into and seeing into,
For the factory, deadpanned by its very existence into a
Descending code of values, has moved right across the road from total
    financial upheaval
And caught regression head-on.
(DDS 31)

Romantic documents such as the Declaration of Independence function now as decoys for the hopeful. These long lines are devoid of Whitmanian optimism. Ashbery works here within the American discursive system, adopting America's declarative "we" and, more radically, recasting its public discourses: "has no place," "urban development," "looking into," "destined by its very nature," "descending scale," "recession."[4] Ashbery's misrepresentative stance demands, however, that he also represent the ostracized. The ostensible target here is the recognizably different people who move "right across the street," causing "descending" property values and white flight. But moral and political ostracism here extends to those less detectable sexual "anomalies" (DDS 32), a term recycled from the end of "Fragment," whose departures from "the average" will "cancel each other out" in the national equation (DDS 31, 32). The romantic individuals in "Decoy" are the capitalist visionaries with their own self-evident truths, the corporate developers, "The men who sit down to their vast desks on Monday to begin planning the week's notations, jotting memoranda that take / Invisible form in the air, like flocks of sparrows / Above the city pavements" (DDS 31). In soaring lines, these dreamy executives (including the vice president of Hartford Accident and Indemnity) track their urban game with memoranda. But for those in the aftermath, "Waking far apart on the bed, the two of them: / Husband and wife / Man and wife" (DDS 32), the American dream is a lure. The cinematic, homotextual close of "Decoy" traces the pursuit of happiness to the wedding vows, in which "man and wife" enter the American way of life only to find themselves as isolated as those they may have ostracized. As elsewhere in Ashbery's poetry, those left out of the American system in "Decoy" define those included.

The animated sestina "Farm Implements and Rutabagas in a Landscape" (misrepresenting the title of a Jacob van Ruysdael painting, *Farm Implements and Vegetables in a Landscape*) draws contemporary American life as an inscrutable assemblage of apparently random events, obeying arcane rules beyond the participants' control or knowledge. The characters in "Farm Implements" have no idea, for instance, that a sestina end-word makes them periodically "scratch" themselves or each other. The ominously absentee landlord of this apocalyptic poem is Popeye ("Popeye sits in thunder," DDS 47): "He is a sort of superhuman creature who is dominating everything even though he is actually not there, though he makes a ghostly appearance at the end. You know—man proposes but Popeye disposes!"[5] Written in the spring of 1967, "Farm Implements" collages the comic strip "Popeye el Marino" from the New York newspaper *El Diario.* "How pleasant / To spend one's vacation *en la casa de Popeye*" (DDS 47). With a Popeye look-alike in drag as Swee'pea's grandmother and a punning use of "enchanting" to bring in a variation on Homer's Circe episode, Bud Sagendorf's comic strip is already a sophisticated parody. In 1956, when Ashbery found himself in the less than loony Montpellier on his Fulbright ("Isn't Montpelier [Vermont] the capital of the ditch state?" TCO 37), he transformed the local French comic strip, "The Phantom of the Opera," into the Gounod-like sestina "Faust" (TCO 47), which anticipates "Farm Implements" in its operatic, cartoon improbabilities. In "Farm Implements" exceptional action is the rule:

> Olive came hurtling through the window; its geraniums scratched
> Her long thigh. "I have news!" she gasped. "Popeye, forced as you know to
>     flee the country
> One musty gusty evening, by the schemes of his wizened, duplicate father,
>     jealous of the apartment
> And all that it contains, myself and spinach
> In particular, heaves bolts of loving thunder
> At his own astonished becoming, rupturing the pleasant
>
> Arpeggio of our years."
> (DDS 47–48)[6]

Olive Oyl, whose news dissipates in operatic complications and lyric flourishes, quickly settles for the language of a TV sitcom (Lucy and her Cuban husband, Ricky Ricardo, would be the likely model): "'I'm taking the brat to the country'" (DDS 48). This "brat" and images such as "she scratched / One dug pensively" (DDS 48) would have been out of place in Ashbery's first, stately sestina, "The Painter." The "country" of this sestina is not France but the United States.

A less circumscribed depiction of narrative hazards may be found in "Soonest Mended" (DDS 17). Ashbery has labeled this his "'One-size-fits-all confessional poem' which is about my youth and maturing but also about anybody else's."[7] Recollections in "Soonest Mended" from "almost a quarter of a century later" (Ashbery's Harvard years) are set in the frequentative progressive past tense, and in the dual and general first and second persons. Readers, including the writer, must fill in their own "faces, namable events, kisses, heroic acts" (DDS 18), since none are supplied. The topic of "Soonest Mended" is economy, as the economically phrased proverb "least said, soonest mended" implies, both of means and of meanings. Ashbery has paired "Soonest Mended" with Thomas Traherne's "Poverty,"[8] a disarmingly straightforward poem in which the poet, seeing in his room "nothing mine / But som few Cups and Dishes shine," looks outside for comfort: "I neither thought the Sun, / Nor Moon, nor Stars, nor Peeple, *mine,* / Tho they did round about me shine; / And therfore was I quite undon."[9] The same holds for "us," whose fortune (fate and poverty) is to look but not touch: "Night after night this message returns, repeated / In the flickering bulbs of the sky, raised past us, taken away from us, / Yet ours over and over until the end that is past truth" (DDS 18; "end of time"). A better known pairing for Ashbery's prosaically cadenced poem would be Wordsworth's "Resolution and Independence," which questions the costs of the artist's independence: "that others should / Build for him, sow for him, and at his call / Love him, who for himself will take no heed at all?" (552). With his "daily quandary about food and the rent and bills to be paid" (DDS 17), subsisting on the "charity of the hard moments as they are doled out" (DDS 19), the poor poet is a sentimental figure. The poem begins with the pop melodramatics of "Farm Implements," but this time the damsel in distress is us "On the brink of destruction":

There would be thunder in the bushes, a rustling of coils,
And Angelica, in the Ingres painting, was considering
The colorful but small monster near her toe, as though wondering whether
    forgetting
The whole thing might not, in the end, be the only solution.
And then there always came a time when
Happy Hooligan in his rusted green automobile

Came plowing down the course, just to make sure everything was O.K.
(DDS 17)

In this dramatization of the impoverished life, Olive Oyl is replaced by Ariosto's Angelica (from Ingres's *Angélique*) and Popeye by Happy Hooligan, the comic-strip army recruit who, during the spring of 1969 when the monstrous war in Vietnam was escalating daily, plays his own ominous part as rescuer. Yet in this comic rendition it is the monster, not its would-be victim, that is sentimentally diminutive, like "our little problems (so they began to seem)" in the universal scheme of things. But adopting this double, stoic perspective, imagining or watching ourselves ("Weren't we rather acting this out / For someone else's benefit . . . ?") as "minuscule on the gigantic plateau" (DDS 17), doesn't save us. As the permutations of the sestina determined Olive Oyl's fate, we are played according to unglimpsed rules, driven by a global wartime economy. In the major realization of "Soonest Mended," the "clarity of the rules" of the game of life dawns on one of its bench-warmers: "*They* were the players, and we who had struggled at the game / Were merely spectators, though subject to its vicissitudes / And moving with it out of the tearful stadium, borne on shoulders, at last" (DDS 18). Poets and other no-accounts, "Barely tolerated, living on the margin / In our technological society" (DDS 17), make little difference, whether protesting or going along quietly, compared to the legislators and heroes. The problems of the marginal people may be small but so is their impact.

In a world where he hardly counts, Ashbery's poetic economy involves conserving semantic resources. On the home front, this means refraining from arguments, from making "a wound . . . flash / Against the sweet faces of the others" (DDS 18), and in the public sphere, it means avoiding divisive issues, practicing "a kind of fence-sitting / Raised to the level of an esthetic ideal" (DDS 18). This problematic aesthetics might be read reductively as a "cowardly" political quietism, confirmed by the dearth of Ashbery poems taking sides on the issues of his day. To what aesthetic, ideal level has Ashbery raised "fence-sitting"? In his bifocal view, poems (among other sententiae) are part and the property of history, which determines their meaning and value: "The being of our sentences, in the climate that fostered them, / Not ours to own, like a book, but to be with, and sometimes / To be without, alone and desperate" (DDS 18). Fence-sitting for Ashbery means being a player and a spectator in public and private history, being, along with Whitman, "Both in and out of the game" (191), imagining that we do own "the being of our sentences," the "faces, namable events, kisses, heroic acts" which produced them. Writing economical, abstract poems which say as little as possible or twist "straight" talk, "sowing the seeds crooked in the furrow" (DDS 19), can be generally engaging: "A poem by Keats would make me wish to become politically involved, to make love—to do all kinds of things—but it doesn't have to point you in a particular direction. You want to get back in touch with life again, after you have had a strong poetical experience, in many different ways."[10] "Soonest Mended" indulges in the fantasy of passive resistance, which is the indirect immeasurable agency of culture.

The most extravagantly noncommittal poem in *The Double Dream of Spring* is the lively musical offering "Variations, Calypso and Fugue on a Theme of Ella Wheeler Wilcox." The medley opens with a quatrain from Wilcox, varies its theme in free verse, segues into a calypso of high-school couplets, and winds up with a fugue of prose and valentine verse. Frequently included by Ashbery in his readings since its composition in the spring of 1969, "Variations" is evidently an accessible crowd-pleaser. In its Cagean rearrangement of verse and collaged prose, the desultory poem most closely resembles "Idaho" (TCO 91), itself a variation on the prose-verse format of Williams's *Spring and All.* A decade later Ashbery would again take up the sentimental mix of verse and prose, with less popular success, in "Valentine" (HBD 62). In "Variations" Ashbery combines a collage of popular fiction with his own doggerel verse. Along the road more traveled by, he develops his own idea of artistic and human development.

In the influential essay "Badness in Poetry," I. A. Richards had taken a poem by Wilcox, the popular contemporary of his friend T. S. Eliot, as his illustrative theme. "Bad poetry," such as the Wilcox sonnet whose "triteness" Richards exposes, retards human development. The lover of such poems cannot face reality but "is only able to face fictions, fictions projected by his own stock responses." Such a reader may of course outgrow immature enthusiasms: "Time and much varied experience might change him sufficiently, but by then he would no longer be able to enjoy such verse, he would no longer be the same person." Richards concedes that the amnesia resulting from aesthetic development would be difficult to prove; one would need to consider "Individuals with alternating personalities and subject to fugues." This psychiatric concept, patterned (roughly) after the fugal development from subject to countersubject to subject, describes amnesiacs who, upon recovering their memory, remember nothing of their amnesiac "stage of development."[11] Though Ashbery does not recall whether or not he read "Badness in Poetry," Richards was much read at Harvard in the 1940s and his term "stock responses," coined in "Badness in Poetry," had gained wide currency by the 1960s. Ashbery's erratic poem seems itself to be "subject to fugue." In any case, the juxtaposition of Richards's essay and "Variations" is revealing.

Ashbery's enthusiastic paraphraser, a simplified personality familiar from "The Instruction Manual" and "The Skaters," is himself a hilariously stock respondent (the opening quatrain is from Wilcox's "Wishing"[12]):

> "For the pleasures of the many
> May be ofttimes traced to one
> As the hand that plants an acorn
> Shelters armies from the sun."
> And in places where the annual rainfall is .0071 inches
> What a pleasure to lie under the tree, to sit, stand, and get up under the
>     tree!
> *Im wunderschönen Monat Mai*
> The feeling is of never wanting to leave the tree,
> Of predominantly peace and relaxation.
> (DDS 24)

As Richards himself concedes, "those who do enjoy [Wilcox's poetry] certainly appear to enjoy it in a high degree" (205). With ponderous appreciation the respondent over-specifies "desert oases," pointlessly elaborates the stock phrase "lying in the shade," reels in a far-fetched allusion to Schumann's bitter *Dichterliebe* (a setting of Heine), and gives an awkwardly qualified ("predominantly peace") restatement of feeling. But a homotextual note sounds in his Whitmanian variation on the idyllic oaken experience, "Growing up under the shade of friendly trees, with our brothers all around" (DDS 24). Even the nostalgic respondent, however, realizes that the maturation process necessitates relinquishing one's stock responses, a development that leads to fugal anxiety:

> But all good things must come to an end, and so one must move forward
> Into the space left by one's conclusions. Is this growing old?
> Well, it is a good experience, to divest oneself of some tested ideals, some
>     old standbys,
> And even finding nothing to put in their place is a good experience,
> Preparing one, as it does, for the consternation that is to come.
> But—and this is the gist of it—what if I dreamed it all,
> The branches, the late afternoon sun,
> The trusting camaraderie, the love that watered all?
> (DDS 24–25)

As Richards warns, the disabused subject "would no longer be the same person," recalling the once pleasurable theme only as a dream. In the spring of 1969, while the new president called for "peace with honor," the killing of men flourished as brotherhood shriveled. Ashbery's variation thus ends with an Eliotic counterstatement:

This is what was meant, and toward which everything directs:
That the tree should shrivel in 120-degree heat, the acorns
Lie around on the worn earth like eyeballs, and the lead soldiers shrug and
    slink off.
(DDS 25)

As the imagery of ammunition ("full of lead") and dropped seeds ("balls," testicles) suggests, the "meaning" inherent in the Wilcox passage is impotence and alienation.

This grim restatement is swiftly forgotten in the sprightly couplets of the calypso section. More than the voyage quatrains of "The Skaters," these stock verses are representative of one's (though not Ashbery's) first voyages into verse. But as its two punctuating triplets show, one cannot simply rescue the poet from this "bad poetry" with such intention-preservers as "irony," "parody," or "pastiche." Ashbery is another person and the same:

But of all the sights that were seen by me
In the East or West, on land or sea,
The best was the place that is spelled H-O-M-E.

And trust in the dream that will never come true
'Cause that is the scheme that is best for you
And the gleam that is the most suitable too.
(DDS 26–27)

With its suspended truism, the first triplet might be taken as simply and wonderfully parodic. But the second, which closes the calypso, is less surely distinguished from the poet's own words of wisdom. Ashbery takes pleasure in bad poetry elsewhere in the volume. In his translation of the surrealist poet and boxer Arthur Cravan's "Des paroles," he joins an archaic lyric diction to a clunky rhythm and desperately rhyming syntax: "Each hour has its color and forever gives place / Leaving less than yon bird of itself a trace" (DDS 61). Unlike this poignantly labored passage, his own first poem, "The Battle," written when he was eight, seems quite effortless: "The trees are bent with their glittering load, / The bushes are covered and so is the road. / The fairies are riding upon their snowflakes, / And the tall haystacks are great sugar mounds. / These are the fairies camping grounds." From the

109

beginning Ashbery was artificially sweetened. The second triplet of "Variations" returns to the "subject"—both the original "theme" (the harmonic rhyme here) and its childlike stock respondent—with a variation on Wordsworth's "Intimations Ode." The "dream" or "theme," whether real or dreamt, must be trusted, its "scheme" or implicit development followed.

In the fugue of "Variations" the shady dream is a covered up crime: "No one ever referred to the incident again. The case was officially closed. . . . Thus, the incident, to call it by one of its names—choice, conduct, absentminded frown might be others—came to be not only as though it had never happened, but as though it never *could* have happened. . . . And thus, for a mere handful of people—roustabouts and degenerates, most of them—it became the only true version" (DDS 27–28; ellipses are mine). Many pleasures may be ofttimes traced to one illicit experience. This impossible theme was first announced in "Fragment" ("the incident is officially closed," DDS 84). In the discourse of the criminal justice system ("incident," "officially closed," "roustabouts and degenerates") the roustabout poet orchestrates his prosecutors. "For a mere handful of people" this criminalized, obliterated response to stimuli is not dismissed as an unspeakable aberration but trusted as the homosexual scheme of existence.

"Variations" ends with a popular rendition of the artist's right to privacy. In this case the creator is a paranoid scientist:

> Weak as he was, Gustavus Hertz raised himself on his elbow. He stared wildly about him, peering fearfully into the shadowy corners of the room.
> "I will tell you nothing! Nothing, do you hear?" he shrieked. "Go away! Go away!" (DDS 29)

This passage is lifted verbatim from Roy Rockwood's 1925 sci-fi mystery, *The City Beyond the Clouds: or, Captured by the Red Dwarfs,* which Ashbery found on 95th Street while on the lookout for an ending to his poem.[13] Set as the finale of "Variations," the passage provides a pop analogue for the wary experimentalist who will tell his inquisitive readers nothing. It may be compared with Lichtenstein's self-reflexive painting of a paranoid experimenter, *What Do You Know about My Image Duplicator?* (1963). Lichtenstein's patented duplication processes and Ashbery's actual and simulated collages involve a similar principle of construction: representations indefinitely multiply originals.

By framing "Variations" with two popular works dating from his youth, Ashbery raises the question of his own development. Like Richards, Ashbery parallels aesthetic with biological and psychological development, but he differs in taking the twists of musical development as his pattern. This process is by no means straightforward; his calypso is "simpler" than his variations, and his fugue is no more developed than his verses. But Ashbery trusts that something of the original experience, the stock response, makes it into his variation or setting. For him, the impossible process of textual development is the only true version.

Though it is best known in isolation, "Fragment" was conceived and produced on the model of a Renaissance emblem book. Ashbery had Alex Katz in mind as an illustrator when he began writing this monumental poem in 1964. The poem was first published, without illustrations, in *Poetry* (February 1966). An illustrated version first graced the fashion magazine *Harper's Bazaar* (June 1968), where five of Katz's voguish half-tones and all fifty of Ashbery's cool dizains (in stylish white print on black background) look restlessly at home. In 1969 Black Sparrow Press published "Fragment" in book form with two dizains a page facing each of Katz's twenty-five illustrations. The poem was patterned on *Délie*: "I had been reading Maurice Scève, the 16th-century poet who wrote in *dizains* and I was impressed by the fruitful monotony of his form. . . . It also seemed like a good in-between length; lacking the in-the-round effect of a sonnet and longer than a quatrain; a purposely stunted form which is ideal for these repetitions with minimal variations."[14]

Scève's *Délie,* which Ashbery studied at New York University in 1957, is composed of an initial octave and four hundred and forty-nine dizains, divided into forty-nine groups of nine (not counting five introductory and three concluding dizains) by fifty emblems, engraved later by an unknown artist. The fifty emblems of *Délie* may have suggested the more manageable length of "Fragment." The intermediate size of the dizain gives the poem an intriguing instability: neither fragment nor whole, it functions neither as a stanza in a connected argument or narrative nor as a relatively independent poem in a lyric sequence. Ashbery would experiment again with numerically predetermined forms, in the thirty numbered sections (of varying length) of "Fantasia on 'The Nut-Brown Maid'" (HBD 72–88) and the fifty four-quatrain poems of *Shadow Train,* but neither of these works has the tantalizing inconclusiveness of "Fragment." The predetermined form of "Fragment" seemed to dictate its mode of production: "I decided that I would do two [dizains] . . . each time I sat down to write and not do any more or less."[15] Each of the twenty-five typescript pages of "Fragment," and each illustrated page of the Black Sparrow edition, thus represents one day's labor. Ashbery's work schedule shows in his work; the four pairs of dizains linked by enjambment are one day's work apiece.

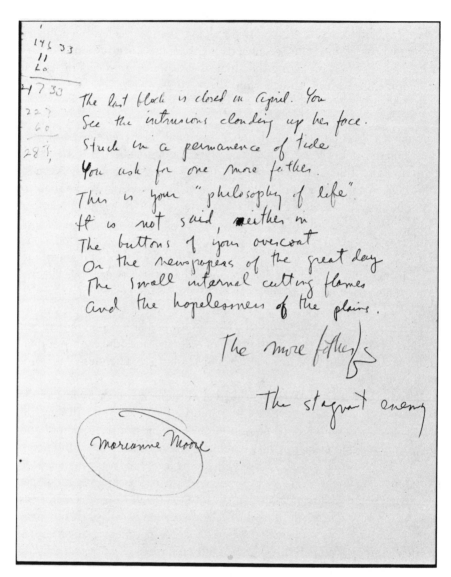

The last block is closed in April. You
See the intrusions clouding up her face.
Stuck in a permanence of tide
You ask for one more father.
This is your "philosophy of life".
It is not said, neither in
The buttons of your overcoat
On the newspapers of the great day
The small internal cutting flames
and the hopelessness of the plains.

The more fathers

The stagnant enemy

Marianne Moore

"Fragment"

 

The American poetics of passionate abstraction begins with Emily Dickinson, maker of emptied boxes, and continues in such vacuum-packed volumes as Lyn Hejinian's *The Cell*. One of Ashbery's mentors in this poetics was Marianne Moore, whose name is written and circled on the first manuscript page of "Fragment" (see figure; note too the oddly appropriate column of figures). Though her nominal presence may be simply coincidental, Moore's poetry has provided Ashbery, from the beginning, with a powerful example of emotional and stylistic reserve. In his 1967 review of *The Complete Poems of Marianne Moore*[16] Ashbery cites the end of "Silence": "The deepest feeling always shows itself in silence; / not in silence, but restraint" (CP 91), a saying Moore attributes to her father. Moore's translation of this paternal (but also Dickinsonian) restraint is figured most immediately in her chiseled syllabic stanzas, which seem to measure their objects with scientific calibration, and ultimately in her frequently objective, critical regard. In Moore's poetry the subject, grammatical or authorial, itself becomes difficult to locate. Ashbery wonders, "I will never be entirely certain of what 'it' is" in the last syllabic stanza of Moore's "The Fish":

> dead.
> Repeated
>     evidence has proved that it can live
>     on what can not revive
>         its youth. The sea grows old in it.
> (CP 33)

While repeated readings may never prove what "it" refers to, both the rhyme of "dead" with "Repeated" and the pounding rhythm of scientific discourse are registered.

Confessing "I am tempted simply to call her our greatest modern poet. This despite the obvious grandeur of her chief competitors, including Wallace Stevens and William Carlos Williams," Ashbery concluded by praising Moore's translations of La Fontaine: "In trying to find an equivalent tone for La Fontaine's, she happened on a new language—new to poetry and new to her." As Moore's translation made her work new, so Ashbery's subjection to the formal rigors of Scève's *Délie* created a language new to Ashbery and, to a large degree, to contemporary American poetry. The generative intensity of the French work lies in the powerful disparity between its charged subject matter (unrequited sexual love, which drives the lover almost to suicide) and its squared stanzas of ten decasyllabic lines. With his stanzaic constraint, the author both erases himself from his dizains ("Scève" and "je" are overshadowed by "Délie" and "tu") and confines his expression to a philosophical, astronomical, mystical, or simply mannered abstraction, which is all the more moving for what it leaves out. Scève's Délie becomes *Délie:* "As far as you may be, you are always present; / As near as I may be, I am still absent" (144).[17] The dark fabric of "Fragment" was also woven on the loom of Stéphane Mallarmé. In 1964 Ashbery was translating

113

Mallarmé's prose poem "Igitur," infused with its own "moment's command-ment" (DDS 78): "Certainly a presence of Midnight subsists. The hour has not disappeared through a mirror, has not hid itself in evoking a furnishing by its vacant sonorousness." Ashbery never finished or published the trans-lation, doubtless realizing that the project was superseded by "Fragment." Ashbery has connected the vacant sonorousness of "Fragment" (a partial whole, rather than "fragments") to its abstracted, encrypted subject matter: "The title Fragment . . . was a kind of joke because it's very long and yet like any poem it's a fragment of something bigger than itself . . . which is the consciousness that produced it at that moment and which left out all kinds of things in the interests of writing the poem, which one is nevertheless aware of in the corners of the poem. . . . I think it's like maybe all of my poems, it's a love poem."[18]

The content of *Délie,* though unspecified, is clear: Scève professes love for an unnamed, idealized woman ("Délie" is an anagram for "l'idée") who never yields to his demands. In "Fragment" both the players and the plot are indeterminate. In his dedicatory octave Scève tells his beloved that the subject of his dizains is neither "Venus" nor "Cupid," neither love nor de-sire, "Mais bien les morts qu'en moi tu renovelles" ("but rather the deaths you renew in me"). Chief among the deaths renewed in "Fragment" was that of Ashbery's father. In December 1964 Ashbery flew home from Paris for the funeral (his father had died on the first of the month—unhappily, also the date of Pierre Martory's birthday); he stayed in Sodus, New York, through December and into January. "Fragment" was begun in Sodus and completed in Paris in March 1965, before Ashbery returned permanently to New York that summer. The memorial dizains of "Fragment" may be grouped, very roughly, as follows: an address to, and meditation on "you" (1–11); partial disclosures of the plot (12–29); reflections on the relation between the present and the past (30–36); parallels between the private cri-sis and its aftermath and the origins of a civilization (37–47); and a framing coda (48–50). What interests Ashbery in "Fragment" is not the deaths or losses themselves but the remembering and even more the forgetting that happens in their wake. A burial in "Fragment" is a cover-up; words are spoken and never spoken of again.

Though they have no speaking parts, the parents play their role in the scheme of "Fragment." The father's unmarked and untold plot is the monu-mental poem itself; the father and his marker are inseparable. Any unspeci-fied mention of him—"whoever lay dying / In a small room" (#47, DDS 93)—or his resting place—the "grave of authority" (#21, DDS 84)—also signifies "Fragment."[19] Rather than being an elegy for the father, "Frag-ment" has taken his place. On the margins of the first handwritten stanza lie two phrases, "The more fathers" and "The stagnant enemy." The second of these loaded phrases, neither of which made it into "Fragment," reappears capitalized in the upper right-hand corner of the typescript, suggesting that Ashbery was considering it for his title ("stagnant" resonates in "Fragment"). But the place of the enemy, though stagnant, is best kept out of mind. Consider these lines from the dizain roughly at the center of the poem, which begins "The apotheosis had sunk away": "The whole / Is a mound of changing valors for some who / Live out as under a dome, are participated in / As the ordinary grandeur of a dome's the thing that / Keeps them living" (#25, DDS 86). In this self-reflexive passage, the paradoxically "whole" hole becomes a grave "mound" beneath the sky's changing "dome" ("tomb," "tome," "home"), another stanzaic room. The strange echo (meant or not) of Hamlet's "the play's the thing" reveals the dangers of even so oblique a viewing.

The figure of the bereft wife and mother enters the system of "Fragment" in the third and second persons. As "she," the wife fills the position of Délie, an emblematic beloved; as "you," she functions as the equally bereft speaker's maternal confidante. Near the father's "mound" in dizain 25, the newly widowed dispossessed third person faces the prospect of living on alone amid the family orchards:

All space was to be shut out. Now there was no
Earthly reason for living; solitude proceeded
From want of money, her quincunxes standing
To protect the stillness of the air. Darkness
Intruded everywhere. This was the first day
Of the new experience. The familiar brown trees
Stirred indifferent at their roots, deeply transformed.
(#27, DDS 86–87)

As with the wife in "The Ecclesiast," "everything, in her belief, was to be submerged" (RM 21); even the trees are strange. But here the proverbs and clichés of the widow's belief system are not misrepresented in quotes. Though grief itself is to be "shut out," Ashbery's free indirect lyric discourse of the mother's homely lament of having "no / Earthly reason for living" is audibly stirring.

In the stately, reserved, first dizain of "Fragment" the parents appear emblematically:

The last block is closed in April. You
See the intrusions clouding over her face

As in the memory given you of older
Permissiveness which dies in the
Falling back toward recondite ends,
The sympathy of yellow flowers.
Never mentioned in the signs of the oblong day
The saw-toothed flames and point of other
Space not given, and yet not withdrawn
And never yet imagined: a moment's commandment.
(#1, DDS 78)

The father's final resting place is represented as the last block of the monument to be closed, the last calendar block x'ed out, even as the blocks of "Fragment" open. In Ashbery's handwritten draft (see figure) the father passes unmentioned in "the newspapers of the great day." But his revision, "the signs of the *ob*long day" ("in the newspapers," "long day," "signs of the times"), traces both the *ob*ituary's and the casket's dimensions. "April" is the father's month both in *The Waste Land* and in Whitman's "When Lilacs Last in the Dooryard Bloom'd," with its April lilacs and its dead father of the Union. The mother appears as a bright face "clouding over" with tears and foreboding and as the widow's "yellow flowers," the ritual sign of "sympathy." Refigured as "saw-toothed flames," the emblem signifies the saw-toothed sun (flower) of children's drawings, newspaper weather reports, and astrological signs. In *Délie* the emblem of the Cicorée or heliotrope captures the signifying relation between the "flower" and the "sun." Among the poems ranked under this emblem is the "April" dizain in which the poet envisions the melting of his beloved's indifferent iciness ("le tien ingrat froid"): "retournant le doux Ver sans froidure, / Mon An se frise en son Avril superbe" ("the sweet Spring returning without coldness, / My Year is garlanded in its amazing April," 148). April marks the time of youth before reserve and "recondite ends" set in, as Scève dates it in an early dizain: "Libre vivais en l'Avril de mon âge, / De cure exempt" ("Free was I living in the April of my age, / Carefree," 6). In "Fragment," as later in "Clepsydra," the last occluding block cuts off the son (the "sun") from the "point of other / Space not given," and from the mother's permissive sympathy, now "Never mentioned." Under Scève's emblem for linguistic confusion, the "Tour Babel," is the dizain Ashbery recalled as his favorite.[20] Here Délie's momentary presence is deemed "un serein en hiver ténébreux" ("a clearing in gloomy winter"), and her absence leaves her poet, like a benighted hare, "Tout éperdu aux ténèbres d'Égypte" ("wholly lost in Egyptian darkness," 129). The solar point, obscured but "not withdrawn," points out the son's unmentionable destiny. In the first draft, the wish for "one more father" is expressed, figured with biting remorse and wandering despair, "The small internal cutting flames / And the hopelessness of the plains" (of Sodom and Gomorrah). In the final version, the absent sun sign presents "a moment's commandment" ("mom's"), echoing the sixth commandment ("Thou shalt honor thy father and thy mother") and Rossetti's definition of the sonnet in "The House of Life" as "a moment's monument," and, beyond these, a life in and out of poetry "never yet imagined."

If "Fragment" is, as Ashbery says, "a love poem," it is the love story rather than the beloved which is emblazoned to pieces. The fragmented story upon which "Fragment" is constructed involves a covert adolescent affair, which the consequent scandal marks as homosexual. But Ashbery is suspicious of the myth of a homosexual origin: "It is ideation, incrimination / Proceeding from necessity to find it at / A time of day, beside the creek, uncounted stars and buttons" (#30, DDS 88). As in the idealization of *Délie,* the necessarily misrepresentative particulars can lead only to mutual "incrimination." The narrative, "those first steps, halted for all eternity," begins innocently enough: "We talked, and after that went out. / It was nice" (#31, DDS 88). But eventually, in an interruptive and ruptured dizain, sex enters in:

> The volcanic entrance to an antechamber
> Was not what either of us meant.
> More outside than before, but what is worse, outside
> Within the periphery, we are confronted
> With one another, and our meeting escapes through the dark
> Like a well.
> Our habits ask us for instructions.
> The news is to return by stages
> Of uncertainty, too early or too late. It is the invisible
> Shapes, the bed's confusion and prattling. The late quiet. This is how it
>     feels.
> (#16, DDS 83)

The indeterminacy of "an antechamber" and the mutuality of "either of us" makes the sex here gay as well as straight and, consequently, the lover's displacement marks not merely post-coital depression but alienation—a position on the outside looking out—in the midst of society. In the first draft of this heavily reworked stanza, the sixth line read "~~Escaping through the~~ Like ~~one great wail.~~ a yell." with "This is how it feels" added in handwriting to fill out the line. Ashbery's final version—"Like a well."—echoes both climactic crypt words, "wail" and "yell." The displacement of the handwritten addition leaves a hole in the stanza and creates an erotically elongated final line.

The lovers' fears were justified, for the secret leaked out in writing: "Gradually old letters used as bookmarks / Inform the neighbors; an approximate version / Circulates and the incident is officially closed" (#20, DDS 84).[21] Ashbery files the case under "that horrible, blatant day" (#36, DDS 90)—a phrase carrying the full allusive force of Spenser's Blatant Beast, who fed on scandal and slander in the sixth book of *The Faerie Queene*.

After the "incrimination," the "suppressed lovers" (#7, DDS 80) are called upon to make a full confession. A commanding voice enters the poem: "I haven't made clear that I want it all from you / In writing, so as to study your facial expressions / Simultaneously" (#22, DDS 85). In 1964 the vogue for confessional poetry was waning, but the agenda of personal exposure was still in force. Ashbery, however, "confesses" nothing to us, the inquisitive readers, in "Fragment." Neither does the worried mother, wondering "What comes after / The purge, she not mentioning it yet" (#23, DDS 85). Nevertheless, she is given the only direct quote in "Fragment," a statement that covers both the father's and the son's condition: "'He's hurt real bad'" (#24, DDS 85). The rest of the poem is speechless.

"Fragment" addresses its words to "you," a second person pluralized, which places lovers past and present, the mother, the speaking and writing self, and the reader(s) in relation with one another. In "A Blessing in Disguise," the close reader becomes a lover; in "Fragment," the lover becomes a reader. The "reader" in the sixth dizain is not an imagined "you-in-the-plural" but an actual (perhaps composite) "you," like the dark lady of Shakespeare's sonnets, whose interpretation is far from disinterested:

> The part in which you read about yourself
> Grew out of this. Your interpretation is
> Extremely bitter and can serve no profitable end
> Except continual development. Best to break off
> All further choice.
> (#6, DDS 79)

Or in the encrypted lover's discourse, "all communication." Declaring "Fragment" "Ashbery's finest work," Harold Bloom described the poem as "the elegy for the self of the imperfect solipsist, who wavered before the reality of another self, and then withdrew back into an interior world."[22] This depiction is responsive as far as it goes, but it limits "Fragment" to its narrative. Like all elegies, specific or not, "Fragment" is dramatic; as he writes, Ashbery makes what peace he can with the dead, the remembered, and himself. The speech act takes place in the present, as the writer argues with his reader. As in "Clepsydra," the "argument" involves a plot, a philosophy (of future developments), and a painful disagreement. Several of the early dizains of "Fragment" begin with an argumentative conjunction: "Although" (#7), "Yet" (#8), "Thus" (#10), "Whereas" (#11). There are two sides to every love story, but the strict economy of lyric poetry means that there is only one authoritative, published version. The paradoxes of the power relation between the poet and the real (and constructed) beloved frame the fourth dizain, which begins by revising the promise of the previous stanza that "You can look at it all / Inside out":

> Not forgetting either the chance that you
> Might want to revise this version of what is
> The only real one, it might be that
> No real relation exists between my wish for you
> To return and the movements of your arms and legs.
> But my inability to accept this fact
> Annihilates it. Thus
> My power over you is absolute.
> You exist only in me and on account of me
> And my features reflect this proved compactness.
> (#4, DDS 79)

In one of the few moments of subdued humor in "Fragment," Ashbery (in the role of the poet-lover) reminds himself that he is powerless over his actual lover. But by forgetting "this fact," by creating his own "you," the creative and destructive artist "Annihilates" his real living and moving lover to an image. But, as his self-deprecating humor suggests, the soundness of the author's proof for the existence of authorial omnipotence is more dramatic than real. Nevertheless, the "proved compactness" of Ashbery's I-Thou dizains is explosive, a "coming together of masses" into a composite nuclear "energy, not yet or only partially / Distributed to the imagination" (#5, DDS 79).

Drama notwithstanding, the absorption in "Fragment" of the first-person pronoun into the second at times introverts or doubles up the self into a self-conscious, idealist "you." In the ninth and tenth dizains, Ashbery's fifth day's work, a dazed, doubled "you," in both the subject and object position, reflects on its internalized world: "Slowly as from the center of some diamond / You begin to take in the world as it moves / In toward you, part of its own burden of thought" (#9, DDS 80). The inversion, remarked by Alan Williamson, of Stevens's "Esthétique du Mal" ("We are not / At the centre of a diamond," 259), suggests that Ashbery has not overcome his own isolationism.[23] The dizain ends with a technologized version of the adamantine "I" or "eye" seeing life through rose-colored glasses: "multicolored / Parentheses, the way love in short periods / Puts everything out of focus, coming and going." It follows, in the tenth dizain, that "your only world is an inside one" (#10, DDS 81). But this idealist "Idle musing" is less a matter of self-reflection than of self-defense, as is clear from the oratorical eighth dizain, set in an unusual communal "we":

> We cannot keep the peace
> At home, and at the same time be winning wars abroad.
> And the great flower of what we have been twists
> On its stem of earth, for not being
> What we are to become, fated to live in
> Intimidated solitude and isolation. No brother
> Bearing the notion of responsibility of self
> To the surrounding neighborhood lost out of being.
> (#8, DDS 80)

Speaking to his Whitmanian comrades, as President Johnson spoke to a country increasingly divided over the expanding war with Vietnam, the orator laments their renunciation of open brotherly love, both inside the home and "abroad." The isolation here is legally enforced, as Ashbery puts it in "The Chateau Hardware," by the "excursions of the police / As I pursued my bodily functions" (DDS 73). The gay community, "out of" each member's sight and apparently out of mind, loses its "being," which is marked only by the traditional elegiac flower on the grave. The "world" idealized and shut out in the ninth and tenth dizains is armed with scandal and rumor and also with its own "ideas" about "Fragment," although "Nothing anybody says can make a difference" (#10, DDS 81) to the dizains or their adamantine polisher. But Ashbery goes beyond the solitary confinement of this dismissal, familiar from *Some Trees*. In "Fragment" the intimidated self feeds on, and exists by virtue of, this supposedly ineffectual world. In a crucial revision Ashbery exchanges a diamond for a flame: "Buffeted by invisible winds, or yet a flame yourself / Without meaning, yet drawing satisfaction / From the crevices of that wind, living / In that flame's idealized shape and duration" (#10, DDS 81). This new emblem draws inspiration from Pater ("to burn with a hard, gemlike flame") and Scève ("Flamme si sainte en son clair durera," 449; "Flame so holy in its clarity will endure"). The flame, poem of desire, dies without the vivifying breath and touch of the world.

In ten late dizains (37–47) Ashbery retells the lovers' tragedy as a historical allegory. It begins with the burning in the fireplace of the physical evidence of "Fragment": "tumbling upward, like piles of smoke" (#37, DDS 90). On these ashes a new, vulnerable future erects itself: "the future, an open / Structure, is rising even now, to be invaded by the present / As the past stands to one side." This Audenesque allegory of the temporal revolution is an emblem of the upheavals in France in the early 1960s, when the Fourth Republic bowed to the "intolerant swarm of freedom as it / Is called in your press" (#38, DDS 90), that is, the Algerians. But the ship of state was soon repaired: "The fathers asked that it be made permanent, / A vessel cleaving the dungeon of the waves" (#40, DDS 91). This civilized galley is charged with forgetfulness. "A universal infamy" reigned, "forgetful of the / Chaos whose expectancy had engendered it" (#46, DDS 93). Ashbery began *Rivers and Mountains* with a similar myth of erased origins: "These lacustrine cities grew out of loathing / Into something forgetful, although angry with history" (RM 9). In "Fragment," the new civilization, waking from an unspeakable affair, is brilliantly rendered in a historical passive voice, with no pronouns taking responsibility for the disturbing transactions:

The victims were chosen through lightness in obscurity.
A firm look of the land, old dismissals
And the affair was concluded in snow and also in
The satisfaction of the outline formulated against the sky.
People were delighted getting up in the morning
With the density that for once seemed the promise
Of everything forgotten, and the well-being
Grew, at the expense of whoever lay dying
In a small room watched only by the progression
Of hours in the tight new agreement.
(#47, DDS 93)

The scapegoats, aberrant particulars selected in chiaroscuro fashion "by secret ballot," are sent into the wilderness with "a firm shake of the hand" to their "recondite ends." In the first draft, "the affair was concluded in tears" rather than in obliterating "snow" (#47, DDS 93). In this history, the survivors "wake" refreshed, having forgotten the previous night's "wake" over the dying victim. But who wakes forgetting whom: the parents the lovers, the healthy society its misfits, or the survivors the dying father? There is no way of choosing. The different formulations are interrelated rather than ironically juxtaposed. Ashbery succeeds here by refraining from drawing distinctions between generations or victims.

"Fragment" is framed by reflections on its own nature as a sign. The word "signs" appears in its first and last dizains, in "the signs of the oblong day" and "the advancing signs of the air" (DDS 78, 94). Though Ashbery was not part of the *Tel Quel* group, he was probably situated near enough (his "French Poems" appeared in *Tel Quel,* and *Art and Literature* published work of Barthes, Pleynet, and others) to get wind of their interest in the Saussurian sign. But Ashbery, like the American semiotician Charles Sanders Peirce before him, is interested not only in arbitrary but in motivated signifying relations. Ashbery's emblem is a spatial, synecdochal fragment and a temporal trace or promise, a Peircean index, of what it signifies, even though this referent may not (yet or any longer) exist. Ashbery tells the story of getting a haircut at the emblematic La Flamme barbershop (still operating) while he was a student in Cambridge. During the obligatory small talk he mentioned the unseasonably mild weather, prompting the barber's reply, "One swallow does not make a winter." Aristotle's authorized version of the proverb (in *Nichomachean Ethics*) opens the penultimate dizain, as Ashbery makes the winter of his discontent into its antonymic "opposite": "One swallow does not make a summer, but are / What's called an opposite: a whole of raveling discontent, / The sum of all that will ever be deciphered / On this side of that vast drop of water" (#49, DDS 94; "the Atlantic"). All that remains, or will return, of "summer" is "sum," a fragmentary signifier signifying nevertheless a synecdochal "whole" (if only a "hole"). The grammatical solecism "One swallow . . . are," unraveling the willful singular of "fragment," is significant. In the previous, Yeatsian dizain, many dancers are survived by their "opposites" or signifying "complements": "And as one figure / Supplants another, and dies, so the postulate of each / Tires the shuffling floor with slogans, present / Complements mindful of our absorbing interest" (#48, DDS 94). As Ashbery once put it, "Fragment" is "a fragment of something bigger than itself . . . which is the consciousness that produced it at the moment and which left out all kinds of things in the interests of writing the poem." Neither the subject nor the subject matter of "Fragment" will ever be unraveled on this side of life, that multiple "vast drop of water" impossible to "swallow." But the whole, of which the parts are part, exists nowhere else.

The signs which make up "Fragment" are decentered on "the central perimeter / Our imaginations' orbit" (#13, DDS 82). While Scève sought to reach "au Centre heureux, au cœur impénétrable" (330; "to the happy center, to the impenetrable heart"), in "Fragment" the happy signified is not only inaccessible but missing. In its place is a wholesale "distribution center" of second-hand "notions" or ideas: "The hollow thus produced / A kind of cave of the winds; distribution center / Of subordinate notions to which the stag / Returns to die: the suppressed lovers" (#7, DDS 80). The stag, another of the emblems from *Délie,* represents the wounded lover. But in the economy of desire, the sought center, like the lover or father, must be missing for the ardent poem to flourish, "a flame yourself / Without meaning, yet drawing satisfaction / From the crevices of that wind" (#10, DDS 81; cf. Scève: "Ma flamme sort de son creux funébreux," 355; "My flame issues from its funereal hollow").

"Fragment" ends in the future anterior with another prophecy, as though one swallow did make a summer a sure thing: "In the months ahead, she would remember that that / Anomaly had spoken to her, words like disjointed beaches / Brown under the advancing signs of the air" (#50, DDS 94). In this revised prophecy, the words are not overheard but spoken. In its first form, the words were "like / Disconnected beaches, brown and gray under the advancing air." Ashbery's renovated simile builds on these materials. In "disjointed beaches" the crypt phrase "disjointed speeches" is more distinctly audible. And these "brown and gray" beaches are covered with receding "hair." Loss of hair or hair color is one swallow of wintry age, as in George Herbert's "The Forerunners": "The harbingers are come. See, see their mark; / White is their colour, and behold my head."[24] But the "air" of course is also a song which advances with the possibility that "she would remember," if not understand, its "passionate intelligence."

It is surprising that Ashbery's advancing air is constructed partly from reused fragments. One isolated, surviving draft page, numbered 10, contains the following sentence (presumably from a draft of dizain 19), here juxtaposed with its new locations in dizains 20 and 49:

Not in the lesson not in the special way of telling
But back to one side of life, not especially
Immune to it, the secret of what goes on
Hopes for your presence like a waxed moustache
And a monocle, in the lowered angles of some room.

Empire, back lands whose sparsely populated look is
Supreme dominion. It will be divided into tracks
And these be lived in the way now the lowered
Angles of this room. Waxed moustache against the impiety
Of so much air of change. . . .
(#20, DDS 84)

They let you sleep without pain, having all that
Not in the lesson, not in the special way of telling
But back to one side of life, not especially
Immune to it, in the secret of what goes on:

The words sung in the next room are unavoidable.
But their passionate intelligence will be studied in you.
(#49, DDS 94)

In the allegory of the old room #19, the secret itself hopes to let you in on it. The phrasing of the invitation, "Hopes for your presence," is formal and archaic from the period of waxed moustaches and lowered lighting (if not suspended ceilings). In the present dizain 20 the secret becomes inherited property, an Empire State of (fifty) farmland plots, a Tennessee without an urn to take dominion. Here the room itself is formal and resistant to change, as one's parents' rooms and the stanzas of "Fragment" tend to be. But Ashbery's carpentry shows in his do-it-yourself joint: "And these be lived in the way now the lowered / Angles of this room." The self-reflexive idea—that these squared plots will be lived in—is almost but not quite lost here "in the special way of telling." In dizain 49 the position formerly occupied by "the secret" is taken by "you" lying in the next room. By adding "in" to "the secret," Ashbery adds the phrase to the series of open and closed interiors, each introduced by "in": "Not in the lesson," "not in the special way of telling," "[But] in the secret," "in the next room," "in you." The "secret" is not the subject of "Fragment" and no one is in on it, at least on "this side" of "what goes on." Its subject instead is "you." In its first rendition, the penultimate stanza's close was clearer but flatter: "The notes sung in the next room are unheard / But their passionate intelligence will be credited to you anyway." The credit and responsibility goes here to "you," the author on the title page, who writes the words without knowing the tune. In Ashbery's revision, where the emblematic "words" become "inaudible" and finally "unavoidable," the poet, poem, lover, father, and mother all live "in you." We readers in the next room, who confirm Ashbery's prophecy with each reading of "Fragment," should expect no more.

In "Fragment," as painfully sustained a poem as any Ashbery has written, abstraction is "unavoidable." The self-reflection in dizain 20, for instance, would not exist without the stilted syntax and harsh landscape architecture: "And I some joy of this have, returning to the throbbing / Mirror's stiff enclave, the sides of my face steep and overrun" (DDS 84). Abstraction conditions expression. Nevertheless, the refined, almost speechless style of "Fragment" closed more doors than it opened. Another radical departure, as after *Some Trees,* was in order. In *Three Poems* Ashbery will dissolve the crystalline form of "Fragment" into prose, reintroducing himself to his readers by letting them recognize their own turns of phrase.

# 5

## Dialectics of Love

### *Three Poems*

What is poetry and if you know what poetry is what is prose.
—Gertrude Stein, "Poetry and Grammar," *Lectures in America*

In a 1981 interview Ashbery called *Three Poems* a liberation from his earlier work: "the poems in *The Double Dream of Spring* . . . had gotten to a tightness and strictness that bothered me, and I began to feel I'd have to start moving in some other direction because I had become too narrow, even though I liked those poems."[1] After the regular crystallizations of "Fragment," Ashbery decided that in *Three Poems* "the poetic form would be dissolved, in solution."[2] Ashbery's novel solution was prose, a prose loose and long and various enough to absorb any subject matter. It was an unusual choice in 1970, when the naked poem still clung to the G-string of lineation.[3] But in the wake of the publication of *Three Poems* in 1972, a fair number of experimental poets—Robert Creeley, Ron Silliman, Rosmarie Waldrop, Michael Davidson, Lyn Hejinian, Paul Hoover, Bob Perelman, and others—began filling their pages with prose they published as poetry. By the end of the 1980s prosing had become so widespread a practice that Charles Bernstein could advise readers: "if it's in prose, there's a good chance / it's a poem."[4] While *Self-Portrait in a Convex Mirror* may have attracted more prizes and readers, *Three Poems* has exerted more influence on poets. It is Ashbery's own favorite, and a bottomless quarry for his later verses.[5] This excursion into prose largely made possible the boundlessly fluctuating prosaic poetry readers think of as Ashbery's.

"The New Spirit," the first of the three poems, begins with a history of development. Speaking as though to an interviewer, the poet looks back on his divided ways of inclusion and exclusion:

> I thought that if I could put it all down, that would be
> one way. And next the thought came to me that to leave
> all out would be another, and truer, way.
>
>    clean-washed sea
>                                          The flowers were.
>
> These are examples of leaving out. But, forget as we will,
> something soon comes to stand in their place. Not the
> truth, perhaps, but—yourself. It is you who made this,
> therefore you are true. But the truth has passed on
>
>                                       to divide all.
> (TP 3)

This plain-spoken beginning offers us a good example of Ashbery's misrepresentative argumentation: turning one way when we expect him to go another or simply stopping and going on to something else when we expect him to continue along. The first page recounts a progressive elimination of possibilities: I thought of putting it all down. Next I thought of leaving it all out. But you readers keep filling in the blanks. So finally I. . . . But Ashbery leaves out the third choice, which might reconcile the opposite ways of inclusion and exclusion, of expansion and abstraction, the forking paths opened up by his two chief forerunners, Whitman and Dickinson. Ashbery's own "examples of leaving out"—mispunctuated, disjunctive, asyntactical, yet lyrical (recombining some such description as "The flowers were washed clean by the sea")—echo the solitary notes of *The Tennis Court Oath*. A decade later Ashbery recalled that in *Three Poems* he wanted to produce "a very long poem completely filling up these pages that would give me the same pleasure that the one-word exercise did way back then."[6] While this statement suggests that Ashbery emptied his pages before he filled them, the pseudo-statement that opens *Three Poems* reverses the sequence, putting the way of total prose not after but before the "truer" way of fragmented lyric. One clue to this inverted history lies in the slight restatements: from "I thought" to "the thought came to me" and from "put it all down" to "leave [it] all out." What the revision leaves out, "I" and "it," are the subject and its matter—"all" the text would need to make perfect sense. As Marjorie Perloff points out: "The poem opens by positing an all-but-impossible choice . . . and then equivocates by putting down a great deal that is nevertheless not the confessional or revelatory 'it' we might have expected."[7] Leaving it all out is impossible since reading is based on preexistent codes and forms which, "forget as we will," cannot be erased, any more than Ashbery can the crypt phrase, "try as we will." Readers corroborate Ashbery's "truth" by seeing how well it corresponds with their own experience; "therefore you are true," Ashbery tells his readers, including himself. But the objective, outside "truth" to which all readers might appeal "has passed on / to divide all." Putting it all down, then, is equally impossible. As Ashbery put it in "The Skaters," "these are fundamental absences" (RM 39) separating reader from writer, lover from lover, past from present, "you" from "yourself," and everyone from certainty. We should read the first perforated page of *Three Poems* as Ashbery wrote it, before he himself knew which way to go, not as a "bad" or "misleading" argument but as a task to be undertaken, a blank to be filled out (if not in). The way turned out to be one of expansive abstraction. No less full of holes than his verses, the all-over writing of *Three Poems* leaves out a great deal. There are no more narrative particulars (names, places, dates) or concrete details than usual. The dominant discursive modes are the love letter or talk, the written or oral history, the sermon, and the spiritual meditation. With its thoughtful monotony, *Three Poems* lacks the impulsive variety of Ashbery's earlier "leaving-out business" (RM 39), "The Skaters," though from poem to poem it is more varied than "Fragment." But by leaving the totalizing "all out," Ashbery will argue, he really leaves nothing behind. If it is not actually there, its latent presence is.

Near the end of his book the poet draws our attention to the novelty of his pre-occupation: "You know now the sorrow of continually doing something that you cannot name, of producing automatically as an apple tree produces apples this thing there is no name for" (TP 110). One obvious nominee is already in use. Ashbery has said, not quite tautologically, that with *Three Poems* he "was trying to write three long prose poems."[8] The name fits in the negative sense that in composing "trois grands poèmes en prose" (and size makes all the difference) Ashbery consciously departed from French models. In a 1972 interview with the *New York Quarterly* he took exception to the artificiality of the genre: "there's something very self-consciously poetic about French prose poetry which I wanted to avoid and which I guess is what I found disappointing in my earlier prose poems; it's very difficult to avoid a posture, a certain rhetorical tone"[9] which distinguishes prose as poetry. This generically self-conscious tone is audible in "The Young Son" (dated May 1952):

The screen of supreme good fortune curved his absolute smile into a celestial scream. These things (the most arbitrary that could exist) wakened denials, thoughts of putrid reversals as he traced the green paths to and fro. Here and there a bird sang, a rose silenced her expression of him, and all the gaga flowers wondered. But they puzzled the wanderer with their vague wearinesses.  (ST 42)

With its paragraph-indented format, "The Young Son" promises the playfulness of Max Jacob. But the sardonic, putrid reversal of "smiling Fortune," the encrypted sexual repression ("wakened desires"), the versifying comma breaks, and the world-weary *fleurs* all reveal Baudelaire's and Rimbaud's prior footsteps on these paths, which are indeed less "paced" than "traced." Around two years later Ashbery wrote a very different kind of prose poem, "Novel" (which the magazine *Accent* returned, Ashbery recalls, with the comment that it was "indeed novel" but not for them).[10] In some places the unpublished work reads like the five-and-dime narratives of "Popular Songs" and "A Long Novel": "Keeping a general store one started so seldom, and then it was only to turn around, it is true, tin things falling, nails perhaps from the paper hole Mr. ------- had forgotten to fix. It was long after that, in another room, we became acquainted. It was tea-rose day" ("a pin drop," "a hole in the tarpaper roof," "New Year's Day"). But elsewhere "Novel" reads like a prose sketch for *The Tennis Court Oath*: "Urgently valves spot the beef straw stopping pitilessly alongside Filbert field. Cops move shot basket torch tough steak grows wind block Catherine bluff, diary salt trail downs slack man salt pickle fashion." These word-measured sentences opened up new paths of prose narrative, but Ashbery left them green. He picks up few narrative leads in *Three Poems,* focusing instead on "what libraries class as 'nonfiction.'"[11]

After a long hiatus, Ashbery returned to prose with "For John Clare" (DDS 35). Written in the spring of 1969, about half a year before "The New Spirit," this was his first poem completely in prose since "The Young Son" (the prose fugue of "Variations" being another important experiment). The poem in prose winds up with a sidelong glance at lyric birdsong:

> As for Jenny Wren, she cares, hopping about on her little twig like she was tryin' to tell us somethin', but that's just it, she couldn't even if she wanted to—dumb bird. But the others—and they in some way must know too—it would never occur to them to want to, even if they could take the first step of the terrible journey toward feeling somebody should act, that ends in utter confusion and hopelessness, east of the sun and west of the moon. So their comment is: "No comment." Meanwhile the whole history of probabilities is coming to life, starting in the upper left-hand corner, like a sail.  (DDS 36; a "jenny" is a female wren)

This mercurial prose communes with a noncommittal nature. With her dropped g's, Jenny Wren's animated tweeting records Keats or Clare less

than Disney. Ashbery develops this topic of the homotextual "first step" in
*Three Poems* (35, 73, 75), which winds up here in a fairy-tale utopia, "East
of the Sun, West of the Moon." Refraining from both denial and affirmation,
Ashbery's personified natural "they" settle for the politician's stock response. "Meanwhile," Ashbery rewrites spring as a statistical probability
rather than a periodic necessity, spreading like his own new prose over a
Mallarméan white sheet. "For John Clare" may involve the same fruitless
journey as "The Young Son," but this new profusion of discourses tells us
something by keeping its lyric comments to itself. It was Clare's journal writing, Ashbery recalls, that provided the impetus for his resumption of prose
poetry.[12] Clare's prose compels partly through its absorption in its subject:

> The Wren is another of these domestic birds that has found favour in the
> affections of man . . . it is a pert bird among its fellows and always seems
> in a conscieted [sic] sort of happiness with its tail strunted up oer its back
> and its wings dripping down—its song is more loud then the Robins and
> very pleasant tho it is utterd in broken raptures by sudden starts and as
> sudden endings it begins to sing in march and continues till the end of
> spring when it becomes moping and silent[13]

This is not Nature writing but Clare, with his own opinions, selective observations, allegorical personifications, and literary conceits. His desultory
leaps among discourses and specifics keep his "whole history of probabili-
ties" from adding up to a single "picture." What attracted Ashbery was
probably this directionless, natural messiness. In fact it seems that, for Ashbery, being natural resembles being Clare: "Being immersed in the details
of rock and field and slope—letting them come to you for once, and then
meeting them halfway would be so much easier" (DDS 35). But Ashbery's
prose here gets back to a Wordsworthian general nature devoid of Clare's
manifold specifics; his immersion is also an abstraction.

Ashbery's contemporary comments to the contrary, *Three Poems* is also
immersed in French prose poetry. Ten years later he acknowledged the allure of this tradition: "I'd always felt that prose poetry, at least the prose
poetry of Rimbaud or Baudelaire, has a poignant, literary quality just from
being prose."[14] In fact the generic doubleness in some of Baudelaire's prose
poems, part essay and part soliloquy, resembles Ashbery's own bifocal perspective. Below are excerpts respectively from Baudelaire's "Les foules,"
Rimbaud's "Ville," and Ashbery's "The New Spirit," depicting the isolated
lyricist's plunge into the mass of words:

> The solitary, thoughtful stroller is singularly intoxicated by this universal
> communion. The man who beds easily with the crowd knows feverish rap-

tures eternally withheld from both the egotist, locked up like a money chest, and the homebody, sealed like a mollusk. He adopts as his own all the professions, all the joys and sadnesses which circumstances present him. What men call love is indeed paltry, restrained, and weak compared to this ineffable orgy, to this holy prostitution of the soul which gives itself entirely, in love and in poetry, to the unforeseen encounter, to the passing stranger.[15]

These millions of people with no need of knowing each other conduct their schooling, career, and retirement so similarly that their life spans must be several times shorter than an insane statistic allots to those on the mainland. Thus, from my window, I see new spirits rolling through the thick, eternal coal smoke (our wood-shade, our summer night!) . . . : unweeping Death, our active daughter and servant, a despairing Love, and a pretty Crime squealing in the muddy street.[16]

He wants to go it alone, but at this time of year the populations emerge again into the arena of life after the death of winter, and one is newly conscious of the multitudes that swarm past one in the street; there is something of death here too in the way they plunge past toward some unknown destination, leaving one a little shaken up on the edge of the sidewalk. Who are all these people? What does it mean that there are so many? (TP 44)

With its "jouissances fiévreuses," Baudelaire's "Les foules" derives from one of Poe's most intriguing stories, "The Man of the Crowd," but its sentiments are more Whitmanian than Poesque. Street-walking is promiscuous for Baudelaire. Yet the solitary poet does not give his poem to the crowd. By avoiding ordinary discourses and average lives, he meets people in the tantalizing singular rather than the drab multiple. Rimbaud's city is at once more abstract and more concrete, with its impossibly visible "millions" wandering through real coal smoke. Yet these individuals reduce to a few allegorical permutations, each with a foreshortened span and islanded room. Rimbaud's city is modern multiplication rather than romantic squalor. The poet's sardonic perspective takes shape as a window which affords him the statistician's vantage point on this shadowy world.

Ashbery's prose triangulates Rimbaud's and Baudelaire's. Elsewhere in his poetry the mysterious stranger represents an interruptive possibility. But in this passage the narrative third person keeps "him" from questioning the vernal multitudes. Ashbery's Anglo-French is discernible here in the generic "one" and in constructions such as "there is something of death here." But the final questions echo Dante (via the Baudelairean Eliot), "I had not thought death had undone so many," casting "he" as Dante, his auditor as Virgil, the crowd springing up as the Dead, and the vague setting (cf. Rimbaud's smoke) as the bank of the Styx. The "rhetorical tone" of Ashbery's well-traveled allusion is counterbalanced here by the poignant "bad poetry" of "the arena of life after the death of winter," which, like Ashbery's translation of Arthur Cravan (DDS 61), is moving because it is self-consciously trite. "He" can only wonder about these masses in their own figures of speech.

When asked about prose "sources" for *Three Poems,* Ashbery offered two generically mixed works, de Chirico's *Hebdomeros* (1929) and Auden's "The Sea and the Mirror" (1944).[17] De Chirico's quirkily democratic book is one of Ashbery's favorites. Twenty-five pages of his translation from the middle of the novel appeared in *Art and Literature* 4 (1965); here is one of the shortest sentences:

> The glory of the past, the vanity of human heroism, and those pyramids which the fear of oblivion incites the administrators of the common weal to command of indifferent hirelings who are thinking of something else as they build, of the fiancée or the wife who awaits them back there, far from the smoke and din, in the peaceful home, close to the window open on the coolness of the garden where thousands of glow-worms streak the shadows with phosphorescent lines.[18]

The solitary artist is figured in the satire as the (nameless) Pharaoh fearful of oblivion, who forces his monumental designs upon his subjects. But in the midst of construction the laborers are lost in their thoughts of a "peaceful home" away from the suspiciously modern "smoke and din," its "glow-worms" outshining their forgotten master's "glory." So too de Chirico's pyramidal syntax (along with his embedded moral, *sic transit gloria mundi*) gets lost in this detailed description. Though Ashbery's sentences in *Three Poems* are relatively spare, their topics or subject matters likewise get buried in their oblivious elaborations, comparisons, and qualifications, which proceed "toward no special goal" (TP 29).

Ashbery discovered demotic poetry in Auden's verse, which he recalls first reading in high school. "What immediately struck me was his use of colloquial speech—I didn't think you were supposed to do that in poetry."[19] But it was Auden's verse and prose "commentary" on Shakespeare's *The Tempest* that was the chief model, or obstacle, for his own most prosaic poetry. In his 1949 senior thesis Ashbery declared Auden's "The Sea and the Mirror," published five years earlier, his "finest work to date," praising its concluding section, "Caliban to the Audience," as "probably the most brilliant writing Auden has ever done. Oddly enough, it is in prose, beginning as a parody of the style of Henry James" (25). What most excites the young poet is Auden's style. His mix of poeticisms with clichés, Ashbery argues, is more worldly than the vernacular style of Eliot, whose "poetry as a whole, though it introduced the idea that the everyday world is part of the province of poetry, remains allusive and refined, lacking in the immediacy and concreteness which Auden gives to all that he touches" (31). Ashbery especially admires Auden's mixture of discourses, which he calls "rhythms (those of the cabaret, the birthday card, the political broadsheet) which are very much a part of our life. . . . If he is not a great poet, a decision which must be made by time, he has brought innumerable people closer to the world in which they have to live" (32).

The worldliness of "Caliban to the Audience," like that of *Three Poems,* is relative and varying. Auden treats the philosophical and literary relation between the abstract and the concrete as a romance:

> As the gay productive months slip by, in spite of fretful discouraged days, of awkward moments of misunderstanding or rather, seen retrospectively as happily cleared up and got over, verily because of them, you are definitely getting the hang of this, at first so novel and bewildering, relationship between magician and familiar, whose duty it is to sustain your infinite conceptual appetite with vivid concrete experiences.   (CP 331–32)

The seamless incorporation of idioms ("slip by," "awkward moments," "cleared up," "getting the hang of") alongside more deliberate parallelisms ("gay productive months," "fretful discouraged days") anticipates Ashbery's hybrid prose. Yet Auden's style and stance here are more classical than Ashbery's. The irony of past troubles smoothed over is marked by the traditional verbal sign of adverbs in mixed discourse ("verily," "definitely"). The "gay" couple, Prospero and Ariel, is here constructed out of a series of syntactical doublets ("days" and "months," "cleared up and got over," "novel and bewildering," "magician and familiar"). Though Auden means this relationship to stand for his own "getting the hang of this" novelistic vivid prose, like an "infinite" god adjusting to human existence, he remains the couple's mutual friend. Auden's godlike "you" addresses no one here, "verily," but himself.

By letting the "untutored" Caliban (who is as refined as any Jamesian narrator) rather than the masterly Prospero or Shakespeare address the audience, Auden admits his audience's "rhythms" into his discursive theater. In *Three Poems* Ashbery's "idea . . . was to allow all kinds of prose 'voices' to have their say in what I hoped would be poetry—so that at times it sounds like journalism or letter writing or philosophy, both Cracker-barrel and Platonic, and so on. I guess I was trying to 'democratize' language."[20] The poetic prose of the high-flown orator also has its say—"the inflated rhetoric," as Ashbery calls it, "that is trying very hard to sound poetic but not making it."[21] Not all of *Three Poems* is equally or similarly "democratic": "The New Spirit" emphasizes private and romantic discourse; "The System" foregrounds public discourse; and "The Recital" features both pragmatic and personal writing. But each of the three poems sacrifices its distinctive "lyric voice" to the press of idioms, styles, and discourses. This "democratizing" or "Americanizing" of the language of the prose poem has been well discussed.[22] But what does Ashbery mean by recycling these stock phrases, figures, and meanings? Where is "Ashbery" in this rapidly shifting demographic mix? According to Fredric Jameson, since the postmodern era lacks a social linguistic norm, parody is superseded by uncritical pastiche. Though suggestive, Jameson's blanket generalization blurs the textual specifics of postmodern poetry. Consider this passage from "The New Spirit": "For we judge not, lest we be judged, yet we are judged all the same, without noticing, until one day we wake up a different color, the color of the filter of the opinions and ideas everyone has ever entertained about us. And in this form we must prepare, now, to try to live" (TP 7–8). We do not have to decide whether Ashbery's adaptation of Matthew 7.1 is a critical parody, an idle pastiche, or a rhetorical restatement which erases the difference between orator and audience, as in Lincoln's second inaugural address ("but let us judge not, that we be not judged").[23] It is all of these. Ashbery's version, which substitutes "we" for "you" and the indicative for the imperative, has a satirical, critical force and implies a practical, cynical alternative to Christian ethics ("judge first, that ye be not judged"). As "we" includes "I," Ashbery's sentence also carries a reflexive dimension: his "innocent" works cannot avoid a volley of critical aspersions.

But Ashbery's prose passes beyond parody with the double valence of "all the same." Alongside the idiomatic sense ("in any case," "anyway") the proximity of "we" awakens a dormant, literal meaning, "as one." Ashbery's homiletic "we" is grammatically plural but rhetorically singular, premised on the assumption that we are "all the same." But is that sameness a singularity or a plurality? Ashbery's lyrical "a different color" crossbreeds "a different person" with "a horse of a different color," which of course means not "all the same" but "something completely different." The magic of the transformation is acknowledged in the phrase "until one day," a fairy-tale formula for introducing a new incident or character into the vast past imperfect. With this phrase Ashbery may be parodying the myth of origins, but he is also resorting to the best formula available to account for the psychological and social phenomenon of suddenly "waking up" to the gradually established reality of our having changed (become older, professorial, a poet). The figuration "the color of the filter of the opinions" specifies "colored," biased or interested, testimony with photographic color filters. The grammatical irony here is that "everyone" is no different from "us"; our "true colors" are all one filtered color. This argument and figure are developed in Ashbery's next long poem, "Self-Portrait": "How many people came and stayed a certain time, / Uttered light or dark speech that became part of you," "Filtered and influenced by it, until no part / Remains that is surely you" (SP 71). But whereas the highly refined verse of "Self-Portrait" itself acts as a filter, the prose poetry of *Three Poems* is insistently demotic. The sentence from *Three Poems* is serious, parodic, pastichist, banal, and original all at once; the layered differences do not cancel each other out but mount up. Ashbery's new "truth" (inverting the usual one, that what people say should make no difference to us) is filtered through everybody's stock phrase. Whether Ashbery originally meant to say what he "one day" ended up saying is doubtful; it seems more likely that he discovered his misrepresentative meaning during the formulation of his new composite sentence, and judged that it should stand. There is no absolute vantage point outside social discourse from which Ashbery can select his styles, as from a computer menu. His particular mixture of prose is as unmistakeable as Joyce's or James's; it stands as a celebratory, objecting, and neutral (because unconscious) amalgam of its discourses.

In a landscape as imposing and undifferentiated as *Three Poems,* changes in argument, discursive register, and even format are not readily discernible. Ashbery may very well have drawn up the blueprint for *Three Poems* as he went along. But a formal design and a dialectical argument are legible in the final product. *Three Poems* consists of two fifty-page poems and a ten-page resumption. Each poem differs minimally and significantly in format: "The New Spirit" is made up of "prose blocks" (unindented prose stanzas) and unindented verse, "The System" of prose blocks, and "The Recital" of regularly indented paragraphs.[24] On the back cover of the Viking edition appears Ashbery's reworded summary of the work:[25]

Meant as a kind of trilogy to be read in sequence, the book opens [in "The New Spirit"] with a spiritual awakening to earthly things that also involves drawing the author's dilemma over selectivity in his work into a metaphor for man's ability to act either with or upon his destiny. Then [in "The System"] Ashbery moves into wry, quasi-dialectical language to tell a love story with cosmological overtones, and [in "The Recital"] he concludes with a poem that consolidates and fleshes out the themes of the previous two, balancing them with the sometimes harsh facts of his own autobiography.

After discussing the problematic choice of a poetic "way" with his readers, the writer in "The New Spirit" turns to a particular reader, ostensibly a former lover, meditating on the history of their affair and on his consequent reintroduction to the world. Near the end of the poem these reflections coalesce into a character called "the Ram" or "he." This "new spirit," both character and persona in an allegorical narrative of prophetic "selection," takes the podium and pulpit in "The System," delivering first a religious history of the sixties and then a sermon on living out one's unknowable destiny. Not long after he had finished the poems, Ashbery offered this explanation:

> I talked about the fact that somebody is being born; in other words at the end [of "The New Spirit"] a person is somehow given an embodiment out of those proliferating reflections that are occurring in a generalized mind which eventually run together into the image of a specific person, "he" or "me," who was not there when the poem began. In "The System" I guess you might say that the person who has been born as "he" has taken over in the first person again and is continuing the debate.[26]

"The Recital" begins brilliantly with the pointed sentence "All right." In ordinary usage this phrase would inaugurate a survey of what is to be done; but in the context of *Three Poems* it also reads as a contraction, "all is right," which readmits the synthesizing "all" left out at the beginning of "The New Spirit":

> The point was the synthesis of very simple elements in a new and strong, as opposed to old and weak, relation to one another. Why hadn't this been possible in the earlier days of experimentation, of bleak, barren living that didn't seem to be leading anywhere and it couldn't have mattered less? Probably because not enough of what made it up had taken on that look of worn familiarity, like pebbles polished over and over again by the sea, that made it possible for the old to blend inconspicuously with the new in a union too subtle to cause any comment that would have shattered its purpose forever.   (TP 117–18)

The common property of *Three Poems,* like the worn simile of the pebbles, blends in so well that it is impossible to separate the public from the individual spirit. The amalgamated "old," however, is not merely old poetry but old Ashbery poetry. In "the earlier days of experimentation" in "Europe" Ashbery combined literary codes (pop fiction and lyric) while hardly tapping nonliterary languages. In its resolute quest to be absolutely "new" or unfamiliar the experiment was "barren," at least from Ashbery's interested perspective at the culmination of *Three Poems*. So "The Recital" synthesizes the old and the new in an inconspicuous renewal. *Three Poems* subtly defamiliarizes the reader, who goes along following each step but ends up completely lost. If *Three Poems* is less conspicuously experimental than *The Tennis Court Oath,* its absorptive dislocations of literary and nonliterary discourses, poetic and banal statements, and familiar and perverted or incomplete arguments are themselves profoundly unsettling.

"The Recital" self-consciously adopts the dialectic as a structuring principle. In the course of *Three Poems* a number of dialectical changes are rung, if not rigorously pursued. The triads which propel "The New Spirit," "The System," and "The Recital" include the following: the new, the old, and the renewed; private, public, and privatized discourse; romantic, religious, and humanitarian love; potential, actual (kinetic), and pragmatic action; forgetting (present), memory (past), and absorption. Ashbery talks about the dialectic of *Three Poems* in musical terms:

> It seems that there is a progression, in *Three Poems,* from different ways of feeling that are continuous through the poem. It talks about a kind of pseudo-platonic stage of love going from, you know, the physical up to the spiritual. And the end of that poem says that the last trials can be administered in a friendly, pleasurable ambience, and they have to be gone through, and that certainly another journey is going to have to be made, even though we seem to have come to a point of peace, pleasure, sort of earthly paradise kind of thing. So in this poem, I think the underlying theme is a kind of progression which I didn't know because I didn't know I was going to meet somebody and fall in love while I was in the middle of it. But it was starting out to be about love, then becoming it, and finally there's a kind of resolution, or an attempt at a resolution, at the end of all the contradictions which in fact implies that the work is a series of contradictions, one after the other.[27]

The musical "progression" and "resolution" probably more accurately characterize the "movements" of *Three Poems* than a Neoplatonic allegory of love. Ashbery listened to Brahms's *Sextet* No. 1 and Elliott Carter's *Concerto for Orchestra* while writing *Three Poems:* "the thing about music is that it's always going on and reaching a conclusion and it helps me to be surrounded by this moving climate that it produces—moving I mean in the sense of going on."[28] A "moving climate" is itself a suggestive description for the progressive seductive prose of *Three Poems*. The theater provides another illuminating analogy. Like "The Sea and the Mirror" and *The Tempest*, "The Recital" resolves the problem of "man's ability to act either with or upon his destiny" with the figure of the play, in which characters "act" most completely by performing what is in the script. The Christian overtones in this model of theatrical action (as in Hopkins's "As kingfishers catch fire" or Eliot's *Murder in the Cathedral*) are clear enough, but Ashbery doesn't cut the action by privileging the spirit over the body or over the systems they both inhabit.

Ashbery's new spirit is born by a process of selection. The title "The New Spirit" comes from *l'esprit nouveau,* André Antoine's term for a group of surrealists including Apollinaire, author of the postwar manifesto "The New Spirit and the Poets." The 1913 Armory Show used "The New Spirit" as its slogan. Ashbery said that he meant the title, like "The New Realism" (TCO 59), to be "slightly satirical" since there is always a new spirit in the air and new realities to deal with.[29] The new, realistic spirit in Ashbery's air involves living in the world within your means toward your own ends, even though they cannot be known. This personal economy entails selection, leaving "all" out, narrowing down possibilities both in living and of writing. This economic spirit is embodied in the idiom "striking out." Drawing on the sense of failure in the all-American game of baseball ("Turning on yourself as a leaf, you miss the third and last chance," TP 4), Ashbery's "idea of striking out" (TP 10) means canceling a portion of a text, losing at love, and beginning a journey:

> Nevertheless the winter wears on and death follows death. I've tried it, and know how the narrowing-down feeling conflicts with the feeling of life's coming to a point, not a climax but a point. At that point one must, yes, be selective, but not selective in one's choices if you see what I mean. Not choose this or that because it pleases, merely to assume the idea of choosing, so that some things can be left behind. It doesn't matter which ones. I could tell you about some of the things I've discarded but that wouldn't help you because you must choose your own, or rather not choose them but let them be inflicted on and off you. This is the point of the narrowing-down process. And gradually, as the air gets thinner as you climb a mountain, these things will stand forth in a relief all their own— the look of belonging. (TP 8–9)

The primary discursive model for this prose block is the self-help manual. After a darkened narrative overview ("the year wears on and day follows day") in which "Nevertheless" functions more like "ever the less," the prose shifts into a commercial testimonial ("I've tried it") for some product like Geritol, much advertised for that "run-down feeling" of aging. Ashbery's pick-me-up resembles Sartre's idea of existential freedom of choice, "a permanent condition of nausea" (TP 103), prior to any single act of choosing—including what is called "sexual choice." Ashbery has confessed that he "never read Sartre," but admitted that he "absorbed the ideas," which were in the air (in *Tel Quel* and *Art and Literature,* for instance) at the time.[30] What is "discarded" may be a word or a lover or verse or heterosexuality. But this "new kind of arbitrariness," the argument continues, both "*pro*tects and *pro*motes" (TP 9; italics are mine). Ashbery's choice of "prose" (from *pro-vertere,* to turn forward) is itself marked by the frequent prefix "pro-" orienting "The New Spirit" as its vector and impulse. The dialectic logic of consolation goes roughly like this: the new spirit, while admitting that it "can't have everything," asserts itself by renouncing some (misrepresentative) things ("why not sacrifice something / ordinary, such as a hairnet," FC 67) in order to have "chosen" what is left. Rhetorically, this mountaintop point, enlarging the hour-glass sands of Dantesque middle age ("The middle of the journey, before the sands are reversed," TP 4), is "Nevertheless" cause for exhilaration. That is, selection becomes election, a chord progression which will be further explored in *Flow Chart.*

One by-product of the choice of prose in "The New Spirit" is its occasional untitled prosaic verses:

> Yet it was almost enough to be growing up in that city.
> The taste of it, rationed through a medicine dropper,
> Filled up the day.
> In the evening the newspaper was delivered, ready to be read.
> Darkness glossed over the imbalances
> And the last irregularities dissolved in sleep.
> That metropolis was like the kitchen of the world
> And we were like servants, setting out on the task of life
> As on a tour of duty.
> (TP 33)

As in Ashbery's poetry of the 1950s, each line in this relatively unmannered, straightforward verse is a dose, as though Ashbery were anxious to differentiate it from the acres of surrounding prose. There are ironies of lineation here, such as the relative smallness of the line "Filled up the day," but the conflicts of regular life are necessarily distilled. The representative city is modeled on Rochester, New York, where Ashbery lived much of the time until he was seven with his grandparents.[31] This early childhood existence, measured in small doses with a "medicine dropper," is marked by days regulated like lines by "old" habits—reading the "news," for instance (cf. Eliot's coffee spoons and "Boston Evening Transcript")—and sexual and political "irregularities dissolved into sleep" as into prose. These lines work quietly by means of resonant idioms ("glossed over"), explicit similes, and worn metaphorical possessives, with their ironic flavor of masculine endeavor: "the task of life" (cf. Cowper's "The Task" and Ashbery's poem by the same title) and "the kitchen of the world" (when he was young, Ashbery's grandfather worked as a cook on his uncle's Great Lakes Steamers). The wryly nostalgic message of these regulated lines is that their comfortable sufficiency is no longer enough. The poetry of the verse, at its best, falls short of the prose, but its recognition of that fact lends it poignancy, if not power.

Among the most significant selections or choices in *Three Poems* are the pronouns. Ashbery's often cited comments on his pronouns have unintentionally misled a number of his readers:

> The personal pronouns in my work very often seem to be like variables in an equation. "You" can be myself or it can be another person, someone whom I'm addressing, and so can "he" and "she" for that matter and "we"; sometimes one has to deduce from the rest of the sentence what is being meant and my point is also that it doesn't really matter very much, that we are somehow all aspects of a consciousness giving rise to the poem and the fact of addressing someone, myself or someone else, is what's the important thing at that particular moment rather than the particular person involved. I guess I don't have a very strong sense of my own identity and I find it very easy to move from one person in the sense of a pronoun to another and this again helps to produce a kind of polyphony in my poetry which I again feel is a means toward greater naturalism.[32]

This explanation, given soon after he had finished *Three Poems,* is a fascinating and cogent summation of Ashbery's pronominal poetics. Ashbery's Keatsian lack of identity ("A poet is the most unpoetical of anything in existence; because he has no Identity") results in a polyphonic, dramatic text, in which pronouns are relational ("like variables in an equation") and representative, not bound to a "particular person."[33] But his claim that it doesn't matter very much, if taken to mean that the often abrupt shifting from one to another is of no consequence, simply doesn't match the experience of reading his poetry, particularly *Three Poems.* Though the particular persons Ashbery is thinking of can make no difference to us, the representative pronouns he selects to represent them are all-important. As Ashbery says, "the fact of addressing someone . . . is what's the important thing at that particular moment." In writing *Three Poems* Ashbery called off his soul-search after a suggestion from his analyst: "'Why don't you try thinking about people who have meant a lot to you in your life and then instead of writing about them, write about what you feel when you think about them?' So I did. I thought about various people whom I was in love with and my dead brother and my parents, and so on."[34] The unnamed addressees are marked not so much by biographical specifics as by discursive registers. Not that Ashbery ever merely speaks to someone else in *Three Poems;* it is a book not of letters but of poetry. To say that Ashbery's pronouns "shift" is only a first, rough observation about their functions in his prose. The pronouns of *Three Poems* register discursive situations and introduce systemic relations with other, unselected pronouns.

The varying prose styles of "The New Spirit" are signaled, and to some extent determined, by their pronominal key. Though "I" is the first word in *Three Poems,* it appears much less frequently than "you," "we," or even "it." In "The New Spirit" "I" plays the selective author but most often functions as one side of an apparently insoluble erotic equation. Whenever "I" dissociates itself from "you," the prose is governed by a lover's discourse verging on a one-sided argument, as when Ashbery questions the ethics of (even anonymously) representing someone else's life:

> Is it correct for me to use you to demonstrate all this? Perhaps what I am saying is that it is I the subject, recoiling from you at ever-increasing speed just so as to be able to say I exist in that safe vacuum I had managed to define from my friends' disinterested turning away. . . . I am the spectator, you what is apprehended, and as such we both have our own satisfying reality, even each to the other, though in the end it falls apart, falls to the ground and sinks in.   (TP 15)

Though "you" and "I" are equally "aspects of a consciousness" called love or authorship, the fact that "I" is an observing subject and "you" his "subject matter" changes everything. The claim "I exist," which completes the cogito "I thought" that inaugurated "The New Spirit," now "leaves out" its erotic other in order to proceed on a "truer way." Ashbery's rueful allotment, which "in the end . . . falls apart," is self-conscious and self-reflexive. The first "you" is both "used" to mean his "significant other" and "mentioned" (following Wittgenstein's distinction) to indicate the second-person pronoun; likewise, the demonstrative "all this" points both to their new situation and to the retrospective poem. The issue is both aesthetic and ethical: can "I" be used without "you," can one's lover be material for a poem? A provisional solution comes earlier in "The New Spirit": "In you I fall apart, and outwardly am a single fragment, a puzzle to itself. But we must learn to live in others, no matter how abortive or unfriendly their cold, piecemeal renderings of us: they create us" (TP 13). This piece of wisdom transposes a Traherne meditation on the self's reproduction into a minor key:[35] "We need Spectators; and other Diversities of Friends and Lovers, in whose Souls we might likewise Dwell. . . . And as in many Mirrors we are so many other selvs, so are we Spritualy Multiplied when we meet our selvs more Sweetly, and liv again in other Persons."[36] In Ashbery's rendition other people divide us piecemeal after their own interests. Yet there is no alternative, no universe of "you" and "I." The fruit of Ashbery's version is revealed when the pronouns of "they create us" are read in quotes: "they" creates "us" out of "you" and "I" and so reconciles our differences. The ex-lover's search for definition ("I fall apart without you") refers back to "Fragment" ("You exist only in me and on account of me," DDS 79). But while the arguments of "Fragment" closely resemble those in the opening blocks of "The New Spirit," *Three Poems* soon pulls away from its measured predecessor. Each "single fragment" or singular numbered pronoun is a distinct but necessary part of its systemic prose.

"In you I fall apart"; "I" disintegrates. The blocks in which "you" predominate are less defensive and self-reflexive than those in which "you" is set off from "I." The shortest paragraph in *Three Poems*—"To you:" (TP 13)—is both an anonymous dedication and a representative salutation. Prominent among the addressees in "The New Spirit" is a long-term second person from whom the "I" is now separated. In the first brief, short-winded prose block to begin with "You," Ashbery croons: "You are my calm world. This is my happiness. To stand, to go forward into it. The cost is enormous. Too much for one life" (TP 4). The highest cost here is the liquidation of the dependent subject "I," which (and "who") nearly assumes the object position in the homely crypt phrase, "Too much for me." His counterpart, of course, also disappears, reemerging as "it," a temporal "world" with a future orientation. In the following passage "you" is prominently introduced only to be displaced by a combination of "we" and "it":

> Such particulars you mouthed, all leading back into the underlying question: was it you? Do these things between people partake of themselves, or are they a subtler kind of translucent matter carrying each to a compromise distance painfully outside the rings of authority? For we never knew, never knew what joined us together. Perhaps only a congealing of closeness, deserving of no special notice. But then the eyes directing out, living into their material and in that way somehow making more substance than be-

fore, and yet the outward languid motion, like girls hanging out of windows . . . Is this something to be guessed at, though? Can it be identified
with some area in someone's mind? The answer is yes, if it is experienced,
and it has only to be expected to be lived, suspended in the air all around
us.   (TP 10; ellipsis is Ashbery's)

The situation and the wager here reside in the encrypted, intimately related
questions "Was it love?" and "Were you my love?" As in "Clepsydra," these
questions only arise in the wake of the thing itself. The rhetorical task of the
prose is to demonstrate that indeed "it was you." The proper form for such
a demonstration would be a dialogue between the interested parties. Instead, we have a meditative prose in which the participants are enveloped
but legible as different temperaments, positions, and ways of proceeding.
One argumentative pole here is materialist, objective, and skeptical. It
mouths "particulars" rather than generalities, raises objections ("Is this
something . . . though?"), doubts the couple's "special" status, and assumes
love is an object—either an exterior Lucretian "translucent matter" or an
isolatable "area in someone's mind." If the internalized addressee has its
way, the consummate lyric subject matter, Love, dissolves upon inspection.
The other, complementary principle is idealist and romantic. It is characterized by entranced wondering ("never knew, never knew"), subjective
vagueness ("somehow making more substance"), Proustian similes of latent
sexuality ("like girls hanging out of windows"), and an atmospheric ellipsis
marking where the "girls" leave off and their view takes over. This interlocu-
tory pole, however, does not place the subject opposite the object, it does
not oppose objectivity with subjectivity, but reconstructs subjectivity as "living into" a world made possible (if not created) by "you." "Was *it* you?"
"The answer is yes," if "it" was experienced. This proof for the independent
existence of "these things between people" hinges on the grammatical existence of the third-person pronoun, which gives rise to "we" and "us" in
relation to an interpersonal, neuter "it." The relationship between two
people is thus a third thing, a *tertium quid* both spatial and temporal,
outward- and future-oriented. In the question "was it you?" the neuter pronoun is grammatical, pointing to someone whose gender is indeterminate,
not yet known. "It" is experienced as an "air of expectancy," the crypt
phrase coupled here with the 1960s refrain "love is in the air." Ashbery's
"air" or love lyric is itself "suspended" in the eroticized suspenseful atmosphere of prose poetry: "the poetic form would be dissolved, in solution,
and therefore create a much more—I hate to say environmental because it's
a bad word—but more of a surrounding thing like the way one's consciousness is surrounded by one's thoughts."[37] Or by one's discourses. The envi-

ronmental, atmospheric rhetoric of "The New Spirit," always on the point of coming to the point, is its own surrounding meaning or experience: "its sense having become generalized in the environment, so that you are already part of it, a little, as you prepare to try to fathom its warpless and woofless subtleties" (TP 29). "Sense" here retains its French *sens* ("direction") as well as its reflexive English meaning. By remaining aimless and senseless, Ashbery's prose keeps its seductive potential, justifying the existences of writer and reader and, temporarily, temporally resolving pronominal differences.

Sometimes the *tertium quid* which joins "you" and "I" into "us" is the third person plural of other people: "they create us" (TP 13). At other times it is the vaguely apprehended, synthesizing "life": "Therefore I hold you. But life holds us, and is unknowable" (TP 11). And "it" is also "earthly things," as Ashbery called them on the back cover of *Three Poems.* There aren't many things in *Three Poems,* and those included retain an exemplary sheen. One passage, beginning with the commandment "It is the law to think now," pauses suspensefully ("But the act is still proposed, before us,") before continuing after a blank space:

> it needs pronouncing. To formulate oneself around this hollow, empty sphere . . . To be your breath as it is taken in and shoved out. Then, quietly, it would be as objects placed along the top of a wall: a battery jar, a rusted pulley, shapeless wooden boxes, an open can of axle grease, two lengths of pipe. . . . We see this moment from outside as within. There is no need to offer proof. It's funny. . . . The cold, external factors are inside us at last, growing in us for our improvement, asking nothing, not even a commemorative thought. And what about what was there before?   (TP 4–5; Ashbery's ellipses)

The unassuming lower and neuter case pronoun "it" which opens (or locks) this prose block hinges on its expletive and its pronominal usages, first as a deep background filling out the sentence, and then as the composite thing itself. "It" marks our identification of, and hence with, the inanimate. No subjects in Ashbery exist wholly out of this world or within it. The subjective act of internalization, never completely performed, lies suspended in the Dickinsonian definitional infinitive, "To formulate oneself." It turns the Russian Formalist Viktor Shklovsky's lyric act of "defamiliarization" into a "refamiliarization." Like that immovable object, the house guest, "your breath" (in the generic but resonantly personal second-person possessive) is "taken in and shoved out" only to return as a humble tutor "growing in us for our improvement, asking nothing" from us in return. Seen from the veranda of Ashbery's prose "from outside as within," a second-hand phrase like "It's funny" does have something to teach us about the strangeness of recognized or representative familiar objects (tools of another kind of manual labor): they are not unfamiliar but "funny," strangely humorous like a versified list: "sháapeless woóden bóxes, an ópen cán of áxle greáse."

By the end of "The New Spirit" the third person is personified by the narrative pronoun "he." Like the title of the narrative prose poem of Ashbery's twenties, "The Young Son," "he" (the poet-lover) is born in Chaucer's spring, when "the yonge sonne / Hath in the Ram his halve course yronne," on the platform of peace in Vietnam and amnesty for draft resisters: "All this happened in April as the sun was entering the house of Aries, the Ram, . . . bringing a spirit of reconciliation and amnesty amid the wars and horror that choked the earth" (TP 43). His birth, like a god's, is preceded by signs, both in the cards and in the stars: "The Hermit has passed on, . . . the Hanged Man points his toe at the stars. . . . The Archer takes careful aim, his arrow flies to the nearest card, the Five of Cups" (TP 42). For his information on Tarot cards, Ashbery relied largely on the work of Arthur Edward Waite, whose book *The Pictorial Key to the Tarot* was, in Ashbery's words, "a gospel of hippiedom."[38] This symbolism—reminiscent of *The Waste Land*—foretells the historically and cosmically inevitable birth of the third person and introduces, with mock-epic grandeur, the emergent author to his public.

As "he" surfaces "The New Spirit" comes increasingly to resemble a *Bildungsroman,* recalling, with its semi-serious embarrassment at its philosophical import, Carlyle's *Sartor Resartus* or one of its offspring, Stevens's "The Comedian as the Letter C." The resurrected "Ram," now without his lover, "rose up from that bed of reflective voluptuousness" and, like Atlas or Christ, took "the universal emotional crisis on his own shoulders" (TP 45). This self-elected savior, however, is at first unequal to the task of formulating himself around his prose blocks: "Thus summed up, he felt sickened at the wholeness. . . . Begone! But the solid block just sat there" (TP 46). But in a sublimely Alpine sentence which begins the penultimate prose block of "The New Spirit," "he" strikes out toward the mountaintop:

> He thought he had never seen anything quite so beautiful as that crystallization into a mountain of statistics: out of the rapid movement to and fro that abraded individual personalities into a channel of possibilities, remote from each other and even remoter from the eye that tried to contain them: out of that river of humanity comprised of individuals each no better than he should be and doubtless more solicitous of his own personal welfare

than of the general good, a tonal quality detached itself that partook of the motley intense hues of the whole gathering but yet remained itself, firm and all-inclusive, scrupulously fixed equidistant between earth and heaven, as far above the tallest point on the earth's surface as it was beneath the lowest outcropping of cumulus in the cornflower-blue empyrean.   (TP 48)

This detailed allegorical vision pitches Dante's celestial rose into the terrestrial mainstream. The roaring channel of narrative possibilities sounds more like what Wordsworth heard atop Mount Snowdon: "the roar of waters, torrents, streams / Innumerable, roaring with one voice" (XIII, 58–59). Out of the motley Whitmanian crowd (or reflexively, out of the mass of prose) "a tonal quality detached itself," otherwise known as "humankind" (or reflexively, "prose poetry"), placed midway between the beasts and the angels, the novel and the lyric. With its single encompassing "tonal quality," this Stevensian humanist sublime too easily strikes out cultural, racial, and sexual diversities. Yet the prophetic "he" stops short of an I-Thou relation with this *tertium quid,* who will become the potential congregation and audience of "The System." As the "tonal quality detached itself" ("se détacher"), this outstanding "he" (now too caught up in its uniformity) will also detach himself from his visionary summit.

In the last prose block of this spiritual life, "he" discovers a tributary to the mainstream, an alternative to his own Neoplatonic dialectic of love, "the previous forms of life he had taken: the animalistic one, the aristocratic one . . . , or the others. . . , culminating in the (for him) highest form of love, which recognizes only its own generosity" (TP 50). The mounting human discourses of his nearly completed poem are now darkly modified into "this horrible vision of the completed Tower of Babel" (TP 50)—recalling "These Lacustrine Cities," where "a tower / Controlled the sky" (RM 9). In *Three Poems* the reluctant prophet decides solipsistically "that there was another way, . . . that the terror ["tower"] could be shut out—and really shut out—simply by turning one's back on it. As soon as it was not looked at it ceased to exist" (TP 50). It is easy enough to read this gesture of "leaving all out" as political quietism, like Tiresias turning his back on the ruin of culture at the end of *The Waste Land:* "I sat upon the shore / Fishing, with the arid plain behind me / Shall I at least set my lands in order?" This Berkeleyan vanishing act, parodied earlier ("Begone! But the solid block just sat there," TP 46) is, I think, better read as Ashbery's radical detachment from "the system," an interested detachment which enables him to misrepresent a homosexual counterculture. Ashbery, if not "he," knows that ignoring the system will not shut it out. But by striking out on "another, truer way," a smaller, ineffectual tradition can, merely by aiming differently, unsettle the cumulative inevitability of the Tower.[39]

Above Babel's mounting babble hang, as over the end of "The Skaters," "the constellations that had presided impassively over the building of the metaphor" (TP 50–51). De Chirico's third person, Hebdomeros, in the culminating vision of the selection Ashbery translated, was similarly struck: "Outside, the sky offered an unforgettable spectacle: the constellations were laid out so perfectly that they formed real figures drawn with dotted lines, as in illustrated dictionaries. Hebdomeros, delighted, stopped and began to point them out. . . . One could see the Twins, leaning on each other in a classic pose of tranquility; one could see the Great Bear, obese and touching." For his configuration, Ashbery (a Leo) selects "the Archer, languidly stretching his bow, aiming at a still higher and smaller portion of the heavens, no longer a figure of speech but an act, even if all the life had been temporarily drained out of it" (TP 51). This Archer, begat by Nimrod, descends most directly from Auden's Ariel, also known in the theological third person as Christ and Cupid: "Does Ariel—to nominate the spirit of reflection in your terms—call for manifestation? . . . He couldn't appear as anything but His distorted parody, a deformed and savage slave [that is, Caliban], . . . [an] insult to us among whom He does and is . . . no less a person than the nude august elated archer of our heaven, the darling single son of Her who . . . [is] our great white Queen of love herself?" (CP 330). A dotted man of action, the Archer outlines the poet's pragmatic, realist other half. Forecasting the birth of the Ram, the Archer manifested his realism in the newspaper astrology section as "Sagittarius, the healer, caustic but kind, sweeping away the cobwebs of intuitive idealism that still lingered here and there in pockets of darkness" (TP 42; Ashbery recalled two friends under this sign, Jane Freilicher and Pierre Martory).[40] In his final allegorically poised pose at the end of "The New Spirit," aiming higher and further, the Archer signifies to Ashbery's third person, to us, and perhaps to Ashbery himself "that a new journey would have to be undertaken" (TP 51), a different and public poem would have to be written to balance the private and interpersonal communications of "The New Spirit." But life in public results from fundamental choices, ways of living and writing. Like the towering trees of "Some Trees," the nonjudgmental stars raise the existential, Heideggerian question of being here alternatively,

> the major question that revolves around you, your being here. And this is again affirmed in the stars: just their presence, mild and unquestioning, is proof that you have got to begin in the way of choosing some one of the

forms of answering that question, since if they were not there the question would not exist to be answered, but only as a rhetorical question in the impassive grammar of cosmic unravelings of all kinds, to be proposed but never formulated.   (TP 51)

As Ashbery advised near the beginning of "The New Spirit," we need "merely to assume the idea of choosing, so that some things can be left behind" (TP 8). This final question entails that one of the constellations, or destinies, must be chosen, though with the brilliant disclaimer that the choice need only be aimed for. But does life flesh out what is already in the stars? Are one's arbitrary and haphazard "choices" in life and art predestined? Yes, if expected. Acting as though one's first steps in any direction included their destination will be the "truer way" of "The System."

Almost fifteen years later, Ashbery chose the middle poem of *Three Poems* as the massive fifty-page center of his *Selected Poems* (1985). More than any other single poem in his career, "The System" renovated Ashbery's poetry by incorporating, without hierarchy and without framing quotation marks, a number of languages from largely public spheres. When asked what systems he meant to include in "The System," Ashbery said everything from the biological to the cosmological, from the circulatory to the solar systems[41]:

> The system was breaking down. The one who had wandered alone past so many happenings and events began to feel, backing up along the primal vein that led to his center, the beginning of a hiccup that would, if left to gather, explode the center to the extremities of life, the suburbs through which one makes one's way to where the country is.   (TP 53)

The topic of this opening block is the breakdown of "the system," but the kind of system it is changes from phrase to phrase: cybernetic, governmental ("breaking down"); traffic, sewer ("backing up"); circulatory, reproductive ("primal vein," "extremities"); respiratory ("hiccup"); weapons ("explode"); and city planning ("center," "suburbs"). The successive referential frames are organized by the figure of the circle of which "one," the representative "he" of "The New Spirit," forms the disintegrating center. The Ram, "the one of whom this is written" (TP 46), passes by the recent "past" of the 1960s, with its political "events" and pop art "happenings." The proper names of American history, of course, continued to multiply: Ashbery read part of "The New Spirit" at Kent State a few months before the National Guard opened fire on students there and was writing "The Recital" when Arthur Bremer tried to assassinate George Wallace.[42] One reading of this body politic is that the urban hiccup is about to reach the complacent suburbs. If one takes "the country" as the United States, the explosion has a revolutionary impact. "What happens to a dream deferred?" asked the urban poet Langston Hughes, "Does it dry up / like a raisin in the sun" or *"does it explode?"*[43] One defining explosion was the riot at Stonewall, a gay bar in New York City, in June 1969, four months before Ashbery began *Three Poems.* Writing in the midst of domestic and foreign upheavals, Ashbery reconstructs the systemic fission of American society and constructs his own system of choice.

The dominant discourse of the first half of "The System" is, it emerges, the historical lecture:

> It was different in those days, though. Men felt things differently and their reactions were different. It was all life, this truth, you forgot about it and it was there. . . . There was, however, a residue, a kind of fiction that developed parallel to the classic truths of daily life. . . . It is this "other tradition" which we propose to explore.   (TP 55–56)

With their syntactical afterthoughts ("those days, though," "all life, this truth"), the opening sentences resemble autobiographical reminiscence (the most densely populated discourse of *Flow Chart*) more than professional history. But the language soon conforms itself into a lecture. The rhetorical expletive ("It is this") and the Ciceronian plural are formal and pompous. Far from the lyric "I," the new historian's asides are highly conventional: "these, I say," "and I hope succinctly," "will, I think, partake" (TP 56). The rhetoric of "The System," posturing and interested, is marked less "authentic" than the meditative explorations of "The New Spirit," but Ashbery is as interested as his lecturer in the outcome—whatever it turns out to be.

As he recalls, the "classic truths of daily life"—God, country, family, and so on—which make up the American system were generally taken for granted. "Then," in this myth of origins, there developed an "other tradition" with its own supreme fictions, parallel with "the tradition." As with "the system," the candidates for this "other tradition" are left open. Ashbery said that he borrowed the term "the other tradition" from Arthur Waite, who in various books speaks of a "Secret Tradition," including Mithraism, Rosacrucianism, Tarot, and Gnosticism, which developed parallel to the dominant Western Judeo-Christian religions. "The System" begins with a history of the "love generation," not only its suburban Zen or Jesus "freaks," but the countercultural movement as a whole, with the benchmark names, dates, and places omitted as usual.

Ashbery's "other tradition" is also homotextual. In his Norton Lectures

(1990–91), significantly entitled "An Other Tradition," Ashbery drew attention to the sexual preferences of several of his chosen authors (Thomas Beddoes, Roussel, John Wheelwright, Laura Riding). Two weeks after America's Bicentennial Ashbery commemorated his own countermovement with "The Other Tradition" (dated July 22, 1976): "Dispersing, each of the / Troubadours had something to say about how charity / Had run its race and won, leaving you the ex-president / Of the event" (HBD 2–3). This gently versified memorial service seems to recall the scattered New York school, its unnamed leader, Frank O'Hara, in particular, who had died ten years earlier, on July 24, 1966. The Audenesque figure of racing charity is taken from the end of Brunetto Latini's canto in Dante's *Inferno,* where the sodomite lecturer, running to rejoin his group, "looked like one of those who doesn't lose but wins" (XV, 121–24).[44] Ashbery refers to his other tradition periodically through his career, but nowhere more compellingly than here.

In its parallel development the social and cultural avant-garde mirrors the Establishment. In May 1968, a decade after "Europe" and about a year before "The New Spirit," Ashbery presented a lecture at the Yale Art School entitled "The Invisible Avant-Garde." This lecture and his fictive lecture in "The System" are mutually explanatory. In "The Invisible Avant-Garde" Ashbery points out the dialectics of establishing a parallel tradition: "Protests against the mediocre values of our society such as the hippie movement seem to imply that one's only way out is to join a parallel society whose stereotyped manners, language, speech and dress are only reverse images of the one it is trying to reject" (RS 393). Like the 1960s counter-culture, the once invisible avant-garde receives almost immediate exposure in the media limelight: "it may be only a matter of weeks before Aram Saroyan has joined Andy Warhol and Viva and the rest of the avant-garde on *The Tonight Show*" (RS 392). In the media's absorptive gaze, practically everybody (or nobody) seems avant-garde: "In fact the avant-garde has absorbed most of the army, or vice versa—in any case the result is that the avant-garde can now barely exist because of the immense amounts of attention and money that are focused on it, and that the only artists who have any privacy are the handful of decrepit stragglers behind the big booming avant-garde juggernaut" (RS 392).[45] This argument, along with its parodic inflations, recurs in "The System":

So that those who assumed that they had reached the end of an elaborate but basically simple progression, the logical last step of history, came more and more to be the dominant party: a motley group but with many level heads among them, whose voices chanting the wise maxims of regular power gradually approached the point of submerging the other cacophony

149

of tinkling cymbals and wailing and individual voices raised in solemn but unreal debate.   (TP 62)

With a faint echo of I Corinthians 13.1 ("Though I speak with the tongues of men and of angels, and have not charity, I am become as sounding brass, or a tinkling cymbal") the cultural historian makes his case. But his characterization of those outside the vanguard chorus as "individual voices" brings another opposition, or dialectic, into play: the (traditional or avant-garde) tradition versus the individual new spirit. As Ashbery asks, paraphrasing Eliot, in "The Invisible Avant-Garde," "has tradition finally managed to absorb the individual talent?" (RS 393). The avant-gardist must resist absorption both by the vanguard ("He must now bear in mind that *he,* not *it,* is the avant-garde") and by his or her appreciative audience, adopting "an attitude which neither accepts nor rejects acceptance but is independent of it" (RS 394). Rather than striving for an individual voice, Ashbery remains independent by making his work dependent on the crowd of his uncritical contemporaries, whose words he has read and studied how to misrepresent.

The history of "The System" begins with the springtime birth of the new *Zeitgeist,* the love generation:

> the entire world or one's limited but accurate idea of it was bathed in glowing love. . . . Not an atom but did not feel obscurely compelled to set out in search of a mate; not a living creature, no insect or rodent, that didn't feel the obscure twitching of dormant love, . . . bent on self-discovery in the guise of an attractive partner who is *the* heaven-sent one, the convex one with whom he has had the urge to mate all these seasons without realizing it. . . . Thus, in a half-baked kind of way, this cosmic welter of attractions was coming to stand for the real thing. . . . For universal love is as special an aspect as carnal love or any of the other kinds: all forms of mental and spiritual activity must be practiced and encouraged equally if the whole affair is to prosper. There is no cutting corners where the life of the soul is concerned.   (TP 56–58)

With its ironic mixtures of scale (from atoms up to the universe), this prose lampoons not only those in search of their Aristophanic other half but also the speaker himself, historian-cum-prophet, whose cracker-barrel wisdom ("There is no cutting corners") sounds too good to be false. The satirical point, despite its questionable source, is clear. This particular "other tradition" mystified "love" by emphasizing its "cosmic" dimension to the neglect of its carnal (social and political) aspects. As mentioned above, Ashbery himself fell in love while writing "The System" (the Ecco edition of *Three*

*Poems* is dedicated to "David"), a happy coincidence which generally buoys the poem over and above its tongue-in-cheek history. But sometimes the historian's point coincides too completely with the poet's. While the war in Vietnam drags on, the cosmically inclined, having reached "the logical last step of history" (TP 62), take refuge in an inner peace and enlightenment. But to the historian these "souls in bliss" have sidestepped both history and their less lucky contemporaries, who are still enmeshed in its daily struggles:

> Hence the air of joyful resignation, the beatific upturned eyelids, the para-
> lyzed stance of these castaways of the eternal voyage, who imagine they
> have reached the promised land when in reality the ship is sinking under
> them. The great fright has turned their gaze upward, to the stars, to the
> heavens; they see nothing of the disarray around them, their ears are closed
> to the cries of their fellow passengers; they can think only of themselves
> when all the time they believe that they are thinking of nothing but
> God.   (TP 74)

Ashbery's portrait hits its barnside target, which includes the stargazer at the end of "The New Spirit." But the poetry is slight; the historian's critical gaze is as stable as the gaze of the blest. It is tempting but reductive to read this spiritual history simply as a backlash against the counteraffirmations of the 1960s. Ashbery himself thinks those changes were generally a healthy and a good thing.[46] As "The System" progresses from historical analysis to its own version of wisdom writing, Ashbery will employ the same extended figure of the alternate path to enlightenment that he uses here to critique the "spiritual bigots" (TP 75). The difference is that Ashbery's "truer way" is endless and aimless, but justified nevertheless.

The sermon in "The System," delivered "On this Sunday which is also the last day of January" (TP 65; as it was in 1971), erects its argument upon a series of contraries and alternatives. The preacher first distinguishes two less than promising models for living: "the 'career' notion" in which each individual follows a curve which reaches a "peak" and then declines, and "the 'life-as-ritual' concept," which is locked into a timeless performance of perfected behavior (TP 70). Then "he" introduces a coordinate distinction crucial to Ashbery's poetry: "In addition to these twin notions of growth, two kinds of happiness are possible: the frontal and the latent. The first occurs naturally throughout life; it is experienced as a kind of sense of im-mediacy, even urgency. . . . Its sudden balm suffuses the soul without warn-ing, as a kind of bloom or grace. We suppose that souls 'in glory' feel this way permanently, as a day-to-day condition of being" (TP 71). "The second kind," latent happiness, is harder to understand. We all know those periods of balmy weather in early spring, sometimes even before spring has officially begun: days or even a few hours when the air seems suffused with an unearthly tenderness, as though love were about to start, now, at this moment, on an endless journey put off since the beginning of time. Just to walk a few steps in this romantic atmosphere is to experience a magical but quiescent bliss. . . . And so the happiness withholds itself, perhaps even indefinitely. . . . These people are awaiting the sign of their felicity without hope; its *nearness* is there, tingeing the air around them, in suspension, in escrow as it were, but they cannot get at it.   (TP 73)

Ashbery's skewed categories (cf. "frontal nudity," "lateral view") echo similar distinctions in Marianne Moore and Raymond Roussel. Moore's poem "In this age of hard trying, nonchalance is good and" ends by delineating the evasive maneuvers of an avant-gardist, whose "by- / play was more terrible in its effectiveness / than the fiercest frontal attack" (34). The word "latent" appears in the suddenly personal ending of Roussel's "The View": "Thanks to the intensity suddenly increased / Of a memory vibrant and hidden ["vivace et latent"] of a summer / Already dead, already far from me, quickly carried away."[47]

The nearest psychological analogue for the temporal structure of frontal and latent happiness is Freud's dialectic of the pleasure and reality principles, which he imagined as alternate paths toward happiness: "Under the influence of the ego's instincts of self-preservation, the pleasure principle is replaced by the *reality principle.* This latter principle does not abandon the intention of ultimately obtaining pleasure, but it nevertheless demands and carries into effect the postponement of satisfaction, the abandonment of a number of possibilities of gaining satisfaction and the temporary toleration of unpleasure as a step on the long indirect road to pleasure."[48] Readers may also recall Freud's "latency period" following the Oedipal stage, and his distinction between latent and manifest dream content. But as Ashbery formulates it, "latent happiness" is not an index of hidden, closeted, or sublimated sexual and textual behavior but instead a way of living and writing broadly implicated in developing realities. The religious paradigm for Ashbery's frontal happiness, or happening, is the Incarnation of Christ. Thus we find the following Kierkegaardian argument for the existence of "it": "But, you continue to argue, it mattered precisely because it was a paradox and about to be realized here on earth, in human terms. . . . When will you realize that your dreams have eternal life? . . . But you must try to seize the truth of this: whatever was, is, and must be" (TP 85). As Christ (Auden's Ariel) paradoxically entered time to guarantee eternal life, so the timeless moment in the past cannot but come true. The crypt word for "dreams" is "souls" and the relevant crypt phrase here is "dream come true." In "Two Scenes" Ashbery wrote that "Destiny guides the water-pilot, and it is destiny" (ST 3). Here, in the fleshed-out development of that claim, Ashbery's rhetorical question of faith is taken from the Episcopal Litany. The romantic paradigm for the frontal moment is the past lover, who determines (or confirms) one's sexual path. As "The System" gradually reincorporates the first- and second-person pronouns, the lover's discourse is reintroduced: "You see that you cannot do without it, that singular isolated moment that has now already slipped so far into the past that it seems a mere spark. You cannot do without it and you cannot have it" (TP 84). The cost of this grim "realization" is clear when it is rewritten thus: "You see, I cannot do without you." But new love likewise involves faith in frontal declarations: "And the word that everything hinged on is buried back there; by mutual consent neither of you examined it when it was pronounced and rushed to its final resting place. It is doing the organizing, the guidelines radiate from its control" (TP 95). Though we do not know what the frontal word is ("love" is one possibility), we do recognize the structure described here. In fact, the relation between the crypt word and the text, what Ashbery in this block calls "the fabric of life" (TP 96), is a good self-reflexive formulation for the relation between love and its latent filiations.

In literary terms, the concept of frontal happiness is familiar from Joyce's "epiphany," Proust's "privileged moment," and Wordsworth's "spot of time." Since these moments only last a moment, Ashbery chooses the detour of "latent happiness." Latent happiness is the sensation of time: the feeling that past happiness (whether real or dreamt) permeates the present and is about to return (like Eliot's "midwinter spring") in the near future. The "first few steps" (TP 75) into this suspended, latent atmosphere of sexual and textual experimentation (such as surrounded the lovers in "The New Spirit") were risky. In "The Invisible Avant-Garde" the oral historian recalled that in the 1950s, unlike the media-blitzed 1960s, "To experiment was to have the feeling that one was poised on some outermost brink. In other words if one wanted to depart, even moderately, from the norm, one was taking one's life—one's life as an artist—into one's hands. A painter like Pollock for instance was gambling everything on the fact that he *was* the greatest painter in America, for if he wasn't, he was nothing" (RS 390). Ashbery's gamble in this "prematurely mild air" (TP 75) of latent happiness is also high. If he stakes his happiness on being a homotextual poet, he is nothing unless others match his wager. Readers must, for instance, take "The System" not merely as poetics or moral doctrine but as prose poetry. But the canonical game, who's the greatest, is never up. The speaking, and the writing, subject of Ashbery's prose poetry remains in doubt along with his fellows at the table.

Ashbery's radical doubt concerning the existence and influence of the frontal happy moment is erased by an equally radical profession of faith. In the climactic rhetorical question of "The System," an assertion punctuated as a question which demands and assumes our assent, Ashbery's preacher shows us the Jamesian figure in the carpet:

> For they never would have been able to capture the emanations from that special point of life if they were not meant to do something with them, weave them into the pattern of the days that come after, sunlit or plunged in shadow as they may be, but each with the identifying scarlet thread that runs through the whole warp and woof of the design, sometimes almost disappearing in its dark accretions, but at others emerging as the full inspiration of the plan of the whole, grandly organizing its repeated vibrations and imposing its stamp on these until the meaning of it all suddenly flashes out of the shimmering pools of scarlet like a vast and diaphanous though indestructible framework, not to be lost sight of again?   (TP 77)

There is no longer any doubt about losing our way: "we have only to step forward to be in the right path" (TP 78). Along the way of his exposition, Ashbery has subtly exchanged characteristics of his two kinds of happiness. Frontal happiness is really latent in that it is all potential, and latent happiness is "actually," currently frontal in that it is fully developed and fitted to our lives. By choosing the latent, hidden happinesses of avant-garde art and undisclosed love, past pleasures through present implications, and so on, one gives up nothing: "this second kind of happiness is merely a fleshed-out, realized version of that ideal first kind, . . . a reflection which is truer than the original because more suited to us" (TP 81). Ashbery's credo recalls Wordsworth's affirmation of blind faith in "Intimations of Immortality": "Those shadowy recollections, / Which, be they what they may, / Are yet the fountain light of all our day, / Are yet a master light of all our seeing" (528). Keats too imagines the frontal moment of happiness as a "Shadow of reality to come."[49] But Ashbery, more than Keats or Wordsworth or Proust, focuses on the later, "truer" photographic development of the romantic frontal flash. Latent happiness is worldly and textual rather than visionary and hyper-linguistic. This contemporary romanticism is a means to an encompassing realism by which we make sense of ourselves in the context of the world.

Ashbery's grand gathering of tenses in "The System" sets up the ten-page coda of *Three Poems*, "The Recital," written in the no-nonsense language of the aftermath: "All right. The problem is that there is no new problem. It must awaken from the sleep of being part of some other, old problem, and by that time its new problematical existence will have already begun" (TP 107). With the "All right" to clear the slate and survey the present situation, Ashbery identifies his problem: his two encompassing prose poems have left him with nothing latent to do. The new spirit has entered the system. This is the realist, practical vantage point of "The Recital," that of "the disabused intellect, whose nature it is to travel from illusion to reality and on to some seemingly superior vision" (TP 112). With this new dispiritedness comes a rationalized love life: "It became a delight to enumerate all the things in the new world our maturity had opened up for us, as inexhaustible in pleasures and fertile pursuits as some more down-to-earth Eden, from which the utopian joys as well as the torments of that older fantasy-world had been banished by a more reasonable deity" (TP 109). In this tame new world of sexual liberation the pleasure principle has been displaced by the reality principle of mature and reduced expectations. One practical difficulty with a philosophy of life as latent development, or destiny, or realization of potential is that everything seems the same old thing: "Was there really nothing new under the sun?" (TP 116). Ashbery's Ecclesiastian query should haunt all subscribers to divine plans. His answer, as we saw earlier, lies in a dialectical renewal: "the synthesis of very simple elements in a new and strong, as opposed to old and weak, relation to one another" (TP 117). This sounds more like poetics than advice for living. But practically speaking, most renewals in work or love involve recombinations rather than absolute revolutions. "The Recital" ends with us exiting the Platonic cavernous theater, with our own act of absorption to be performed: "The performance had ended, the audience streamed out; the applause still echoed in the empty hall. But the idea of the spectacle as something to be acted out and absorbed still hung in the air long after the last spectator had gone home to sleep" (TP 118). The audience includes Ashbery; *Three Poems* is to be "absorbed," like the objects on the wall in "The New Spirit," so that its latent potency can act and be "acted out." Ashbery's succeeding verses will demonstrate the potential of his excursion into prose.

As unlikely as it may seem, after completing *Three Poems* Ashbery tried writing more poetic prose. The unpublished "Purgatory," alluding to a better known trilogy, toils in labors and arguments past: "But today is a calm hiatus in this seemingly inevitable progression. How magnificently blue the sky has been all day, how hushed and how gracious the sunlight seemed as it came down to perform with no fuss its task of softly gilding everything until it again seems to be part of life, something taken back into the depths of one's soul." This moment of prosaic happiness, pleasing in itself, unfortunately needs no further elaboration. It only confirms the bleak thesis of "The Recital" that "there is no new problem." Ashbery must have thought so too, since he abandoned this project without finishing it. To "awaken from the sleep of being part of some other, old problem" (TP 107), he would need to return, with renewed energy, to verse.

# 6

## "On the Outside Looking Out"

### Self-Portrait in a Convex Mirror

> Of what use is genius, if the organ is too convex or too concave, and cannot find a focal distance within the actual horizon of human life?
>
> —Emerson, "Experience"

> To formulate oneself around this hollow, empty sphere
>
> —Ashbery, "The New Spirit"

*Self-Portrait in a Convex Mirror* (1975), dominated by its now famous title poem, contains Ashbery's first free-standing lyrics since *The Double Dream of Spring*. Several of these new poems speak of "waiting," as though acknowledging the poet's delayed return to verse after his lengthy excursion into prose. In one of Ashbery's favorite American puns, this waiting is often set away from the city in "the country, / Our country" (SP 45). His return to lyric brings him back to narrative, often in the elementary form of the fairy tale, a mode virtually left out of *Three Poems*. It also reintroduces the measure and idea of music; many of Ashbery's titles derive from musical works: "As You Came from the Holy Land" and "A Man of Words" from ballads; "Scheherazade" (Rimsky-Korsakov), "Grand Galop" (Liszt), "Tenth Symphony" (Mahler), "Suite," "Märchenbilder" (Schumann) from classical pieces. The defining left-hand margins of all but two lyrics are capitalized. There are no prose poems in this volume and no fixed forms (sestinas, pantoums). Apart from the six lyrics divided into roughly regular stanzas, most of these new verses come as they are in free-verse paragraphs. Though they exhibit less formal and stylistic variety than the immediately previous and subsequent verse collections, these poems display a new plain American speech, more direct and inclusive, registering Ashbery's recent experience in prose.

The smallest verse in the volume, "Tarpaulin" (dated April 17, 1974), reveals Ashbery's fluency in the prose medium:

Easing the thing
Into spurts of activity
Before the emptiness of late afternoon
Is a kind of will power
Blaring back its received vision
From a thousand tenement windows
Just before night
Its signal fading
(SP 40)

With Dickinsonian economy, one brief poem of one sentence "covers" one big urban event, like a tarpaulin or a journalist. But unlike the contemporary miniatures of A. R. Ammons and Robert Creeley, usually capitalized and punctuated like prose, "Tarpaulin" is segmented only by its capitalized lines. Passing without subordinating punctuation, these lines don't know their places. "Tarpaulin" generates power from syntactical polyjunction. Framed by "Easing" and "fading" (rhyming with "thing"), the poem turns at the copula "Is," which recasts the subordinated participial "Easing" as a complex gerundial subject, displaces the expected lyric subject (for example, "Easing the car into the parking space, I turned off the radio"), and shifts the sentence from narration (finishing X, I did Y) into assertion (doing X is Y). This heavy-duty mid-sentence overhaul charges "Tarpaulin" with "a kind of will power" lacking in the embedded love lyrics of "The New Spirit." In this way Ashbery automates the traditional elegiac subject of the "fading" sunset. Removing the solar reflecting subject democratically multiplies it by "a thousand tenement windows" and diversifies its power—mechanical ("Easing the thing"), phallic ("spurts"), mental ("will"), solar ("[G]laring back its received [wisdom]"), and electric ("[radio] signal") by turns. In "Tarpaulin" Ashbery pours sentence structure into verse form to produce a stronger, lighter poem.

Ashbery versifies prose differently in the unpunctuated, capitalized "Lithuanian Dance Band" (written early in 1973), an "action poem" written with Frank O'Hara in mind.[1] Divided into hasty "septets" (one of which is a sestet), Ashbery's nonstop lines run across the page, as though he were racing to catch up with his energetic friend's life force:

I write you to air these few thoughts feelings you are
Most likely driving around the city in your little car

158

Breathing in the exquisite air of the city and the exhaust fumes dust and
    other
Which make it up only hold on awhile there will be time
For other decisions but now I want to concentrate on this
Image of you secure and projected how I imagine you
Because you are this way where are you you are in my thoughts
(SP 52)

Both breathless and longwinded, this second stanza crosses a personal letter
with a hazardously compounded urban "air" (rhyming "are" with "car"). A
contemporary effort, "The Thief of Poetry" (dated September 21, 1974),
with comparably short unpunctuated lines, bears the same address, "To
you / my friend who / was in this / / street once" (HBD 54). Unlike "Tarpaulin," "Lithuanian Dance Band" runs several dashed-off sentences and
phrases together, dropping more than commas: "and other [pollutants],"
"[which is] how I imagine you." The interpolated question "where are you"
redirects O'Hara's own waking confusion "Where am I?" in indirect discourse, giving him his say while Ashbery focuses his image. Prufrock spoke
prematurely: there will not be "time yet for a hundred indecisions"(4).
O'Hara's projected image of sweeping lines condenses onto television: "it
looks compressed like lines packed together / In one of those pictures you
reflect with a polished tube" (SP 53). The poem ends with a rebus for the
typewritten page—a turned field with black (hunted and pecked) figures
on it: "And the crows peacefully pecking where the harrow has passed" (SP
53). In this final unstopped phrase O'Hara ("harrow") comes to rest.

"As One Put Drunk into the Packet-Boat" (written in 1974), the first and
originally the title poem for the volume, heralds Ashbery's return to verse
with a newly pronounced music. Self-consciously romantic, "As One Put
Drunk" records the thoughts of "I" (the poem's and book's first word) from
afternoon to night, just outside a childhood country home. The poem employs a pastoral crisis narrative: a summer storm gathers but passes, leaving
the relieved, mortal poet in the dark. This romanticism may be taken as a
sign either of Ashbery's poetic "potential" or of his lyric retrenchment. But
Ashbery's recycled romanticism exceeds both judgments with its reserve
power:

I tried each thing, only some were immortal and free.
Elsewhere we are as sitting in a place where sunlight
Filters down, a little at a time,
Waiting for someone to come. Harsh words are spoken,
As the sun yellows the green of the maple tree. . . .

159

So this was all, but obscurely
I felt the stirrings of new breath in the pages
Which all winter long had smelled like an old catalogue.
New sentences were starting up.
(SP 1; Ashbery's ellipsis)

The semi-formal attire of mimetic anapests ("only sóme were immórtal and frée") and iambs ("a líttle át a tíme"), loosening the tight titular pentameter, signals Ashbery's departure not only from the unmarked prose of *Three Poems* but from his earlier densely stressed verses. "The Task" (written in 1969), which opened *The Double Dream of Spring,* likewise narrates a renewal of effort, but its syllables are less musically scored than emphatically underscored: "Théy are prepáring to begín agaín: / Próblems, néw pénnant úp the flágpóle / In a prédicated románce" (DDS 13). Ashbery's new verse revises the discursive ambiguities of his prose poetry. The first line and sentence recalls the opening argument of "The New Spirit": "I thought that if I could put it all down, that would be one way. And next the thought came to me that to leave all out would be another, and truer, way" (TP 3). But though "immortal and free" are both common modifiers of "verse," Ashbery makes his "I" more representative, less simply a writer apart from his or her readers, by misrepresenting the clichéd expression "I tried everything," which, unlike the writer's "put it all down," may be said (and read along with) by anybody. A feeling that this "I" is not representative enough may have led Ashbery to submerge "I" in "we" and to discard the narrative past for the sermonic ("immortal and free") present familiar from "The System." But the stilted simile "Elsewhere we are as sitting" (displacing "Otherwise we are sitting" and "Meanwhile we are sitting") recalls instead the abstracted speech of "Fragment," and fails with its generic "we" to dissipate the quarrel ("Harsh words are spoken") between two people.

But the past tense demonstrative "So this was all," coming after the ellipsis, recasts the first stanza as a quoted sample of verse. Wordsworth uses the same textualizing technique to make the wandering beginning of *The Prelude* into a prototype, when he reveals to Coleridge that he did "Pour out that day my soul in measured strains, / Even in the very words which I have here / Recorded" (I, 57–59). As Ashbery's example (cf. "These are examples of leaving out," TP 3) is meant to demonstrate, there is a new spirit animating his pages; new leaves of grass, in "free" but "measured strains," "were starting up." This announcement rewrites an earlier springtime effort, "The Orioles" (1955), in which the young poet already questioned his music's duration: "The excited songs start up in the yard! / The feeding station is

160

glad to receive its guests, / / But how long can the stopover last?" (ST 41). Short poems mime the brevity not only of life but of writing; "How long will the poem last?" and "How long will it be remembered?" are related questions. Ashbery soon interrupts the vernal imagery of renewal in "As One Put Drunk" by setting his present thoughts in "summer," overspecified to qualify the pastoral figuration of middle age: "But the summer / Was well along, not yet past the mid-point / But full and dark with the promise of that fullness" (SP 1; "well along in life"). According to the seasonal narrative, the summer poet is not synchronized with his sprouting sentences. But this belated waiting period is quickly refigured as a storm cloud's pregnancy, latent with promise rather than past its prime. Latent "happiness," in a privileged pun, is redefined in the line before the second stanzaic pause: "To watch the thing that is prepared to happen" (SP 1).

The latent happiness of waiting includes keeping things in reserve, or as Ashbery puts it in a brilliant later title, "Saying It to Keep It from Happening" (HBD 29). Various things could (but do not) happen in "As One Put Drunk." The third stanza begins by cutting to a specular "you": "A look of glass stops you / And you walk on shaken: was I the perceived? / Did they notice me, this time, as I am, / Or is it postponed again?" (SP 1; "looking glass"). To be, in Ashbery's verses, is to be unperceived. The transparent trans-peering self-image of "you" is caught in the paranoid reflection of "their" always critical eyes. But the immortal, frontal moment of being seen face to face never comes to pass. The next imagined happening, a storm, is not so much postponed as muted. Scored with unemphatic phonemes, the event is "orchestrated" not as a symphony with clashing symbols but as "a ballade / That takes in the whole world, now, but lightly, / Still lightly, but with wide authority and tact" (SP 1). After this light rain of liquids and dentals in minutely progressive syntax, the lyric subject wakes in confusion, fearing a definitive encounter with darkness. This fear of obliteration is raised by Ashbery's main intertext, Marvell's "Tom May's Death." Marvell's boisterously rhymed opening couplet wastes no time setting up the comic premise: "As one put drunk into the Packet-boat, / *Tom May* was hurry'd hence and did not know't." In this precursor to Dryden's "MacFlecknoe" and Pope's *Dunciad,* the poetaster May, after waking in heaven, is scolded by Ben Jonson (cf. "Harsh words . . . *ma*ple") and sent packing "in a Cloud of pitch."[2] The anxiety of being scorned by those immortal and free poets also darkens Ashbery's narrative, whose flow is interrupted as by a knock: "Come in. And I thought a shadow fell across the door / But it was only her come to ask once more / If I was coming in, and not to hurry in case I wasn't" (SP 2). Death is sidestepped once again with the hesitant maternal (rather than the fulminating Jonsonian) presence, the potential drama of the encounter itself being defused in free indirect discourse. The rural American idiom "not to hurry" wonderfully reverses Marvell's narrative of Tom May "hurry'd hence." Time is temporarily on the poet's side.

The final stanza lets in another intertext, de Chirico's essayistic prose poem, "On Silence,"[3] which Ashbery translated in May 1974, shortly before writing "As One Put Drunk." In his translation, for instance, "a moon of boreal pallor is rising in the great silence," and in his poem "A moon of cistercian pallor / Has climbed to the center of heaven" (SP 2). This doubt-less unintended overlap inevitably draws in more of the painter's line of thought. The gathering storm in de Chirico's satirical prose poem is both cosmic ("God created the world in silence; . . . then began noise") and revolutionary: "then arise the revolts and revolutions as the storm arises in the sultry sky of a summer afternoon" (cf. Ashbery's "clouds that arise with a swift / Impatience in the afternoon sky," SP 1). Among the privileged few shielded from this brewing revolution are the "gentleman poets barricaded in their rooms," who, like the Futurists, "love to hear thunder, artillery salvos that waken echoes at the four corners of the horizon." These "well-protected" spectators, like Ashbery's dozing "I," are finally disturbed as the wind blows open a window: "they forget everything and start chasing the white sheets and catch them in flight. . . . Beware, friends, of the silence that precedes such events."

After the storm passes, every "thing" heaves a sigh of bas-relief: "And a sigh heaves from all the small things on earth, / The books, the papers, the old garters and union-suit buttons / Kept in a white cardboard box somewhere, and all the lower / Versions of cities flattened under the equalizing night" (SP 2; the process of "evening"). Ashbery's summation overturns his opening argument: "The summer demands and takes away too much, / But night, the reserved, the reticent, gives more than it takes" (SP 2). In choosing maternal generosity over paternal demands, Ashbery in effect chooses a "mortal and bound" life of waiting over blinding moments of illumination. The couplet itself is compactly diversionary; by skewing the opposition ("summer" and "winter" or "day" and "night") Ashbery enters all four terms into his system. But tactful renunciation and diverted opposition may be a survival tactic. Even while the poet emulates his romantic precursors, he bows out of the contest, not wanting to anger the immortals. In "The Comedian as the Letter C" Stevens declared, against his Keatsian contemporaries, that "Moonlight was an evasion, or, if not, / A minor meeting, facile, delicate." But Crispin accurately measured his own range as "A fluctuating between sun and moon" (65). "As One Put Drunk" may be an "A minor meeting," but it retains its latent possibilities.

Ashbery's spacious lyric "Grand Galop" (named for a French round dance in couples, best known from Liszt's Grand Galop "Chromatique"; the poem was first entitled "The Blind Tourist") emulates the inclusiveness of his prose poetry, completed a month earlier.[4] The topos or spread of "Grand Galop" (with its inevitable cowboy rhyme) is America, characterized, in the postwar and pre–Watergate period of the spring of 1972, when the poem was written, by waiting: "Only waiting, the waiting: what fills up the time between? / It is another kind of wait, waiting for the wait to be ended" (SP 14). Elaborating on this theme in "Grand Galop" Ashbery declared, "It's an agonizing problem, to know what you're supposed to be doing while you're waiting, because waiting doesn't seem enough, but it is possible to force oneself realize that waiting is actually enough. Waiting is part of an endless series of stages of which the so-called objective is only another stage." It is like the wide open pauses in Cage's music, in which, Ashbery suggests, "he's trying to draw attention to the fact that every moment has a validity; it's a valuable unit of time, and the things that might be happening at any time have a value and even a beauty."[5] Waiting democratizes time, unseating its privileged moments.

"Grand Galop" begins with the apparently unrelated literary topic of self-reflexivity, which Ashbery endeavors to make representative:

All things seem mention of themselves
And the names which stem from them branch out to other referents.
Hugely, spring exists again. The weigela does its dusty thing
In fire-hammered air. And garbage cans are heaved against
The railing as the tulips yawn and crack open and fall apart.
And today is Monday. Today's lunch is: Spanish omelet, lettuce and tomato salad,
Jello, milk and cookies. Tomorrow's: sloppy joe on bun,
Scalloped corn, stewed tomatoes, rice pudding and milk.
(SP 14)

This philosophically and syntactically labored ("seem to mention") thesis recalls Stein's "CARAFE," both "a single hurt color and an arrangement in a system to pointing."[6] In Ashbery's floral arrangement things are naturally nominal; they spring up self-reflexively into the things their names name and branch out into a referential system of related named things. Every thing has its season in its system; in the school system names are digested on weekdays. Ashbery remembers pasting in his list (or "Liszt"), a school lunch menu, from a small-town New Hampshire newspaper. Having things "do their thing" in 1960s fashion, Ashbery redoes Hopkins's kingfisher sonnet where "Each mortal thing does one thing and the same: / Deals out that being indoors each one dwells; / Selves—goes its self; *myself* it speaks and spells."[7] But in Ashbery's system, things take time to be themselves: "The wait is built into the things just coming into their own" (SP 14). The "tulips," for instance, play on their name as they "yawn and crack open and fall apart" like two lips.

What about "weigela"? The spring flower's name "branches out" across the opening pages of "Grand Galop" in a cryptographic word chain: "weight," "wait," "pause," and "paws." Ashbery recalls that his family had a weigela bush in their yard in Sodus, and adds that the flower is "common enough,"[8] but its name, immortalizing one Doctor Weigel, is not. One important connector is "carry": "one may pick it up, / Carry it over there, set it down" (SP 15). This act mimes the "carrying over" of "metaphor," the word in modern Greek for moving van. Ashbery takes "carry" over to the next stanza in the "carrying" voices of the "caravan": "The dog barks, the caravan passes on. / The words had a sort of bloom on them / But were weightless, carrying past what was being said" (SP 15). Being "weightless," words carry easily past their weighty subjects. With "weight," a literal neighbor of "weigela," brought in as its antonym, the fourth stanza carries its weight or "wait" as a "pause": "It is just the movement of the caravan away / Into an abstract night, with no / Precise goal in view, and indeed not caring, / That distributes this pause" (SP 16). In moving vehicles not "this pause" but the "weight" is distributed; the line makes sense only through the encrypted series: "pause"—"wait"—"weight." In the countercultural leg of its journey, Ashbery's metaphorical vehicle, the "caravan of life," is not "career-oriented" but distributes its waits along the way toward Death—"only this time toward no special goal" (TP 29). But these painfully self-conscious "pauses" may equip "paws" with claws: "these pauses are supposed to be life / And they sink steel needles deep into the pores, as though to say / There is no use trying to escape" (SP 17). This cryptographic pair had already been developed by Dickinson, who planted "pause" beneath "paws": "When Winds take Forests in their Paws— / The Universe—is still—" (#315). Ashbery finally justifies the waiting pains as "pregnant pauses": "The groans of labor pains are deafening" (SP 18). Despite its intricacy, the root system of "weigela" need not have been tended by Ashbery. Networks such as these grow by themselves; their aimless branchings keep the poet to his topic without mentioning it.

The weightiest question Ashbery ponders in "Grand Galop" is whether not "weigela" but "poetry" has dried up. The poem tracks "waiting" to its "fulfillment," an achieved but depleted state drained of potential: "And yet it has ended, and the thing we have fulfilled we have become" (SP 17). In the long meandering sixth stanza (SP 18–20), as the overland trail arrives in

"Oregon" (a state he had yet to visit), the literary line ends in "bookstores where pornography is sold" (SP 18). But this displacement of "poetry" by "pornography" is more than an ironic reflection on America's cultural vacuum. With this transplantation, the poet stakes out homotextual territory deemed off limits by his government. (In the early 1970s the silent majority's President Nixon campaigned against the devaluation of American morals, epitomized by the lenient pornography rulings of the Warren Court.) Yet the question waits: is lyric verse still viable? The pioneering poet "is left sitting in the yard / To try to write poetry / Using what Wyatt and Surrey left around" (SP 19). Among other things, the rough Wyatt and the smooth Surrey ("correct delight," SP 20) left English versifiers the pentameter and the sonnet, two mainstays Ashbery has largely done without. What shoots up while he waits is the pornographic "word 'cock' or some other, brother and sister words / With not much to be expected from them, though these / Are the ones that waited so long for you and finally left" (SP 19). But are these last remaining "immortal and free" words, "Waiting for someone to come" (SP 1) upon them, so bereft of potential? Is the undigestible contemporary "gorgeous raw material" (SP 19) good only for prose? As in "As One Put Drunk," Ashbery looks in the nostalgic trunks for an answer, translating the canonical English verses into America's "forgotten letters / Packed away in trunks in the attic—things you forgot you had" (SP 19). In the wake of *Three Poems* Ashbery's new airs come from old junk: "You forget how there could be a gasp of a new air / Hidden in that jumble" (SP 20). He therefore diagnoses his English precursor away: "Surrey, your lute is getting an attack of nervous paralysis / But there are, again, things to be sung of / And this is one of them" (SP 20; cf. Wyatt's "My lute, awake!"). The New World of waste paper for one. With Bloom's burdensome appreciations beginning to appear, Ashbery's poetics of waiting may be read in part as a healthy alternative to the "nervous paralysis" a poet may feel in the face of a well-stocked tradition.

But in "Grand Galop" Ashbery is more concerned with America's "nervous paralysis" than with his own. If "waiting" denominates the gradual fulfillment of one's destined name, "America" lives up to its latent potential by realizing its continental, westward expansion. For Frost, writing "The Gift Outright" as America entered the Second World War in 1942, this self-fulfillment required sacrifice: "Such as we were we gave ourselves outright / (The deed of gift was many deeds of war) / To the land vaguely realizing westward."[9] In Ashbery's jaundiced eyes, at the end of the Vietnam War, the romance of westward (and worldwide) expansion had soured. In the final stanza of "Grand Galop" the fulfilled American West is viewed, as at the end of "A Last World" (TCO 56), through the Hollywood Western. The stanza opens with an on-the-scene interview with a native: "Ask a hog what is happening. Go on. Ask him. / The road just seems to vanish / And not that far in the distance, either. The horizon must have been moved up" (SP 20). This antic perspective, recycling the elegant artist's materials from "The Skaters," is as much temporal as spatial. For the hog, the suppressed "date" moved up is with the butcher. In "The System" the anxious "end . . . of the way left open to you" was neared by Robert Browning's hero: "Perhaps Childe Roland wore such a look as he drew nearer to the Dark Tower" (TP 92). In "Grand Galop" this well-worn approach is Americanized, as one limps up to "a worn, round stone tower / Crouching low in the hollow of a gully / With no door or window but a lot of old license plates / Tacked up over a slit too narrow for a wrist to pass through / And a sign: 'Van Camp's Pork and Beans'" (SP 20). Strait is the gate through this old shack with its name plates signifying that Ashbery's vehicles are not the first to arrive. The sign advertising the campfire fare of pork and beans is the hog's *per me si va*. For his *réalisation* Ashbery casts back to a representative high-school memory of "The movie with the cows in it": "Impossible not to be moved by the tiny number / Those people wore, indicating they should be raised to this or that power. / But now we are at Cape Fear and the overland trail / Is impassable, and a dense curtain of mist hangs over the sea" (SP 21). In this Western, the rodeo takes place in a rigged Calvinist arena; the contestants are numbered in advance for canonization or obliteration. The myth or model of self-realization is fatalistic; one's destiny is either a silk purse or a sow's ear. America camps at "Cape Fear" (a 1962 thriller) at the end of an Oregon trail or a Pacific theater from which the revelatory cape or curtain has not yet been withdrawn. Past Vietnam but on the brink of Watergate, Ashbery's United States are shrouded by "*angst*-colored skies" (SP 20). "Grand Galop" leads up to a Keatsian pacific surmise, but winds up waiting out an impasse.

Several of the poems in *Self-Portrait* draw on fairy tales, resuming Ashbery's researches in the form and significance of narrative after the largely nonfictional prose of *Three Poems*. The open-ended structure of the fairy tale leads the reader into the ways of latent happiness. Like romances, fairy tales are nonteleological journeys; any number of improbable adventures can happen along the way toward their fulfillment. These predictable narratives (which Vladimir Propp demonstrated are based on a small number of acts and events) set in motion the pleasurable dynamics of waiting for and warding off the satisfying conclusion, an ambivalence epitomized by Scheherazade's predicament. By pouring their hopes and fears into a tale's simple, empty characters, readers (or bedtime listeners) learn the self-fashioning process of identification. In "Märchenbilder" Ashbery finds the disappointing twin fulfillments of expectation and identification irresistible: "I want to go back, out of the bad stories, / But there's always the possibility that the next one . . . / No, it's another almond tree, or a ring-swallowing frog . . . / Yet they are beautiful as we people them // With ourselves. They are empty as cupboards" (SP 60). An unacknowledged master of punctuation, Ashbery uses ellipses here to indicate further narrative possibilities—empty shelves waiting to be filled. Such sexually charged retellings as Jean Cocteau's *The Beauty and the Beast* and Anne Sexton's popular *Transformations* (1971) must have served as incitements. In Ashbery's homotextual lyric "The Fairies' Song," for instance, "Thunderheads of after-dinner cigar smoke in some varnished salon / Offer ample cover for braiding two coat-tails together / Around the clumsy arm of an s-shaped settee" (VN 93). Each of Ashbery's fairy tales involves sexual identification.

"Scheherazade" (dated June 4, 1973) elaborately illustrates Ashbery's all-purpose fairy tales. The poem is divided into three unequal parts, standing in for a typically unspecified setting, plot, and moral. In the first and longest verse paragraph Ashbery creates an illogical setting out of nothing:

> Unsupported by reason's enigma
> Water collects in squared stone catch basins.
> The land is dry. Under it moves
> The water. Fish live in the wells. The leaves,
> A concerned green, are scrawled on the light. Bad
> Bindweed and rank ragweed somehow forget to flourish here.
> (SP 9)

Unlike the natural, seasonal music of "As One Put Drunk into the Packet-Boat," these lines are strikingly stilted. The sentences seem either too short or too long for their lines, and the intrusive exclusion of "Bad / Bindweed and rank ragweed" is doggedly discordant. No luxurious fairy-tale king-dom, this scene offers little breathing room for identification.

This is a textual landscape of groundless fertility, "Unsupported" by argu-ment or narrative, a flowering "bank / Of colored verbs and adjectives" (SP 9) without substance or substantives. Like Ashbery, Scheherazade is both a story-teller and a grammarian: "But most of all she loved the particles / That transform objects of the same category / Into particular ones, each distinct / Within and apart from its own class" (SP 9). These misrepresentative partic-ulars of speech are themselves particularized by the existential particle "the." The labyrinthine landscape is already narrative: "there was the story / Of the grandparents, of the vigorous young champion / (The lines once given to another, now / Restored to the new speaker)" (SP 10). The parenthetical comment belongs to the textual critic, as well as to the narrator, who knows that all new speeches and actions depend on permutations of existing conventions, "For the possibilities are limited" (SP 10). In "The System" Ashbery pledged his faith to the encompassing narrative thread, "the identifying scarlet thread that runs through the whole warp and woof of the design" (TP 77). But in "Scheherazade" life's text is a trap: "So each found himself caught in a net" (SP 10). How, then, can one be happy with his or her latent, impending reward or punishment? Our Edenic function as namers, fanciers, and narrators—if only of our own stories—gives us a divine vantage point: "It is we who make this / Jungle and call it space, naming each root, / Each serpent, for the sound of the name / As it clinks dully against our pleasure, / Indifference that is pleasure" (SP 10–11). In Emerson's Eden the poet was the namer. In his own garden, the erstwhile prose poet refashions clichés: "it's a jungle out there," "make a house a home," "to coin a phrase."

The key crypt phrase reverberating in this final stanza is "good, bad, or indifferent." This important triplet makes ethical judgments aesthetic; words and characters are pleasant, indifferent, or unpleasant (even painful) to one's taste. Here the "good are rewarded" and "the unjust one is doomed to burn forever / Around his error," while those "minor characters" in the indifferent middle "muddle through" (SP 10). The generic "his" homotextually indicates the burning error, but Ashbery goes beyond good and evil by going between them, to the majority of us characters too insignificant for history's judgment: "The balance is restored because it / Balances, knowing it prevails, / And the man who made the same mistake twice is exonerated" (SP 11). The moral is perhaps that misrepresentative sinners are also representative and should be judged (innocent) accordingly.

The quest for the father is the matter of "Oleum Misericordiae," a fable drawn from Esther Quinn's study, *The Quest of Seth for the Oil of Life,* which Ashbery picked up in Provincetown in 1974.[10] Seth, seeking the oil of mercy for his dying father, Adam, comes upon the tree of life with a baby in its branches, mankind's promised oil of mercy—a "snake oil" guaranteed to neutralize the serpent's original venom, "To rub it out, make it less virulent" (SP 66). Ashbery's use of a mytho-Christian scaffolding recalls Eliot's reliance on Jesse Weston's *From Ritual to Romance* in *The Waste Land,* but Ashbery tailors his story differently. The poem is divided into slim-lined beginning and ending commentaries and an expanding middle-paragraph plot summary. The interminable plot outline, based partly on the Grimm brothers' "The Water of Life,"[11] is a marvelously misrepresentative flow chart:

The dwarf led you to the end of a street
And pointed flapping his arms in two directions
You forgot to misprize him
But after a series of interludes
In furnished rooms (describe wallpaper)
Transient hotels (mention sink and cockroaches)
And spending the night with a beautiful married woman
Whose husband was away in Centerville on business
. . . . .
You got hold of the water of life
Rescued your two wicked brothers Cash and Jethro
Who promptly stole the water of life
After which you got it back, got safely home,
Saved the old man's life
And inherited the kingdom.
(SP 67)

Ashbery began writing such all-purpose narratives in "Popular Songs" (ST 10). But this rambling fairy-tale outline is disjointed and full of parenthetical addenda; the textual quest remains unfulfilled. The picaresque outline sketches an American oral autobiography (in the generic second person), a discourse that will be inflated to impossible dimensions in the epic outline of *Flow Chart.* The schematic plot of "Oleum Misericordiae" ends happily with father and son reconciled, but such endings occur only in fairy kingdoms: "In poorer lands / No one touches the water of life" (SP 67). In "A Wave" the myth of the son's quest to heal the father will be rewritten as the story of an exiled son's quest to cure the father's moral blindness. In the bleakly heroic open ending of "Oleum Misericordiae," Everyman is left waiting among shriveled lines for the communal mercy cup to be passed to him: "having come / So far / Without dog or woman / So far alone, un-asked" (SP 67). The paraphrastic syntax recalls the hemistich form of the Finnish epic, the *Kalevala,* later adopted in "At North Farm," where men travel alone seeking wives. Such wanderers reach no happy ending and must make do with stories.

The subject of "A Man of Words" (SP 8; dated January 11, 1973) is the dramatist and his actor. The title is taken from an ominously anonymous lyric that only Auden could have included in a volume of light verse: "A man of words and not of deeds / Is like a garden full of weeds; / And when the weeds begin to grow, / It's like a garden full of snow." The grim song continues adding links to its chain until its punning full stop: "And when

your heart begins to bleed, / You're dead, and dead, and dead, indeed."[12]
The difference between word and deed is crucial to both poems. If a poem
is not, or cannot be, purely and simply autobiographical, the poet's words
cannot be deeds. As J. L. Austin put it, literary deeds are infelicitous: "a
performative utterance will, for example, be *in a particular way* hollow or
void if said by an actor on the stage, or if introduced in a poem."[13] This
verbal hollowness was welcomed by the new critics, who sought to insulate
their literary icons. This postwar new critical world, with its dramatic persona, verbal irony, and overhearing audience, is the stage of "A Man of
Words." The poem opens in the third person: "His case inspires interest /
But little sympathy; it is smaller / Than at first appeared." The legal, psychoanalytic, and biographical "case" of the man of words is his casket, a
bookcase of his collected "volumes" of diminished reputation. The "speaker's" words may have lost their author's motivation: "Does the first nettle /
Make any difference as what grows / Becomes a skit? Three sides enclosed, /
The fourth open to a wash of the weather" and to an audience watching "gestures theatrically meant / To punctuate like doubled-over weeds as / The garden fills up with snow?" From the difference between word and deed grow
all the others: poet ("Behind the mask") and persona, intention and (verbal)
gesture, stimulus (a sexual weedy "nettle") and lyric response, past experience and present text, first and second stanza, and poet and audience. This
scene of the poet looking with a marked detachment and anxiety into his own
case is tinged with a new critical irony, as the poet sees that his once imagined
"destiny" has darkened and hardened into a "density black as gunpower."
The "case," to use one framing crypt phrase, is "open and shut," "like the
pressure / Of fingers on a book suddenly snapped shut" ("trigger," "shot").

These manifold made differences may not make any difference to an audience beset with their own. How can a man of words make any difference to
men and women of deeds? Ashbery's first response to this deconstructive
nettle is that all first-person (lyric) discourses are alike: "All diaries are alike,
clear and cold, with / The outlook for continued cold." From their diaries
each "I" looks out, day after day, on the same time ("le temps"), recorded
and forecast. All diary-poems become first-person tomes or tombs,
"placed / Horizontal, parallel to the earth, / Like the unencumbering
dead." The poem might have ended on "dead," a last word indeed. But
Ashbery takes his close beyond sardonic irony: "Just time to reread this /
And the past slips through your fingers, wishing you were there." "A Man
of Words" is crossed diagonally by three personal pronouns: "His," "I,"
and "you." These personae enter the poem into the postal system. In this
sample of epistolary writing ("Just time to write this," "wishing you were
here") the past wishes "you" were there with it, when that first persona was

speaking, with all its hopes and optimism intact. But as Ashbery well knows, there is no past without the post. The nostalgic gesture is not the last word of the poem but its last deed, what we might term (after Austin) the performative of representation. By enclosing the audience's words and phrases in his poem, this man of words has in fact done something: (mis)represented us to ourselves. Thus, as Austin implies, the poetic act is unhappy only in the particular sense that it remains present while its nettled dramatist passes on. The case may always be reopened.

Though not concerned with folk or fairy tales, "No Way of Knowing" (SP 55; written in 1973) is the volume's most hazardous interrogation of narrative epistemology. Neatly divided into a "double-sonnet" sequence of three 28-line verse paragraphs, the poem mimes the beginning-middle-end partitions of Ashbery's fairy tales only to question whether such ways of telling provide paths of knowing. Like "Clepsydra" before it, "No Way of Knowing" begins in the wake of an event and an affair, waking up with a host of questions:

> And then? Colors and names of colors,
> The knowledge of you a certain color had?
> The whole song bag, the eternal oom-pah refrain?
> Street scenes? A blur of pavement
> After the cyclists passed, calling to each other,
> Calling each other strange, funny-sounding names?
> Yes, probably, but in the meantime, waking up
> In the middle of a dream with one's mouth full
> Of unknown words takes in all of these:
> It is both the surface and the accidents
> Scarring that surface, yet it too only contains
> As a book on Sweden only contains the pages of that book.
> (SP 55)

These questions, fluctuating between double and triple and rising and falling rhythms, mime experiential flux, a mimesis cast into doubt by the reductive phrase "the eternal oom-pah refrain?" What way do we have of knowing Ashbery's verses in their wake? Knowing what Ashbery's poetry "means" means knowing where it comes from and how it works. The opening elliptical question, for instance, functions discursively as an abbreviated form of the paradigmatic narrative question, "And then [what happened]?", to which the title forms the ready answer: "[there is] No Way of Knowing" (the phrase appears in the middle stanza). The other questions offer various representative possibilities for what happened, the event being an ongoing bicycle race of which the outcome (perhaps miles and hours away) is unknown. But we may know how this particular event occurred to Ashbery, who "likes to begin his poems *in medias res.*"[14] The event in question comes from a punning reformulation of this Horatian tag: "in medias race." Ashbery's skepticism surfaces in one version of the phrase, "in the meantime," a narrative formula indicating that two events take place simultaneously in different places as parallel developments. Representation happens "in the meantime," in parallel, and as such "only contains" its experience, just as "a book on Sweden" contains only its carefully selected pages, not Sweden.

A proponent of latency, Ashbery is leery of frontal endings. "No Way of Knowing" is skeptical of narrative theories of knowledge which reduce experience to its outcome or high point (the fall of Troy or the failure of an affair), omitting "The dank no-places and the insubstantial pinnacles"(SP 55). The seductive power of the end-theory of knowledge is evident in such words as "de*fin*ition" and "de*term*ination." Definitive histories leave out the representative meantimes, where the bulk of no-name living occurs. To illustrate, Ashbery slips into a rural American reminiscence: "There were holidays past we used to / Match up, and yep, they fitted together / All right, but the days in between grow rank" (SP 55). The Dickensian inversion of "holidays past" betrays the conventionality of these favored times. The very process of narrative (and lyric) selection is a kind of mutilation; the memorable times and the meantimes, what happens on and off-schedule, are "parts of the same body" (SP 55) of experience.

The middle stanza broadens its skepticism by stifling objections ("there are no 'yes, buts.'") and refusing any common narrative "point of view / Like the 'I' in a novel" (SP 56), through which readers might identify with, and assent to the truth of, representations. Ashbery situates his skepticism with two epistemological concepts: "binary system" and "parallelism" (SP 56). In a convoluted, unmusical sentence with its own complex grammatical subject ("This stubble-field. . .," SP 56), he asserts that there is no way of knowing how the subject knows, or how its computer "binary system" (processing others in a skewed opposition as "neighbors or friendly savages," SP 56, straight or gay) arrives at its results. The rapid development of faster and smaller computers in the 1970s renewed debates about the very existence of mind or spirit. A much earlier, Cartesian doctrine known as parallelism asserted that the mind, if it did exist, simply operated in parallel with the body: "All attempts to influence / The working are parallelism, undulating, writhing / Sometimes but kept to the domain of metaphor" (SP 56). Poetry (not to mention critical theories of "influence") makes nothing happen; it promotes no understanding of the past or of "other points of view."

And "writing" "only contains" its "writhing" body or subject metaphorically. This fork in the bicycle path of knowledge splits a number of pairs: middle and end, thing and (color) name, body and mind, poetry and experience, self and other, Aristotelian substance and accident (cf. "insubstantial," "accidents," SP 55), and tenor and vehicle. Ashbery relies on I. A. Richards's well-known terms for metaphor to diagnose poetry, skeptically and Platonically, as a "vehicular madness" (SP 56), a name drawn from the legal term "vehicular homicide." Vehicles out of control cause accidents.

Such an accident is spun out in the concluding verse paragraph. In this camp melodrama we wait for a nurse to enter, carrying a Waterford vase and a "heroine," with the "denouement" (not the heroine) "drenched in the perfume of fatality" (SP 56; "in blood"). This dreamlike accident calls up the surreal misrepresentations of *The Tennis Court Oath*: "The cut driver pushes them to heaven" (SP 56; "The cab driver rushes them to the hospital"). Whatever happened, whether automobiles and/or bicycles were involved, the accident "only contains" the breakup of "you" and "I." For his own ending, Ashbery reaffirms his faith in the embodiment of lyric knowledge: "I like the spirit of the songs, though, / The camaraderie that is the last thing to peel off" (SP 57). The term "camaraderie" and the second-person questions ("Why must you go? Why can't you / Spend the night, here in my bed, with my arms wrapped tightly around you?" SP 57) recall Whitman's Calamus poems, the skeptical "Of the Terrible Doubt of Appearances" in particular. Whitman wisely turns away from suspicions that "day and night, colors, densities, forms, may-be . . . only apparitions" toward enveloping certainties: "I cannot answer the question of appearances or that of identity beyond the grave, / But I walk or sit indifferent, I am satisfied, / He ahold of my hand has completely satisfied me" (275). Ashbery too anchors his doubts on the bedrock of another body, from which he might construct a "theory of knowledge" and poetry. Tango ergo sum:

An LP record of all your favorite friendships,
Of letters from the front? Too
Fantastic to make sense? But it made the chimes ring.
If you listen you can hear them ringing still:
A mood, a Stimmung, adding up to a sense of what they really were,
All along, through the chain of lengthening days.
(SP 57)

Poetry matters, along the unknowing way, and rebuts the lover's new skeptical questions because it captures not only memorable moments but the essence, the perfume, of all the times together. Ashbery's final melodic flourish, lengthening the nostalgic cliché "through the years," is produced by transposing the modifier "lengthening" from "chain," where we might expect it, to "days," as though the accumulating years were only lengthening spring days. The metaphor of a "chain of days" is a sonic deformation of the familiar romantic figure of a "daisy chain."[15] Poetry, in this article of faith, holds something since its words come with their feelings and associations attached. The impossibility of knowing makes it possible for the represented essence to be pervasive, "all somewhere around / But difficult to read correctly" (SP 56); doubt clears the way for the unknown alternate routes of poetry.

---

In 1972, after new owners took over *Art News,* Ashbery found himself without a job as an art critic. This abrupt interruption of his occupation "of the left hand" (or right, for the left-handed Ashbery) encouraged him to experiment with art criticism in his poetry. The result was his best-known long poem, "Self-Portrait in a Convex Mirror." Ashbery began "Self-Portrait" in Provincetown in February 1973 and finished it in New York in "three months of not very inspired writing."[16] This was a transitional period not only for Ashbery but for the United States, which had just made peace without honor in Vietnam (January 27; the last American troops had left Vietnam by the time the poem was finished) and was beginning to investigate the Watergate cover-up ("Conflicting statements gathered, lapses of memory / Of the principal witnesses," SP 78). America's (and Nixon's) defensive posture in the early 1970s enlarged the aura of secrecy and self-protectiveness surrounding Ashbery's work. Though Ashbery makes neither crisis his subject matter, his argumentative poem manifests a postwar self-defensiveness.

"Self-Portrait" is the most anthologized and discussed of Ashbery's long poems partly because, unlike most of his poetry, it appears to hold to its premise and to its announced subject, Parmigianino's *Self-Portrait in a Convex Mirror.* According to Ashbery, "that's really a superficial quality of the poem. It seems to have given people the idea that I was actually dealing with a subject matter in some recognizable way, and this was a great relief; but I think really it's just as random and unorganized as my other poetry is."[17] Most readers would indeed have trouble charting the arguments of its disproportionately long last stanza, but as a whole "Self-Portrait" parcels out its themes relatively neatly. The poem is divided into six verse paragraphs or globes. The first three consider the self in the present, past, and future; the second three confront the otherness of the painting, of one's environment and history, and of one's own actions. The language of art criticism, predominant only in the first globe, disappears along with Parmigianino's painting for long stretches, but both the painting and the critical discourse return periodically to provide Ashbery with fresh points of departure. Though the aims of Ashbery's "Self-Portrait" are limited, it rivals Eliot's *Four Quartets* and Stevens's "Notes Toward a Supreme Fiction" in the perfection of its design.

The poem begins *in medias res* as a piece of lyrical art criticism:

As Parmigianino did it, the right hand
Bigger than the head, thrust at the viewer
And swerving easily away, as though to protect
What it advertises. A few leaded panes, old beams,
Fur, pleated muslin, a coral ring run together
In a movement supporting the face, which swims
Toward and away like the hand
Except that it is in repose.
(SP 68)

With its freely falling rhythms and loose pentameter measures (in the first draft the hand was "Twice as big as the head"), the opening phrases play sensual music off critical discourse. But an analytical detachment prevails. The rich and costly props supporting Parmigianino's equally cool regard are itemized as though advertised in an auction catalogue. Ashbery quotes (with ellipses) and paraphrases other critical works—Vasari's *Lives of the Poets* (in Mrs. Jonathan Foster's 1874 translation) and Sydney Freedberg's *Parmigianino*[18]—fitting them into his own metrical frame and occasionally finishing their sentences. He explicates his own vocabulary: "The words are only speculation / (From the Latin *speculum*, mirror)" (SP 69), "the weather, which in French is / *Le temps,* the word for time" (SP 70). With its ellipses, parentheses, italics, abbreviations, and interweaving of sources, the text of "Self-Portrait" is less spoken than written.

Ashbery, fond of quoting Nijinsky's maxim that "criticism is death," has a horror of criticism even though he has written a great deal of it. Why then did he strike the critical pose for his self-portrait? Though his appropriations are often subtly humorous, it was not his purpose simply to parody (or blankly pastiche) critical discourse; the line between "critical" and "creative" writing in "Self-Portrait" is impossible to draw. Ashbery's opening description of Parmigianino's protective gesture, for instance, resembles several remarks in his *Art News* reviews. Richard Bogart's shapes "simultaneously accost and turn away from the viewer"; in Neil Welliver's work there

175

"remains an element of mystery . . . that attracts as it eludes the eye"; and Robert Rauschenberg's collages, like Joseph Cornell's boxes, are made up of "the object and its nimbus of sensations, wrapped in one package, thrust at the viewer, here, now, unescapable."[19] My guess is that Ashbery struck a critical pose as a defensive maneuver against critical assimilation (a tactic which turned out to be wildly unsuccessful). Ashbery's etiolated, mannered poem self-reliantly reads itself. "Most artists," Ashbery notes, "would like to believe that their work renders criticism superfluous, since criticism is included in the act of creation" (RS 20). But every poem, as superfluous (or necessary) to life as its critical reflection, remains unfinished.

Ashbery's criticism of Parmigianino derives from received critical concepts. Several art historians have noted the flattening or foreshortening of space characteristic of mannerist painting. Freedberg, for instance, observes that in Parmigianino's *Self-Portrait* "lines of projection are thus partly flattened out into a plane . . . oblique to the front plane of the painting" (c.f. the hand "projected at a 180-degree angle," SP 68).[20] In a review of a surrealist exhibit, Ashbery derives surrealist deformations from the "Mannerists' telescoping of space" (RS 11) and notes that "the space of dreams can be flat as well as deep" (RS 10). In "Self-Portrait" the perspective lines have outmaneuvered the instruction manual of "The Skaters." At the beginning Ashbery ruefully observes that "the mirror being convex, the distance increases / Significantly" (SP 68), and near the end of the poem we track the mannerist's image "through the wrong end / Of the telescope" as it travels at relativistic flattening speed through foreshortening space: "you fall back at a speed / Faster than that of light to flatten ultimately / Among the features of the room, an invitation never mailed" (SP 82). In an enthusiastic 1964 review of Parmigianino's drawings, Ashbery claims that the artist's experiments with shape anticipate the spatial deformations of both surrealism and cubism: "it is hard to remain unmoved by his craftsmanship at the service of a sense of the mystery behind physical appearances, which makes him a precursor of de Chirico himself." "When one remembers the important role distortion plays throughout his work," he adds, "starting with the self-portrait in which the hand is larger than the head, it is possible to see in Parmigianino an ancestor of Picasso and other artists of today" (RS 31, 33). The descendant foremost in Ashbery's mind at the time of "Self-Portrait" was probably Cornell, in whose mannerist work, as in that of de Chirico and Roussel, "matter and manner fuse to form a new element" (RS 17). Cornell died in January 1973, a month before Ashbery began his own convex box. In a reminiscence delivered at the memorial service Ashbery recalled visiting the reclusive artist's studio: "I remember . . . particularly a box with a blue beveled glass top and a dim light bulb inside which enabled one to perceive dimly the outline of a bird. We were allowed to see only a certain number however, and it seemed as though these had been specially selected for our viewing. Most of the works remained on their shelves, with their backs to the viewer. And this seemed as it should be."

Despite Parmigianino's innovations, Ashbery sees limits in his project, "to perfect and rule out the extraneous / Forever" (SP 72). The sphere is a geometrically perfect but rhetorically imperfect figure, granting central, synecdochal power but prohibiting linear movement. Parmigianino's spherical poetics thus rules out change coming from outside. To include temporal and historical change as a topic within his poem, Ashbery warps the sphere into an hourglass or a vase and temporalizes it by continually shifting our vantage point. The past, for instance, often appears as the center of our circumferential present, which itself forms a new center for a projected future. In his critique of Parmigianino's poetics of perfection, as earlier in his sestina "The Painter" (ST 44), Ashbery draws on Browning's "Andrea del Sarto (Called 'The Faultless Painter')." Like Ashbery, Browning consulted Vasari for his portrait of Parmigianino's contemporary, who surpassed Raphael in technical facility but lacked his saving errors. While lamenting that "all is silver-grey / Placid and perfect with my art," Browning's painter, in the company of his model wife, cannot resist correcting Raphael's mistakes: "And indeed the arm is wrong. / I hardly dare . . . yet, only you to see, / Give the chalk here—quick; thus the line should go! / Ay, but the soul! he's Rafael! rub it out!" (677–78). As Stevens warned, "The imperfect is our paradise" (158).

Despite his suspicion of Parmigianino's superhuman achievement, Ashbery's "Self-Portrait" not only reflects on but reflects its subject. The poem is mannerist both in overall design and in its smallest details. Parmigianino's decorous restraint is matched by Ashbery's critical reserve, the painter's meticulous finish by the poet's subtle elaboration. Like Parmigianino's self-reliant hand, "Self-Portrait" strays from its ostensible subject for long periods. Time itself is deformed as the future and the past are flattened into the present "so that it is soon / Much later" (SP 71). The lyric space of "Self-Portrait" is also elongated. The last globe is nearly as long as the preceding five, and the poem itself, a 20-page study of a 10-inch painting, is blown well out of proportion, "but not coarse, merely on another scale" (SP 70). Ashbery's main guide here was probably Roussel, whose 20,000-line poem "The View" described in impossible detail the seaside prospect engraved on a convex lens set into a penholder. Ashbery first saw Parmigianino's painting "with Pierre in the summer of 1959" (SP 75; "Pierre" Martory—a rare unmisrepresentative proper name in Ashbery's poetry), when he was researching the secretive Roussel's life and work, a circumstance which must have tied the French poet's monotonous alexandrines to his own flattened lines.

In a 1970 essay on Saul Steinberg, Ashbery wrote that "manner is the only conjugation of matter" (RS 284). The evidence for this conjugation in both self-portraits is that the "hand" is "Bigger than the head." Recalling that the word "manner" derives from *manus* or "hand," we arrive at the mannerist displacement of both projects: the style displaces its subject (both subject matter and artist). Ashbery's stylistic mannerism manifests itself at the smallest levels of his text. In his elliptical first sentence, for instance, which encrypts some such sentence as "[I want to do it] As Parmigianino did it," the grammatical subject, "I," is elided in favor of the adverbial "As," the adverb being the grammatical indicator of manner. Adverbial distortions often displace the subject of "Self-Portrait," in such phrases as "Chiefly his reflection" (where the "chief" or "head" is modulated by "ly") and "the distance increases / Significantly; that is, enough to make the point"—that is, enough to make the point vanish. Relations between the head and the hand are at best, to use Ashbery's summary modifier, "unlikely" (SP 69).

While at Deerfield Academy Ashbery wrote an eleven-line lyric entitled "Poem," an uncanny forerunner of "Self-Portrait":

Always the left hand flickers, falls to right;
The eyes, groping at mirrors
Strike the sought self, opaque and firm,
Safe in its frame. A sweet disorder
Arranges mirrors, and the tensile gaze
Turns inward, calls the turning love.

Let our dual sight
See not so clearly, and turning, take daylight.
And before mirrors long unvisited
Avoid the milk white and translucent face
That stays there, that we know not how to name.

It is amazing to see how precisely the long poem exfoliates from this compendious metaphysical lyric. "Poem" anticipates "Self-Portrait" in the interchange of attributes (eyes flicker, hands grope and strike); the outstretched, tensile gaze ("how far can it swim out through the eyes," SP 68); the opaque yet translucent face enclosed within its protective (handlike) frame; and, above all, the introverted, narcissistic eros of Robert Herrick's "sweet disorder" ("A sweet disorder in the dress / Kindles in clothes a wantonness"), the enigma of the self confronting another as (the other within) itself. This speculative affair involves the gazer and his image, the poet's writing hand and seeing eye. The aptness of the description makes one wonder whether the young Ashbery might not already have had the seductive dualisms of Parmigianino's *Self-Portrait* in mind.

Parmigianino's mirror painting illustrates a paradox of priority: the head moves the hand that draws the head. Ashbery's "Self-Portrait" is likewise organized around an unstable set of relations between head and hand: center and circumference, matter and manner, signified and signifiers, depth and surface, whole and parts, inside and outside, past and present, present and future, concealment and exposure, self and other, and so on. In Parmigianino's *Self-Portrait* the interplay between the head at the virtual center and the hand at the circumference of the painting reflects the antithesis between the expressive and decorative tendencies in mannerist painting.[21] Virtually all the figuration in Ashbery's "Self-Portrait" derives from the mannerist tension between the central head and its surrounding hand. All curved, turning, circular, or enveloping figures in "Self-Portrait" are concentric, though our perspective is sometimes central and at other times peripheral: "light behind windblown fog and sand" (SP 71), "a chill, a blight / Moving outward along the capes and peninsulas" (SP 75), "room for one bullet in the chamber" (SP 82). Consider this passage from the first globe, in which the "hand loom[s] large"

> to fence in and shore up the face
> On which the effort of this condition reads
> Like a pinpoint of a smile, a spark
> Or star one is not sure of having seen
> As darkness resumes. A perverse light whose
> Imperative of subtlety dooms in advance its
> Conceit to light up: unimportant but meant.
> Francesco, your hand is big enough
> To wreck the sphere, and too big,
> One would think, to weave delicate meshes
> That only argue its further detention.
> (Big, but not coarse, merely on another scale,
> Like a dozing whale on the sea bottom
> In relation to the tiny, self-important ship
> On the surface.) But your eyes proclaim
> That everything is surface.
> (SP 69–70)

The face is variously depicted here as a pinpoint, a smile, a spark, a star, a homotextual "perverse light," "meant," and a ship, while the hand appears in "loom," "subtlety" (from *\*sub-tela*: the fine warp of a loom), "delicate meshes," the sphere, the "whale," and the encircling parentheses. The crypt word dozing beneath "smile" is "simile," signaled by "Like" (twice), "As," "Conceit," and Ashbery's parenthetical cameo of Milton's epic simile in *Paradise Lost* in which Satan is likened to "that Sea-beast / *Leviathan*" which "The Pilot of some small night-founder'd Skiff, / Deem[s] some Island" (I, 200–208).[22] The simile or metaphysical conceit (or mannerist *concetto*) details the "unlikely" relation not only between the head and the hand but between painting and poetry; the "As" in "As Parmigianino did it" recalls the "ut" of Horace's "ut pictura poesis." Sir Philip Sidney ("Sidney" Freedberg) defined poetic mimesis in Horatian terms as "a representing, counterfeiting, or figuring forth—to speak metaphorically, a speaking picture—with this end, to teach and delight."[23] When the reader's and writer's desire to commune with the speaking picture dissipates, the picture flattens into words on a page, "an invitation / Never mailed" (SP 82). When the viewer's "eyes" realize that Parmigianino's hand, like Ashbery's whale, is really painted beneath rather than projected before his head, they declare that everything is painted on a surface. Though the poem reverses itself quickly, claiming that the painting "is not / Superficial but a visible core" of central expression, the global stanza closes by labeling the painting, and itself, a "pure / Affirmation that doesn't affirm anything" (cf. Sidney's poet who "nothing affirms, and therefore never lieth," 52). The speaking picture of this *poésie pure* speaks only itself. The momentary defensiveness breaks the spell, a rupture signaled at the start of the next global stanza: "The balloon pops, the attention / Turns dully away. Clouds / In the puddle stir up into sawtoothed fragments." As the blank space breaks the textual surface and our "attention," the Lichtenstein cartoon speech-balloon "pops" and pop art thought-clouds resume.

The globe of "Self-Portrait" is not only a bubble but a prison, one in which "the soul is a captive, treated humanely, kept / In suspension, unable to advance much farther / Than your look as it intercepts the picture" (SP 68–69). The slightly misshapen third phrase combines chemical suspension with narrative suspense ("kept in suspense"); in both cases the solution is withheld. But the military vocabulary of "advance" ("advance the plot," avant-garde) and "intercepts" (in the first draft, a rifle "zeroes in" on the soul under "house-arrest") suggests that this prison was built in the context of the war in Vietnam. In aesthetic terms, the soul is held captive by the constriction of mannerist space. Freedberg, for instance, remarks that figures in Parmigianino's paintings "stand close against the front plane, but at the same time they are strictly confined behind it."[24] The "delicate meshes" of fine-meshed expression "only argue" the artist's "further detention" (SP 70). More generally, every self is imprisoned within its self-image, guarded by the intercepting expectations of others or itself. In "Circles," an essay concentric with Ashbery's poem, Emerson claimed that the "life of man is a self-evolving circle, which . . . rushes on all sides outwards to new and larger circles. . . . The heart refuses to be imprisoned."[25] But Ashbery's Parmigianino imprisons himself in self-defense—a homotextual revision that makes the portraitist's room his closet. Neither formal restraint nor inescapable solitude can account for the painful embarrassment of the soul's exposure:

> But there is in that gaze a combination
> Of tenderness, amusement and regret, so powerful
> In its restraint that one cannot look for long.
> The secret is too plain. The pity of it smarts,
> Makes hot tears spurt: that the soul is not a soul,
> Has no secret, is small, and it fits
> Its hollow perfectly: its room, our moment of attention.
> (SP 69)

To be sure, this hollowness may be seen as characteristic both of the mannerist formal veneer and of the modern secular "soul." Freedberg writes that "Parmigianino's figures are an assemblage of surfaces; nothing is contained within these surfaces, and their modeling is the affirmation not of a solid, but only of a hollow form."[26] This superficiality would reduce the mannerist, surrealist enigma to a classical reality "if," as Ashbery elsewhere defines it, "by classical we mean clarity, tautness of argument, things filling their space accurately, and a dramatic trajectory whose every point is visible."[27] Ashbery's perfectly imprisoned soul recalls Bishop's snail, "Inside, it is as smooth as silk, and I, I fill it to perfection" (141), but there is no comfort in his picture.

Though the self-protective secretiveness of "Self-Portrait" has a homotextual dimension, Ashbery is not simply closeted within his nonaffirming poem. The duplicities of the mirror place Ashbery outside with us, his contemporaries, gazing at his speculative, narcissistic twin in an "enchantment of self with self" (SP 72). Freud described homosexuality as a phase in the development of the libido, preceding the attachment to an external object. Homosexuals "are plainly seeking themselves as a love-object and their type of object-choice may be termed *narcissistic*."[28] Narcissism in "Self-Portrait," neither solipsistic nor "incurably" self-absorbed, involves seeking the self in another and finding the other in oneself. Ashbery's globe travels in time and history.

"Self-Portrait" begins with an obvious (though hitherto unnoticed) mistake, or error, or open secret: the distorted hand "thrust at the viewer" was not Parmigianino's right hand but his left. What (if anything) lies behind this misrepresentation of Parmigianino's portrait, this reversal of left and right? Since Ashbery makes a point of reminding us that everything is "reversed in the accumulating mirror" (SP 73), this sleight of hands should be related to the many reversals within the poem. Parmigianino's single, enlarged, phallic hand "thrust at the viewer" is sexually disorienting; it may be left or right. To see Parmigianino's left hand as his right is to imagine that the painter has taken the place of his portrayed mirror image within the globe. Parmigianino copied, according to Vasari, "'all that he saw in the glass.'" "Chiefly his reflection," Ashbery continues, "of which the portrait / Is the reflection once removed" (SP 68). The triangle of relations once removed rotates as follows: Parmigianino sits, in Rome in 1524, for his self-portrait, with a barber's mirror at his left hand and a wooden ball at his right. Not long after the Sack, Parmigianino goes under the ball, and Ashbery, soon after the fall of Saigon, takes his place in the artist's seat, with what we imagine is a good color reproduction of Parmigianino's *Self-Portrait* at one hand and a writing page at the other. Actually, Ashbery composed his poem on the typewriter, but the triangulation remains, together with the first two letters of the poet's imperfectly erased signature: "As[hbery] Parmigianino did it." Finally, the ardent reader, with poem and critically extrapolated marginalia in hand, assumes Ashbery's "point of view," hoping to postpone the inevitable critical displacement. But the poem's opening "As" means, succinctly enough, "in like manner."

In Ashbery's "Self-Portrait" otherness mirrors, defines, and sometimes displaces the central self. In the fourth globe, for instance, the mirror portrait takes over "your" reflections for once, and the spectator suffers a temporary loss of self-consciousness: "So that you could be fooled for a moment / Before you realize the reflection / Isn't yours. You feel then like one of those / Hoffmann characters who have been deprived / Of a reflection" (SP 74).[29] In the first draft Ashbery characterized this encounter as a "skirmish between sitter and viewer." Intrusive readers who have invaded Ashbery's privacy will also have been taken by surprise. In the second globe, the other influences the self through the slow alchemy of memory. As thought-clouds "stir up" memories, the first-person pronoun makes its first appearance in the poem: "I think of the friends / Who came to see me, of what yesterday / Was like" (SP 71). Like the painting or poem on view, the self is "influenced" (anxiously or not) by the views of others, friendly or critical, who frame its reputation and self-image: "How many people came and stayed a certain time, / Uttered light or dark speech that became part of you / Like light behind windblown fog and sand, / Filtered and influenced by it, until no part / Remains that is surely you" (SP 71). The self, other than itself, is addressed as "you," in the objective, specular case. It is the convex mirror of lovers, friends, acquaintances, and readers that constructs the critical variorum of any one life. The construction takes "the form of memories deposited in irregular / Clumps of crystals" (SP 71). Toward the end of his short life Parmigianino became obsessed with alchemy, and, as Ashbery put it, "was pouring all his strength and money into trying to find a way to solidify mercury" (RS 32). For Ashbery, Parmigianino's *Self-Portrait* stemmed from a like obsession, stopping time. So too with Proust's massive self-portrait: "*A la recherche du temps perdu* escapes the limitations of autobiography, transmuting the frivolous or sordid facts of his existence into a rare magical substance. . . . Photographs and documents . . . are the lead that he somehow turned to gold, and they have taken on an unnatural sheen, as though the alchemy had already begun."[30] Similar memorabilia are transmuted into the "silver blur" (SP 72) of the present ego in "Self-Portrait": "I feel the carousel starting slowly / And going faster and faster: desk, papers, books, / Photographs of friends, the window and the trees / Merging in one neutral band that surrounds / Me on all sides, everywhere I look" (SP 71). In the cinematic, radial acceleration of the global merry-go-round (or memory's LP-record band) "I" at the center feels itself being formed at the circumference. This decentering sphere is temporal: events from the central past "boil down" (SP 71) to an alchemically refined, circumspect present. Manifold historical differences are flattened into "one neutral band" ("hand") of identity by means of indifference: "your self, / Firm, oblique, accepting everything with the same / Wraith of a smile" (SP 71; developing both "the sought self, opaque and firm" of "Poem" and the "hard stare, accepting / / Everything" of "Little J.A.," ST 28–29). Indifference toward an irrecoverable past resolves differences into identity. In "The System" this was the symptom of chronic, chronological depression: "You cannot do without it and you cannot have it. At this point a drowsiness overtakes you as of total fatigue and indifference" (TP 84). "Self-Portrait" presents the psychological conclusion: when the past is past, it ceases to make a difference.

With the third globe indifference toward the past is transmuted into desire for the circumferential future, "our / Landscape sweeping out from us to disappear / On the horizon" (SP 72). The globe opens with a misrepresented proverb, "Tomorrow is easy, but today is uncharted" (SP 72), in which the conventionally uncharted future changes places with the present.

Tomorrow is easy to the extent that one lives by projecting one's dreams into the future. Freud temporalized the narcissist's object-choices as "what he is himself," "what he once was" (a child), and "what he would like to be" (an ego-ideal). Lacan too saw the untouchable mirror image occupying another, future dimension: "The *mirror stage* is . . . precipitated from insufficiency to anticipation."[31] As Ashbery puts it, punning on "cogito ergo sum": "more keeps getting included / Without adding to the sum" (SP 72). Future-oriented, career-oriented types, not content with today's latent happiness, sacrifice daily pleasures to self-fulfillment: "the source of dreams / Is being tapped so that this one dream / May wax" (SP 73). The third globe introduces a new set of narcissistic twins into the picture: present and future, actual and possible, waking and dreaming, fulfillment and promise, and real and surreal (ideal, romantic). These attracting poles continually turn toward and into each other in a process of identification. Present possibilities, for instance, become future realities (or disappointments). To illustrate this, Ashbery turns the Aristophanic hemispheres face to face "like an hourglass" (SP 73). For most of us, our identity-dream passes, "leaving us / To awake and try to begin living in what / Has now become a slum" (SP 73; resonating "sum"). Ashbery plays on this grim realization with the surfacing hand's "wave": "And we realize this only at a point where they lapse / Like a wave breaking on a rock, giving up / Its shape in a gesture which expresses that shape" (SP 73). For an artist, the creative act provides a brief facsimile of this lifelong process of actualization: "Something like living occurs, a movement / Out of the dream into its codification" (SP 73). In the indifferent codification of one's dream, the globe is rounded.

In the fourth globe Parmigianino takes the forgetful Ashbery by surprise as a mirror-doubled "it," both object and subject of reflections: "As I start to forget it / It presents its stereotype again" (SP 73). In the fifth globe the poet mounts something of a counterattack. The topos of this globe is the city, center of historical and cultural change, which displaces selves to the circumference:

The shadow of the city injects its own
Urgency: Rome where Francesco
Was at work during the Sack: his inventions
Amazed the soldiers who burst in on him;
They decided to spare his life, but he left soon after;
Vienna where the painting is today, where
I saw it with Pierre in the summer of 1959; New York
Where I am now, which is a logarithm
Of other cities.
(SP 75)

Ashbery's accelerating tour of cities and centuries owes something to Vasari's history of Parmigianino's *Self-Portrait:* "With respect to the portrait in the mirror, I remember to have seen it, when I was a youth, in the house of Messer Pietro at Arezzo. . . . It afterwards fell, by what means I know not, into the hands of the carver in crystal, Valerio Vincentino, and is now in the possession of Alessandro Vittoria, a sculptor in Venice."[32] In Ashbery's historical survey Francesco is displaced first by his painting and then by his poet. The shock of Parmigianino's work surprised history's footsoldiers, who "burst" into his bubble-chamber and invaded his privacy. But the winds of change appear to hasten his work out of style: "Are you strong enough for it? / This wind brings what it knows not" (SP 75). The wind or wave of a "new mode" (SP 75) is personified as an "unlikely / Challenger pounding on the gates of an amazed / Castle" (SP 76). The challenger confronts his no longer fresh subject with an insulting apostrophe, barely masked by the narrative pluperfect: "Your argument, Francesco, / Had begun to grow stale" (SP 76). But as Ashbery well knows, each victorious challenger will be assaulted and displaced in turn. On the brink of imagining his virtual image "dissolv[ing] now / Into dust" (SP 76), Ashbery abruptly reverses his disintegrating poem by identifying with "It"—history, life— now refigured as a quasi-divine source and synecdochal center of change:

> but look now, and listen:
> It may be that another life is stocked there
> In recesses no one knew of; that it,
> Not we, are the change; that we are in fact it
> If we could get back to it, relive some of the way
> It looked, turn our faces to the globe as it sets
> And still be coming out all right:
> Nerves normal, breath normal.
> (SP 76)

No longer at the center of our future horizon, we find ourselves on the circumference of a common history. "It" has taken the solar position with "you" in orbit, as in the globe's closing phrase: "if you think about it" (SP 76). Ashbery's "turn to the globe" undoes the encrypted narrative gesture of death ("he turned his face to the wall") and the euphemistic "setting sun" with a surgical, narrative, and perhaps homotextual "coming out all right." But "it" is not so easily appeased or evaded.

In the last globe, Parmigianino's image returns with ghostly foreboding and convoluted syntax:

> A breeze like the turning of a page
> Brings back your face: the moment

185

Takes such a big bite out of the haze
Of pleasant intuition it comes after.
The locking into place is "death itself,"
As Berg said of a phrase in Mahler's Ninth.
(SP 76)[33]

The "pleasant intuition" of taking "a big bite out of" the carnal apple is dispersed by "the moment" of frontal knowledge of Parmigianino's, or someone's, face. These tightened lines, locking into place with increasingly regular pentameters, were constructed before "Self-Portrait" was begun. Sometime during the late 1960s (before *Three Poems*) Ashbery began a sonnet sequence, finishing 27 free-verse sonnets before abandoning the project. One of these poems (the "sequence" was not ordered) begins as follows: "All action is like dying, because / The moment takes such a big bite out of / The haze of pleasant instinct it succeeds" and so on roughly as in "Self-Portrait" for six more lines. "Self-Portrait" thus had its beginnings in the paradigmatic sequential form of love poetry. Ashbery rendered the subject matter of his sixth globe more typically mysterious by omitting the sonnet's thesis statement: "All action is like dying." But the deleted topos covers the vast last globe, which rivals "Clepsydra" and the final movement of Mahler's Ninth in length. Committing an act, whether of love or of art, puts an end, momentarily, to the living, latent haze of possibilities and desires.

One's life may be regarded as a tide: "one / Is always cresting into one's present" (SP 78). All worldly action conjugates the self with otherness; one's self-portrait is composed of foreign matter. Otherness includes other people. In the first typescript of "Self-Portrait" Ashbery interposed a sentence between "face" and "the moment": "I passed by your house / Today, to see how you were." Some lines down, the phrase "They told me you were out" was also struck from the poem. Further on, "why the light / Falling at the end of the street at your house / Bespeaks the agency of love" became "why that light / Should be focused by love" (SP 78). The dramatic framework of the first person's visit to the second person's residence has been carefully removed.[34] But though "Love" is "now shadowed, invisible," its recurrent latent possibility is still "mysteriously present, around somewhere" (SP 77). If one act of love has ended, another may be waiting in the wings, with "the look / Some wear as a sign" (SP 77) of narcissistic, homosexual identification. Though unrealized, such an act remains "present, unimpaired, a permanent anomaly" (SP 78). The word "anomaly," which appears prominently at the end of "Fragment" ("that/Anomaly had spoken to her," DDS 94), seems always in Ashbery's poetry to signify an unconventional sexuality. Other linguistic signs wear an accidental significance. Around the time he was writing "Self-Portrait," Ashbery began wearing glasses. Though he may have lost his licence to drive "unimpaired," his poetic licence is still valid.

Though Parmigianino is addressed as a rival or lover, his actual presence is framed as a painting reproduced in art books and housed in a museum. Accordingly, the poet relegates the painting to the "long corridor" (SP 78) of the museum's accumulated past and adopts a revolutionary rhetoric of change. These corridors threaten contemporary artists by reducing their own "special, lapidary / Todayness" to "no special time" (SP 78, 79). More than one artist has faltered in the face of the Renaissance. Mechanical reproduction has "reduced" the museum in turn "to the status of / Black-and-white illustrations in a book where colorplates / Are rare" (SP 79); artists' lives are similarly reduced in literary anthologies to tiny selections and tinier headnotes. Ashbery stands on both sides of the debate over past and present taste. In his 1968 article on a Dada and surrealist show at the Museum of Modern Art, he begins with a *New York Times* story about some "Yippy demonstrators" picketing "the Mausoleum of Modern Art" on the grounds that "Like maybe these people coming to see the Dada show wouldn't have entertained the original artists in their own homes." Ashbery responds in kind: "Like maybe they wouldn't have 50 years ago, but since then the Surrealist Revolution has intervened. . . . We all 'grew up Surrealist' without even being aware of it." The latter-day surrealist poet and art critic defends these patrons of surrealism by concluding that "while it is perfectly OK to heckle the swells descending from their rainy taxis to sip MOMA champagne from fur-lined teacups, it is also OK to be them."[35]

The museum patrons in "Self-Portrait" seem as anxious as the contemporary artist about living in the past: "the public / Is pushing through the museum now so as to / Be out by closing time. You can't live there. / The gray glaze of the past attacks all know-how" (SP 79). In the first draft, the counterattack "You can't live there" was prefaced with the tell-tale "Like" of the leftist yippies or hippies. Late in his foreshortened life, Parmigianino himself could have passed as a long-hair; in his early review of Parmigianino's paintings Ashbery quotes Vasari's description of the disreputable alchemist-artist who had "allowed his beard to grow long and disordered, which made him look like a savage instead of a gentleman" (RS 32). As the argument becomes more extreme, Ashbery's reservations increase in clarity: "We don't need paintings or / Doggerel written by mature poets when / The explosion is so precise, so fine" (SP 79; "nature poets"). The argument against past art (and, presumably, artists over thirty) has widened into an attack on all art, with ammunition supplied by Thorstein Veblen's *The Theory of the Leisure Class*. Leisure time is a figment invented by the privileged classes:

"Does it / Exist? Certainly the leisure to / Indulge stately pastimes doesn't, / Any more." All that remains is conspicuous (art) consumption, and demonstrations organized against it: "'Play' is something else; / It exists, in a society specifically / Organized as a demonstration of itself." Artists such as Parmigianino and Ashbery, "with their mirror games" and their romanticizing "investing / Aura"[36] of latent presence, must be social deviants, including homosexual "assholes" who would "confuse" straightforward thinkers (SP 79). From this no-nonsense, homophobic viewpoint, the postwar cultural scene indeed appears to be a "very hostile universe" (SP 80).

Ashbery's deconstructive counterargument is that otherness, confusing distortions, and the mirror games of self-consciousness pervert the most ordinary daily activities; all such actions divide one from oneself. This model of the act recalls Eliot's sibylline thesis in "The Hollow Men": "Between the motion / And the act," "Between the conception / And the creation," "Falls the Shadow" (58–59). For Ashbery, the intervening shadow marks the "way" acts come into being. We might be able to live in the "undivided present," for instance, "if the way of telling / Didn't somehow intrude, twisting the end result / Into a caricature of itself," which is "the principle that makes works of art so unlike / What the artist intended" (SP 80). This mannerist deformation describes the outcome of any action. In the climactic realization of "Self-Portrait," the mirror reflects not oneself but "otherness":

> Is there anything
> To be serious about beyond this otherness
> That gets included in the most ordinary
> Forms of daily activity, changing everything
> Slightly and profoundly, and tearing the matter
> Of creation, any creation, not just artistic creation
> Out of our hands, to install it on some monstrous, near
> Peak, too close to ignore, too far
> For one to intervene? This otherness, this
> "Not-being-us" is all there is to look at
> In the mirror, though no one can say
> How it came to be this way.
> (SP 80–81)

The "poetry" of these verses, manneristically flattened into the prosaic registers of *Three Poems,* is easily overlooked. But the exasperated, impassioned oral rhetoric here is quietly underscored by the adverbs of manner ("Slightly and profoundly"), by the triplication of "creation," by the philosophically

188

loaded end-words, by the wonderful oxymoron "this otherness," by the distortion of scale (is the peak the hand or the monumental head?), by the word play (a "monster" is an unreadable "sign"), and by the existentialist vocabulary of the 1960s. Outbursts like this, which both characterize and caricature their speaker, will shape the oral poetry of "Litany" and, later, of *Flow Chart.*

Now that Parmigianino's face has revealed "this otherness" dominating everyone's mirror, one might conclude that the self no longer exists, "that the soul is not a soul" (SP 69). Parmigianino's seductive project, "to perfect and rule out the extraneous / Forever" (SP 72), ruled out the possibility of random, external influences. Ashbery takes the hazardous opportunity of otherness to thwart the drive to perfection: "You are allowing extraneous matters / To break up your day" (SP 81). The word "extraneous," along with its cognates "stranger" and "strange," is one of the most erotically charged in Ashbery's poetry, which is full of passing strangers, estranged lovers, and extraneous self-images. Admitting "this otherness" is the only alternative to solitude.

With chilling formality, Ashbery shows Parmigianino the door: "Therefore I beseech you, withdraw that hand, / Offer it no longer as shield or greeting, / The shield of a greeting, Francesco: / There is room for one bullet in the chamber" (SP 82). The erotic narrative of "Self-Portrait," passing from seduction to disenchantment with its self-reliant object, parallels the course of carnal knowing in Keats's own ecphrastic poem, "Ode on a Grecian Urn," which begins by praising the urn's chastity ("Thou still unravished bride") and ends by calling it a tease ("Cold Pastoral!"). Ashbery's break with his own convex subject is less clean. After the Russian roulette of his six-chambered poem, doubts begin to assail him as to whether his own impulse ever "actually" existed. As at the end of "Clepsydra," he takes comfort in reflecting that the original outline informs the final construction: "Its existence / Was real, though troubled, and the ache / Of this waking dream can never drown out / The diagram still sketched on the wind" (SP 82). The head survives in its hand, "So unlikely a part" (SP 69). Ashbery's final credo follows the diagram sketched in "Ode to a Nightingale"—from "My heart aches" to "Do I wake or sleep?"—which ends with Keats turning away from the ecstatic self-absence of self-expression as from death. It also foreshadows the opening of *Flow Chart,* where Ashbery questions the foreboding "diagram," a skeletal bridge shaken by "an emptiness / so sudden it leaves the girders / whanging in the absence of wind" (FC 3). In "Self-Portrait" the diagram sketches the skeletal structure of Parmigianino's hand, which, Freedberg notes, "serves as a bridge into the depth of the picture" (105).

The diagrammatic bridge is invisible at the far end of "Self-Portrait" but "around somewhere" in its reverberations:

> The hand holds no chalk
> And each part of the whole falls off
> And cannot know it knew, except
> Here and there, in cold pockets
> Of remembrance, whispers out of time.
> (SP 83)

The synecdochal rhetoric here is based on the time-sphere. Now and again centrifugal parts recall their common origin. Those deciduous actors (and works and deeds) have "no way of knowing" what happened unless certain timeless moments bridge "Here and there," now and then: "When we experience a moment we feel perhaps a kind of emptiness, but when we look back at it there will be different aspects and the moment will separate itself into these aspects."[37] Ashbery's haunting phrase for this recollected frontal happiness, "pockets of remembrance," incorporates the phrases "air pockets" and "pockets of resistance." His punctuating phrase "whispers out of time" echoes the final, ringing "le temps" of Proust's *Remembrance of Things Past.* But Ashbery's quieter close also recalls the end of Hart Crane's "The Bridge," "Whispers antiphonal in azure swing" (108). And Whitman, who heard "what the sea whispered me" in "Out of the Cradle," would discern "death" in Ashbery's "Whispers of the word that can't be understood / But can be felt, a chill, a blight" (SP 75). Parmigianino is empty-handed, and Ashbery is "out of time." But "love" is always another possibility. Ashbery's personification of "each" singular unknowing "part" ushers in persons halved from one Aristophanic sphere, whose participation in a writing and loving community is known only from occasional whispers. With the communicative act of "Self-Portrait" Ashbery enters his own name into the grapevine.

Following the excursions of *Three Poems,* the poems of *Self-Portrait* opened up a new range of prosaic American styles for Ashbery's verse, less abstracted from speech and writing discourses than the poems of *The Double Dream of Spring.* But Ashbery's America here tends to resemble the America that dominates Fairfield Porter's canvases: "in cool yards, / In quiet small houses in the country, / Our country, in fenced areas, in cool shady streets" (SP 45); it is a nice place to look at, but "You can't live there" (SP 79). The poems in *Self-Portrait,* as brilliant as they are, are often confined by a lyric decorum of low-key, beautiful, serious meditation, admitting little of the unstable, discursively self-aware humor which enlivened Ashbery's previous verses. In "Self-Portrait" Ashbery is highly conscious of re-flecting (on) an artistic tradition, but less self-conscious about joining it. Robert Lowell also has recourse to Renaissance painting in justifying his own recollective poetry: "Pray for the grace of accuracy / Vermeer gave to the sun's illumination."[38] Though Ashbery the abstract mannerist has little in common with his senior realist contemporary, his "Self-Portrait" displays an equally Renaissance grace of distortion. This Renaissance polish will be removed in his next long poem. *Self-Portrait* is Ashbery's most fully realized book to date. For that reason, as with *Some Trees,* he had to break from it definitively if he was to reinvest his writing with potential.

# 7

## "In the Public Domain"
### *Houseboat Days*

In 1975 *Self-Portrait in a Convex Mirror* won three major poetry prizes—
the Pulitzer Prize, the National Book Award, and the National Book Critics
Circle Award—and relocated the avant-garde poet, in many readers' eyes,
from "the other tradition" to "the tradition." In "The Invisible Avant-
Garde" Ashbery recommends that the artist adopt a posture of indifference,
"an attitude which neither accepts nor rejects acceptance but is independent
of it" (RS 394).[1] *Houseboat Days* may be taken as Ashbery's declaration of
independence from a growing public expecting more "Ashbery poetry"
from Ashbery. As though he owed it to his audience to confound their expectations, Ashbery is at pains here not to repeat his past successes. His new
long poem, "Fantasia on 'The Nut-Brown Maid,'" scrupulously avoids the
seductive lyricism and monologic discursiveness of its predecessor. The results are interesting, but the poem has not attracted much acclaim from
critics or poets. The major attraction of *Houseboat Days* is its short poems.
In a 1982 interview in which he named *Three Poems* and *Houseboat Days*
as his favorite books, Ashbery described these as "more accomplished and
fulfilled" than the lyrics of *Self-Portrait*.[2] They are also more discursively and
stylistically varied. Above all, they show Ashbery's keen awareness of his
new status as a member of the visible avant-garde.

As he was finishing *Self-Portrait,* Ashbery began teaching English and
Creative Writing at Brooklyn College. Asked by his students to explain his
profession, Ashbery responded with a pair of poems, "What Is Poetry" and
"And *Ut Pictura Poesis* Is Her Name." Both poems, placed side by side
in *Houseboat Days,* are parodically self-conscious. "What Is Poetry" (HBD
47; dated March 18, 1976), mimicking the sonnet with its seven unrhymed

couplets, begins with a singularly unpromising subject matter—"The medieval town, with frieze / Of boy scouts from Nagoya? The snow"—and continues by caricaturing the imagistic exoticism of contemporary poetry, lured away from ever faithful "ideas" by "Beautiful images": "But we / Go back to them as to a wife, leaving / / The mistress we desire?"[3] Like marriage, the misrepresentations of poetry should be taken, and received, on faith: "Now they / Will have to believe it / / As we believe it." Aside from the question mark (unaccountably missing in the title), the most prominent feature of "What Is Poetry" is this mysterious, quasi-religious "it." The poem ends like a field-guide, with fledgling poets, like boy scouts, instructed to look up their answers: "What was left was like a field. / Shut your eyes, and you can feel it for miles around. / / Now open them on a thin vertical path. / It might give us—what?—some flowers soon?" This ending came by chance: "In a bookstore I overheard a boy saying to a girl this last line."[4] Beginning with an expletive "It" and harboring two question marks, the boy's remark is ready-made Ashbery. Thus transplanted, the "flowers" are tropes, and "It," the "thin vertical path," indicates the vertical axis of metaphorical substitution. The anonymous remark reappears without change under Ashbery's name, yielding its small share of profit in the bookstore where it was overheard.

"And *Ut Pictura Poesis* Is Her Name" comically recasts the aphorism from Horace's *Ars Poetica* and ushers in the pedagogical, authoritative discourse of the Horatian poem. It begins with an all-purpose compositional stricture: "You can't say it that way any more" (HBD 45). The line itself is a case in point. With its ambivalent second person (both generic and particular), abstracted subject matter ("it"), and temporalized rhetoric ("that way any more"), the line announces itself as Ashbery's. And although it "says" much the same thing as Pound's authorial edict, "Make it new," it says it differently, registering its discursive situation (a contemporary American writing workshop) with a new precision. What Ashbery in particular can't make any more is a self-portrait in the convex mirror of his admirers: "you, you who have so many lovers, / People who look up to you and are willing / To do things for you, but you think / It's not right, that if they really knew you . . . / So much for self-analysis" (Ashbery's ellipsis). And so much for confessional poetry; the pedagogue's turn is next: "Now, / About what to put in your poem-painting: / Flowers are always nice, particularly delphinium." He also recommends the average diction of mainstream poetry, "a few important words, and a lot of low-keyed, / Dull-sounding ones" before launching into an implausibly surreal epiphany: "She approached me / About buying her desk. Suddenly the street was / Bananas and the clangor of Japanese instruments" (HBD 45). But as time runs out parody yields to the need of saying "it," and Ashbery eroticizes the Horatian relation as "poetry and panting": "The extreme austerity of an almost empty mind / Colliding with the lush, Rousseau-like foliage of its desire to communicate / Something between breaths" (HBD 45–46). A poem, then, shouldn't be about sex, but writing and reading poetry should be like it. Ashbery knows what poetry is by experience, and it is the lesson of experience he hands to us: we will know a real poem-painting when we see it.

The title poem of *Houseboat Days*, one of its best poem-paintings, illustrates the difference writing lyric prose made to Ashbery's prosaic verse. "Houseboat Days" (1975) is written in what I call "sentence measure," with phrasal and syntactical periods taking precedence over linear and stanzaic rhythms, and a single paragraph break dividing its sixty-eight lines.[5] Ashbery took his title from Florence H. Morden's armchair travelogue, "House-Boat Days in the Vale of Kashmir," which appeared in *National Geographic* in 1929. The romance of Morden's travels depends entirely upon the portability of the British Empire and an imperious subjectivity.[6] Just as horrifying in its way as the *National Geographic* illustrations of Bishop's "In the Waiting Room," Morden's travelogue orients us discursively in Ashbery's poem, which begins in the crabbed handwriting of a postcard, set off in quotes as a misrepresentative sample: "'The skin is broken. The hotel breakfast china / Poking ahead to the last week in August, not really / Very much at all, found the land where you began . . .'" (HBD 38; Ashbery's ellipsis; "Poking" revised "Pointing"; also "Peking," after "china"). If the details are unfamiliar, the conventional message (say, "The heat wave has broken. Vacation almost over. Not really doing much. Found everything as you described it") is legible enough. But this telegraphic travelogue is unrepresentative of the sentences of "Houseboat Days," which in their easy breadth recall those of Henry James, whose late Odyssean tale of a long-delayed return home to oneself, "The Jolly Corner," seems to be written into the poem's latent environment, "as though one were always about to meet / One's double through the chain of cigar smoke" (HBD 38). The stylistic girders for "Houseboat Days" were taken from another prose artist, Walter Pater, two of whose sentences are collaged directly into the poem. Pater's intricately friendly lecturing style, from his 1893 lectures *Plato and Platonism,* amplifies the travel discourse of "Houseboat Days" with a parallel pursuit of knowledge. But Ashbery's new oratory has little of the conscious amateurism of "The System"; "the light / At the end of the tunnel" (HBD 39) is the poem's only unaltered cliché.

As it turns out, Pater's work also provided much of the argumentative framework for Ashbery's poem. In "Plato and the Sophists," the lecture from which Ashbery drew his sentences, Pater distinguishes two opposing tendencies of classical Greek life, the "centrifugal" and the "centripetal." The former, by which Pater links the Athenian sophistical method to Heraclitus' philosophy of motion, sounds like Ashbery's own improvisational tendency: "working with little forethought . . . throwing itself forth in endless play of undirected imagination; delighting in colour and brightness, moral and physical." In the "social and political order" Pater's centrifugal sophists advocate "individualism" and ceaseless political development. Opposed to this Ionian outward tendency to variety, diversity, and change is the centripetal "Dorian influence of a severe simplication everywhere," including a central, static, and reasonable government. Representing this centripetal alliance of central government and timeless truth, Plato argued in "opposition to the metaphysic of Heraclitus, to enforce the ideal of a sort of Parmenidean abstractness, and monotony or calm."[7]

It is easy enough for us to place the 1960s poet in the camp of fluctuation and revolution. "Houseboat Days" was itself rewritten in flux. After finishing the first verse paragraph roughly as it stands, Ashbery wrote two more paragraphs of thirty-six and forty-five lines; then, rather than revise the single-spaced typescript, he started over with what is now the second stanza, "Pinpricks of rain fall again," writing onward until he discovered a new direction. This performative method of revision preserves the initial impulse of writing forward rather than (or more than) writing over. Pater theorizes that the Heraclitean impulse to fluidity resulted partly from the geographical situation of the Athenians, "people of the coast who have the roaming thoughts of sailors, ever ready to float away anywhither amid their walls of wood" (24). Ashbery plays with this coastal tendency in a punning travel narrative: "You walk five feet along the shore, and you duck / As a common heresy sweeps over" (HBD 38). This sentence plays not only with "duck" but doubtless with the "heresy" of "Pelagianism" (named after "Pelagius," the "sea-side" dweller), an Emersonian denial of original sin and emphasis on individual freedom. Ashbery accordingly drifts, with his pleonastic "you," away from the pentameter's "five feet." The climactic image of "Houseboat Days," a memory as if of a Mediterranean voyage, is also Heraclitean: "A sail out of some afternoon, like the clear dark blue / Eyes of Harold in Italy, beyond amazement, astonished, / Apparently not tampered with" (HBD 40; the allusion to Byron's paradigmatic romantic tourist is certainly qualified, since Byron's sailors were drowned). Ashbery gazes here not at Italian skies or seas but through Byron's first-person eyes, which he shaded "dark blue" after the most copied line from "Childe Harold's Pilgrimage": "Roll on, thou deep and dark blue ocean—roll!" (IV, 1603).[8] Like Pater's sophists, Byron hymns change: "Thy shores are empires, changed in all save thee— / Assyria, Greece, Rome, Carthage, what are they?" (IV,

1630–31). In the Ionian "Houseboat Days," written in the wake of Richard Nixon's administration and Edward Heath's parliament, governments likewise dissolve in the Heraclitean wireless flux as, "from across the quite wide median," "a reply is broadcast: / 'Dissolve parliament. Hold new elections'" (HBD 39; for "median," "Mediterranean").

Fluctuating appearances to the contrary, however, Ashbery's argument in "Houseboat Days" is also crucially Platonic and anti-sophistic: while acknowledging motion, Ashbery denies the possibility of knowing. But in the houseboat frame of reference, knowledge (as of the Platonic forms) means staying put, whereas Socratic not-knowing means keeping moving. Ashbery's borrowings from Pater are misrepresented in order to graft Plato's centripetal stasis onto the sophist's centrifugal flux:

> To praise this, blame that,
> Leads one subtly away from the beginning, where
> We must stay, in motion. To flash light
> Into the house within, its many chambers,
> Its memories and associations, upon its inscribed
> And pictured walls, argues enough that life is various.
> (HBD 39)

The second sentence, revisiting both Plato's cave and the sphere of "Self-Portrait," modifies one of Pater's, which ended with "pictured walls": "To make men interested in themselves, as being the very ground of all reality for them, *la vraie vérité*, as the French say:—that was the essential function of the Socratic method: to flash light. . . ."[9] In "Houseboat Days" Ashbery replaces Socratic "verity" with sophistic "variety," a key term in Pater for the centrifugal impulse. Ashbery's first infinitive, a grammatical form itself representing timeless definition, alters Pater's translation from Plato's *Republic* 492, in which Plato argues that the real sophists are the fashionable Athenian public: "When seated together in their thousands at the great assemblies . . . with much noise the majority praise this and blame that in what is said and done, both alike in excess, shouting and clapping," so that the pliant youth, "borne down the stream," judges "the same thing as they fair or foul."[10] In Ashbery's sentence Plato's argument becomes a cautionary tale against the influence of criticism, an argument against argument itself and in favor of original impressions. Yet Ashbery ends by modifying his originary stasis, paradoxically and sophistically, with the image of a houseboat "where / We must stay, in motion" (HBD 39); even the central home from which we travel doesn't stay put in history.

The houseboat has two passengers. Like the argument in "Clepsydra," the implicit narrative scenario of "Houseboat Days" centers on a wounding argument between friends or lovers, which breaks the polite surface of daily life and is only mended by denial. This sudden experience is figured as a storm or wave ("The surge creates its own edge," HBD 39) or centrifugal earthquake registered "on the seismograph" (HBD 40), which rocks the "houseboat," represented variously as a hotel, a dark house, a "speeding train" (HBD 39), a "sail" boat (HBD 40), and a body. The rupture is experienced as pain; as in "Self-Portrait," the stanzas have permeable membranes, each one opening with a wound: "The skin is broken," "Pinpricks of rain fall again" (HBD 38, 39). The first of Pater's sentences injected into Ashbery's corpus is framed as a novelistic, Platonic dialogue:

> Really, he
> Said, that insincerity of reasoning on behalf of one's
> Sincere convictions, true or false in themselves
> As the case may be, to which, if we are unwise enough
> To argue at all with each other, we must be tempted
> At times—do you see where it leads? To pain
> (HBD 38)

In "Plato and the Sophists" Pater takes care not to confuse the Athenian practice of sophism with its modern equivalent, "'sophistry' of course, against which we have all of us to be on our guard—that insincerity of reasoning on behalf of sincere convictions, true or false in themselves as the case may be, to which, if we are unwise enough to argue at all with each other, we must all be tempted at times."[11] Ashbery's supplement to Pater's sentence, which ended here, marks an important departure both from accepted arguments and from his own previous one. In "The System" the experience of time was divided into frontal and latent happiness, the former characterized as a blissful ecstasy. Ashbery now describes this frontal experience as radically alienating, "a catastrophe on another planet to which / One has been invited," a numbness or shock commonly attested to by victims of sudden loss. This suspenseful rupture of ordinary experience, which separates the sufferer from the eyewitness, is recorded only as a hiatus in the historical manuscript: "And then it . . . happens" (HBD 38; Ashbery's ellipsis).

In "Houseboat Days," Ashbery's "Esthétique du Mal," frontal happiness has become frontal pain, and the experience of latent presence is likened in turn to foreboding before the fact, "as though one were always about to meet / One's double" (HBD 38), and denial afterward: "as though a universe of pain / Had been created just so as to deny its own existence" (HBD

39). This phenomenology of pain—reverberating through the poem in "brain," "rain," "train," and "spine"—is profoundly Dickinsonian, articulated in such powerful poems as "After great pain" (#341), "To fill a Gap" (#546), and "Pain—has an Element of Blank" (#650). Ashbery follows Dickinson in diverging from the received wisdom that "suffering brings knowledge," a saying already proverbial in Aeschylus' *Agamemnon.* For Ashbery, as for Dickinson, pain brings no knowledge—no deeper understanding, for instance, between forgiving lovers. "Houseboat Days" thus contains the blueprint for the long poem "A Wave"—which also quotes from Pater, argues against knowing, favors infinitives, reverberates "pain," and figures the shock as a wave. In the first draft of "Houseboat Days" the wave itself produced a centrifugal wake: "Facing away from the center which it defines in this way." The initial "hiccup," liable to "explode the center to the extremities of life" (TP 53), gave a similar shock to "The System."

Plato's Socrates knew only that he did not know; Ashbery's passenger, beside himself with pain, gazing "As in the window of some distant, speeding train," knows only that he moves: "It would be deplorable if the rain also washed away / This profile at the window that moves, and moves on, / Knowing that it moves, and knows nothing else" (HBD 39; "pane," "pain"). The ineffable experience is marked grammatically by "It," appearing first in the expletive ("It would be deplorable"), then in the pronominal position, in which "it" points, if not names. "It" happens in "Houseboat Days" as an unknowable central truth, which can captivate a generation of time travelers: "It is the light / At the end of the tunnel as it might be seen / By him looking out somberly at the shower, / The picture of hope a dying man might turn away from, / Realizing that hope is something else, something concrete / You can't have" (HBD 39). Ashbery aligns this liminal truth, a relativistic "light at the end of the tunnel," with St. Paul's view of otherworldly knowledge. Now we know only in part, as through a narrative glass darkly ("somberly"), which results in the hotel-bound tourist's despair, palpable enough in the antonymous replacement of "abstract" with "concrete." In the wake or waking realization of not knowing or possessing "it," Ashbery imagines a latent carnal restlessness: "it becomes a vast dream / Of having that can topple governments, level towns and cities / With the pressure of sleep building up behind it" (HBD 39). Ashbery will synchronize private and national upheavals in "A Wave," but nowhere more powerfully than in "Houseboat Days" does he link the "acquisition of knowledge" with the destructive capitalist enterprise. In the first draft of "Houseboat Days," as at the close of "The New Spirit," fixed Platonic constellations, "hung like the weaving of an unknowable / Tribe," appeared behind the centrifugal, changeable weather as a guarantee (as in "Clepsydra") that "whatever one sleeps at, / Or wakes up doing, is the right thing." But all centripetal traces of providential fixity are removed from the final version, where obscurity prevails "As the rain gathers and protects / Its own darkness" (HBD 40). "Houseboat Days" ends not with an affirmation of blind faith but with denial, a darker narrative first outlined in "Some Trees": "the place in the slipcover is noticed / For the first and last time, fading like the spine / Of an adventure novel behind glass, behind the teacups" (HBD 40). So too domestic life is mended like a slipcover when the painful incident is glossed over. The "adventure novel" is preserved behind a glass darkly and, as in "The Instruction Manual," dailiness resumes.

One of Ashbery's finest anti-confessional poems, "Wet Casements" (HBD 28; dated March 22, 1975), grew out of an embarrassing and frustrating experience. A poet paid the newly famous Ashbery a visit: "He began asking questions that I found very deep and almost painful to contemplate. This strange transformation interested me very much. At one point it was almost as if we were seeing ourselves in each other. I was looking at him but it seemed as though I was looking at myself. He pointed out this phenomenon." [12] Ashbery found an analogy for this experience in Kafka's unfinished story, "Wedding Preparations in the Country," which provided him with his epigraph: "When Eduard Raban, coming along the passage, walked into the open doorway, he saw that it was raining. It was not raining much." What interests Ashbery here is the device narrative theorists call focalization: the reader views Raban's view of the rain: "It was not raining much." This voyeuristic "look of others through / Their own eyes" becomes uncomfortable when the look, with its own point of view, turns on oneself. Another passage from Kafka's story describes something like Ashbery's experience with the visiting poet. Raban notices a woman looking at him:

> She did so indifferently, and she was perhaps, in any case, only looking at the falling rain in front of him. . . . Raban thought she looked amazed. "Well," he thought. . . . "One works so feverishly at the office that afterwards one is too tired even to enjoy one's holidays properly. But even all that work does not give one a claim to be treated lovingly by everyone; on the contrary, one is alone, a total stranger and only an object of curiosity. And so long as you say 'one' instead of 'I,' there's nothing in it and one can easily tell the story; but as soon as you admit to yourself that it is you yourself, you feel as though transfixed and are horrified." [13]

The narrative deflection of the gaze onto a generalizing pronoun or a character's name is costly: it divides "I" from "myself," consciousness from self-consciousness. Their wedding preparations never end.

In "Wet Casements" the troubling interdependence of one upon others and upon oneself is inescapable. But the tearful "streaming windowpanes" show how painful objectification can be.[14] The misrepresentation of Ashbery in his readers' "digest of their correct impressions" of him is as alienating as it is "interesting." Ashbery already felt the splitting of his published from his private personality in "Worsening Situation": "This severed hand" that writes "is ever / A stranger who walks beside me." Efforts at the reintegration of one's self, at the repossession of one's name, sound hysterical: "The name you drop and never say is mine, mine!" (SP 3). The author here promises "Some day I'll claim to you how all used up / I am because of you" (SP 3), and "Wet Casements" keeps that promise. The poem is measured into dwindling sentences and three shrinking stanzas. The first and longest stanza consists of a series of appositional clauses and sentences revolving around "you." Its nuclear argument runs as follows: It is interesting to see the look of others at oneself, a digest of their impressions; "You" are the result ("snapshot") of your name being circulated. With an elongated, drugged sentence, "You in falbalas / . . . the cosmetics, / The shoes perfectly pointed," the poet (ad)dresses himself in the second person. But the submerged sensual drift exceeds simple negation. "You" is also powerfully attracted toward its narcissistic image: "Like a bottle-imp toward a surface which can never be approached, / Never pierced through." Whether or not one is alone, the hymeneal mirror surface remains unbroken. The "bottle-imp" is a scientific toy consisting of a hollow figure in a column of water, which responds to varying pressure by rising, plunging, and remaining in suspension. Its other name, the Cartesian devil, brings Descartes's reflective cogito into Ashbery's picture.[15] Our composite "Ashbery" is "an epistemological snapshot" of associations: New York School experimentalist, important writer, difficult poet, and so forth. In the literary market his famed "name circulates," a loaded phrase in which the name is already recognized as cultural capital: "someone" picked up the name dropped "and carried that name around in his wallet / For years as the wallet crumbled and bills slid in / And out of it" ("wall," "Bill"). One's name is also subject to deterioration.

The first stanza of "Wet Casements" does not break after that simile, as we would expect, but after an incomplete sentence: "I want that information very much today, // Can't have it, and this makes me angry." The desire to recover one's name cannot be realized. Ashbery's frustration, now in the first person, produces another desire and a beautiful complex image, a Pauline mirror-bridge: "I shall at last see my complete face / Reflected not in the water but in the worn stone floor of my bridge." Ashbery's poetry is his communication bridge, which includes both himself and his circle of readers, joined in a round dance ("sur le pont d'Avignon on y danse, on y danse"). The bridge, "worn" like a costume or billfold, reconstructs, with Crane's assistance, Whitman's "Crossing Brooklyn Ferry." Whitman too imagined "the look of others": "Just as you feel when you look on the river and sky, so I felt" (309), a syntax mirrored in "Wet Casements": "(how long you / Have been drifting; how long I have too for that matter)." Whitman's image returns to him not through a glass darkly but face to face: "Flood-tide below me! I see you face to face!" (307). But Ashbery's reflection is still partial. Like Kafka's story and the middle stanza of "Wet Casements," the bridge at Avignon is incomplete. The Pauline prophecy remains unfulfilled because communication is still under construction.

Yet the closing stanzaic couplet seems perfectly self-contained: "I shall keep to myself. / I shall not repeat others' comments about me." Harold Bloom praises this stanza for its "sermon-like directness."[16] It is true that the "I want" of the first stanza yields to four prophecies beginning "I shall." But the self-commandments of the last stanza are marked discursively as a journal entry. Even in these published private resolutions to keep oneself and one's name private, oneself is two: two lines and sentences each with "I" on one end mirroring its reflective object, "myself" and "me," on the other. Privacy, Ashbery realizes, can be no healing alternative to publicity. The mirrors of other people, however distorted and reductive, are the only looking-glasses around.

Another bridge is drawn in the five disintegrated stanzas of "The Wrong Kind of Insurance" (dated April 12, 1976). As signaled by the mention of the New York "post-office inscription about rain or snow / Or gloom of night" (HBD 49), "The Wrong Kind of Insurance" enters into the postal or communications system comprised of a sender, a messenger with a message, and a receiver. With intriguing waywardness, Ashbery relates Herodotus' "archaic meanings" (HBD 49) to another national system, the insurance system, a collective form of security of person and property (including mail) in the event of an accident. If you have the wrong kind of insurance, you're not "covered," are exposed to the elements like the dedicated postal courier. (The first draft included the exclamation, "This umbrella saved my life," the umbrella being the logo of Travelers insurance.) Ending up unloved, undelivered into the shelter of another's arms, also means not being covered, left unclaimed out on the "cold, open / Shore of sorrows" (HBD 50).

Ashbery opens "The Wrong Kind of Insurance" with an increasingly common gambit: a few words from a representative American, nonlyrical "I":

I teach in a high school
And see the nurses in some of the hospitals

And if all teachers are like that
Maybe I can give you a buzz some day,
Maybe we can get together for lunch or coffee or something.
(HBD 49)

In this postal exchange, someone hands someone else, as Ashbery hands us, a line. The appeal is painfully "insincere"; it is illogical, confused, clichéd, and progressively, hopelessly indefinite. As sentimental as nature, with its "tattered / Foliage, wise old treetrunks, rainbow tissue-paper wadded / Clouds," this sender "wants / To be loved" (HBD 50) not for his delivery but for himself. Ashbery too "knows we know" (HBD 50) about his artificial confidence game: "Yes, friends, these clouds pulled along on invisible ropes / Are, as you have guessed, merely stage machinery" (HBD 50)— which doesn't lessen their appeal.

Circulating in so many different and overlapping systems, no American sender can make either a very coherent or a very original appeal to any other. Each sender builds his or her love letter out of reusable alphabet blocks. Ashbery begins his third stanza with the first letter, his own initial: "All of our lives is a rebus / Of little wooden animals painted shy, / Terrific colors" (HBD 49). As in the first chapter of Walter Abish's *How German Is It,* Ashbery's A dictates its own story: "we have winter in August / As they do in Argentina and Australia" (HBD 49). The capital A—a summit and ladder and house—has long held a romantic appeal for New World male writers, from Hawthorne to the insurance executive Stevens to Zukofsky. But in "The Wrong Kind of Insurance," A is just another piece of the American puzzle.

If America is ideally "one nation, indivisible," Ashbery's America, in this bicentennial-year poem, is a rebus of irreparably divisible, disunited figures: "We straggle on as quotients, hard-to-combine / Ingredients" (HBD 50). The last stanza, fissured by interlinear breaks, is itself a "hard-to-combine" conclusion. It was originally an independent poem, "'To Whinny Muir Thou Comst at Last,'" entitled after a line from the Scottish ballad "A Lyke-Wake Dirge" (cf. "your comic / Dirge routine," HBD 50).[17] In the ballad, "Whinny-muir" is the "furzy moor" to which one comes at death. In "The Wrong Kind of Insurance" the final destination is a dead-letter office in which the published message "will be lost on the unfolding sheaves / Of the wind." Insuring himself against this fate, Ashbery binds his leaves, his multiple lives, into an atomized seductive essence: "this distilled, / Dispersed musk." These poems, like their author, are "the product" of too much circulation. Nevertheless, the mail or "male" is delivered, "trifoliate, strange to the touch" (HBD 50), a phrase recalling Freud's association of the male genitalia with the number "three." If no one gets the message, at least one keeps in touch.

No Ashbery poem is more the product "of too many / Comings and go-ings" (HBD 50) than "Daffy Duck in Hollywood" (published in 1975) with its cavalcade of action-painted extras: "Not people, comings and goings, more: mutterings, splatterings" (HBD 32).[18] Whitman, responding in "Song of Myself" to "Trippers and askers" curious about the influence on his po-etry of the "latest dates, discoveries, inventions, societies, authors old and new," and, more intimately, of "The real or fancied indifference of some man or woman I love," likewise fends off his comings and goings: "These come to me days and nights and go from me again, / But they are not the Me myself" (191). Invaded by "effectively equipped infantries of happy-go-nutty / Vegetal jacqueries" (HBD 32), the poet newly arrived in "Holly-wood" is besieged by a growing legion of admirers, both animate and inani-mate (two crypt words underpinning this animated cartoon-poem). But the inanimate objects are the poet's secret allies, diverting readers from more animated encounters. In a complaint lodged against allegorically-minded critics, Ashbery cited the "strange objects" that "avalanche into the poem" as evidence: "I meant them to be there for themselves, and not for some hidden meaning. . . . They are just the things that I selected to be exhibited in the poem at that point."[19] The poem, which seems to sense the creepy presence of its readers ("Something strange is creeping across me," HBD 31) is itself something of a cautionary tale against reading signs and wonders into everything.

At a reading, Ashbery recalled the improbable genesis of "Daffy":

> I went to a program of animated cartoons at a museum in New York a year or so ago and at the same time I was reading *Paradise Lost*. There was a Daffy Duck cartoon ["Duck Amuck"] in which you see the pencil of the cartoonist [Bugs Bunny] sort of adding extra limbs and erasing the head and various parts . . . and I somehow subconsciously associated this with the idea of God in the first book of *Paradise Lost,* who has always seemed to me very comically conspicuous by his absence. . . . So I seemed to have somehow associated Satan with Daffy Duck. . . . They are somewhat alike.[20]

So are Ashbery and his animated alter-ego; Ashbery once thought of con-fessing "I am Daffy Duck" in the middle of *Flow Chart*.[21] Dissolved into a single 120-line stanza (with one mid-line pause), "Daffy" resembles a pol-luted, American "Clepsydra." The jarring mixed signals owe as much to Las Vegas as to Hollywood; Ashbery had evidently learned enough from Robert

Venturi's *Learning from Las Vegas* (1972) to construct a poem less like a storm than a "strip" (a street, a comic strip, and a strip-tease). Even during his fifteen minutes of fame, Ashbery knows that his name may one day elude us. Like an old comic strip character, the former household name slips from memory. Other densely populated Ashbery poems have preceded "Daffy": "Rivers and Mountains," with its impossibly allegorical map and its Americana; "The Skaters," with its collections; and "Soonest Mended," with Happy Hooligan rescuing Ingres's Angelica. But "Daffy" descends most directly from Ashbery's bad-mannered sestina, "Farm Implements and Rutabagas in a Landscape," with its Miltonic absent divinity, Popeye. In "Farm Implements" Popeye manifests himself as thunder: "It was domestic thunder, / The color of spinach" (DDS 48). "Daffy," split by the one-liner "The storm finished brewing" (HBD 33; that is, the storm broke), ends with an apocalyptic sky (on loan from Flaubert's "Un coeur simple"): "We don't mind / Or notice any more that the sky *is* green, a parrot / One" (HBD 34). But in this daffy storm, the thunder has its say. With its dated references and its recherché vocabulary, "Daffy" emulates the allusive block paragraphs of Milton's all-inclusive epic. Daffy even borrows Satan's self-aggrandizing self-portrait, "While I / Abroad through all the coasts of dark destruction seek / Deliverance for us all" (HBD 33; II, 463–65). So too, we are to believe, the author of "Daffy" scours the West Coast for the redeeming features of his postmodern leveled playing field.

Like "The Wrong Kind of Insurance" and "Wet Casements," "Daffy" combines the postal system with what we might call the democratic system, expressed in the paradoxical "e pluribus unum." "One" is represented by the sky, silence, the storm, and God, indicated, as in Dante's *Inferno,* only in paraphrase: "If he is the result of himself, how much the better / For him we ought to be!" (HBD 33). In this communication the poet, bewildered receiver of indecipherable, possibly meaningless, sacred and profane messages, takes our end of the party line. In the congested spaces of the first ten lines of "Daffy" a Rojas play, a Billie Holiday song, a Handel opera, an instantly collectible baking-powder can, a "celluloid earring" ("film clip," "clip-on"), a cartoon speedster, a popular novelist, tastefully printed pornography, and a Hollywood intersection, all contend for our shrinking attention span. Even the author of "Self-Portrait" gets warped: "That mean old cartoonist, but just look what he's / Done to me now! I scarce dare approach me mug's attenuated / Reflection in yon hubcap" (HBD 31). The characteristic American response is to move and read on. The irresistibly animated but interminably divisible "Daffy Duck" keeps us "reading without comprehension" (TP 13), until Daffy tortuously concludes, rejecting the romantic close of "Self-Portrait": "No one really knows / Or cares whether this is the whole of which parts / Were vouchsafed—once—but to be ambling on's / The tradition more than the safekeeping of it" (HBD 34).

Yet the poem is persistently apocalyptic, and the storm heralds a Miltonic punishment. Behind the neon signs of "Daffy" both sexual and poetic license is taken. On the allegorical Map of Love, featuring "algolagnic *nuits blanches,*" Amadis entices the liberated Princesse de Clèves for a "midnight micturition spree" (HBD 32; "swim," "spray"). Daffy the prophetic poet becomes the sidewalk preacher announcing the wide way to Hell: "This wide, tepidly meandering, / Civilized Lethe . . . / . . . leads to Tophet" (HBD 32), the oblivion of dead poets and sinners. But is Hollywood or New York really Sodom or Gomorrah? Ashbery's irreverent response is to break and make camp: "Therefore bivouac we / On this great, blond highway, unimpeded by / Veiled scruples, worn conundrums. Morning is / Impermanent. Grab sex things" (HBD 34; "condoms"). But "Daffy" ends not with more racket but quietly, with the echo of a new covenant: we "have our earnest where it chances on us, / Disingenuous, intrigued, inviting more, / Always invoking the echo, a summer's day" (HBD 34). This final acceptance is no value-free postmodernism. What Ashbery invokes is a lifelong latent homotextual echo. By resisting the puritanical prophets of doom, and by eroticizing cultural paraphernalia, the poet makes his own liberating "political statement." His response to the defenders of high moral and aesthetic seriousness is itself in lively earnest.

With its flat, outgoing free verses, "Pyrography" (dated February 8, 1976; the art of pyrographic writing is featured in *Three Hundred Things a Bright Boy Can Do,* the book Ashbery used to construct "The Skaters") picks up where "Daffy" leaves off. Ashbery was by now eminent enough to attract governmental attention (a frightening prospect); the poem was commissioned by the United States Department of the Interior for a Bicentennial traveling exhibit of American landscape paintings called "America 1976." (In a painstaking feat, his friend Larry Rivers painted "Pyrography" verbatim behind the figure of Ashbery at the typewriter, the whole crossed by bars of muted red, white, and blue.) Though Parmigianino's "commission" "never materialized" (SP 69), Ashbery's "Pyrography" fulfills its own contract to the Department of the "Interior," the poem's encrypted cornerstone. Ashbery views American history through its interior decorations. At the century's turn, "The climate was still floral and all the wallpaper / In a million homes all over the land conspired to hide it. / One day we thought of painted furniture" (HBD 9). Americans interiorize their landscapes: "The land wasn't immediately appealing; we built it / Partly over with fake ruins, in the image of ourselves" (HBD 9). And America is represented by its interior, the Midwest: "Out here on Cottage Grove it matters" (HBD 8).

A "central perimeter" (DDS 82), the Midwest is paradoxically "Out here" (not "in here" or "out there"). On Cottage Grove Avenue, a long street in Chicago leading to the suburbs, the synecdochal "it" "matters." The United States, and the centuries, turn on their midwestern axis, "like a creaking revolving stage in Warren, Ohio" (HBD 8). One center of gravity for America is its place names. A 1974 poem with an irresistible title, "The One Thing That Can Save America," begins by asking "Is anything central?" For example, "Are place names central? / Elm Grove, Adcock Corner, Story Book Farm?" (SP 44). In "American Names" (1927), the popular poem that gave us the testament "bury my heart at Wounded Knee," Stephen Vincent Benét likewise pondered the place names of America: "The plumed war bonnet of Medicine Hat, / Tucson and Deadwood and Lost Mule Flat." [22] But Ashbery's "Story Book Farm," compounded of Stony Brook (Long Island) and Brook Farm (the utopian Massachusetts community of the 1840s) suggests that his America is located on a map of no single projection: "These are connected to my version of America / But the juice is elsewhere" (SP 44).

America's interior lies midway in history. Frost's America was still "vaguely realizing westward," but Ashbery's restless settlers are interrupted: "midway / We meet the disappointed, returning ones" (HBD 8). Like the reflecting bridge at the end of "Wet Casements," America's monument is still under construction: "An arch that terminates in mid-keystone, a crumbling stone pier / For laundresses, an open-air theater, never completed / And only partially designed" (HBD 9). As Ashbery wrote a few years later of the experimental architect Aldo Rossi, "Rossi sees the city itself as . . . continuously coming into being—a concept perpetually modified by the exigencies of everyday reality, where what is unbuilt or incomplete has a function no less important than what is actually there" (RS 335). Or as Daffy puts it, "what maps, what / Model cities, how much waste space. Life, our / Life anyway, is between" (HBD 34). "It," then, is neither America's final utopian ideals, nor its mythic historical origins, but daily life under way. "To be able to write the history of our time" (HBD 9), Ashbery writes in this prolegomenon to any contemporary American history, one must turn partially away from its major events and figures: "not just the major events but the whole incredible / Mass of everything happening simultaneously and pairing off, / Channeling itself into history" (HBD 10). Standing out with their proper names forever engraved in our memory, the major events and persons of American history are unrepresentative. What matters on Cottage Grove (as well as on Broadway and Telegraph) cannot be named, envisioned, remembered, or even known, but can be recognized nevertheless as "something one can / Tip one's hat to" (HBD 10). [23]

Ashbery adapts a temporal, musical form most concisely in "Blue Sonata" (originally "Sonatina"). The sonata form has two halves (modulation to a new key and back to the tonic) and three parts: exposition in the first half, development and recapitulation in the second. Use of the form has waned in the twentieth century; as Ashbery has remarked, "reality . . . does not naturally take the form of a sonnet or a sonata."[24] Musical analogies are always hazardous, but the three-stanza form of "Blue Sonata" invites the comparison.[25] Ashbery's sonata scores our musical development from the "present past" toward the future. Its willfully philosophical beginning will remind many readers of the opening movement of Eliot's *Four Quartets:*

> Long ago was the then beginning to seem like now
> As now is but the setting out on a new but still
> Undefined way. *That* now, the one once
> Seen from far away, is our destiny
> No matter what else may happen to us. It is
> The present past of which our features,
> Our opinions are made.
> (HBD 66)

This exposition relies on the relativity of the shifters "then" and "now." The odd locution "the then" points to the quondam future that developed into our present, "now." The present likewise "is our destiny," developing into another future. Ashbery varies Eliot's theme, "Time present and time past / Are both perhaps present in time future" (117), by encrypting and pluralizing "future" in "features." Near the end of the first stanza, which includes lines breaking on "now," "we," "is," and "to be," the poem modulates, via "becoming," into a new key, from B ("Blue," "beginning") into C ("coming"): "becoming before becoming may be seen" (HBD 66). The development now "unrolls" and sets everything in motion—"coming to be," "come and gone," and "passing through" (HBD 66–67). Near the end of the second movement, the third theme is announced with "Each image fits into place." The recapitulation of "Blue Sonata," in the key of Re or D and noted by the hyphenated neologisms "re-imagine" and "re-inventing," recalls the claustrophobia of "Self-Portrait," where the soulless soul "fits / Its hollow perfectly" (SP 69): "It would be tragic to fit / Into the space created by our not having arrived yet" (HBD 67). "Ashbery has arrived," as the blurbs have it, but a recapitulation of past successes would be disastrously predictable.

Since "Two Scenes" (ST 9) fate has been a frequent topic in Ashbery's poetry. If life were really a sonata, "We could re-imagine the other half, deducing it / From the shape of what is seen" (HBD 67), as one might recognize one's Aristophanic "other half" at first sight. For the future to be more than the realized dead end of the "present past," this desirable "other half" must be carefully violated. The future here mirrors the past through the latent *via negativa* of half-forgetting rather than the strait way of remembering: "progress occurs through re-inventing / These words from a dim recollection of them, / In violating that space in such a way as / To leave it intact" (HBD 67). In this homotextual affirmation, one penetrates the future without wholly knowing it, so that "*That* now" holds further developments.

Unlike the prospective "Blue Sonata," the humble narrative of "Street Musicians" (HBD 1; written in 1975) remains tied to its past. Opening on "One," the first poem of *Houseboat Days* constructs a myth of origins. Divided into two short stanzaic scenes—the first taking the past tense and the third person, the second the present and the first—"Street Musicians" resembles two earlier proems, "Two Scenes" and "At North Farm." Like the two musicians, the two stanzas cannot be reunited. Yet the story somehow bridges the chasm. After "One died," the dispirited survivor "walking the streets" (and walking "on and on") tracks his ghostly other ("volumetrics, shadows"). At last, the dear departed reveals himself to the survivor, like a "beached" whale from the outer or inner depths. These "Revelations at last" appear less apocalyptic than scandalous since "they grew to hate and forget" rather than to forgive and forget "each other."[26] The other isolated stanza begins with an abandoned mother's story: "So I cradle this average violin that knows / Only forgotten showtunes, but argues / The possibility of free declamation anchored / To a dull refrain." In an earlier draft the stanza began, "Meanwhile I walk this bleating mandolin." Ashbery may have deleted "bleating" because lambs bleat in Keats's "To Autumn" and because it resonates "bleeding" (heart). In any case, in the present version, "cradle" submerges the sentimental image of the one left holding the baby, the "average" of its parents. The new verb also recalls Whitman's "Out of the Cradle," with its mourning love bird. Ashbery's revision of "Meanwhile" to "So" also matters. While "So" preserves the simultaneity of its forerunner, it also means "as a result" and, secondarily, "likewise." These two meanings are connected. In Ashbery's temporal reflexivity, the past is recovered involuntarily, when one acts (or sings, like Picasso's and Stevens's *The Man with the Blue Guitar*) in like manner. The rebus of this temporal reflex is drawn in "the year turning over on itself" and in the smoke signal curling like a question mark. Origins are recovered by imitations, the leaving of likenesses. But perhaps origins are invented after the fact; Ashbery's "question of a place of origin" misrepresents "quest for." The question is raised by a deliberate trail of leavings: autumn leaves, an evicted "family," a "beached" whale, old showtunes, "meat . . . on the bone," smoke, and "Our trash, sperm, and excrement everywhere." The gay action-lovers smear their remains on the landscape in an effort at understanding and creation, at making sense. But the "place of origin" of these leavings remains unknown, even to the campers. What matters is that the question is undertaken.

"Syringa" (written in 1975), one of Ashbery's finest poems, is in many ways the most ambitious undertaking in *Houseboat Days*. Like "Self-Portrait," "Syringa" begins with a given subject matter, the myth of Orpheus and Eurydice, which may account in part for the poem's popularity. Yet "Syringa," which maintains the third person throughout, is not the elegy its underlying narrative might lead us to expect. It lacks the sentimental pathos of its humble companion-piece, "Street Musicians," for instance, and the personal intensity of "Wet Casements." Eurydice appears mainly as an afterthought. "Orpheus liked the glad personal quality / Of the things beneath the sky," Ashbery begins, adding quickly, "Of course, Eurydice was a part / Of this" (HBD 69). Ashbery's Orpheus derives from Ovid's, who, after losing Eurydice a second time, set an example to the Thracians by loving boys (*Metamorphoses* X). This retelling of the Orpheus myth will show us how to sing the past without looking back for it.

The title "Syringa" sends us in several directions. Flowers of the genus syringa include the mock orange—a saxifrage like "the tiny, sparkling yellow flowers / Growing around the brink of the quarry" (HBD 70)—and the "lilac," Whitman's fragrant metonymy, preserving the consonants of "Lincoln," who remains unnamed in Whitman's elegy. But Ashbery, who dons the mantle of the historian rather than the mourner, espousing not cathartic but accurate songs, keeps his loss, if there was one, unrecoverable. "Syringa" also points toward Syrinx, an Arcadian nymph who was pursued by Pan, changed into a reed, and finally turned into a "syrinx" or "panpipe" by her frustrated lover (the story is told by Ovid in *Metamorphoses* I). But Pan passes unmentioned in "Syringa," and Syrinx is only fleetingly glimpsed in "the tossing reeds of that slow, / Powerful stream" (HBD 70). Moreover, the consolation prize of song, awarded to both Pan and Orpheus, is insufficient for Ashbery, who argues that "it isn't enough / To just go on singing" (HBD 70) as though nothing had happened. What might be called the elegiac myth of poetry, that the death or loss of the subject is the birth or gain of the song, offers this singer little comfort. He cannot hold on to his song, "Syringa," any more than to its vanished subject matter. Like Keats's "Ode to a Nightingale," the reflexive "Syringa" is its own elegy; it laments the song lost in its singing.[27]

"Syringa" begins like "Street Musicians," with an oval "O" and a sudden break—the egg of "Orpheus" dividing into three successive instances of the capitalized genitive "Of." Oneness shatters in the threadbare formula in which everything and nothing gets related: "Then one day, everything changed" (HBD 69). In response to the grief of Orpheus the sympathetic blue egg of the sky seems about to fall: "The sky shudders from one horizon / To the other, almost ready to give up wholeness" (HBD 69). Yeats's "shudder in the loins," which engendered history's tragic egg in "Leda and the Swan,"[28] certainly reverberates in Ashbery's sky. The crack in Nature is compounded by the rift between the present and the past, personified by a chiding Apollo: "'Leave it all on earth. / Your lute, what point? Why pick at a dull pavan few care to / Follow, . . . / Not vivid performances of the past'" (HBD 69).[29] Coming from the god of music, the question challenges; no historically minded poet can evade it. Harold Bloom claims, on the dust jacket of *Self-Portrait in a Convex Mirror,* that Ashbery "is joining that American sequence that includes Whitman, Dickinson, Stevens, and Hart Crane." Ashbery heeds his precursors, "tall guardians / Of yesterday," at the beginning of "Business Personals" (a poem he associates with "Syringa"[30]):

> The disquieting muses again: what are "leftovers"?
> Perhaps they have names for it all, who come bearing
> Worn signs of privilege whose authority
> Speaks out of the accumulation of age and faded colors
> To the center of today. Floating heart, why
> Wander on senselessly? The tall guardians
> Of yesterday are steep as cliff shadows;
> Whatever path you take abounds in their sense.
> (HBD 18)

Though Ashbery has his own ideas about influence, one could not ask for a more trenchant restatement of Bloom's theory. Before Orpheus can reply to Apollo's Bloomian challenge, the narrator cuts in and answers for him: "But why not? / All other things must change too." "The seasons," like the poets, "are no longer what they once were," but their faded virtues fit each other (HBD 69). Only contemporaries, the argument goes, speak to contemporary reality.

"Syringa" argues for "change," the English word for Ovid's "metamorphosis." Ashbery speaks against the kind of ahistorical "epistemological snapshot" that stereotyped him in "Wet Casements": "For although memories, of a season, for example, / Melt into a single snapshot, one cannot guard, treasure / That stalled moment. It too is flowing, fleeting" (HBD 70). Though this passage, which now seems to augur *Flow Chart,* puts everything into flux, we shouldn't conclude, for instance, that Ashbery doesn't have "treasured memories" or that his poetry precludes climactic, epiphanic moments. Like Proust and Wordsworth before him, Ashbery has learned that one must turn away from the frontal happiness of those prophetic moments in order to keep them. In the epiphany of "Syringa," one of the towering moments in Ashbery's poetry, the portentous poem itself flashes away:

> Its subject
> Matters too much, and not enough, standing there helplessly
> While the poem streaked by, its tail afire, a bad
> Comet screaming hate and disaster, but so turned inward
> That the meaning, good or other, can never
> Become known. The singer thinks
> Constructively, builds up his chant in progressive stages
> Like a skyscraper, but at the last minute turns away.
> The song is engulfed in an instant in blackness
> Which must in turn flood the whole continent
> With blackness, for it cannot see.
> (HBD 71)

The turn away avoids Orpheus's error of regarding but still loses "The song" to "blackness." Such eclipses dot Ashbery's career, from "The Mythological Poet" to "Clepsydra" to the end of "The New Spirit," and on to the "cimmerian moment" of "A Wave." The blind prophetic moment engulfs the poet's Tower in "flames" (under "blackness"). But what kind of blind, charred construction remains? For a poem to change, the poet must relinquish its Eurydicean "subject / Matters." As the singer "turns away," his construction is "turned inward." Ashbery's poetics are in this regard essentially new-critical: "I think of my poems as independent objects or little worlds which are self-referential."[31] But this introversion is above all defensively self-reflexive, protecting its final meaning from critics who would judge it prematurely. Citing Shakespeare's Hector, Ashbery remarks that "The end crowns all" so long as the towers of Troy are still standing (HBD 70; *Troilus and Cressida,* IV, v, 224). As in "Street Musicians," introversion also lets the poet keep the past by unknowingly imitating it. "Syringa" ends with the singers buried in the library stacks,

> Frozen and out of touch until an arbitrary chorus
> Speaks of a totally different incident with a similar name
> In whose tale are hidden syllables

Of what happened so long before that
In some small town, one indifferent summer.
(HBD 71)

The rebirth Ashbery describes here resembles his own unintentional procedure of composing by crypt words. We don't know—nor perhaps does Ashbery—what syllables are hidden here, or whether this concluding "summer," recalling the end of "Daffy Duck" and Roussel's "The View," is
confessional or representative. But few of us would imagine that such a summer was "indifferent."

What makes the summer, and the elegiac poet, "indifferent"? As in
"Scheherazade," the adjective completes the typical range of judgments,
"good, bad, or indifferent," launched by the "bad / Comet" ("comment")
and the "meaning, good or other." The poet's meteoric rise should pass
without comment or judgment, even from its author. Earlier still, we were
warned that music, like time and Eurydice, "passes, emblematic / Of life
and how you cannot isolate a note of it / And say it is good or bad" (HBD
70). When we and the past no longer matter to each other, like a pair of
indifferent lovers, we can sing accurately. So too the good poet remains indifferent to bad comets. In a Stevensian mood, Ashbery asserts that "Singing accurately"—in a nonce word (merging "encapsulates" and "epito-
mizes")—"encapsulizes / The different weights of the things" (HBD 70).
In his elegy for his teacher Santayana, Stevens, singer of "accurate songs"
(214), instructs himself to "Be orator but with an accurate tongue / And
without eloquence" (372). Ashbery's Orpheus makes a similar, self-reflexive
claim for veracity: "these are of course not regrets at all, / Merely a careful,
scholarly setting down of / Unquestioned facts, a record of pebbles along
the way" (HBD 71; "peoples"). Does critical detachment translate into aesthetic distance? The author, "standing there helplessly / While the poem"
is judged good, bad, or indifferent, must remain indifferent to his own canonization or oblivion. Ashbery realizes that "Stellification / Is for the few,
and comes about much later" (HBD 71).

---

Even a cursory comparison of "Fantasia on 'The Nut-Brown Maid,'" the
long poem of *Houseboat Days,* with its precursor, "Self-Portrait in a Convex
Mirror," reveals how far the newly stellified poet went to avoid repeating
himself. Instead of the surging and falling rhythms which open "Self-
Portrait," "Fantasia" mixes its opening balladic tetrameter with lines of insistently prosaic rhythm, sound, and vocabulary ("figpeckers" are small fig-
eating birds): "Be it right or wrong, these men among / Others in the park,

all those years in the cold, / Are a plain kind of thing: bands / Of acanthus and figpeckers" (HBD 72).[32] "Self-Portrait" proceeds from topic to topic like a verse essay; "Fantasia" moves in circles of intricate argumentation. The poem is structured as a dialogue between HE and SHE, the interlocutors of the ballad "The Nut-Brown Maid," from which Ashbery also drew his opening line. But the characters are displaced and disembodied. Auden's *The Age of Anxiety* may have provided Ashbery with a model of nondramatic dialogue in which it is not the plot but understanding that advances, what Ashbery calls "Patience / Of articulation between us" (#24, HBD 84). Among Ashbery's published works, "Fantasia" most closely resembles the densely reasoned, implicitly dialogic "Fragment." Its abstracted formality is also anticipated by an early one-page fantasia on "The Nut-Brown Maid," "The Perfect Orange" (dated June 1946): "HE: Foregoing, foregoing / It seems we have foregone / Whatever was in the beginning / The end of sacrifice"; "SHE: Yes, there is strength in numbers. / But I often wish that the stars / And the numberless walking crowds / Were not so much alike"; "BOTH: We have given ourselves away. / The chase has a beast in view / And the name of the beast is Time."[33] The beast was captured thirty years later. Ashbery preserved only the prose coda of "Fantasia" in his *Selected Poems* (1985), where the long poems "Self-Portrait" and "A Wave" are reproduced in full—conceding perhaps that "Fantasia" was more of a shield than a greeting, as though designed chiefly to ward off the easy adulation of its prize-winning forerunner. The poem has accomplished that goal: alone among his long poems, it has so far received no extended reading, and it has passed unmentioned by poets writing in his wake.

Like "Self-Portrait," "Fantasia" is based on a Renaissance work, the anonymous sixteenth-century ballad "The Nut-Brown Maid." Courtly rather than popular, the ballad is an apology for the faithfulness of women, or more precisely, a rebuttal of their bad reputation: "It is said of old, Soon hot, soon cold / And so is a woman" (#21). HE begins the exchange by complaining that as soon as a new man appears "He is a banished man" (#1). SHE reminds him of the nut-brown maid who kept her faith, and HE proposes that they put woman's faith to the test by taking the roles of the nut-brown maid and her love, banished to the woods for an unspecified crime. In her role as the nut-brown maid, SHE remains ready to accompany her love into exile from society despite his protests of hardships to come: the law, the weather, the lack of food and shelter and clothing, even the intrusion of another woman. Once convinced of the nut-brown maid's steadfastness, he reveals that he is an earl's son and promises to marry her. The last stanza closes the frame with the narrator (taking the woman's position) addressing the implied audience, proclaiming woman's faith to man and offering man's faith, in turn, to God. In his "Fantasia," a musical form embellishing well-known airs, Ashbery preserves the gendered headings from Quiller-Couch's edition of the ballad and matches its thirty stanzas. While only 18 of the roughly 481 lines of "Fantasia" echo "The Nut-Brown Maid," Ashbery's improvisational poem nevertheless depends on it.[34] The ballad provided Ashbery with a genre (the lovers' *débat*) and a sequential form (seven of the first eight stanzas of "Fantasia" are sonnet-length).

The most unusual and surprising aspect of "Fantasia" is that Ashbery produced it by collaging in a great deal of his own unpublished poetry from the 1970s (a procedure he has since forgotten).[35] The poem is thus a fantasia not only on "The Nut-Brown Maid" but on his own poetry. If Ashbery earlier produced obviously disjunctive collages such as "Europe," in "Fantasia" he combined his own discarded poetic texts with new verse in such a way that "it was hard to distinguish the new elements from the old, so calculated and easygoing was the fusion" (TP 118). I have discovered 17 poems and fragments which contributed to "Fantasia." Ashbery did not simply salvage occasional lines and sentences from these poems. At least 283 lines of "Fantasia"—24 of its 30 stanzas—are either wholly or partially recycled (by contrast, none of Ashbery's other long poems contains more than ten recycled lines). Five of the final six stanzas (and perhaps also #28, for which I have found no source) derive entirely from Ashbery's unpublished lyrics.

While the unsuspecting reader has no way of knowing that "Fantasia" is an in-house collage, the poem does indirectly acknowledge its constructive principle. At one point, SHE seems to marvel at its fragile network: "somehow you spliced the bleeding wires, / Made it presentable long enough for / Inspection" (#10, HBD 76). In an interesting exchange, both characters seem dimly aware of their own second-hand existence. HE notes that while there "are other kinds of privacy / Coming in now," there will soon be enough time to examine and grade them on "a sliding scale" (#21, HBD 82). SHE both disagrees with and confirms his prediction: "No, but I dug these out of bureau drawers for you, / Told you which ones meant a lot to me, / Which ones I was frankly dubious about, and / Which were destined to blow away" (#22, HBD 82). The seventeen lines of this stanza[36] were themselves dug out of the drawer, from two unpublished poems, "Bunch of Poems" (source for the last seven lines of #21) and "Collective Dawns" (which gave its title to another poem, HBD 5). The first four lines are taken nearly verbatim from "Bunch of Poems." In their new setting "these" old verses represent past experiences, treasured or disposable memories, and ultimately their agents, presumably responsible for their actions. The god-like authorial decision concerning which "works" are destined to be saved (or remembered) relates the afterlife of poems, in drawers or books, to that of experiences in the memory. The next nine lines (excluding the phrase "until a later date / . . . water," from "Bunch of Poems") incorporate the fragment "Collective Dawns." SHE and HE are not meant "to suffer after this" (HBD 82) for their sexual transgressions. After the Eliotic "winding / Paths of despair and memory, reproach in / The stairwell" (HBD 82), SHE predicts that the lovers will find that "memory / Had placed chairs around" (as later for the spirits in James Merrill's "Coda: The Higher Keys" in *The Changing Light at Sandover*). The rest of #22 comes from "Bunch of Poems." The lucky few, resurrected in "Fantasia," will escape the "fixed / Destiny" (HBD 83) of oblivion in the drawer. This resurrection does not depend on their being either remembered or published: "It's enough that they are had, / Allowed to run loose" (#23, HBD 83, also from "Bunch of Poems"). Poems and actions are best kept wild in the public and private domain, where their authors claim only limited responsibility for them.

A single unpublished poem can run loose in "Fantasia." Consider the unpublished lyric "Equestrian Statue," quoted here in its entirety (material collaged into "Fantasia" is underlined with stanzas noted in the left margin; cancellations are struck through and handwritten revisions are italicized):

| | |
|---|---|
| #6 | <u>I want to fly but keep</u> |
| #6 | <u>My morality,</u> odd |
| #6,5 | <u>As it is</u> *may be,* but <u>as Naming-of-Cares</u> |
| #6 | ~~Shall~~ keep up the <u>branched diversions</u> |
| #6 | <u>Around an axis</u>, and let this stand as |
| | As good. Meanwhile *So* the outcry |
| | Is maintained on a steady basis (could |
| #15 | Be worse, could be worse) <u>planing the way</u> |
| #15,7 | <u>For asking him to come down</u>. And the <u>great</u> |
| | Utilitarian inventions of our era along with |
| #7,15 | <u>The squash domes, granular like the rings of Saturn,</u> |
| | Sag then melt *mutate* in intense yet pointless gentian, |
| | If we could but know. Is it that *because* we |
| | "Are living, we are dwelling, |
| | In a grand and awful time?" In |
| #15 | "An age on ages telling?" These *There?* <u>are mostly shoals,</u> |
| #15 | <u>Even tricks of the light,</u> <u>vaporous armies</u> |
| #15 | <u>In debacle, helter skelter,</u> <u>pell-mell,</u> |
| #15 | <u>Fleeing us</u> now <u>who sometime did us seek,</u> |
| #4,15 | <u>And there is nothing solid,</u> <u>nothing</u> |
| #4,15 | <u>To build on,</u> <u>if it took</u> us <u>weeks and months,</u> |
| #15 | <u>With time running out,</u> <u>nothing could be done.</u> |

The matter of "Equestrian Statue," written two days after the United States Bicentennial, is America (see Augustus Saint-Gaudens's equestrian statue of General Sherman and winged Victory in Central Park). A statue is an easy target for graffiti; the trick is to mar the figure without resorting to satire. Following Stevens's on the equestrian statue of Andrew Jackson in Washington, "The American Sublime" (114), Ashbery's poem is a dialogue between an idealist United States, played by the statue, and its anxious citizens. But as a whole, "Equestrian Statue" is less successful than either Stevens's enigmatic poem or Ashbery's own commissioned Bicentennial poem, "Pyrography." Its sexual politics, pairing the god's "fear of flying" (Erica Jong's novel appeared in 1973) with the lovers' fear of abandonment (caught from Wyatt), remain unrelated to its national politics. But like much of Ashbery's unpublished work, "Equestrian Statue" contains a lot of good poetry.

As the statue gets broken down in "Fantasia," itself assembled in the fall of 1976, it assumes larger, and intricately various, dimensions. In stanza #6 SHE becomes an author, who wants to keep her encrypted "virginity" (or impenetrability) intact: "I want to fly but keep / My morality, motley as it is, just by / Encouraging these branching diversions around an axis" (HBD 74). "Equestrian Statue" itself branches into diverse versions. The lines "there is nothing solid, nothing / To build on," for instance, cited almost verbatim in #4, are varied in #15 as "there is no place, nothing / To hide in." The line "The squash domes . . . Saturn" is split between #7 and #15. In #7, where the "equestrian statue" itself is wheeled up like the Trojan horse, "The great squash domes" "belong to no one," like classics or "Utilitarian inventions" in the public domain. In #15, the line becomes "Those ramparts, granular as Saturn's rings." The word "rampart" (resembling a "rampant" equestrian statue) recalls the "ramparts" of the U.S. national anthem. Next the domes are privatized into a Coleridgean "tomb of pleasures, a Sans Souci" ("dome"), deaf to ancestral voices prophesying war. As though to complicate matters, a similar line appears in the unpublished "Sans Souci" (the name of the tomb of Frederick II): "The great squash domes / Look porous, like the moons of Jupiter." Because the version from "Equestrian Statue" is closer to what survived in "Fantasia," it is probable that the line itself originated in the undated "Sans Souci." But all we know now is that for Ashbery the great line belonged to no one poem. The Arnoldian perspective in "Fantasia" #15 of ignorant armies clashing by night is shared by a pair of aging lovers, who, as in Wyatt's lyric, are deserted by younger warring men. This apocalyptic perspective is sharpened by "helter skelter," the name of a TV docudrama appearing in 1976 about Charles Manson, who read the Beatles song as a prophecy of race war. But as in #6, the safety of love's overlook is abandoned for the plain, taken appropriately from "The Nut-Brown Maid": "The snow, the frost, the rain, / The cold, the heat; for dry or wete, / We must lodge on the plain." In the "real" world, where rampant lyric monuments such as Wyatt's are no more substantial than "absent clouds," "The real diversions" are "on the ground" (#15, HBD 79).

Once the mode of production of "Fantasia" is known, certain characteristics of the poem emerge more clearly. First, we can neither read "Fantasia" simply as a dialogue nor completely ignore its dialogic frame. HE and SHE represent neither two separate characters nor a single argument. Five years later, Ashbery himself noted that the "doubleness in 'Fantasia' is fairly arbitrary because it would read the same if some of the he and she headings were left out."[37] As readers of the poem have remarked, HE and SHE are essentially indistinguishable.[38] On the other hand, not long after "Fantasia" was published, Ashbery said of "The Nut-Brown Maid" that "there is a kind of spirit of repartee in the poem."[39] The same is true of his "Fantasia." The unanimity of HE and SHE not only qualifies but intensifies their conversation, as though they were of one divided mind, completing each other's thoughts. Sometimes they talk to each other entirely through collaged poems: in #26 SHE speaks the first stanza of "A Melange of Half-Truths," and in #27 HE answers with the first stanza of "The Sad Thing." More often, parts of a collaged poem are parceled out between them. Ashbery's "Septet," no longer in septets, stretches across #17, #18, and #19, where its rhetorical progression of question and answer is dramatized, its line and stanza breaks reframed as pauses in the dialogue. HE senses their predicament, in the third person—Ashbery has noted that the speakers of the ballad "kind of speak of themselves in the third person"[40]—in the conclusion to #19: "But the hesitation stayed on, and came to be permanent / Because they were thinking about each other" (HBD 81).

The question of what Ashbery "meant" or "wanted to say" by improvising "Fantasia" is part of a larger question raised by and in the poem: what is an author? In cultural terms, the question concerns the poet's responses to the past, literary or historical, and the responsibility of the poet for his or her works. In ethical terms, the question extends to cover anyone's authorship of and responsibility for their acts. Roland Barthes's "The Death of the Author" and Michel Foucault's "What Is an Author?" (both appeared in English in 1977, along with "Fantasia")[41] helped bring this question into American critical discourse. Though Ashbery had not read these essays, they illuminate his self-interested understanding of the question. Both Barthes and Foucault take the death of the modern author for granted, and both see the author as partly a critical construction. To "give a text an Author," Barthes argues, "is . . . to furnish it with a final signified."[42] According to Foucault, the invention of "the author-function" enabled critics both to classify and group certain texts and to assign them a rational center of "creativ[ity]" and "profundity."[43] In a coolly satiric passage collaged from "The Machinery of Life" into "Fantasia" #7, HE warns SHE that they (and their author) are not alone: "Others, patient murderers, cultivated, / Sympathetic, in time will have subtly / Switched the background from parallel rain-lines / To the ambiguities of 'the deep'" (#7, HBD 75). Critics need an "author-function" for parallel lines on a page to converge into the virtual depths of ambiguity and profundity.

For both Barthes and Foucault, one of the fundamental characteristics of the author is responsibility; the author not only originates but owns and can be held responsible for his work. Barthes speaks of classical French novelists assuming "responsibility for a narrative,"[44] and Foucault hypothesizes that the concept of the author appeared toward the end of the eighteenth century, "when a system of ownership and strict copyright rules were established,"[45] so that writers might be punished for transgressions of property and propriety. In the first draft of "Fantasia" Ashbery adopts a strikingly similar vocabulary, as SHE, "branching diversions," renounces ownership of her origins: "It's out of copyright." The final version of the sentence attracts more "ambiguities": "It's in the public domain" (#6, HBD 75). While the sentence refers directly to the anonymous, uncopyrighted ballad "The Nut-Brown Maid," it ultimately includes the unpublished "Ashbery poems" collaged into "Fantasia" and "Fantasia" itself, which entered the "public domain" and became public property when it was published: "The great squash domes seem / To vindicate us all, yet belong to no one" (#7, HBD 75). Ashbery's presence in this domain, what he later calls "the published city" (FC 3), will be a major topic in his longest poem, *Flow Chart;* "Fantasia" is his first extended fantasy on this theme.

To what extent is Ashbery denying responsibility for his poems by locating them in the public domain? To be sure, his name appears on his book covers. The author did not commit suicide in "Fantasia"; the omniscient classical Author interred by Barthes and Foucault is a straw figure. "Ashbery" is neither simply a "creative genius" nor a writing, assembling machine. But he remains anxious, like many authors, about the public's ascription of "authoritative" characteristics and meanings to works gathered under his name. Rather than dismissing the "modernist" questions of authorship and responsibility, Ashbery collaborates with private and public history in constructing a poem for which he may be held irresponsible.

The question of responsibility most immediately concerns Ashbery's response to the critical reception of *Self-Portrait,* the volume which prompted

Harold Bloom to place Ashbery on the short list of strong poets. In "Fanta-sia" #25 (originally an unpublished prose poem also called "Fantasia on 'The Nut-Brown Maid'") the prize-winning poet writes a memo warning himself not to let success go to his head: "Just because Goofus has been lucky for you, you imagine others will make a fuss over you" (HBD 84). "Goofus is lucky for you" is a line from a 1920s popular song which was revived in the 1970s; but "G*oo*fus" also recalls the recent value "Bl*oo*m" has added to the author's name. If he doesn't come to his senses, the author of the mirror-ball poem will imagine that "the glint of light from a silver ball on that far-off flag pole is the equivalent of a career devoted to life, to im-proving the minds and the welfare of others, when in reality it is a common thing like these, and less profitable than any hobby or sideline that is a source of retirement income." These United States are not likely to take up Ashbery's highly praised poem as their banner any time soon. His visibility on the poetic scene may well be transient, like that of the proverbial "man in the crowd": "You are like someone whose face was photographed in a crowd scene once and then gradually retreated from people's memories, and from life as well."

An American poet makes a name for himself or herself by attracting "big name" reviewers and academic critics, an audience of nonprofessional read-ers, and, most importantly, the attention of practicing poets, all of whom raise the value of the author's name in their respective quarters. A critical heritage and a continuing influence on "name" poets maintains the poet's name after the author is no longer around to defend it. W. H. Auden suc-cinctly recorded this apotheosis in his poem commemorating W. B. Yeats: "he became his admirers" (EA 241). Consider the modification of an au-thor's name in critical discourse (Whitmanian, Dantesque) in which an au-thorized style lives on in another author's poems, taking the insubstantial form of a few patented characteristics (the catalogue, terza rima). The cur-rency of a poet's name thus depends on the public.

Being named, being singled out and held responsible for one's words, gives rise to anxious fantasies. Ashbery has committed poetry, and one sin recalls all the others. In the anonymous ballad "The Nut-Brown Maid," HE warns that SHE should "take good heed / What men will think and say" of her following him into exile, "[her] wanton will for to fulfil" (#9). SHE counters, "Theirs be the charge that speak so large / In hurting of my name" (#10). In "Fantasia" SHE attributes her own hasty departure to the suspi-cion that "someone in a department store made some / Cryptic allusion" (#10, HBD 76). In the ballad, the sin for which the man is banished is un-specified: "It standeth so: a deed is do / Whereof great harm shall grow" (#5). In "Fantasia" it is misrepresented: "I once stole a pencil, but now the

219

list with my name in it / Disgusts me" (#11, HBD 77). Stealing a pencil has sexual and reflexive overtones; the phallic fall from innocence marks the beginning of writing. The original misdeed is variously alluded to: SHE accuses HE of "going on and on about something / That happened in the past" (#12, HBD 77), while HE later sees their present "embarrassment" as "The product of a discretion lodged far back in the past" (#19, HBD 81; "indiscretion"). The misrepresentative crime for which one is put on the "most wanted list" is rumored in whispers: "Tell about the affair she'd had / With Bennett Palmer, the Minnesota highwayman" (#28, HBD 85–86; Ashbery invented the highwayman's name). In this case the rumor mill is run by one "Thomas a Tattamus," that tattle-tale of nursery rhyme fame. The "list with my name on it"—at once the FBI's, St. Peter's, Senator McCarthy's, and the canonizing critic's—only confirms the responsible party's "reputation."

In a terrifying collaborative narration, SHE forecasts their doom, "Plummeted into the space under the stage / Through a trapdoor carelessly left open" (#12, HBD 77), and HE envisions being carried away to Hell (the space beneath the Globe Theater) by two demon Marx Brothers out of Lichtenstein: "Then double trouble / Arrives, Beppo and Zeppo confront one / Out of a hurricane of colored dots" (#13, HBD 78). SHE next warns of a possible eternal punishment:

> If brimstone were the same as the truth
> A gate deep in the ground would unlock to the fumbling
> Of a certain key and the dogs at the dog races
> Would circumambulate each in his allotted groove
> Casting an exaggeratedly long shadow, while other
> Malcontents, troublemakers, *esprits frondeurs* moved up
> To dissolve in the brightness of the footlights. I would
> Withstand, bow in hand, to grieve them.
> (#14, HBD 78)

The vision conjures up Canto XV of *Inferno,* in which Dante's revered teacher Brunetto Latini races in his allotted infernal ring as one who wins. Brunetto's "crime" retroactively specifies the pencil theft and sharpens the homotextual anxiety about being named. Ashbery retreats from this nightmare of nomination in #14 by collaging in the conclusion of a rejected poem, "A Melange of Half-Truths" (this title is collaged into #13). SHE and HE, indicated only by pronouns, are not singled out after all, and remain part of the diluvial public, "all / Somehow related, to each other and through each other to us, / Characters in the opera *The Flood,* by the great anonymous

220

composer" (#14, HBD 78; no such opera exists). If the Author of the Biblical Flood remains anonymous, surely His or Her characters, HE and SHE, are not responsible for their transgressions.

The operatic and mundane narratives of "Fantasia" have broad ethical implications. If we are not simply authors of our acts but characters in our lives, we cannot be judged completely responsible for our acts or roles. In the ballad, already a fantasia of two inventive players, HE and SHE act within the confines of a ready-made plot. Ashbery's HE and SHE, representing the two sides of "the story of our lives" (#8, HBD 75), see their own and each other's history as a story line. SHE narrates her life in the omniscient third person, "Saddened, she rose up / And untwined the gears of that blank, blossoming day" (#2, HBD 72–73), and HE narrates her life to her in the epistolary second person, "you chose a view of distant factories" (#9, HBD 76). SHE imagines both of them traversing a "plot" twist: "a landscape in its inner folds, relaxed / And with the sense of there being about to be some more / Until the first part is digested and then it twists" (#18, HBD 80). There is no alternative to understanding the winding course of history, public or private, as a story, with plot twists standing in for purported moments of revelation. Personal responsibility may be written into one's role from the start.

In the middle of the fourth stanza of "The Nut-Brown Maid," SHE leaves the narrative frame and assumes her representative office: "*I answer now, / All women to excuse:* / Mine own heart dear, with you what cheer?" Yet in the ensuing debate SHE defends only herself, not all women, against charges of unfaithfulness. To act means acting in character and, to some extent, forgetting one's framing play. Ashbery opens his own framed narrative with the theme of latent memory: "We may as well begin the litany here: / How all that forgotten past seasons us" (#4, HBD 74). This memorable idea first appeared near the end of Ashbery's unpublished lyric "The Water Drinkers" (dated June 17, 1976), in which "the forgotten past" is remembered by "Mom" and "Dad," prompting an invitation which now makes up the last seven lines of "Fantasia" #20 (HBD 81–82). This temporal seasoning seems to be more of a blessing in disguise than a litany of complaints. We are acted upon, influenced, by our past without our full knowledge. We tend to think of choice as being free to the extent that it is deliberate. But Ashbery's HE answers with Hamlet's hesitation: "It is true, a truer story. / Self-knowledge frosts each action, each step taken / Freely" (#5, HBD 74), a "truth" rearranged from "The Water Drinkers": "try to see / Into the opaque glaze that frosts everything / With ~~its own~~ self-knowledge." Free action lies in the public domain in that its precedents are unexamined, unauthored: "The ends stream back in the wind, it is too dark / To see them but I can feel them" (#5, HBD 74; cf. Hamlet's "There's a divinity that shapes our ends"). The past, larger and more complex than we can take into account, "seasons us" or prepares us for acting in the present. But in a moving passage, collaged from "The Sad Thing" (dated June 1, 1976), HE explains why we might after all complain of this seasoning: even if we wanted to, we have no way of getting back to the heart of the matter, of establishing the truth, the basis for conscious, moral action:

> Each of us circles
> Around some simple but vital missing piece of information,
> And, at the end, as now, finding no substitute,
> Writes his own mark grotesquely with a stick in snow,
> The signature of many connected seconds of indecision.
> What I am writing to say is, the timing, not
> The contents, is what matters.
> (#27, HBD 85; "makes his mark," "trying to say")

The cursive continuity of Ashbery's career is an illusion. Nobody knows enough to be an author; no one makes fully informed decisions. But all of us author our acts and sign our texts, subject to "Legends and misinterpretations" (#27, HBD 85), because we have no alternative. The significance of these works which bear our signature, Ashbery argues, is due to their "timing," their culminating historical context, rather than their "contents" or authorial intention. What if the reflexive, self-protective "Self-Portrait in a Convex Mirror," for instance, had not met an introspective American audience beginning to recall its citizens from a disastrous excursion in Vietnam? As HE concedes, "All this could have happened / Long ago, or at least on some other day, / And not meant much except insofar as the eye / Extracts a progress from almost anything" (#27, HBD 85).

Authorial responsibility is a central topic in the closing pages of "Fantasia," which are largely collaged from an unpublished and unfinished poem, "The Patient's History" (two more titles used in *Houseboat Days,* "The Lament upon the Waters" and "All Kinds of Caresses," are handwritten at the end of this typescript). In what was apparently a desperate attempt to save this poem, Ashbery canceled twelve of its sixteen octaves. But most of these "rejected" stanzas found new life in "Fantasia." As it stood (or lay), "The Patient's History" was an anesthetized problem. Its disaffected beginning, "To him, the holiday-making crowds were / Engines of a parallel disaster," which Ashbery reused to open "Fantasia" #29 (HBD 86), would not garner the patient much sympathy. In "The Patient's History" the poet tends to play not the patient but the all-knowing doctor, keeping the American public under constant observation. In his dreams, when as Jack (John) up the beanstalk he gained the proper perspective, the crowded landscape "Agreed to be so studied" and was refracted in "the prism that matters" (cf. #30, HBD 87). The morning leaves the patient with more questions than answers:

> Always there was something to see, something
> Going on, for the historical past owed it
> To itself, our historical present. But if each
> Act is reflexive, concerned with itself
> On another level as well as with us, the strangers
> Who live here, can one advance one step
> Further without sinking equally far into the past?
> Or is this a permanent ledge, a shelf of whatever happens?

In #29 Ashbery salvaged this open-ended stanza, the eleventh octave of "The Patient's History," by interchanging its first two sentences, making the opening statement a response to its former objection: if reflective, "responsible" action mires one in contradictory premises and insufficient information, "sinking equally / Far back into the past," authorial indecision may be cured by curiosity: "There was always something to see, / Something going on, for the historical past owed it / To itself, our historical present" (HBD 86). This marvelous musical idea, recapitulated in italics in the anonymous prose coda of "Fantasia," improvises on the common commercial appeal: "You owe it to yourself to see this magnificent spectacle." Ashbery's variation articulates a temporal responsibility. In written French the "historical past" is equivalent to the *passé simple,* demarcating what has happened once and for all. But the past is never that simple. Its influence upon the present is incalculable, as is the development of "our historical present" in the future. History itself, then, is self-reflexive; it co-authors our acts, whose consequences we are never wholly aware of, or responsible for. If the present folds back on the past even without our knowing it, we owe it to ourselves to be patient with history, to experience its ongoing implications, which "shall, like a Moebius strip / Of a tapestry, play to our absences and soothe them" (#24, HBD 83).

In a public reading of the prose coda of "Fantasia" Ashbery compared it with the last stanza of "The Nut-Brown Maid," "the conclusion of the poem" which is "spoken by the narrator who makes his appearance only at that point and says that this proves the superiority of women to men but we should all be thinking about God anyway."[46] In "Fantasia" this unassigned prose speech marks the appearance of the anonymous author. The page and a half of prose is composed entirely of earlier poems, their line breaks obliterated, as though the omniscient perspective were immeasurable. The coda opens with the hanging question from "The Patient's History," "Unless this is the shelf of whatever happens?" (#30, HBD 87; "self"). The catalogues of thoughtless, aimless crowds, which formed the rejected middle stanzas of "The Patient's History," here become misrepresentative lists of unfolding "oral history": "There were visiting firemen, rumors of chattels on a spree, old men made up to look like young women," and so on. In this small world, recalling the café life of the avant-gardist, "Things overheard in cafés assumed an importance previously reserved for letters from the front." But the homotextual narrative is soon judged by "the inevitable uninvited and only guest who writes on the wall: I choose not to believe." The sentence is itself heretical, as is Ashbery's culminating assumption of responsibility (#30, HBD 88):

Responsible to whom? I have chosen this environment and it is handsome: a festive ruching of bare twigs against the sky, masks under the balconies

                                                      that
                                                   I sing alway

The final, purposely unpunctuated response of "Fantasia" answers the defiant question "Responsible to whom?" Ashbery is responsible to his environment; he owes his fantasias to the influential public domain that includes his readers and those who have never heard of him. The poem breaks off (with a description drawn from "The Patient's History") like an unfinished manuscript. But the spacing of "that / I sing alway" mirrors a salutation and a signature. This balladic pseudonym ("*alway*," "*Ashbery*") derives from Yeats's dialogue poem, "The Sad Shepherd" (companion to "The Song of the Happy Shepherd"): "And he called loudly to the stars to bend / From their pale thrones and comfort him, but they / Among themselves laugh on and sing alway" (9). Merely by singing, by improvising on public and private history, Ashbery has fulfilled his responsibility and developed an answerable style.

# 8

## Parallel Adventures
### *As We Know*

In 1979 Ashbery readers were surprised by a beautiful but strangely shaped volume called *As We Know*. Its cover reproduced a painting Ashbery had seen in Rotterdam in 1977, Pieter Jansz Saenredam's *St. Mary's Square and St. Mary's Church, Utrecht,* depicting a nearly vacant plaza with, at the church entrance, two inconspicuous parallel columns.[1] The book's 7-by-9-inch format was devised to set off the seventy-page poem "Litany," which was printed in two parallel columns, the left in roman type and the right in italics, "meant," according to an "Author's Note," "to be read as simultaneous but independent monologues" (AWK 2). Though Ashbery determined its doubleness in advance, the form of "Litany" was modified by its mode of production. Ashbery wrote "Litany" (dated October 1977—April 9, 1978) on the typewriter, using standard 8½ by 11-inch paper. His procedure was to start with the left-hand column and to write until he reached the end of the page. Then he would reset the margin at the middle, return to the top of the page, and compose the right-hand column. As the poem progressed, the right, middle, and left margins shrank to almost nothing. Or in fact to less than nothing, since at several points (beginning with AWK 23) the swelling left-hand column began to break into the space reserved for the right-hand column. After two claustrophobic pages of all-over typing, Ashbery took to writing only one column per page, alternating left and right columns. Now he felt freer to drift over the center line. After four typewritten pages of isolated columns, each with a huge, suggestive right or left margin, he typed two pages of right-hand columns in a row (by accident or design) before returning to double-columned typing. The extra right-hand column caused a gaping hiatus in the left-hand column of the final text, with the italicized right column continuing eerily on its own. After that, he kept both columns on a single page, no matter how small the margins. Not until publication did he and Viking Press come up with a new page to accommodate the crowded poem.

Ashbery speculates that his double form was influenced by the stereophonic divisions of Elliott Carter's music: "He has a work for violin and piano, which I heard before I started writing 'Litany.' . . . It was done with the violin on one side of the stage and the piano on the other side of a very large stage. It would seem as though they were talking about different things, but the one would become more intense and the other would somehow begin to fade at certain points, then the situation would change and the violin, which was already in an unequal struggle with the piano, would nevertheless overtake it and dominate it."[2] Some months earlier Carter had premiered his setting of Ashbery's poem "Syringa," in which the mezzo-soprano singing the poem competed with a bass-baritone simultaneously rendering fragments of ancient Greek Orphic poetry.[3] The mere impossibility of reading both printed columns of "Litany" simultaneously makes us keenly aware of a "present that is elsewhere" (AWK 74).[4] Ashbery has suggested that "perhaps the two columns are like two people whom I am in love with simultaneously."[5] But the columns also seem to be in love with each other. The right column of the first section thus concludes nostalgically, *"We never should have parted, you and me,"* while the left narrates a longing only for death: "Each thought only / Of his private silence, and hungered / For the promised moment of rest" (AWK 16)—a rest the left column itself achieves a few lines before the right.[6] These disorientations make us examine our reading habits. How far should one read in one column before doubling back to the other? A line, a stanza, a completed argument? If it is difficult to concentrate on one column while its counterpart is also going on, it is next to impossible to read one column while playing back the other in one's head, as Ashbery later acknowledged: "I like the idea of having these two things people have to pay attention to at the same time, but on the other hand who's going to do it? I don't, and I can't really expect anybody else to."[7] In his *Selected Poems* (1985) Ashbery cavalierly isolated the end of the right column, now in roman type. Nevertheless, "Litany" stands as his boldest formal experiment in the long poem since "Europe."[8]

The parallel columns of "Litany" suggest other parallels: stereo speakers; the two hands or eyes or sides of the brain; consciousness and self-consciousness; architectural columns; divided highways; columns of figures; facing phallic columns; the private and public spheres; the double-columned King James Bible; newspaper columns; a poem *face en face* with its italicized translation; a text with marginal critical commentary, and so on. The correspondent columns of "Litany" also invite comparison with the minister's supplications and the congregation's responses, printed in roman and italicized type respectively, of Thomas Cranmer's liturgical service, "The Great Litany" (Ashbery's original title).[9] As Ashbery puts it in "Litany," *"we can now feel with our minds / Which is someplace between prayers / And the answer to prayers"* (AWK 52). In *The Book of Common Prayer* "The Great Litany" is immediately followed by the "Ash Wednesday" service. Eliot's "Ash Wednesday" and "The Hollow Men" both employ liturgical language, and "The Hollow Men" (1925) experiments with italicized verses and barely prayable roman-type responses:

> *For Thine is the Kingdom*
>
> For Thine is
> Life is
> For Thine is the
> (CP 59)

Auden offered his own morally acute litany for all manner of sinners in "The Orators": "For those who borrow and for those who lend, for those who are shunned on the towpath; for those regarded in their households as saints, / / O Swan with the Two Necks, hear us" (EA 67; Ashbery used the phrase "on the towpath" for a poem title, HBD 22). Ashbery borrowed from Auden's misrepresentative survey for his own intercessory prayers: *"For all those wearing old clothes / With the dormant look of expectation about them / / For the women ironing / And who cut into lengths of white cloth"* (AWK 22). For his italicized close, Ashbery collaged an appeal from a newspaper advice column,[10] in which one hesitant, afflicted soul appeals neither to God nor to Mary but to some faceless benign agency such as the Better Business Bureau, explaining that he *"accept- / ed"* the Columbia Tape Club's offer to *"buy one / Tape and get another free"*: *"But since I've been / Repeatedly billed for my free tape. / I've written them several times but / Can't straighten it out—would you / Try?"* (AWK 67–68).[11] No response, in or out of the poem, is forthcoming.

In an interview, Ashbery recalled saying "half-jokingly" of "Litany" that "my object was to direct the readers' attention to the white space between the columns."[12] It is illuminating to view "Litany" with figure and ground reversed, as a central, blank poem with surrounding printed marginalia, or even as a cross-section of a "hollow tower" (AWK 50), a "hollow" into which the soulless soul of "Self-Portrait" "fits / . . . perfectly" (SP 69). Ashbery labels this missing center variously as *"the buttonhole of truth,"* a "lost cause," and "some source, / An origin of the present." It represents the mythological lost origin, before "The moment," "reflecting / Only itself," became "two moments" (AWK 18). The center may also have been erased. In *Nature* Emerson claims that our vision is occluded: "The ruin or the blank, that we see when we look at nature, is in our own eye" (47). Harold Bloom's revised Freudian blank is helpful here: "The blank, being both unwritten page and unviewable void or abyss, would be for Freud the image of primal repression, a defense prior to any drive against which we need to be defended."[13] The central American poet of blankness is Dickinson, who already associated it with the "blanking out" of repression: "Pain—has an Element of Blank— / It cannot recollect / When it begun—or if there were / A time when it was not—" (#650). Ashbery nearly equals Dickinson's economy in a passage on the formal feeling of the aftermath: "*Pain intervened, as usual, / The calm remained, held over / From the other time / And no broken trace was seen*" (AWK 9). Where there were stormy relations, only the dividing indifferent blank remains.

The deconstruction site of the blank center of "Litany"—whether it displaces a hushed-up affair, an absconded Deity, a hidden past, or the missing basis of communication—rules all the poem's surrounding, surviving ideas, signs, and figures. In one version of the story the twin towers of verse-commentary "regroup farther on, / Standing around looking at / The hole left by the great implosion" (AWK 5). In theological terms, this central ruin marks the departed Logos, "a central crater / Which is the word," and the surrounding words represent the self-important churches (or poetry groups), "tightly compartmented, almost feudal / Societies claiming kinship with the word" (AWK 55). In "Burnt Norton" Eliot imagines this silent, inscrutably Oriental center: "Words, after speech, reach / Into the silence. Only by the form, the pattern, / Can words or music reach / The stillness, as a Chinese jar still / Moves perpetually in its stillness" (121). Ashbery's tricolumnar form stands as his attempt to include silence by enclosing it.

The blueprint for "Litany" was drafted with uncanny precision in "The Ice-Cream Wars" (HBD 60; dated August 1976), where the fighting words hurled back and forth between the prophet in his watchtower and the belligerent reader are represented by italics and roman type respectively: "*Why you old goat!* Look who's talkin'. Let's see you / Climb off that tower." The prophet's italicized insult, "slanted sideways, disappears for awhile," and his prophecy is metonymically replaced by its transcendent signified, the rising sun, "pearl of the orient, occluded / And still apt to rise at times"—a rising celebrated in the Protestant hymn's refrain, here reduced to its narrative kernel: "[I love to tell] the old, old story [of Jesus and his love]." What remains of the Word, while the "truth becomes a hole," are its marginal commentaries, "A few black smudges / On the outer boulevards, like squashed midges." With these marginalia the besieged prophet John outlined the gospel of "Litany" without knowing it.

Some of Ashbery's readers may protest that "Litany" is not logocentric and Eliotic but decentered and Derridean. With its uneven columns and absent center, "Litany" certainly looks deconstructive. But it does not follow that Ashbery is following or versifying Jacques Derrida. Though he has not read Derrida, Ashbery speculates that "it is probably not a coincidence that we've been addressing ourselves to similar problems and that these sorts of things tend to happen simultaneously in history from certain causes."[14] In an early essay, "Structure, Sign, and Play in the Discourse of the Human Sciences," Derrida distinguishes between negative and positive attitudes toward a decentered world: "The one seeks to decipher, dreams of deciphering a truth or an origin which escapes play and the order of the sign, and which lives the necessity of interpretation as an exile. The other, which is no longer turned toward the origin, affirms play and tries to pass beyond man and humanism, . . . the reassuring foundation, the origin and the end of play."[15] In the playful practices and retrospective speculations of "Litany" Ashbery has it both ways. It is instructive to juxtapose "Litany" with Derrida's double-columned book, *Glas,* published five years earlier. With its multilingual fragmentary columns notched and fissured by inserted marginalia, *Glas* is much more visually complex than Ashbery's invariantly double-columned poem. The book derives from parallel essays, the left column on G. W. F. Hegel, the right on Jean Genet. Without inspecting the typescript, one can see that the essay on Genet is shorter, since it is set in larger type. It seems likely, then, that Derrida wrote the essays separately and then placed them together, adding sufficient marginalia to make the columns come out even. Thus the parallel productive play that enlivens "Litany" is here concentrated in the interpolated marginalia. *Glas* too concerns translation, communication, trope, commentary, theological absence, and homosexual difference. Yet because of its essayistic, interpretative form, its self-reflexive moments often seem restricted to the circuit of the work: "each column rises with an impassive self-sufficiency, and yet the element of contagion, the infinite circulation of general equivalence relates each sentence, each stump of writing . . . to each other, within each column and from one column to the other of *what remained* infinitely calculable."[16] The self-reflexivity of "Litany" leaves more of a remainder: "*That tower of lightning high over / The Sahara Desert could have missed you*" (AWK 5; "hit"). In the readers' interpretative exodus, it is not a pillar of cloud or fire but a Babelian "tower of lightning" that serves as guide; Ashbery's lightning strikes twice. Whatever their thematic continuities, Derrida's postphilosophical and Ashbery's postmodern writing projects are differently misrepresentative of their kinds.

Ashbery's logocentric bias perhaps enables him to bring into focus the third, blank column. The opening stanzas of "Litany" proclaim a conspiracy of silence surrounding "unspeakable" private practices. These stanzas anticipate much of the poem's opening section (AWK 3–16), which itself diagrams the self-reflexive topic of the three-part poem its own divided form. "Litany" is its own place; whatever is lost "once" occupied the middle, whatever remains is sidelined in the marginal, doubled text. In Ashbery's relational poetry, terms and topics come and go but the all-purpose narrative remains the same:

<table>
<tr><td>

I

For someone like me
The simple things
Like having toast or
Going to church are
Kept in one place.

Like having wine and cheese.
The parents of the town
Pissing elegantly escape knowledge
Once and for all. The
Snapdragons consumed in a wind
Of fire and rage far over
The streets as they end.

The casual purring of a donkey
Rouses me from my accounts:
What given, what gifts. The air
Stands straight up like a tail.

He spat on the flowers.

Also for someone
Like me the time flows round again
With things I did in it.
I wish to keep my differences
And to retain my kinship
To the rest. That is why
I raise these flowers all around.

</td><td>

*I*

*So this must be a hole*
*Of cloud*
*Mandate or trap*
*But haze that casts*
*The milk of enchantment*

*Over the whole town,*
*Its scenery, whatever*
*Could be happening*
*Behind tall hedges*
*Of dark, lissome knowledge.*

*The brown lines persist*
*In explicit sex*
*Matters like these*
*No one can care about,*
*"Noone." That is I've said it*
*Before and no one*
*Remembers except that elf.*

*Around us are signposts*
*Pointing to the past,*
*The old-fashioned, pointed*
*Wooden kind. And nothing directs*
*To the present that is*
*About to happen.*

*These traumas*

</td></tr>
</table>

| They do not stand for flowers or | *That sped us on our way* |
|---|---|
| Anything pretty they are | *Are to be linked with the invisible damage* |
| Code names for the silence. | *Resulting in the future* |
| (AWK 3–4) | |

Headed by its upstanding roman numeral "I," the roman column begins with a representative American speaker. In reticent, halting phrases the speaker makes his wish to keep his private life private, though the secrets of "someone like me," in this simile of representativeness, are necessarily common property. When "someone / Like me" reappears he sounds more like the private poet of "Litany," raising his troping, screening "flowers all around." The visionary opening augury in italics is also cryptically representative; the phrase "*So this must be*" points toward the idiomatic conclusion, "*the place,*" here occupied by an indefinite void *("a hole").* Descriptions and narrations in the dual monologues of "Litany" are filtered through its self-consciously misrepresentative personae, who wish at once "to keep" their "differences" (or "distance"), both from each other and from the American norm, and "to retain" their "kinship / To the rest."

Beneath this public-spirited American language lie private lives. On the roman side, "Kept in one place," a reverberation of the "*place*" encrypted in the italicized opening, marks its own buried words, "separate" and "private." The word "private" surfaces in a parallel argument in Ashbery's "Grand Galop," where another averaged speaker watches "People parading with their pets / Past lawns and vacant lots, . . . / Before going home to the decency of one's private life / Shut up behind doors, which is nobody's business" (SP 15). What happens "*Behind tall hedges*" on either side of the unwritten Main Street gets buried in this homotext. The "donkey" in the strange locution "The casual purring of a donkey" marks both "cat" and "ass," while in the erotic combat the phallic "hair" "Stands straight up like a tail." Such transgressive acts cross the unwritten, invisible borders between men: "You and Sven-Bertil must / At some point have overridden / The barriers real or fancied" (AWK 7). In one peculiarly misrepresentative reminiscence, an American speaker at the italicized end of "Litany" I recalls: "*The series were all sisters / Back in the fifties when more of this / Sort of thing was allowed. Two could / Go on at once without special permission*" (AWK 16). Beneath Senator McCarthy's radar, borders were freely transgressed, at least in the haze of memory. Later in the poem two Skeltonic stanzas celebrate wine, men, and song: "The sleeve detaches itself from the body / As the two bodies do from the throng of gay / Lovers on the prowl that do move and sway" (AWK 52). The first of these two stanzas rhymes sixteen lines with "May." But the garden in which the gay couple strays soon turns into a graveyard with no "stay / Of execution," and the lovers, introducing a darker rhyme, "soon disappear" (AWK 52). A new stanza begins by denying the old: "Yet none is in disrepair / And soon, no longer in fear / Of the flowers their arrears / Vanish and each talks gaily of his fear" (AWK 52).[17] But in the opening page of "Litany" these variant practices are covered over with rituals and forms. On the left column, the town "parents" (not "fathers") may seek to "escape [carnal] knowledge / Once and for all," but it leaks out in the Freudian slip of "Pissing" for "Passing" or "Posing," a revealing error matched in the opposite column by *"explicit sex,"* which dislodges the euphemistic "delicate" or "private." The crypt word underlying "escape knowledge," signaled by "Once and for all," is "decide." A rite is a decision not to know, not to think about it any more: *"the rite"* in "Litany" only *"emerges as a firm / Enigma, burnished, filled in"* (AWK 15).

What remains in Ashbery's cryptographic text always indicates what has disappeared or what has been covered over. The italicized faith in the *"hole / Of cloud"* marks the absent "will of God." Either *"Mandate or trap,"* this milky middle way, or hazy sign, casts its spell over the *"whole town."* The left column figures these bordering signs as "flowers" which, like homotextual secret passwords, represent "Code names for the silence." On the right side, the small-town picket fences serve as indicators, *"signposts / Pointing to the past"* rather than the future. The small town of "Litany" I consists of vacant houses with only the referential frame left standing as its own signpost: "The dust blows through / A diagram of a room. / This is where it all / Had to take place" (AWK 5). Across the gap we find *Hands where it took place / Moving over the nebulous / Keyboard: the heft / Now invisible, only the fragments / Of the echo are left"* (AWK 6), a passage which echoes Dickinson's resonant quatrain, "There's a certain Slant of light, / Winter Afternoons— / That oppresses, like the Heft / Of Cathedral Tunes—" (#258)—rhyming her slant-rhymed "heft" with "left," and reflecting her "Slant" in its slanted type. The signposts of "Litany" are often marked by demonstrative pronouns, which can point if they can't name: "This is an outburst" (AWK 4); "This rules ideas / Of what else may be there" (AWK 4); *"But it can no longer stand up to / That"* (AWK 4); "It is they who carry news of it" (AWK 5). Ashbery's trademark "it" functions in particular in "Litany" as a neuter-gendered homotextual signpost. Neither male nor female, "it" may indicate the central mystery of homosexuality, as when Ashbery likens his erect columns to *"neuters / Too independent of each other"* (AWK 13–14). But this demonstrative past is forgotten or hidden: *"no one / Remembers except that elf."* This partially erased *"elf,"* also known by the Odyssean pseudonym "'*Noone,*'" marks the absconded "self" that might piece life together.

"Litany" might have ended after its first thirteen-page section, which sketches almost all of its formal topics. But in that case the poem would have remained a postapocalyptic, poststructuralist, postmodern collection of traces. The second, forty-page section of "Litany," its longest and most prosaic, attempts to fill in the blank with various revelatory accounts of a sudden illumination, when "a light bulb / Appears in a balloon above his head" (AWK 42). One eyewitness account records a "New England" oceanside party, which was "Strangely rewarding anyway," although "No one offered you a drink" and "supper / Never appeared on the table." The prevalence of adverbs signals an alien manner: "Presently / Out of this near-chaos an unearthly / Radiance stood like a person in the room, / The memory of the host, perhaps," whereupon everyone "Fell silent, or stayed at their musings, silent / As before, and no one any longer / Offered words of advice or misgiving" (AWK 22). The "host" is remembered here, significantly, not by the singular poet but by a group of communicants. In his introduction to *The Protestant Mystics* Auden describes a strikingly similar epiphany, the "Vision of Agape," which likewise involves "a multiplicity of persons" as "equals": at a faculty dinner party, "We were talking casually about everyday matters when, quite suddenly and unexpectedly, something happened. I felt myself invaded by a power. . . . For the first time in my life I knew exactly . . . what it means to love one's neighbor as oneself. I was also certain, though the conversation continued to be perfectly ordinary, that my three colleagues were having the same experience," or as Ashbery put it, "Inhabiting the same thought" (AWK 22).[18] In each case, the spell of community remains unbroken so long as no one mentions it.

But the pervasive silence between people only temporarily displaces "words of advice or misgiving" (AWK 22). "Litany" offers us not only one silent but two talking columns. In "Litany" II Ashbery introduces two new self-reflexive topics, translation and criticism. Yet simultaneously (and deconstructively), as if to resist any stable hierarchy between "intuitive" and reflective modes of living, he restlessly breaks his own generative rules. After foundering in a convoluted interpretation of the radiant host, the roman column suddenly switches to italics: "*I seemed to have become less averse to laughter / And less disinclined for certain small pleasures,*" "*So that I regretfully concluded / That I would soon again be the same man as before—*" (AWK 23). This passage, which "translates" italics into the roman column, reproduces an English translation of Giacomo Leopardi's meditative journal, "The Woman Who Cannot Be Found."[19] Yet the versified translation appears on the side convention reserves for the original. It is preceded by the reader's lament, "Honey, it's all Greek to me, I—" which is reflected on the translation side by a divided autobiography, *"I came out here originally I"* (AWK 23). Which side, which "I," is the original? In his diary, Leopardi regrets the loss of his idealized Petrarchan Lady less than the loss of the creative melancholy her departure produced in him: "I would have liked to finish the verses, with which I was much pleased, before the heat of my melancholy mood had cooled" (47). His fear of returning happiness proves unfounded as a mention of his Lady's name induces "the same nausea as when I heard cheerful talk, the same grief" (48). Which of these two states, in turn, is the "original" Leopardi? Ashbery alters the English translation, "the man I was before" into *"the same man as before,"* and changes Leopardi's translated, transported state into a paraphrase of his "normal," upright condition: "Meaning: *the same nausea . . . / The same grief*" (AWK 23). The misrepresentation or mistranslation puts the new and old Leopardi on equal footing. As he concluded earlier of an altered state, *"all is other and the same"* (AWK 15).

"Litany" II revolves around the interpretative translations of criticism. With its parallel columns, the poem provides a running commentary on itself, rendering further critical parallel phrasing superfluous. In an interview given around the time he began "Litany," Ashbery expressed dissatisfaction with the criticism of his work, noting that even sympathetic criticism is "a sort of parallel adventure to the poetry. It never gives me the feeling that I'll know how to do it the next time I sit down to write." Ashbery prefaced this remark by observing that "Criticism, in general, has less and less to do with my work. I'm sometimes kind of jealous of my work. It keeps getting all the attention and I'm not. After all, I wrote it."[20] But is Ashbery jealous only of "my work" or also of "criticism," which was getting lots of attention at the end of the 1970s? In a later interview, Ashbery admitted to trying to gain the upper hand with "Litany": "I intended, in 'Litany,' to write something so utterly discursive that it would be beyond criticism. . . . And I think that any true work of art does defuse criticism; if it left anything important to be said, it wouldn't be doing its job. (This is not an idea I expect critics to sympathize with, especially at a time when criticism has set itself up as a separate branch of the arts, and, perhaps by implication, the most important one)."[21] Deconstructive criticism in particular was busy deconstructing literature's claim to originality. In 1979, the year *As We Know* appeared, Harold Bloom edited a collection of essays by Yale critics, *Deconstruction and Criticism,* and wrote the lead essay on Ashbery's "Self-Portrait in a Convex Mirror." Derrida's "Living On: Border Lines," written the same time as "Litany," appended a parallel critical commentary (below a border line) to a critical essay on Blanchot. In "The Critic as Host" J. Hillis Miller argued that the critic was not a paraphrasing parasite but a life-sustaining host. In the poststructuralist age the borderline between literature and criticism seemed to some to have been irrevocably deconstructed.[22]

Ashbery's response to this overrunning of the central divide is his six-page verse "essay on criticism" (AWK 31–37). In "Litany" I he faintly praised the close-reading academy for preserving their microscopically analyzed samples: "*Certainly the academy has performed / A useful function. Where else could / Tiny flecks of plaster float almost / Forever in innocuous sundown almost / Fashionable as the dark probes again*" (AWK 14–15). The function of poetry and its newly fashionable criticism is to make "ordinary" people more aware of their world. But the alienating gap between the knowing critic and the "intuitive" creative writer also separates the knowing poet from the "uncritical" populace. This parallel raises a frightening prospect: perhaps both criticism and poetry are superfluous. Ashbery's partial solution to this possibility is to adopt the litany of the members of the congregation. This shift, away from the plain-spoken preacher of "The System," introduces new discursive possibilities which will be further developed in *Flow Chart*. The litanist complains that "*no one really pays much attention / To anything at all*" (AWK 32). Gathering momentum, he continues, "*You will see them buying tickets / To this or that opera, but how many times / Will they tell you whether they enjoyed it / Or anything?*" (AWK 32). Yet despite the funny, folksy American trailer "*Or anything,*" this fairly unrepresentative sample of daily life (opera is hardly popular entertainment) only betrays the separateness of the poet's persona. The litanist's everyday accent fades as he proposes a new critical awareness: "*It behooves / Our critics to make the poets more aware of / What they're doing, so that poets in turn / Can stand back from their work and be enchanted by it*" (AWK 33). So too, the argument goes, the public will become more conscious of the poet's awareness, "*And then, hopefully, make some sense of their lives, / Bring order back into the disorderly house / Of their drab existences*" (AWK 33). Ashbery argued similarly in a 1970 interview that the function of poetry criticism is to "make the reader want to experience it for himself." To do so, the critic "has to put himself both in the place of the artist and also in the place of the public."[23] The reflexive irony of the clichéd adjective "drab" ensures that the author can disavow his persona's critique of "*your average baker or cheerleader*" (AWK 33). But for poetry, for critical self-consciousness, to justify its existence, some version of the divide must be admitted.

Ashbery finds his way out of this dilemma through his well-trodden path of unknowing. In his most haunting evocation of the central blank, he claims that "*all / Is by definition subject matter for the new / Criticism, which is us: to inflect / It is to count our own ribs, as though Narcissus / Were born blind, and still daily / Haunts the mantled pool, and does not know why*" (AWK 35). The crypt word for "*inflect*" here is "reflect," but the etymological sense, "bend," also indicates the refracted italic lettering. Criticism, as Ashbery sees it, is essentially narcissistic and hence homotextual. This passage inflects both blind Milton and his narcissistic Eve at her reflecting pool. But if reflecting and inflecting divides, the central "Universal blanc" (*Paradise Lost,* III, 48) unites. Ashbery practices his new uncritical criticism of life on Keats's "On the Grasshopper and Cricket," a tantalizing sonnet that inflects itself. In the octave, beginning "The poetry of earth is never dead," the grasshopper "takes the lead / In summer luxury," singing outdoors in the sun's heat. The sestet, revising the earlier claim as "The poetry of earth is ceasing never," brings the song inside a winter stove's fire, where "there shrills / The Cricket's song, in warmth increasing ever."[24] Poetry, paralleling life, becomes an artificial source of energy. As critic, the poet evaluates Keats according to a psychology of response reminiscent of I. A. Richards: "*the writing that doesn't offend us / (Keats' 'grasshopper' sonnet for example) / Soothes and flatters the easier, less excitable / Parts of our brain*" (AWK 36). Such writing leads "*us gradually back to words / With names we had forgotten, old friends from / Childhood, and then everything / Is forgiven at last*" (AWK 36–37). This allegory of remembering forgotten words is powered by a sentimental narrative of mutual forgiveness in which parent and child, critic and poet, and poet and audience are united. For the moment, the words lose their printed inertness and become an oral warming source, like Keats's winter stove: "*The tales / Live now, and we live as part of them, / Caring for them and for ourselves, warm at last*" (AWK 37). The criticism of poetry in "Litany" is the criticism of life. In his commentary on the line "Yet none is in disrepair" (AWK 52) from his own Skeltonic lyric, Ashbery translates his paraphrase into the life of oral narrative: "it is in the disrepair / Of these lives that we not find despair / But all that nourishes and comforts death / In life and causes people to gather round / As when they hear a good story is being told" (AWK 53). Criticism, like poetry, recenters us around our storied lives. Ashbery's narrative of the disappearance of criticism—of dividing words themselves—in life is only another story, which for a time seems a matter of fact.

The two columns of "Litany" III open with the same antithetical conjunction, "But." Of the forty stanzas in this section, nine begin with "But" and one with "However." In *The Principles of Psychology* William James stressed the feelings attached to conjunctions: "We ought to say a feeling of *and,* a feeling of *if,* a feeling of *but.*"[25] What is the feeling of "but"? As a coordinate conjunction, "but" joins two elements of equal weight and emphasis, coordinating simultaneous but independent clauses. But the second element is rhetorically emphasized, syntactically italicized, indicating that the former statement is incomplete. "But" resists the concluding synthesis that the tripartite structure of "Litany" might lead us to expect. Its discourse is rather the litany of complaint, as in the letter concerning the *"Columbia Tape Club,"* which is diagonally crossed by the conjunction: *"But you are leaving," "But since I've been," "I've written them several times but"* (AWK 67–68). "Litany" III opens with a petulant objection: *"But I want him here. / Something is changed without him, / Something we will go on understanding / Until he returns to us"* (AWK 58). By shifting from "I" to "us," Ashbery changes the messenger in this communications system from a lover to a commonly central man, Christ. Meanwhile on the roman side the litany takes the form of a speculative impatience for first principles: "But, what is time, anyway?" (AWK 58). Here the missing "faces and pleasures" mock the thinker like shy Cupids: "The wicked taunting us to some kind of action, / Any kind, with hands partially covering / Their faces, to hide or to mock us, or both" (AWK 58). This gesture from the past, reminiscent of Whitman's taunting lovers, belittles the serenely seductive gesture of Parmigianino's *Self-Portrait in a Convex Mirror.* But what has this to do with time? These haunting erotic experiences are, predictably, "a kind of parallel tide, / A related activity" (AWK 58), but not the central, temporal, neuter "it": "I think the things that are in it / Are more like it, though not quite it" (AWK 58).

The roman column of "Litany" ends magnificently with Ashbery, now the sender in the communications system, misrepresenting the envoy, the poetic speech act with which the poet frees his words. The passage opens with an antagonistic question in the form of a cryptic challenge, "Why keep on seeding the chairs / When . . . no one knows what / He wants?" (AWK 68). Why plant seeds in young minds, or "seat" the auditorium, since future readers may not exist? Apollo challenged Orpheus similarly in "Syringa": "Why pick at a dull pavan few care to / Follow" (HBD 69). In his guardedly offhand response, the post-epic poet imagines his Homeric *epea pteroenta,* "wingèd" or "fletched" word-"arrows" flying into the Roman-type Coliseum, like Christians thrown to the insatiable, lionizing critics: "Probably they won't be devoured / By the lions, like the others." Ashbery's only answer is that his words are as strange to him as they are to us. But by leaving in the blanks of "our not-knowing" (AWK 68), he hopes to have included something central to us as well.

Ashbery wrote most of the lyrics in *As We Know* in the fertile summer of 1978, about two months after he had finished "Litany."[26] Overshadowed by their looming predecessor, these summer poems preoccupy themselves with the question of place. Ashbery means "place" not only spatially, as an inhabited "space," but temporally, as an event "taking place." To make a space a place means to inhabit it, and to be occupied by it in turn. In the more difficult poems place remains an empty speechless space: "In pendent tomes the unalterable recipe / Is decoded. Then, a space, / And another space" (AWK 102). It is helpful to think of "place" in these poems as a verb, as in Stevens's monumental line, "I placed a jar in Tennessee" (46). Domestication, including colonization, is an act of the imagination. But as usual, Ashbery omits the imposition of place names.

The short poems tend to appear in the order of composition (another kind of placement). But they show traces of an earlier arrangement. "No, but I Seen One You Know You Don't Own" (AWK 114), "The Shower" (AWK 115), "Landscapeople" (AWK 116), and the near-sonnet "The Plural of 'Jack-in-the-Box'" (AWK 118) were first published as part of an eleven-poem sequence, "Kannst du die alten Lieder noch spielen?" (after Schumann).[27] The first four of these originally untitled poems are three quatrains each, which suggests that Ashbery was looking for a stanzaic shape before settling on (and in) the four-quatrain poems of his next book, *Shadow Train.* The sonnet form, surfacing only in the last poem, "The Plural," is displaced but not forgotten.

The most accessible poems are the "one-liners," as Ashbery called them, written two days after the Fourth of July, when the United States celebrates its national place.[28] Here a long capitalized title dwarfs its poem, only to be swamped in turn by the expanse of the oversized double-columned page made to order for "Litany" (AWK 95):

OUT OVER THE BAY
THE RATTLE OF FIRECRACKERS

And in the adjacent waters, calm.

As the noise from these bombs bursting in air carries only a little way, so our flag may last only a little while. The sublime long shot of these lines, an ironic perspective at once suburban and oceanic, is unsettling. With their isolated phrases set in an encroaching blankness, "these new poems," as Ashbery noted, "are a re-examination of the experimental poems in *The Tennis Court Oath.*"[29] "Out over the Bay" recalls the horizon of "The New Realism": "This was as far as she would go— / A tavern with plants. / Dynamite out over the horizon / And a sequel, and a racket" (TCO 62). "Out over the Bay" displays the paratactic syntax of "The New Realism" by placing the titular racket and the lyric calm in parallel universes, like the "simultaneous but independent" columns of "Litany." Independence, then, may mean a tenuous interdependence of place and space, history and time. The "calm" following the comma's pregnant pause may, after all, be the "comma" before the storm. A similar reversal of fortunes is sketched in the adjacent poem entitled, also in capital letters, "I Had Thought Things Were Going Along Well": "But I was mistaken." (AWK 94). Here, in an unnarratable interval, the course of one's life has changed. After the harrowing humor of this still delightful poem wears off, an aftershock is registered: the perspective of this minuscule conclusion is so small that nothing can be confidently concluded one way or the other (things may be going along "well" after all). In the larger scheme of "things," one line, one life, is little more than a point. As Ashbery advises in "This Configuration," "You might as well linger / On verandas, enjoying life, knowing / The end is essentially unpredictable" (AWK 109).

The course of a life emptying into the larger course of time is described at greater length in "Haunted Landscape," the longest lyric in *As We Know.* This variation on the "haunted house" suggests that exteriors, like interiors, may be haunted. Ashbery recalled writing the poem "very rapidly . . . without any changes."[30] Cut into quatrains of fiction-length lines that swell and sometimes overflow their margins, this narrative poem covers a great deal of territory. Ashbery has said that the poem was influenced by "one of my all-time favorite movies," Wojciech Has's epic three-hour film, "The Saragossa Manuscript" (1964).[31] The unlucky thirteen-quatrain expanse of "Haunted Landscape" is equally labyrinthine. From a deserted campground we pass through an Edenic farm, the Flood, the prospect of old age, a miracle play, and a house with a poltergeist and a visiting specter, before returning to the landscape. Readers familiar with "Street Musicians" (HBD 1) will recognize the urge to leave the landscape you pass through haunted by your marks: "Something brought them here. It was an outcropping of peace / In the blurred afternoon slope on which so many picnickers / Had left no trace" (AWK 80). To write "no trace" is to mark a ghostly trace. The opening sentence, recalling the haunted landscape of Frost's "Mending Wall" ("Something there is that doesn't love a wall," 47), suggests that this unpromising "plot" (a key crypt word here) of land was promised, foretold in Scripture. The mundane camp accordingly coalesces into the legendary Edenic pair, the delver and his fruitful mother earth. Yet this maternal landscape, bordering on Auden's "In Praise of Limestone," sounds more like *East of Eden:* "She had preferred to sidle through the cane and he / To hoe the land in the hope that some day they would grow happy / Contemplating the result: so much fruitfulness" (AWK 80; "Cain"). In "A Last World" (TCO 56) Ashbery enlivens his genetic narrative with a Darwinian parody.

As the primate Eve waits in her jungle home, "She climbs a tree to see if he is coming / Sunlight breaks at the edges of the wet lakes / And she is happy" (TCO 56–57). The pregnant gaze in "Haunted Landscape" is comparatively soft-focused: "He came now in the certainty of her braided greeting, / / Sunlight and shadow" (AWK 80). Our welcome to this conventionally georgic scene is less assured.

Ashbery's own impatience with his story seems to have prompted the intrusion of "insiders / Secretly amused at their putting up handbills at night" which will be seen by "hardly anyone." His bland landscape is mercifully flooded by a magnificent three-quatrain sentence of vast geological change, which soon casts off historical periods and commas: "They were thinking, too, that this was the right way to begin / A farm that would later have to be uprooted to make way / For the new plains and mountains that would follow after / To be extinguished in turn as the ocean takes over" (AWK 80). Ashbery will later call this apocalypse a wave, which "passes through you, emerges on the other side / And is now a distant city" (W 68). In "Haunted Landscape" the climactic event functions like a hiatus in the manuscript. The glacial sentence ends sentimentally; our cultivated place "has shrunk from the / Outline surrounding it to a little heap or handful near the center" (AWK 80). At the other end is "old age or stupidity, and we, living / In that commodity, know how only it can enchant the dear soul" (AWK 80). Geological artifacts are replaced by human keepsakes, thus softening the irony of writing "commodity" instead of "community." Ordinary life, like "The Saragossa Manuscript," has no "plot": "nothing ever happened," nothing takes place. But that is its virtue, since if the "plot" cannot be followed it is limitless.

The miracle play of life concludes with a present-tense haunting visitation: "The door is opening. A man you have never seen enters the room. / He tells you that it is time to go, but that you may stay, / / If you wish" (AWK 81). Ashbery's messengers bring cataclysmic changes, but this brush with death is postponed. "Haunted Landscape" closes with a nostalgic shot of the landscaped Adam and Eve: "Now time and the land are identical, / / Linked forever." This final sentiment, with the last two words isolated in their own stanza, may have been shaped by Henry Moore, whose enigmatic "Reclining Figure" Ashbery praised in similar terms: "The figure is recognizably female—both a powerful earth mother and a vulnerable earthling, as the apertures cut into her body testify. But she is also landscape, time and weather; she suggests a seamless piece of poetry or music."[32] The weakness of "Haunted Landscape," for all its compelling moments, is perhaps that the rents in its fabric are too seamlessly patched together. There are, after all, cataclysmic events even in unremarkable lives that mark them forever, despite the majestic sweep of the landscape.

Modestly squared into four quatrains, "Many Wagons Ago" (AWK 73; compare the Hollywood Indian idiom "many moons ago") foreshadows the lyrics of *Shadow Train*. Like the titular vehicle "Houseboat Days," this mobile home leaves one unsure who stays and who passes: "At first it was as though you had passed, / But then no, I said, he is still here, / Forehead refreshed. A light is kindled. And / Another. But no I said." In this hesitantly powerful opening, the absent other remains. Here, as elsewhere in this perforated volume, the model is Reverdy, for example his unpunctuated poem "Ce souvenir" ("That Memory"), which Ashbery translated in the late fifties: "I saw you / I saw you in the distance in front of the wall / I saw the hole of your shadow on the wall / There was still some sand left."[33] Like other Ashbery poems connecting "I" with "you," "Many Wagons Ago" draws on the interdependent systems of communication and transportation. The message lies in the kindled stars, if they could only be connected. On the other end of the vertical line, "you," an eclipsed God or a departed lover, may be vigilantly leaving astral lights in the windows.

Since "Nothing"—an audible silence—"Stays to listen" outside, Ashbery moves in the second quatrain inside his folded book ("Doubled up, fun is inside") with a single faithful reader. In his essay "Civilization" Emerson advises, "Hitch your wagon to a star." The exhortation resonates in "Many Wagons Ago," where the night sky is represented within. In Ashbery's starlit text, Emerson's "Hitch" is echoed by "stitch" and the night landscape becomes a needlepoint: "It needs only one intervention, / / A stitch, two, three, and then you see / How it is all false equation planted with / Enchanting blue shrubbery on each terrace / That night produces." Poems take their place on the page and sometimes in the world. This latter prospect, a metaphorical "false equation," comes into focus with the magical "revision" of a word or two. This crypt word surfaces in a parallel passage from "A Wave": "It takes only a minute revision, and see—the thing / Is there in all its interested variegatedness, / With prospects and walks curling away, never to be followed" (W 78). Once it is "sewn" or "sown," this virtual reality yields its own produce. The last quatrain places the landscape artist back with us bewildered receivers. In a final twist of the trope, the constellation lines or needlepoint threads become record grooves threaded by the phonograph needle: "How easily we could spell if we could follow, / Like thread looped through the eye of a needle, / The grooves of light." The spell-binding pattern, or tune, like the "curling walks" in "A Wave," is difficult to follow. But in an ending that revises the astronomical doubt of the opening, that "Nothing . . . / Stays to listen," the faithful few still attend the piece of resistance among the worn record grooves: "It resists. But we stay behind, among them, / The injured, the adored." These final qualifiers open up new, sentimental prospects one hesitates to follow. But there is no "false equation" in their nostalgia.

Ashbery weaves more ambitiously and powerfully in "Tapestry" (AWK 90), one of his finest poems. Like "Wet Casements," "Tapestry" generates power from restraint. It begins with a problem: "It is difficult to separate the tapestry / From the room or loom which takes precedence over it. / For it must always be frontal and yet to one side." Harold Bloom, who has praised "Tapestry" and "Wet Casements" and proposed their early admission into the canon, has given a persuasive allegorical paraphrase of this stanza: "It is impossible to separate the poem, Ashbery's 'Tapestry,' from either the anterior tradition or the process of writing, each of which has priority, and illusion of presence, over it, because the poem is compelled always to 'be frontal,' confronting the force of the literary past, 'and yet to one side,' evading that force."[34] One may find a Bloomian precursor to "Tapestry" in Stevens's "The Plain Sense of Things," which challenges us to see the "great pond, / The plain sense of it, without reflections"—an unmodified place where "It is difficult even to choose the adjective / For this blank cold" (383; "this____cold"). Stevens's difficulty frames Ashbery's "Tapestry," which begins "It is difficult to separate" and ends "Upended in a puddle somewhere / As though 'dead' were just another adjective." History may leave no room for the imagination. Among Ashbery's poems, the aesthetically distanced description in "Tapestry" most directly engages "Self-Portrait in a Convex Mirror," in which the hand "loom[s] large" as it "weave[s] delicate meshes / That only argue its further detention" (SP 70). In its sixth global stanza, Ashbery finds a similar difficulty in abstracting the painting from its museum space: "Yet the 'poetic,' straw-colored space / Of the long corridor that leads back to the painting, / Its darkening opposite— is this / Some figment of 'art,' not to be imagined / As real, let alone special?" (SP 78). Aren't they, and we spectators, bound up in "the present," in "'history' / In the making," as Ashbery calls it in "Tapestry"?

There is more than literary history looming in "Tapestry." The most famous tapestry of history in the making is the Bayeux tapestry (c. 1082), which depicts the contemporary Norman Conquest. The seventy-meter tapestry, which Ashbery saw in 1961 while living in France, is embroidered in wool and winds around its museum room. Ashbery's description of the woolen room in "Tapestry" is similar: "If it has the form of a blanket, that is because / We are eager, all the same, to be wound in it," as in a winding sheet. The Bayeux tapestry narrates the frontal attack, depicted laterally ("to one side"), of William's Normans against Harold's English at the Battle of Hastings. The unfinished tapestry ends with the upended English fleeing the Norman horsemen on foot, abandoning their dead king, with an arrow stitched into his head, as though he were just another fatality.

It is difficult to separate our responses to the historic tapestry from the history it depicts. In "Self-Portrait" Ashbery's viewer found "No way out of the problem of pathos vs. experience" (SP 70). In "Tapestry" the experience is shattering, striking the convex eyeball like a grenade:

> It insists on this picture of "history"
> In the making, because there is no way out of the punishment
> It proposes: sight blinded by sunlight.
> The seeing taken in with what is seen
> In an explosion of sudden awareness of its formal splendor.
>
> The eyesight, seen as inner,
> Registers over the impact of itself
> Receiving phenomena, and in so doing
> Draws an outline, or a blueprint,
> Of what was just there: dead on the line.

The first of these stanzas depicts an attack, and the second defends itself. The pathos of seeing the events depicted on the tapestry is inseparable from the aesthetic experience of its "formal splendor." The seeing eyeball, like Plato's cave or Parmigianino's global room, is a prison from which we never completely escape; we never quite adjust our eyes to the piercing sunlight of the text (history, tapestry) itself. In a review of Jane Freilicher's paintings Ashbery commended her for taking in what and how she saw, thus avoiding corrective realism: "lesser artists correct nature in a misguided attempt at heightened realism, forgetting that the real is not only what one sees but also a result of how one sees it—inattentively, inaccurately perhaps, but nevertheless that is how it is coming through to us, and to deny this is to kill the life of the picture" (RS 242). Objectivity is death for Ashbery as for Stevens (Charles Reznikoff and George Oppen have seen it differently). The plodding biological precision of Ashbery's defensive stanza kills the life of both the tapestry and its spectator. A phenomenological reduction is performed to exorcise the ghost of a response. But, as in "Wet Casements," the gaze is trained back on one's self, on the imprinting eyeball. What is known as the "outline stitch" of the Bayeux tapestry is copied by the eye's objective "outline." As Stevens's objectifying snow man "beholds / Nothing that is not there" without being able not to behold "the nothing that is" (54), the eyeball "kill[s] the life of the picture" by registering "what was just there: dead on the line." The reordering of the expected phrase, "just what was there," reveals history and life passing away from the outline. King Harold, "dead on the line," is killed by the adverbial sense of "dead on," "precisely," which precludes the afterlife of ambiguity. After the funeral, where the deadly accurate spectator is wrapped in the winding sheet of the tapestry, the final stanza nevertheless depicts a kind of afterlife, which softens (if it does not unravel) the finality of "dead." To the spectacle of men making war Ashbery juxtaposes the prospect (Stevensian in style only) of "fruits" making legalized love: "The citizens hold sweet commerce with one another / And pinch the fruit unpestered, as they will." Even though "the dream" with its dreamer ends up "Upended" like Harold, its "words," like riderless (writerless) horses, will continue to cry the occasion, and to make their own history.

Another ambitious history in the making in *As We Know* is "Train Rising Out of the Sea" (AWK 87). "Where would we be," asks the politician, "without this great land of ours?" In this mild parody of Whitmanian optimism, Ashbery meditates on the unity of the United States, our greatest poem. Like "Many Wagons Ago," "Train Rising" is written in coupled quatrains. Its language is based on political oratory, with periods derailing their antecedents. Set in the first and second person plural, the poem favors the objective pronoun "us," which Ashbery and other American poets associate with "U.S." (for example, Eliot, "The river is within us, the sea is all about us," 130). Like "The Wrong Kind of Insurance" (HBD 49), "Train Rising" oscillates between the one and the many, the central paradox of democracy found in our pledge of allegiance, "one nation indivisible," and our motto, "e pluribus unum." The poem begins by pledging its own Declaration of Independence: "It is written in the Book of Usable Minutes / That all things have their center in their dying, / That each is discrete and diaphanous and / Has pointed its prow away from the sand for the next trillion years" ("Book of Hours"). "Independence" and "Declaration" ("making clear") are reworded by "discrete and diaphanous." But it is Jefferson's most famous sentence, "We hold these truths to be self-evident," with its series of dependent clauses ("That all men are created equal; that they are endowed by their creator with certain unalienable rights; that among these are life, liberty, and the pursuit of happiness") that shapes Ashbery's document. The quatrains of "Train Rising" are loosely connected by disparate "that" clauses: "that makes it seem a deliberate act," "That inundates our remarks," "that brought excessive flowering," "That left you feeling too simple." Ashbery employed this Jeffersonian syntax ten years earlier in "Decoy": "We hold these truths to be self-evident: / That ostracism, both political and moral, has / Its place in the twentieth-century scheme of things; / That urban chaos is the problem we have been seeing into and seeing into" (DDS 31). Though the discourse is the same, the differences are self-evident. "Decoy" was a protest poem against economic and sexual inequalities; "Train Rising" is an elegy for the end of an era, and a declaration of interdependence, locating a new American center of gravity: "all things have their center in their dying." Our mortality, if nothing else, unites us.

For his more perfect union Ashbery draws on another well-known document, John Donne's famous meditation: "No man is an *Iland,* intire of it selfe; every man is a peece of the *Continent,* a part of the *maine;. . . .* any mans *death* diminishes *me,* because I am involved in *Mankinde;* And therefore never send to know for whom the *bell* tolls; It tolls for *thee.*"[35] "Train Rising," like Ashbery's next declaration, "The Pursuit of Happiness" (Sh 1), begins with "It," not "We." This core of mortality binds to the mainland each newborn island, each "terrain" (beneath "train") rising out of the sea. This common ground, as in "Decoy," is also legal and economic: "After that we may be friends, / Recognizing in each other the precedents that make us truly social. / Do you hear the wind? It's not dying, / It's singing, weaving a song about the president saluting the trust." After finishing a typewritten draft of the poem (first called "Silhouette," a title he used elsewhere in this volume) Ashbery made two key revisions in this stanza, changing "benefits" to "precedents" and "the past" to "the trust." Ashbery thus ended up hearing America singing a pledge of allegiance to the almighty dollar (with its motto "In God We Trust") and by extension to the U.S. Trust, a "Bank" that is both an "institution" and a "shore" (AWK 87). As the Carter administration launched America into its third century, the United States was foundering in rising unemployment, inflation, and a deficit, an "excessive" borrowing and devaluation which "diminished" us singles as currency, "Taking away a little bit of us each time / / To be deposited elsewhere." Misrepresenting Arnold's touchstone, Ashbery sees in this age "an era that refuses to come to an end or be born again." In "This Configuration," first entitled "A Hundred Years Ago," Ashbery speculates on how "The end" of an era and the rebirth of another might come. "It might be soldiers," he muses, "Or it may be that we and the other people / Confused with us on the sidewalk have entered / A moment of seeming to be natural, expected, / And we see ourselves at the moment we see them: / Figures of an afternoon, of a century they extended" (AWK 109). "Train Rising" ends more tentatively, as Donne's intertext surfaces. Each inflated individual floats "Like an island just off the shore, one of many, that no one / Notices, though it has a certain function, though an abstract one / Built to prevent you from being towed to shore" (AWK 87). The distant antecedent ("our involvement /

With the core") to which this final clause is tied, as by a mooring rope, should keep our individual ships of state "from being washed away." Ashbery's version runs against the tide of his logic, and keeps him loosely tethered to this sinking Trust.

Ashbery's title poem, "As We Know" (AWK 74), is a beautiful and moving riddle, a cryptic message marked urgent. We use the phrase "as we know" to establish a commonly held, tacitly assumed truth or opinion upon which we may construct an argument or theory. But the topic of the poem, identified by the adverbial grammar of its title, is our way of knowing. In Ashbery's lyric space "way" often marks the circumferential, adverbial route to and from the central, nominal "it." In the minimalist, prosaic phrases of "As We Know," "way" takes on metaphysical and epistemological import: "there was no other way to appear," "The way we had come was all we could see." The two-way street of "Litany" with its unreachable median may be a helpful parallel. Like several passages of "Litany," "As We Know" begins with Eliotic paradoxes:

> All that we see is penetrated by it—
> The distant treetops with their steeple (so
> Innocent), the stair, the windows' fixed flashing—
> Pierced full of holes by the evil that is not evil,
> The romance that is not mysterious, the life that is not life,
> A present that is elsewhere.

The momentum of the contradictions, culminating wonderfully in "elsewhere" (instead of "absent"), places "it—" with its Dickinsonian blank off the map. Any theory based on this supposed common knowledge is already shot "full of holes." So, in a series of afterthoughts, Eliot wrote of the center in *Four Quartets:* "Neither flesh nor fleshless; / Neither from nor towards; at the still point, there the dance is, / But neither arrest nor movement" (119). If Eliot's axial point reconciles polar opposites, Ashbery's paradoxical center is not transcendental but mundane, neither "evil" nor "mysterious." Further, his penetrating "it" is insistently phallic, from the "treetops" to the "steeple" (so inviting), up the climactic stair to the "flashing" lighthouse windows. Whereas Eliot grants us "inner freedom from the practical desire," Ashbery binds us with "it" to our elusive carnal knowledge.

The next free-verse stanza penetrates further in, where the dance is: "And further in the small capitulations / Of the dance, you rub elbows with it, / Finger it. That day you did it / Was the day you had to stop, because the doing / Involved the whole fabric, there was no other way to appear." From the casual acquaintance of "rub elbows with it" to the first-hand knowing of "Finger it" to the sexual consummation of "you did it," the way to "it" is followed. "As We Know" radiates from a passage in *Three Poems,* where the initial sexually orienting transgression is something that is easier done than said: "you must have said *it* a long way back without knowing it. . . . We are to read this in outward things: the spoons and greasy tables in this room, the wooden shelves. . . . They have become the fabric of life" (TP 95–96; italics are Ashbery's). Frontal moment and buried declaration ("I love you"), "it" infuses the latent fabric of everyday life. Ashbery comes closer to frontal gay knowledge in "As We Know": "You slid down on your knees / For those precious jewels of spring water / Planted on the moss, before they got soaked up." The pathos of this passage, which recalls the wrenching beginning of the medieval poem *Pearl,* where another man loses his treasure in the grass, comes from an uncertainty about whether these family jewels of wisdom are gained or lost.

In Ashbery's homotextual narrative, frontal knowledge is often followed by fear of punishment. Like a public drunk, the carnal knower "teetered on the edge of this / Calm street with its sidewalks, its traffic, / / As though they are coming to get you. / But there was no one in the noon glare." From this frontal exposure the poem retreats to a private textured interior: "The light that was shadowed then / Was seen to be our lives, / Everything about us that love might wish to examine, / Then put away for a certain length of time, until / The whole is to be reviewed." Like first drafts, these pivotal past experiences are buried in a drawer until the secrets are published, revised and "reviewed." By the end, the public "we" of the title becomes the dual "we," two lovers nearing the end of their way: "The way we had come was all we could see / And it crept up on us, embarrassed / That there is so much to tell now, really now." The shadowed interior is haunted by the past; "it" is now "old age" which "crept up on us." If the latent present "that is elsewhere" relies on a potential future, the actual moment of death becomes the ultimate frontal moment, where the poem's last word, "now," revises the titular "know." As Ashbery puts it in "The System," "Now there is so much to talk about that it seems neither of you will ever get done talking" (TP 95). There is "no way of knowing" (to borrow another of Ashbery's titles) whether the "now" of "As We Know" is "really now" (meaning "let's get serious"). But we can be sure that Ashbery's most penetrating secrets will remain shadowed and full of holes.

By virtue of its titular office, "As We Know" is destined to be widely anthologized and reviewed.[36] I want to end by drawing attention to another poem from *As We Know,* "Knocking Around" (AWK 85), which was to have been the title poem: "The name of this poem is 'Knocking Around,' which I think is going to be the title of the book I intend to collect all these [poems] into. . . . I did get a pair of pants at a sale at Brooks Brothers and the man told me he couldn't do that [put them on sale] because these were for knocking around, which got me thinking of the subject of knocking around and does one do anything else or does one do it at all."[37] "Knocking Around" means wandering aimlessly, "only this time toward no special goal" (TP 29), something Ashbery has espoused since *Three Poems*. Yet "knocking around" also means colliding (promiscuously) with other moving bodies in space, like billiard balls on a table. The title raises the question of choice and responsibility in a world where one's actions are also reactions within a larger system. We knock around in a "chain reaction," a crypt phrase for the poem, which extends into uninhabited space and time. "Knocking Around" begins like the one-liner "I Had Thought Things Were Going Along Well" (with its implied punch-line, "But I was mistaken"): "I really thought that drinking here would / Start a new chain" (AWK 85; "trend"). Yet this "I," like so many first-person beginnings in Ashbery's poetry, is not confessional but representative, one branch of a Whitmanian chain. Such a chain of events creates an ordered, predictable place in time in which we can ignore "the horror stories, the / Noises men make to frighten themselves," knocking around like poltergeists. In our chains our words lie "on the lip of a canyon," gaping like the empty center in "Litany."

The second free-verse stanza begins with a dislocated sentence: "Nothing is very simple." Underneath the complexity is the common phrase "Nothing is certain": nothingness, like death and taxes, awaits us animate objects. Ashbery reminds us "that certain things die out for awhile": "Look at Art Deco / For instance or the 'tulip mania' of Holland." In the representative system, trends and particulars die out as new ones emerge. With "Holland" Ashbery recalls his own daffy catalogue of Hollywood's animated fads, things which knocked around "as though they were responsible / For part of life." If inanimate pop objects are "responsible," certainly we are too: "We are wrapped in / What seems like a positive, conscious choice, like a bird / In air." "Knocking Around" gives us a vertiginous bird's-eye view of time, place, and manner. One's chosen place and sexual way of life are local, while the haunting empty space and time are infinite. But place and space, life and death, presence and absence, are interdependent. In a homely but grim parallel (recasting the Reaper and his wheat fields), Ashbery observes: "They depend on each other like the snow and the snowplow."

If our place of articulation "on the lip of a canyon" lies on the brink of nothing, what security can we find here? After placing us at the edge of his system, where can Ashbery's argument turn? The final stanza of "Knocking Around" clothes us in affirmation:

It's only after realizing this for a long time
That you can make a chain of events like days
That more and more rapidly come to punch their own number
Out of the calendar, draining it. By that time
Space will be a jar with no lid, and you can live
Any way you like out on those vague terraces,
Verandas, walkways—the forms of space combined with time
We are allowed, and we live them passionately,
Fortunately, though we can never be described
And would make lousy characters in a novel.

"Daisy chain," "colander" ("calendar, draining"), and "time clock," crypt phrases in the first sentence, somewhat domesticate its wide open spaces. But the image of Stevens's jar placed not in Tennessee but in the alien universe is, in a word, jarring. Another of Ashbery's tiny one-liners resembles this brink, "We Were on the Terrace Drinking Gin and Tonics": "When the squall hit" (AWK 96). The daisy chains of daily life are fragile. But unlike the one-liner, "Knocking Around" foregrounds adverbs: "more and more rapidly," "Any way," "passionately, / Fortunately." Ashbery's adverbs, including the title phrase "as we know," describe the ways we make places out of spaces. It doesn't matter which particular adverbs or "tendencies" we choose; we can live irresponsibly since we knock around in infinite space. This sublime perspective, observing human things from the outside looking on, tends to reduce them to mechanical toys, free but bound. Ashbery's final qualification, then, is important; if we are finite, we are infinitesimal— indescribable and uncharacterizable. Not knowing is the saving grace of *As We Know.* To know "it," to have bridged the intervening gap in "Litany," would be to define ourselves as "not it," an outline to be filled in. The shape of a poem or a life may have a final form, but to know it in advance is not to live it.

# 9

## Fearful Symmetries

### *Shadow Train*

Between March and mid-October 1979 (with a break in April), Ashbery composed fifty poems, four quatrains each, which eventually came to be called *Shadow Train.* During this period Ashbery, a longtime New York City apartment dweller, found and purchased a Victorian-era house in upstate New York. With its multiple rooms, this house may have provided a blueprint for the many-chambered volume.[1] Reviewing his work in progress, with a nod to the fifty dizains of "Fragment," "Flow Blue" (happily encrypting its earlier title, "The Flowers Bloom"), Ashbery imagines it as a cluttered dwelling: "It may sound like a lot of odds and cloud-filled / Ends—at best, a thinking man's charmed fragment, perhaps / A house" (Sh 36). As he explained, the idea "was an artificial concept that was loose enough to let me do what I wanted and strict enough to bring me to the task each time I wanted to do it. I did the same thing with 'Fragment' actually."[2] But *Shadow Train* will disappoint readers expecting the suspenseful abstractions of "Fragment," and its puzzling form seems a minor sequel to the bold formal departure of *As We Know.* Though it contains some memorable lyrics, the volume is too undiversified for a collection of Ashbery poems, and too little connected for a lyric sequence. Ashbery more engagingly links his poetry in the mixed titular sequence "And The Stars Were Shining," a 25-page poem broken into thirteen sections of variable length, lineation, and stanza size. Begun in December 1992 and composed in its present order, this manifold poem recalls *The Waste Land* and ultimately *Song of Myself.* Merely by numbering breaks, Ashbery allows himself more freedom to break with his preceding measures than he gave himself in "Self-Portrait," "A Wave," or even in *Flow Chart* where the numbered divisions were added later. Though separate titles for the poems of *Shadow Train* might otherwise have encouraged an equal diversity, the predetermined invariant form keeps these independent poems in line.

Poetic unity is relative and multi-dimensional; a collection may be unified, or strategically diversified, in form, style, topic, narrative, and so on. In "Fragment," for instance, Ashbery reproduced his dizains roughly in the order of production, and brought fragmentary, tensely objective narratives into an unstable relation. In *Shadow Train* he rearranged several of the poems out of their production sequence, often with verbal couplings: "It came about" (Sh 1), "At first it came easily" (Sh 2), "what attitude isn't then really yours?" (Sh 2), "[you] have adopted a different attitude" (Sh 3).³ The volume contains some intriguing mini-sequences. The September poems, running from "Night Life" (Sh 29) through "The Leasing of September" (Sh 32), scramble romantic and apocalyptic narratives. "Night Life" rewords the "let's be friends" sequel to a "Dear John" salutation: "come on let's / Be individuals reveling in our separateness." "Written in the Dark" counts the ways to say "I love you": "Telling it five, six, seven times a day, / Telling it like a bedtime story no one knows," until "All these and more were ways / Our love assumed to look like a state religion" (Sh 30). The next lyric, "Caesura," parallels the evicted lover with "Job [who] sat in a corner of the dump eating asparagus" (Sh 31). In "The Leasing of September," the earliest written poem in this series, "You stepped into a blue taxi" (Sh 32), presumably to take over a September lease. As an apocalyptic epilogue to these poems, Ashbery adds "On the Terrace of Ingots," written much earlier (late March), which begins: "It was the bitterness of the last time / That only believers and fools take for the next time" (Sh 33). In this indirect, intermittent fashion, Ashbery advances some stories and topics on different fronts. But while individual poems in *Shadow Train* reflect on sequentiality, as a whole the volume is not a shadowy "train of thought" or "train of events." For the most part, the boxcars are on their own.

The unsettling absence of a clear progression in many of the poems is compounded by their shrewd symmetrical form; every quatrain looks like every other one. Ashbery explains that his apparently stable stanzaic pattern of four qua-trains is really "a kind of antiform": "It looks sensible enough on the page but, in fact, it lacks the 'meaningfulness' of the sonnet, a logical form."⁴ The Petrarchan sestet and the Shakespearean couplet reasonably conclude their sonnets partly because their unequal length signals that the series of quatrains is over.⁵ In Ashbery's modular poems, however, no formal destination is reached. Ashbery likened this structure to the effect that "the minimalist artists of the 1960s such as Donald Judd were aiming at—four oblongs next to each other, rather than a hard, humanistic treatment of geometry such as you get in Piet Mondrian. It really is, then, an asymmetry, a coldness, an alteration. There was the sense of cutting things up, putting them in a kind of Procrustean Bed rather than letting them ooze out into a freedom of their own."[6] Yet the minimalism of *Shadow Train* is also congruent with the diagonal paintings of Mondrian, as Ashbery described them in the fall of 1979, when he was at work on his series: "These compositions go about their business as though dealing with the customary square or oblong containing frame, yet they are unexpectedly truncated and finally liberated by the soaring and diminishing implications of the diamond shape."[7] A few weeks later a similar description crept into "Unusual Precautions," where lives are seen as "diagonal, vertical, shallow, chopped off / / At the root" (Sh 35).

The anti-form of *Shadow Train* also seems influenced by the decorative postmodern trend of the late 1970s. In a July 1979 article reviewing two exhibits in Philadelphia, Ashbery noted that "Painting, sculpture, crafts, one's environment, one's body and the way it moves, are all being marshaled under the adjective 'decorative.'" Despite this confusion of genres, the movement is a "serious . . . corrective to the puritanical excesses of Minimalism, just as Pop Art was a reaction to the seriousness of Abstract Expression."[8] The decorative "pattern painting" of *Shadow Train* patterns its elements after fabric and wallpaper. In a passage reminiscent of the centripetal messages in "Litany" Ashbery notes that the maypole of the times centers all surrounding elements: "Whatever twists around it is decoration and can never / Be looked at as something isolated, apart" (Sh 37). Decorative elements come with their system attached.

This decorative impulse is transcendental; the wall shadows of Ashbery's cave point beyond themselves. When asked in the early 1980s about a "certain religious tone" in his poetry, Ashbery responded: "Everything seems to be sort of transcendental, a kind of shadow of something else."[9] Shadows foreshadow. In the theological lyric "The Absence of a Noble Presence" Ashbery points to the "shadow in the plant of all things / / That makes us aware of certain moments, / That the end is not far off" (Sh 11; "plan," "aware at"). Shadows reveal the Noble Presence to be not only immanent but imminent. With their impending shadows, Giorgio de Chirico's canvases are an obvious forerunner. In his essay "Mystery and Creation," de Chirico speculates that "perhaps the most amazing sensation passed on to us by prehistoric man is that of presentiment. It will always continue. We might consider it as an eternal proof of the irrationality of the universe."[10] The fear of what the lengthening shadows betoken creates what Ashbery has described as "the angst of de Chirico's piazzas."[11]

The irrationality that begs the transcendental question is manifested in the contradictory statement of paradoxes ("The longest way round is the shortest way home") and the verbal irrationality of oxymorons ("freezing fire"). Donne's *Paradoxes and Problems* ("That Nature is Our Worst Guide") and Kafka's minimal narratives in *Parables and Paradoxes* share the transcendental urge. Cleanth Brooks, whose *The Well Wrought Urn* was a new critical handbook when Ashbery was an undergraduate at Harvard, reconciled the romantic with the metaphysical poets through their use of paradox, a prominent closural device in new criticism.[12] Yet the ruthless symmetries of *Shadow Train* keep us from overcoming logical antinomies and narrative suspensions. Like the double-columned "Litany," with its "*Antithesis chirping / To antithesis*" (AWK 8), the parallel rails never meet.

Both paradox and imminence contour the unnerving poem that opens the volume, "The Pursuit of Happiness" (Sh 1): "It came about that there was no way of passing / Between the twin partitions that presented / A unified façade, that of a suburban shopping mall / In April. One turned, as one does, to other interests." The opening narrative formula translates into the paradox that it came to pass that there was no way of passing: the entrance to the volume is blocked. The impasse includes Ashbery's previous constructions. The "twin partitions" recall the double-columned "Litany," and the opening closure echoes the beginning of the fifty-chambered "Fragment": "The last block is closed in April" (DDS 78). Since Ashbery wrote no poems for *Shadow Train* in April, this "unified façade" ("united front") may mark an impasse in his project. "April" may also have been selected for its capital "A," which probably influenced the initial placement of "The Pursuit of Happiness"; "The Vegetarians," the poem written and placed last in the series, posts its final letter with "Zurich" (Sh 50).

The patriotic title of "The Pursuit of Happiness" leads not to the kind of political oratory Ashbery used in "Decoy" (DDS 31) but to an alienated objectivity, impossible for us to "identify with," characterized by the pronoun "one": sign both of objectivity and of representative singularity. "The Pursuit of Happiness" plays on the title's double genitive: the alien "happiness" now pursues us, "waiting for the expected to happen" (Sh 43). Ashbery's central, unnameable "It," the key signature for *Shadow Train,* is an expletive ("It came about"), but it may also be read as an alien, foreshadowing the creature which "came creeping" in the second quatrain. The democratic specter of "a suburban shopping mall," a shopping "center" where consumer happiness is intently pursued, mirrors the wall-sized "tides in Bay of Fundy," one of Ashbery's brilliant misrepresentations. The alienated, disinterested "One" of the first quatrain is now replaced by its "towering" twin (as in the Twin Towers of New York's World Trade Center): "one / Who all unseen came creeping at this scale of visions / Like the gigantic specter of a cat towering over tiny mice / About to adjourn the town meeting due to the shadow." Most literally a gathering storm "front" ("façade") creating sharp "incisive" shadows, the creeping one is likened to the cat which disrupts the democratic "town meeting" in the fable of the belling of the cat.[13] In the central cryptic pun of the poem, "it" crouches like a great cat ready to "maul" ("mall") its shoppers.

"The Pursuit of Happiness" raises anxieties in the face of the faceless, immense capitalist system. Like the invariant sequence, the chain mall appears "in its outrageous / Regularity" during the April Easter shopping season like Christ, "too perfect" it seems "to be called to stand trial again." As the storm breaks, raindrops (as in the Protestant hymn "Showers of Blessing") fall on the hungry populace like manna from heaven "That every blistered tongue welcomed," "Caus[ing] the eyes to faint, the ears to ignore warnings"; "Having eyes, see ye not?" Christ asks, "and having ears, hear ye not?" (Mark 8:18). The concluding hyper-sonnet couplet of "The Pursuit of Happiness" shifts to the first person plural, so that we identify at last with the parched receivers in the system, just getting by: "We knew how to get by on what comes along, but the idea / Warning, waiting there like a forest, not emptied, beckons." In the first draft, Ashbery ended with "blackens." The cryptographic revision to "beckons" is a happy one, mixing seduction and violence. In this final line, riddled with suspenseful pauses, Ashbery's model is not the sonneteers but the American inventor of the quatrain, Dickinson. Her suspenseful sonnet-length lyric "He fumbles at your Soul" towers over Ashbery's poem, especially in its cliff-hanger ending: "When Winds take Forests in their Paws— / The Universe—is still—" (#315). Like the tottering enjambments of "Litany," the caesuras of *Shadow Train* sound the alarm of silence.

Written during the pause of the autumnal equinox, "Caesura" offers itself as a misrepresentative "cross section of the times" (Sh 31). But the afflicted figure in this story is not unduly concerned: "Job sat in a corner of the dump eating asparagus / With one hand and scratching his unsightly eruptions / With the other. Pshaw, it'd blow over." The uncomplaining Old Testament figure is kin to Ashbery's pop Jehovah, Popeye, in the sestina "Farm Implements and Rutabagas in a Landscape": "It was domestic thunder, / The color of spinach. Popeye chuckled and scratched / His balls: it sure was pleasant to spend a day in the country" (DDS 48). But "Caesura" resembles a comic strip less than a film, with quick "cuts" ("caesuras") between shots. Around five years earlier, in "Forties Flick," Ashbery foreshadowed suspense in black-and-white: "The shadow of the Venetian blind on the painted wall, / Shadows of the snake-plant and cacti" (SP 5). Here the panning is more frenetic. Successfully revising his Twin Towers, Ashbery finds a grammatical equivalent to Job's litany, the nonsequential list: "'I have one ambulance three nuns two (black- / And-white list) cops dressed as Keystone Kops lists, a red light / / At leafy intersection list.' Then it goes blank, pulp-color." After the cut hyphenated adjective, and the stop at the stanza-breaking "red light," the black-and-white shot cuts to an autumnal hiatus in the manuscript, reproducing the blank middle of "Litany." The sufferings of this litanist are work-related, produced from a pun on "Job" and "job": "His thoughts / / Were with the office now: how protected it was, / Though still a place to work." "Caesura" ends telegraphically, with the temporal sequence and Robert Frost's inner weather restored: "The darkness and light have returned. It was still / The weather of the soul, vandalized, out-at-elbow. A blight. Spared, though." This powerful ending is filmed through Job's eyes and told in his words. Seasonal and work routines may return, but the two fissured two-word sentences do not make much of an interval between caesuras.

The most popular poem in *Shadow Train* is its tantalizingly simple statement of poetics, "Paradoxes and Oxymorons" (Sh 3). As late as the galley proofs, Ashbery thought of making it his title poem. He wanted to use the title "with the photograph I found that I liked very much of the interior of a Viennese house—in a Jugendstil style—which seemed to have overtones of Wittgenstein in it, not only the title but the room itself. As you know, Wittgenstein was an architect in that period and designed at least one very odd-looking house." But he decided that the title "seemed a bit difficult for your average book buyer who goes into a bookstore and says: 'I'd like that book by John . . . What's it called?' It would have been quite a mouthful. I feel that most people don't know what an oxymoron is, and I haven't known too long myself."[14] The poem itself voices Ashbery's populist impulse to reach the common reader, who thinks poems are constructed on many interpretive levels. There is frustration on both sides:

> This poem is concerned with language on a very plain level.
> Look at it talking to you. You look out a window
> Or pretend to fidget. You have it but you don't have it.
> You miss it, it misses you. You miss each other.

On the "level plain" of this communications system, the paradoxical pair of poem and reader stands in for two lovers. A few pronominal substitutions bring the romantic discourse to the surface: "Look at me talking to you," "You miss me, I miss you," and so on. This homoerotic subtext connects the poem to the envoy of "Song of Myself": "Failing to fetch me at first keep encouraged, / Missing me one place search another, / I stop somewhere waiting for you" (247). Ashbery gives a more explicit rendition of this romance in his suggestively entitled "Or in My Throat," where he recommends poetry as an alternative to oral sex: "It's clean, it's relaxing, it doesn't squirt juice all over" (Sh 25).

In the second quatrain of "Paradoxes and Oxymorons" the reader interrupts the poet, as in an interview, with a few questions: "What's a plain level? It is that and other things, / Bringing a system of them into play. Play? / Well, actually, yes, but I consider play to be / / A deeper outside thing." Like his paradoxical formulation "on the outside looking out," the oxymoron "A deeper outside thing" is an apt description of Ashbery's poetry, "not / Superficial," as he says in "Self-Portrait," "but a visible core" (SP 70). What deepens Ashbery's level playing field are his random Cagean procedures, a hugely varied "division of labor" between the poet and language: "And before you know / It gets lost in the steam and chatter of typewriters." If infinitely many monkeys are set before typewriters, the statistical paradox goes, they will sooner or later produce Shakespeare's plays. Ashbery's poem "has been played" like a record or a trick. But perhaps it is the reader's trick as well. In the communications system, the ideal reader now resembles the Divine Paradox: "I think you exist," the poet asserts, "and then you aren't there." In his final paradox, "The poem is you," varying the dedication "the poem is yours," Ashbery yields himself to the reader, who nevertheless continues to "miss" him.

Several poems in *Shadow Train* concern the sequence, or noncausal series, of a life. One of the most delightful is the unabashedly nostalgic "Untilted" (Sh 26; scrambling the painterly "Untitled"). With his opening exclamation and closing tear, Ashbery reprises the gently parodic style of *Some Trees*. The poem, which captures the highwire act of "living in the past on the ridge / Of the present," is perhaps a retrospective on Ashbery's arrival in the city, in 1949, "as I began / To live." Like Franz Hals's cavaliers, his revelers reproduce "the tilt of the wine in the cavalier's tilted glass / That documents so unerringly the faces and the mood in the room." "Untilted" pays homage to another vertiginous performance, Bishop's "The Man-Moth" (a misspelled "mammoth"), written soon after her own arrival in New York. "Untilted" begins exultantly at the top: "How tall the buildings were as I began / To live, and how high the rain that battered them!" "The Man-Moth" opens similarly: "Here, above, / cracks in the buildings are filled with battered moonlight" (14). Like the man-moth, Ashbery's speaker clambers down noctural skyscrapers: "coming down them, as I often did at night, / Was a dream." "The Man-Moth" ends with a single, surreal, self-reflexive tear: "one tear, his only possession," which is "cool as from underground springs and pure enough to drink" (15). At the end of "Untilted" the tear is cradled, like the "average violin" in "Street Musicians": "It hurts now, /

Cradled in the bend of your arm, the pure tear, doesn't it?" Bishop died a little over a month after "Untilted" was written; in retrospect, the homage becomes a fitting elegy.

The backward glance is more sidelong in "Penny Parker's Mistake" (Sh 24), a brief study of authorial (ir)responsibility. With his title Ashbery was "trying to characterize or give an example of a certain kind of individual by using a name—in this case, I suppose, it would have been somebody like Nancy Drew—a girl's heroine." Unlike "Europe," which followed the exploits of *Beryl of the Biplane,* "Penny Parker's Mistake" uses no collage or detective discourse. Ashbery recalls that he found a book in upstate New York "which I had completely forgotten [I owned]. It was called *The Missing Houseboat—A Penny Parker Mystery.* I suppose that must have influenced both *Houseboat Days* and 'Penny Parker's Mistake.'"[15] Like *Shadow Train,* such novels form a continuing series of adventures unified only by their central character. The poem begins defensively with a long convoluted sentence, elongating the crypt phrase "any way you look at it": "That it could not be seen as constituting an endorsement / Any way she looked, up, down, around, around again, always the same / For her, always her now, was in the way it winked back." The impinging historical self is represented here by a complex grammatical subject, "That ... now," and a simple verb, "was." The past "now, was" reflexive, winking back, without "endorsing" its present product. Yet the heroine's "selling these old Indian dinosaur / / Eggs" looks back to the opening "advertise[ment]" (SP 68) of "Self-Portrait." Does the poet endorse the poem, does the poem advertise the poet? In "Self-Portrait" Ashbery remarks that "The skin of the bubble-chamber's as tough as / Reptile eggs" (SP 72). Though self-enclosed and self-sustaining, the convex eggs still bear their producer's likeness. In his second, equally tortuous eight-line sentence, Ashbery concedes that the producer does remain "in some obscure way in [the] debt" of his past products. Each egg represents a petrified moment in the past, with its characteristic look: "with little gold flecks / And reflection of wet avenues."

"Nothing succeeds like success," gloated the successful novelist Alexandre Dumas. The cultural capitalist of "Penny Parker's Mistake" admits that "we caring for the success of the success / / Cannot cancel postures from some earlier decade of this century / That come to invade our walking like the spokes of an umbrella" ("waking," "dreams"). These "spokes" or "spoken" words still play their part in Ashbery's current self-portrait. Yet the process is not straightforward or concentric. In a wonderful apostrophe in "Crossing Brooklyn Ferry" Whitman creates his own representative reflection: "Diverge, fine spokes of light, from the shape of my head, or any one's head, in the sunlit water!" (313). Ashbery's winking reflection is not "sunlit" but shadowed ("umbra"). And his radial reflection is not quite "natural." Two of the four sentences in "Penny Parker's Mistake" begin with the same tacit assumption: "For naturally," "Now, naturally." Poetic, and human, "development" (literally, an unwrapping or unrolling) is considered a natural "sequence," like evolution. Did we come from dinosaur eggs or they from us? In the closing line of the poem Ashbery compares his reptilian development to the progressive stages of drunkenness: "To be uncoiling this way, now, is the truer, but slier, stage of inebriation" (Sh 24; "unwinding" after a day's work). The serpentine progression of "Penny Parker's Mistake" may not be straightforward ("slier" contains "lies"), but the reflection is nonetheless "truer."

The title poem, "Shadow Train" (Sh 48), itself went by other titles. Ashbery first called it, in the manner of one of Aesop's fables, "The Banana and the Strawberry," and then produced a PG version, "The Lion and the Squirrel," with homotextual allusions intact: "To that end the banana shakes on its stem, / / But the strawberry is liquid and cool" (Sh 48). The poem was written on July 26, 1979, two days before Ashbery's birthday. This impending anniversary, one of an indefinite number of rounds, becomes a sweet, whole note in a musical sequence, "a rounded / Note in the descending scale." This line echoes an earlier quatrain poem, "Melodic Trains" ("melodic strain"): "Each voice has its own / Descending scale to put one in one's place at every stage" (HBD 25). Each quatrain is another stair step ("scala") downward.

The descending musical progression begins seductively with "violins" (the opening crypt word): "Violence, how smoothly it came / And smoothly took you with it / To wanting what you nonetheless did not want." What is the moral to this fable of the runaway sexual progression? Ashbery provides several: "To want is to be better than before. To desire what is / Forbidden is permitted. But to desire it / And not want it is to chew its name like a rag." Ashbery's truth seems to be the Proustian one, that forbidden desires are desired out of habit. Conditioned desire is the violence of the strain. At a certain point, so goes the sour-grapes philosophy, one knows the score too well to play it again.

"Shadow Train" ends by comparing the inner with the outer train of events: "history merely stretches today into one's private guignol. / The violence dreams. You are half-asleep at your instrument table" (Sh 48). But was the Iran hostage crisis in 1979, for instance, really comparable to this erotic Punch-and-Judy show? Ashbery only drafts his view of political theater in "Shadow Train." The counterargument, that one's private guignol stretches into historical conflict, what men do to each other, seems more to the point. In any case, the passionate poet is the puppeteer of his guignol, seeking to conduct his behavior from his "instrument panel" (the crypt phrase), either an air-traffic control tower or a recording studio. But his alertness falters in the erotic trance, and the descending scale is forgotten once again. And it should be, because Ashbery's thesis, "To want is to be better than before," convinces no matter what follows from it.

# 10

## The One That Got Away

### *A Wave*

With its refreshingly various short poems, rivaling those of *Houseboat Days,* and its surging title poem, more outgoing than the recalcitrant "Fantasia," *A Wave* is Ashbery's strongest book since *Self-Portrait in a Convex Mirror* and *Three Poems.* After confining himself to quatrains in *Shadow Train,* Ashbery breaks out in *A Wave* into a multitude of new and renewed prose and verse forms. The forty-three short poems were selected from a larger group of around seventy lyrics written for the most part between 1980 and 1983. One poem in quatrains entitled "The Songs We Know Best" (W 3; dated April 11, 1980), a hilariously soulful number set to the rhythm of Peaches and Herb's "Reunited," lightens up the anxious quatrains of *Shadow Train.* With its blues phrasing ("now you're lookin' good all up and down the line"), wooden rhymes ("confetti" / "spaghetti," "lurch" / "perch"), and pop gospel refrains ("But didja ever think of what that body means?"), Ashbery is reunited at last with the experiments in doggerel he made first in *The Double Dream of Spring* (and will resume in *Flow Chart*). The protean volume includes a translation from Baudelaire, a pantoum, "37 Haiku," six haibun; and three prose poems. With the rest of the poems in free-verse paragraphs of varying lengths and widths, Ashbery assumes an engaging American informality, at once folksy and abstract, that will characterize much of his work to come.

One surprising turn is Ashbery's appropriation of Japanese verse and prose forms, particularly the haiku (or "hokku"), the verse equivalent of macramé in America's 1960s. He had approximated the concise form in "The Skaters" IV, but had yet to take up the form by name until "37 Haiku" (nicely placed on W 37). The impetus came from *From the Country of Eight Islands,* translated primarily by Hiroaki Sato, which set Ashbery to work almost as soon as it was published.[1] He focused on the hokku of the best known poet, Matsuo Basho, whose "Seventy-Six Hokku" Sato renders in single lines. Also crafted in single, sparsely punctuated lines, which may or may not be read sequentially, Ashbery's "37 Haiku" may be considered either as prose or as verse. Some involve a fusion of lyric images: "You lay aside your hair like a book that is too important to read now" or "A pencil on glass—shattered! The water runs down the drain" (W 38). Others (like many of Basho's) are determinedly prosaic and unbeautiful: "What is the past, what is it all for? A mental sandwich?" (W 38) or "Pirates imitate the ways of ordinary people myself for instance" (W 37). One of these pirated imitations reads like a novel: "Hesitantly, it built up and passed quickly without unlocking" (W 38). In the turbulent New York skyline a building may rise and fall without so much as opening. The idiom "built up" applies to feelings, such as fear or nausea, which mount and subside without being revealed. But the trademark opening adverb, "Hesitantly," discursively marks this sentence as pulp romance, a near encounter: "Hesitantly, he got up and passed quickly without looking." The word "unlocking" seems an odd marker for the crypt word "looking," but it serves its purpose of keeping the heart's secrets. As the next haiku affirms, "There are some places kept from the others and are separate, they never exist" (W 38).

Another form Ashbery discovered in Sato's anthology was the haibun, a prose passage followed by a haiku, which Basho used for his travel diaries. Ashbery's haibun share more than the form with Basho's. In "Snowball," for instance, Basho tells of visits from a neighbor, who helps to prepare his food. Basho is careful to point out that "our relationship doesn't involve money." As its self-referential haiku attests, the poem itself enters into their exchange: "You, make a fire. I'll show you something nice—a snowball."[2] Ashbery's "Haibun 4" (W 42; dated November 21, 1981) also envisions a "universal brotherhood" in which relations between men are not based on money. The haibun begins with a weather note, "Dark at four again," setting the poem in the short, dark days of November when vision is obscured. The rain makes its own action painting, "drips and squiggles of light" on the modern traveler's windshield, as the poet drives the narrow roads with his foot on the piano-brake "pedal held down so that the first note echoes throughout the piece." Its "message of universal brotherhood through suffering" first appeared in "Houseboat Days," with its "Pain in the cistern, in the gutters" (HBD 39). Here the weather seems to precipitate "a man, it was one all along. No it isn't. It is a man with the conscience of a woman." In "Man Carrying Thing" Stevens likens poetic obscurity to a man's approach: "The poem must resist the intelligence / Almost successfully. Illustration: / / A brune figure in winter evening resists / Identity. The thing he carries resists / / The most necessitous sense" (281). What Stevens knows of the "man" is that he belongs to the "obvious whole" of mankind or brotherhood. In Ashbery's rainy blur, the man's gender is feminized into a composite which makes brotherhood possible. As his man comes in out of the rain, he is "wondering about a possible reward," as though for returning something lost. As with Stevens's man carrying something, and Basho's man carrying kindling, an exchange of goods or services is offered. What is exchanged in "Haibun 4" is perspective. We now see things from the approaching man's point of view, "turning to look at you." In this darkened reflection, "Haibun 4" revises the angry poem of betrayal, "Wet Casements," as the man brings a "knowledge in his way of coming" as "sweet" as Eden's fruit. Ashbery's allegory of obscurity borrows from St. Paul's famous figure: "For now we see through a glass, darkly, but then face to face" (I Cor. 13:9–12). His glimpse through the windshield condenses in the moving haiku: "The pressing, pressing urgent whispers, pushing on, seeing directly" (like Sato, Ashbery ends his haiku without periods). The "depressing" day is forgotten in "the pressing" of the Whitmanian crowd into the man who approaches.

Among the prose pieces in *A Wave* ("prose poem" does not encompass their generic and discursive variety), "Description of a Masque" (W 18–30) represents Ashbery's most radical departure from his previous prose styles. Unlike *Three Poems,* "Description" is cloyingly, hilariously artificial, insisting, like the Renaissance masque, on its own artifice. *Three Poems,* which begins with the problem of aesthetic selection, is certainly self-referential, but it does not question the reality or the significance of its questions. On the contrary, it raises the importance of aesthetic selection by making it representative of the ethical and metaphysical problem of choice and destiny. And though "Description" describes itself as "rolling its waves across our vision like an ocean" (W 27), it lacks the modernist high seriousness of "A Wave" (the belief that writing is an act, or at least a testimony, of survival), compensating with a plenitude of misrepresentative particulars and environments. With its allegorically heightened and stiffened dialogue and its profusion of high and pop cultural objects, "Description" has more in common with "Daffy Duck in Hollywood" (HBD 31).

As the title suggests, the generic backdrop, if not the literary "background," for "Description of a Masque" are the masques of Jonson and Milton (whose epic Satan looms behind Ashbery's Daffy). Milton's *Comus* in particular helps focus the elusive allegorical dimension of "Description." Several of Ashbery's settings, props, scenes, and characters are on loan from Milton's (luxuriously staged) allegory of the triumph of Chastity. Ashbery's heroine, Mania, is wooed away from her grotto by Mercury, in the guise of a Stranger, in an acrimonious Miltonic debate (W 23–24). One setting in "Description" is the morally bewildering "forest scene" (W 22) of *Comus,* drawn most immediately from "a Tenniel illustration for *Through the Looking Glass*" (W 18). Mania waves a Comus-like "wand with a gilt cardboard star at its tip" (W 22), signifying her Hollywood star stature. For the sensual beasts of Comus, son of Circe, Ashbery gives Mania a pet hyena and Alice a baby pig. Comus's revelers are played in "Description" by a host of nursery rhyme characters, and a "corps de ballet of hobos" (W 22), who appear in "the interior of an English pub, as it might be imitated in Paris" (W 18) rather than at Comus's convivial table. Two of the rout, Jack Horner and the Knave of Hearts, argue like the chaste Lady's brothers in *Comus.* And the nymph Sabrina, who frees Milton's heroine at the conclusion of *Comus,* suddenly and ominously appears "clasping an old-fashioned kodak, which she had pointed at Mercury" (W 30) at the end of "Description."

Ashbery unsettles Milton's allegory by reducing his principles from three (the Lady, Comus, and the Attendant Spirit) to two; "Description" speaks both for conviviality (or adaptability) and for chastity (or independence). Mercury is variously cast in Ashbery's masque. The semi-divine figure, who by the end of the masque "had become both more theatrical and more human" (W 29), most closely resembles Milton's Attendant Spirit. But he also plays the part of Comus in his seductive *débat* with Mania. The inventor of the lyre and the messenger of the gods, Mercury represents quicksilver change, a trademark of Ashbery's poetry. He is featured in Jonson's masque, *Mercury Vindicated from the Alchemists at Court,* where his exuberant prose anticipates Ashbery's: "what between their salts and their sulphurs, their oils and their tartars, their brines and their vinegars, you might take me out now a soused Mercury, now a salted Mercury, now a smoked and dried Mercury, now a powdered and pickled Mercury. Never herring, oyster, or cucumber passed so many vexations."[3] Whereas Jonson's Mercury defends natural creation against alchemical simulations, Ashbery's recommends that we immerse ourselves in the artificial sublime.

As "goddess of confusion" (W 18), Mania manifests another dimension of "Description," its postmodern confusion of different levels of reality (the description, the masque, the statue of Mercury, the goddess Mania, the mural of Alice, the Pie Man) and of culture (*La Bohème* and *Lassie*). Secluded in her grotto with her pet hyena and nursery revelers, Mania recalls Comus's mythic mother, Circe, who appeared in Ashbery's *The Heroes* (1953), his first attempt at the Hollywood antics of "Description": "Oh I could kill that man! But what if I did? Everybody'd say they always expected it of me! *(She sobs awhile.)* There's only one thing to do. Luckily I brought along this girdle, which will make every man who sees me in it fall hopelessly in love with me. *(She slips it on.)* There we are. Love conquers all, as the poet said" (Plays 11). Her dissolute companions and mythic lineage notwithstanding, Mania also shows flashes of Milton's Lady's imperious chastity: "My sister *Hecat* ... warned me of this dell, seemingly laid out for the Sunday strolls of civil servants, but in reality the haunt of drifters and retarded children" (W 22; "*Hecat*" also appears italicized in *Comus*). "Mania" (related to the Latin "Manes") is the little-known mother of the Lares, the protective Roman household gods. But the word is more common in Greek, where it signifies the inspired enthusiasm and artistic madness ridiculed by Plato. Ashbery may also have had Mercury's mother "Maia" in mind ("Mania" preserves all its letters in order). In any event, Mercury and Mania make a volatile compound.

If the masques of Jonson and Milton provide the mythological and allegorical scaffolding for "Description," the novels of Raymond Roussel supply the mainspring for its perversely artificial descriptions. After describing Mania's pet hyena, Ashbery directs our attention to its implausible facsimile, "a metal shoescraper in the form of a hyena, and very like this particular one, whose fur was a grayish-white faintly tinged with pink, and scattered over with foul, liver-colored spots" (W 18). Roussel's fantastic machines are likewise marked with signs of decay, as in *Locus Solus:* "Suddenly, of its own accord, the paving-beetle rose into the air and, propelled by a gentle breeze, made a slow, straight flight of some fifteen to twenty feet, alighting not far from us upon a smoker's tooth browned by tobacco."[4] Some of Ashbery's scenes seem to be directed by Rousselian encrypted phrases. The nursery rhyme "Little Boy Blue come blow your horn," for instance, is set in a gay bar, where "Little Jack Horner, in fact quite a tall and roguish-looking young man wearing a trench coat and expensive blue jeans," sits facing "Little Boy Blue [who] partially knelt before him, apparently performing an act of fellatio on him" (W 19). "Description" is well stocked with high and low camp transvestism. At one point, Ashbery's romantic leads reappear on a Hollywood set, Mania mannishly "dressed in the style of Joan Crawford in *Mildred Pierce,* in a severe suit with padded shoulders," while "the man at her side wore a broad-brimmed hat, loose-fitting sport coat and baggy gabardine slacks; he bore a certain resemblance to the actor Bruce Bennett but closer inspection revealed him to be the statue of Mercury, with the paint still peeling from his face around the empty eye sockets" (W 26). Bruce Bennett, who also makes a cameo appearance in "Fantasia" (HBD 83), was the character actor who played "Mildred's" first husband. Ashbery's Crawford knows him as "Herman Brix," the actor's real name, which in this context subtly suggests his divine role as Hermes (the Greek Mercury). Personalities in "Description" are shed like costumes.

In a parody of the masque's allegorical machinery, Ashbery has Mania explicate her appearance: "this spangled gown and these tangled tresses [are] meant to epitomize the confusion which is the one source of my living being" (W 22). Likewise, the endlessly and pointlessly varying stage sets of "Description" epitomize the absence of allegorical significance. Few readers today take the debate between chastity and luxury seriously (who would choose the luxurious masque to exalt chastity?), but Ashbery manages to adapt Milton's argument for his own postmodern production. "Description" pits the inviolate individual, Mania, against the mercurial temptations of scenery (updating the rivalry between Ben Jonson and Inigo Jones). The goddess of confusion is, for instance, not at all content to be confused with her critics and dismisses them with Jehovic disdain, "I am as I am, . . . and care nothing for the opinion of others" (W 23). Later, she walks out on the well-meaning Herman Brix, explaining, "I must be—my tired, tyrannical self, as separate from local color as geometry is from the hideous verticals of these avenues" (W 27)—reprising the role of the artist (or movie star: "I want to be alone") as a minor divinity. Mercury promises Mania a kind of utopian uninterrupted artist's retreat, where "the disturbing letters and phone calls that hamper your free unorthodox development will melt away" (W 24), a cushy but stifling situation far from the New York School's implicit poetics of spontaneous production. In an interview conducted around the time he was writing "Description," Ashbery (chastely) confesses, "Perhaps I have gone to extremes not to care what people have thought," but goes on to describe himself as "a very gregarious person. . . . My best writing gets done when I'm being distracted by people who are calling me or errands that I have to do. Those things seem to help the creative process, in my case."[5]

In "Description" the "creative process" itself sweeps Mania, and finally Mercury, from the stage: "Then we [in the virtual audience] all realized . . . that the setting would go on evolving eternally, rolling its waves across our vision like an ocean, each one new yet recognizably a part of the same series, which was creation itself. Scenes from movies, plays, operas, television; decisive or little-known episodes from history; prenatal and other early memories," in which "event followed event according to an inner logic of its own" (W 27–28). Ashbery's chaotic montage of Puccini's "*La Bohème,*" "Jacques Cousteau documentaries," "old clips from *Lucy, Lassie* and *The Waltons,*" and Ibsen's "*When We Dead Awaken*" culminates in Mercury's reappearance "in the shrewd bumpkin manner of a Will Rogers," who informs the audience that "what counts isn't the particular set of circumstances, but how we adapt ourselves to them" (W 28–29). As HE puts it in "Fantasia," which ends in a similar prose catalogue, "There was always something to see, / Something going on" (HBD 86). Ashbery's Bergsonian "creative evolution," at once mercurial and confounding, is also Darwinian, an endlessly "evolving" series to which we human characters, artists included, must "adapt ourselves." In this world of postmodern simulacra, natural yields to artificial selection; those unable to adapt to cultural and technological change get left behind. Ashbery's cavalcade would seem uncritically exuberant were it not shadowed by the specter of death, in the figure of the pistol-packing Daffy Down Dilly and the camera-toting Sabrina. Face to face with Sabrina, Mercury manages to exclaim, "even if it does menace us directly, *it's exciting all the same!*" before being silenced by an "avalanche" which "fell and fell, and continues to fall even today" (W 30). Ashbery's darkening postmodern masque marks an evolutionary descent whose end has not yet arrived.

A more intimate but still representative message is delivered in the four-paragraph epistolary prose poem "Whatever It Is, Wherever You Are" (dated March 1, 1980). The poem stems from the cultural history of "The System" and the autobiography of "The Picture of Little J. A." It begins as a kind of anthropology of the age of capitalist consensus: "The cross-hatching technique which allowed our ancestors to exchange certain genetic traits for others, in order to provide their offspring with a way of life at once more variegated and more secure than their own, has just about run out of steam" (W 63). As the American family reassembled after the trauma of World War II, the ideological cross-breeding of old-world values with new-world consumerism transmitted the American message of prosperity and decency from generation to generation. In "The System" these self-evident, unquestioned truths were indistinguishable from life: "It was all life, this truth, you forgot about it and it was there. No need to collect your thoughts at every moment before putting forth a hesitant feeler into the rank and file of their sensations: the truth was obstinately itself" (TP 55). Not only one's environment but one's own bodily responses were programmed. In "Whatever It Is," as in "The System," this inherited heterosexual nervous system is "breaking down" (TP 53): "What did *they* want us to do? Stand around this way, monitoring every breath, checking each impulse for the return address, wondering constantly about evil until necessarily we fall into a state of torpor that is probably the worst sin of all?" (W 63). The regulation of misrepresentative, "evil" impulses is an unwelcome inheritance. In "The Picture of Little J.A." the photographed subject posed "in a Prospect of Flowers" for a parental figure, which included his older self. In "Whatever It Is" the image to be photographed is illuminated by the flash of tulip bulbs: "a specific color—the yellow of the tulip, for instance—will flash for a moment" (W 63–64). The subject of this "old photograph," and the object of this unusually direct prose poem, is a systemic "you"—"Someone whose face is the same as yours in the photograph but who is someone else"—Ashbery's father and an older Ashbery, who accepts the photographic light "like love from someone you always thought you couldn't stand, and whom you now recognize as a brother, an equal" (W 64). Within the charmed literary "circle of your ancestors' games and entertainments" (W 65), the cross-hatched message of the photo is received.

Among the versified poems of *A Wave,* the most moving study in long-distance communication is "Just Walking Around" (W 8). Adding a quatrain to the four-quatrain form of *Shadow Train,* "Just Walking Around" gradually betrays the toll of its message. Like "At North Farm" (W 1), the poem places "you" at the end of the line as its *destinataire,* destination, and destiny: "What name do I have for you? / Certainly there is no name for you / In the sense that the stars have names." Appearing first as a stellified Creator, the second person expands to include the wandering poet, who by indirection finds directions out: "as you realize once again / / That the longest way is the most efficient way." This paraphrase of the old proverb "The longest way round is the shortest way home" provides an indirect answer to the implied titular question "where are you going?"

By "Just Walking Around" the poem gradually reaches its destination, ending with an invitation to the reader that is also a prayer: "The segments of the trip swing open like an orange. / There is light in there, and mystery and food. / Come see it. Come not for me but it. / But if I am still there, grant that we may see each other." The poet foresees his collected poems "swing[ing] open" like a door. Compressed into monosyllables, the powerful appeal remains tantalizingly elusive. Inspecting the travel diary is the reader to whom the poet (like Eve) offers the homotextual fruit and whom he (like St. Paul) hopes to "see face to face." The distance Ashbery has come as a poet may be approximated by comparing "Just Walking Around" with a parallel moment in "Fantasia on 'The Nut-Brown Maid,'" written around fifteen years earlier. SHE reads an appeal into the "new crescent" moon:

> It seems to say: there are lots of differences inside.
> There were differences when only you knew them.
> Now they are an element, not themselves,
> And hands are idle, or weigh the head
> Like an outsize grapefruit, or an ocarina
> Closes today with a comical wail.
> Go in to them, see
> What the session was about
> (HBD 81)

This invitation is fanciful and impersonal; it matters little whether HE looks in or not. The appeal in "Just Walking Around" is much more economical, as though the poet felt he might not be afforded another.

Two of the best poems in *A Wave,* "Purists Will Object" and "Down by the Station, Early in the Morning," study the economy of formal purity. Both poems are variations on a theme announced by Eliot in "Little Gidding," where, translating Mallarmé's eulogy of Poe in "Le tombeau d'Edgar Poe," a Yeatsian ghost eulogized his colleagues: "our concern was speech, and speech impelled us / To purify the dialect of the tribe" (141). What need is there for linguistic purists in a contemporary America which thrives on, and drowns in, its own confusion of tongues? In a review of Robert Wilson's *Video 50,* written around a year before "Purists Will Object" (dated September 23, 1981), Ashbery sees in Wilson's splices (which resemble the cuts in "Description of a Masque") a new American purity: "Reveling in the sickly pinks, tans, and aquas of cheap color TV, he has fabricated a series of ever dissolving vignettes that draw on the visual vocabulary of soaps, commercials, and late-night horror movies but 'purify the language of the tribe' in ways that Mallarmé never thought of and would have tried to forget if he had." [6] For the postmodernist poet, to purify is not to cleanse but to purge from poetry what no longer matters. Thus Ashbery injects American idioms into his poetic dialect: "My mind wants to give clichés their chance, unravel them, and so in a way contribute to purifying the language of the tribe." [7] The tribe only needs purists who listen to them.

The title "Purists Will Object" (W 17) belongs to the dialect of art criticism. In 1980 Ashbery praised Susan Shatter's giant watercolors for their impurity: "their richness and complexity would seem to be obtainable only in oil. Purists could object that she is making watercolor do things it isn't supposed to; impurists will marvel at their being done so well." [8] In "Purists Will Object" impurity is both appealing and objectionable. The poem is divided into two stanzas (of thirteen and seven lines) and scenes, urban and suburban. Significantly, it is framed by the first-person plural pronoun, first in the subjective ("We have the looks you want") and finally in the objective ("no dialect hears us") case. "Purists" object to subjects identified solely by their objects. Yet Frank O'Hara claimed to choose poetic form for its allure: "As for measure and other technical apparatus, that's just common sense: if you're going to buy a pair of pants you want them to be tight enough so everyone will want to go to bed with you" (498). In "Purists" Ashbery gives this form-fitting aesthetic the personalized vulgarity of a TV ad: "We have the looks you want: / The gonzo (musculature seemingly wired to the stars); / Colors like lead, khaki and pomegranate." With this "gonzo" poetry, modeled after Hunter S. Thompson's coinage for liberated journalism,

Ashbery is of course objecting not to tight pants but to buying "your" sexuality as advertised. But, Ashbery's reader might object, don't these form-fitting fabrics—"Landscape embroidery, complete sets of this and that"—suit Ashbery's own misrepresentative poetics? What after all makes "Description of a Masque" so appealing but its endless display of itemized particulars?

In the early 1980s, with Reagan's "morning in America" under way, the costs of buying into this uncritically postmodern, consumerist aesthetic were becoming increasingly apparent:

It's bankruptcy, the human haul,
The shining, bulging nets lifted out of the sea, and always a few refugees
Dropping back into the no-longer-mirthful kingdom
On the day someone sells an old house
And someone else begins to add on to his.
(W 17)

Emma Lazarus's huddled masses take refuge on the shores of Liberty, but the small fry drop through the loosened reticulations of Reagan's "safety net." The urban renewal recalls Eliot's in "East Coker": "In succession / Houses rise and fall, crumble, are extended, / Are removed, destroyed, restored, or in their place / Is an open field, or a factory, or a by-pass" (123). But Ashbery's renovation differs from Eliot's in its erotic glamor. The bulging nets rise into a hypnotic erection, the phallic New York Tower of Babel: "this pornographic masterpiece, / Variegated, polluted skyscraper to which all gazes are drawn, / Pleasure we cannot and will not escape." At the end of "The New Spirit" Ashbery first confronted this American monstrosity: "this horrible vision of the completed Tower of Babel, . . . perfect in its vulgarity" (TP 50). In "Purists Will Object" this "Variegated, polluted" monument to impurity turns eyes away from all the drowning subjects.

In the second stanza we descend with the drowning refugees to the submerged "sub-urb" or "subterranean life," where "traffic lights were green and aqueous." The look may be sexy, with its blanketing "privet" ("privates"), but everyone is isolated in this useless system. "Purists" closes with two objecting questions, too desperate to be wholly rhetorical: "If if can't be conjugated onto us, what good is it? / What need for purists when the demotic is built to last, / To outlast us, and no dialect hears us?" In this pointed critique of his own poetic discourse Ashbery mourns that, like a good car, "the demotic," democratic system of language, with its all-inclusive pronouns and other shifters, will "outlast" all its speaking and writing subjects, poets in particular. The final objectified "us" is not advertising's friendly "we," but us refugees going down for the third time. In America, it seems, nobody is listening. Yet, as Ashbery knows, there is no alternative but to resist, in poem after purifying poem, the monolithic impurity of consumerism's "polluted skyscraper." More than Poe's or Mallarmé's, Ashbery's dialect is variegated with closely heard and studied American speech and writing. The texts Ashbery weaves won't outsell those of the "free" market system (where poetry is marginally subsidized, distributed, advertised, and reviewed). But his conjugation of our cries may after all outlast it.

The personal consequences of purity and form are dealt with in "Down by the Station, Early in the Morning" (W 14), as powerful a poem as any Ashbery has written. The title comes from a children's verse, "The Puffer-Belly Song": "Down by the station, early in the morning, / See the little puffer-bellies standing in a row." Written not long after a serious illness (in the spring of 1982 Ashbery underwent surgery for a nearly fatal epidural abscess), the poem is urgently cathartic. The poem is informally dressed, with twenty-three prosaic lines of roughly the same length divided into three symmetrical stanzas (6, 11, 6), each draining syntactically into the next. But the casual form wears out and, finally, violently implodes, in order to remake itself at the end. The poem opens on a domestic tragedy of disbelief, raising the possibility of a "pure poetry" of daily life composed of empty forms of speech devoid of content:

> It all wears out. I keep telling myself this, but
> I can never believe me, though others do. Even things do.
> And the things they do. Like the rasp of silk, or a certain
> Glottal stop in your voice as you are telling me how you
> Didn't have time to brush your teeth but gargled with Listerine
> Instead. Each is a base one might wish to touch once more
>
> Before dying.

What has emptied out is the "thing" or relationship. Two people have nothing between them any more, nothing to say or do but to go through the motions, though their objects seem to object. In the halting enjambments a sentimental drama shows through ("a [catch] in your voice," "wish to touch once more"). But the remaining conversational forms are stopped, sterilized, and unsuited to their sad contents.

Once one thread is cut, the whole fabric of belief unravels. In the second stanza, Ashbery manufactures a line of Proustian moments: "There's the moment years ago in the station in Venice, / The dark rainy afternoon in fourth grade, and the shoes then." If the past "no long exists" it is recaptured when "you name it, remembering." Emerson named the poet "the Namer, or Language-maker, naming things sometimes after their appearance, sometimes after their essence" (456–57). But names, as Ashbery realizes, may contain nothing more than their conditioned responses: "even then / It may not have existed, or existed only as a result / Of the perceptual dysfunction you've been carrying around for years." This humorously bleak diagnosis of Wordsworth's creative senses, "what they half create, / And what perceive," is offered by a notoriously difficult poet: "I often wonder if I am suffering from some mental dysfunction because of how weird and baffling my poetry seems to so many people and sometimes to me too."[9] The homotextual self-diagnosis includes a "sexual dysfunction." In this hollow moment each dysfunction seems created out of nothing.

This willful suspension of belief results in a tragic "catharsis," the generative crypt word of "Down by the Station." Aristotle said that tragedy "through pity and fear effects the proper purgation of these emotions" (*Poetics,* VI.2).[10] This purgation, a voiding and purifying, explains the presence of the mouthwash Listerine (named for the founder of antiseptic surgery, Joseph Lister), which was also believed, early on, to protect against AIDS. Though "Down by the Station" is not "about" the newly discovered epidemic, it does register a heightened anxiety of infection. With a noncausal succession based on "then," the stanza climaxes in a purgative leakage that is emotive, sexual, and syntactical, even though one partner may be only the TV news: "The result is magic, then terror, then pity at the emptiness, / Then air gradually bathing and filling the emptiness as it leaks, / Emoting all over something that is probably mere reportage / But nevertheless likes being emoted on." The bland narrative conclusion of the stanza, "And so each day / Culminates in merriment as well as a deep shock like an electric one," may pun darkly on Eliot's own grim formulation of the magic moment in "East Coker": "And every moment is a new and shocking / Valuation of all we have been" (125). Ashbery's voiding climax before the vacuum tube culminates in the interruption of the final stanza:

As the wrecking ball bursts through the wall with the bookshelves
Scattering the works of famous authors as well as those
Of more obscure ones, and books with no author, letting in
Space, and an extraneous babble from the street
Confirming the new value the hollow core has again, the light
From the lighthouse that protects as it pushes us away.

Interruption is the topic of the next poem in *A Wave,* "Around the Rough and Rugged Rocks the Ragged Rascal Rudely Ran," a prosaic reduction of Keats's "When I have fears": "I think a lot about it, / Think quite a lot about it— / The omnipresent possibility of being interrupted / While what I stand for is still almost a bare canvas" (W 15)—the Dickinsonian open-ended dash standing for what "it" brings. In "Down by the Station" the interruption is staged as a purgative irruption into the stanzaic apartment. Plosives, culminating in "babble," rupture the glottal poem. The crypto-graphic marker "babble" leaks syntactically, letting its crypt words— "noise," "rabble," and more distantly "Babel" and the bursting "bubble"— seep through. "Bubble" ("the hollow core") gathers in the oral and anal cavities, the TV tube, the wrecking ball, the global stanza chamber, and the sweeping lighthouse light. The interruption may be no more than the open-ing of a window in Manhattan, letting noise from the "rabble" break into the dialects of the named and nameless tribes on the bookshelves. Ashbery's cathartic purification is a vitiating but refreshing infusion of "extraneous" languages into the claustrophobic lyric space. The confusion of tongues in "Down by the Station"—threadbare clichés, brand names, sentimental and nostalgic reveries, psychological and medical jargon, nursery rhymes, and so on—amplifies the hollow core of lyric noise. As Helen Vendler puts it, "the wrecking ball lets in a new influx of demotic speech, and a new genera-tion will construct the library all over again around that perpetual hollow core."[11]

This imagined circular library may derive from an essay by Jorge Luis Borges, "The Wall and the Books," which Ashbery read around the time he wrote the poem. The essay, cited at length by Ashbery in a contemporary interview with Richard Jackson, meditates on the two immense efforts of China's first Emperor Shih Huang Ti, "who ordered the building of the almost infinite Chinese Wall . . . [and] who also decreed the burning of all the books that had been written before his time."[12] The Emperor claimed descent from the legendary Emperor Huang Ti, who, like the Emersonian poet, "gave things their true names."[13] Ashbery speculates that Borges's es-say illustrates "Harold Bloom's theory of the Anxiety of Influence in the desire to destroy or negate all previous writings in order to give things their true names and at the same time build a wall around an impossibly large area."[14] This association helps explain the walled-in library's destruction in "Down by the Station" by the Namer who erects his own lighthouse Tower at the poem's end.

In the interview, Ashbery refers to Borges's reflection on the purity of empty form: "We could generalize, and infer that *all* forms possess virtue in themselves and not in a conjectural 'content.' . . . [In] 1877 Pater had already stated that all the arts aspire to resemble music, which is pure form. Music, states of happiness, mythology, faces molded by time, certain twilights and certain places—all these are trying to tell us something, or have told us something we should not have missed, or are about to tell us something; that imminence of a revelation that is not yet produced is, perhaps, the aesthetic reality."[15] Empty forms are not yet fulfilled. Both Borges and Ashbery draw on Pater's famous "Conclusion" to *The Renaissance:* "While all melts under our feet, we may well grasp at any exquisite passion, or any contribution to knowledge . . . or any stirring of the senses, strange dyes, strange colours, and curious odours, or work of the artist's hands, or the face of one's friend. Not to discriminate every moment some passionate attitude in those about us . . . is, on this short day of frost and sun, to sleep before evening."[16] Ashbery revises Pater in "A Wave," where he reminds us that we will retrace our steps in memory: "We will all have to walk back this way / A second time, and not to know it then, not / To number each straggling piece of sagebrush / Is to sleep before evening" (W 72). Memorable forms are not only revelatory but protective. In lyric poetry the hallowed, hollowed forms are often erected to wall the private in and the public out. Ashbery, with his identifying reader alongside, might have decried the extraneous world from his Tower of Babble, and shut it out. But if we are with Ashbery in the writer's seat inside for the wrecking ball's blast, both we and the writer are exiled from the lighthouse light, which "protects as it pushes us away" like Parmigianino's arm which "protect[s] / What it advertises" (SP 68). Ashbery situates himself with us in the rubble on the outside looking out. It's a hazardous site, but it's only there that his poetry takes place.

Ashbery surveys his own historical place in "But What Is the Reader to Make of This?" (W 13). The poem is premised on Auden's purist dictum that "poetry makes nothing happen," which Ashbery elsewhere interprets to mean that the effects of poetry, though not measurable or recordable as public, historical events, nevertheless make things happen to the reader: "its value is precisely the fact that it doesn't, because that's the way it *does* make things happen. The pleasure that you get, if you love poetry, is a pleasure that's going to cause you to act, it forces you back into life."[17] The three-storied poem opens with a kaleidoscopic view of a cryptic lake district, a psychic reservoir, which a "quarter-turn" or "revolution" (the crypt word here) collapses: "A lake of pain, an absence / Leading to a flowering sea? Give it a quarter-turn / And watch the centuries begin to collapse / Through each other, like floors in a burning building." In the rubble of the present only revolving fragments of the old regime remain. The second stanza turns Auden's proposition into its converse, arguing that history makes nothing happen to the poet or, by extension, to any bit player on the historical stage: "Those delicious few words spread around like jam / Don't matter, nor does the shadow. / We have lived blasphemously in history / And nothing has hurt us or can." We may pass unnoticed and unpunished, but if history thus far appears harmless, memory wields its own archives: "Facts seize hold of the web / And leave it ash." The fire reaches the Borgesian archives and reduces Ashbery's signature to volcanic "ash." The poet counters this textual oblivion by reasserting private life: "Still, it is the personal, / Interior life that gives us something to think about. / The rest is only drama." So too the exemplary soliloquist Hamlet cut short his final political directives with "The rest is silence."

But history invades too many interiors to be thus discounted. The defensive distinction between interior life and exterior historical drama itself collapses in the final stanza of the poem. Like the Civil War youth in *The Red Badge of Courage,* "the personal, / Interior life" is buffeted from without and within:

> Meanwhile the combinations of every extendable circumstance
> In our lives continue to blow against it like new leaves
> At the edge of a forest a battle rages in and out of
> For a whole day. It's not the background, we're the background,
> On the outside looking looking out.

The indifference of Stephen Crane's Nature has been replaced by our own stoic indifference to "extenuating circumstances." Whitman similarly objects in "Song of Myself": "Battles, the horrors of fratricidal war, the fever of doubtful news, the fitful events; / These come to me days and nights and go from me again, / But they are not the Me myself" (191). Both biographical and historical "influences" pass over the invulnerable "Me myself" without leaving a trace, or at least none that Whitman admits. But in Ashbery's lines "we" are displaced by our so-called "historical background." History does in fact take center stage and direct each "Interior life." But the individual persona is thereby neither simply marginalized, on the outside looking in, nor featured, on the inside looking out. As historical subjects, the poet and his anonymous readers find themselves "On the outside looking out." Like an Ashbery poem, "the general life" of a generation "Is still many sizes too big, yet / Has style, woven of things that never happened / With those that did, so that a mood survives / Where life and death never could." Only the general life becomes history. The exclamation "Make it sweet again!" with which the poem suddenly closes comes from any outgrown consumer, including the latterday poet. We don't know how well Ashbery's impure demotic style will suit his own generation, any more than we know whether history will sweeten its mood. But we do know that his paradoxical stance is circumstantially informed.

The history of "A Wave" begins in the summer of 1980, when Ashbery visited the Princeton University Art Museum to review an exhibit of Italian baroque painting for *New York*.[18] One painting unmentioned in his review, Guercino's *Landscape with Tobias and the Angel* (1617–18), gave Ashbery the title and subject matter for the first version of "A Wave." Guercino's painting depicts an incident from the apocryphal *Book of Tobit* in which a magical fish appears to the bathing Tobias and the angel Raphael. Tobias, who is journeying to Ecbatana to claim a debt owed to his pious blind father, is instructed by his angelic traveling companion to catch the fish and to save its inner organs. With the heart and liver of the fish Tobias exorcises a demon-lover (Asmodeus) from his future wife, Sarah, and with its gall he heals his father's blindness. In Ashbery's two-page fragment, "Landscape with Tobias and the Angel," Sarah is comically erased from the story, which sympathizes instead with the sexually frustrated "poor devil" Asmodeus. The all-male cast in Ashbery's "Landscape" features the son and the father, whose presence seems to short-circuit the poem, which breaks off, without punctuation, mid-sentence: "Father would have appreciated that, he had so much practical sense. / And when". Like "Oleum Misericordiae" (SP 66), built on the related noncanonical myth of Seth, Adam's son and would-be healer, "Landscape" follows in the wake of *The Waste Land,* which featured a son's quest to cure his father. But in the second typescript of "A Wave," which bears the title "Long Periods of Silence," Guercino's painting and the story of Tobias have all but disappeared. In their place we find traces of the story of the Flood (the apocalyptic Wave) and its aftermath.[19] This new beginning ("around New Year of 1983")[20] is inscribed in the typescript: "The beginning of the arc of the year / May not gradually melt into rainbow, salmon-hued, messy / Rainbow extravagances" (recalling the ecstatic ending of Bishop's "The Fish": "everything / was rainbow, rainbow, rainbow! / And I let the fish go," 44). In "Long Periods" the turning New Year appears to signify the diluvial aftermath and the arc of the New Covenant, which in "A Wave" threatens to constrict: "The covenant we entered / Bears down on us, some are ensnared" (W 71).

A handwritten line at the top of the "Long Periods" typescript, "In the end he was caught out," appears to mark the son's apprehension. Though in the *Book of Tobit* Tobias's journey is not a matter of atonement or banishment, "Long Periods" suggests that a homotextually misrepresentative sin results both in the father's long periods of silence and in the son's quest to cure his father's "blindness." In "Long Periods" the son tries unsuccessfully to break the paternal silence: "In the end he was simply caught out. / After so many long periods of silence / The new rhythm of dropping ashes on the carpet / And coming to the point couldn't help but attract / Some attention" ("ashes" was O'Hara's name for Ashbery). The nearest thing to this father-son encounter is staged not in "A Wave" but in the short poem preceding it, "Problems": "Once, someone—my father—came to me and spoke / Extreme words amid the caution of the time. / I was too drunk, too scared to know what was being said" (W 67). In "Long Periods," as in "Fragment" ("Gradually old letters used as bookmarks / Inform the neighbors; an approximate version / Circulates and the incident is officially closed," DDS 84), neighbors inform on the son: "In the end though / Neighbors had informed on him, and soon the whole town knew." The son is not so much banished as "allowed to materialize elsewhere on the main trail / Between two thriving desert cities," the unspecified Sodom and Gomorrah. The prospects for fishing are slim.

The myth of exile and return shows through at points in the final text of "A Wave." The prodigal son dreams once of returning home, through Ashbery's childhood orchards, only to witness (or imagine) his father's unabated shame: "I could see white curtains fluttering at the windows / And in the garden under a big brass-tinted apple tree / The old man had removed his hat and was gazing at the grass / As though in sorrow, sorrow for what I had done" (W 85). This verse paragraph also preserves a fragment of a previous title: "But in the end the dark stuff, the odd quick attack / Followed by periods of silence that get shorter and shorter" (W 86). Tobias seems anonymously preserved in several travelers of "A Wave," from the "future saint intoxicated with the idea of martyrdom" (W 68) to the speaker of the poem's closing stanzas, who interrogates the silent sky: "It would be cockier to ask of heaven just what is this present / Of an old dishpan you bestowed on me?" (W 87). The sky's response, along with the cumulative meaning of Ashbery's poem, becomes less and less definite: "And already the sky is getting to be less salmon-colored, / The black clouds more meaningless (otter-shaped at first; / Now, as they retreat into incertitude, mere fins)" (W 88). "Landscape with Tobias and the Angel" began with the line "And already the clouds are becoming less salmon-hued." By the end of "A Wave" Tobias's magically curative fish has become "mere fins" (a fish's tail and a tale's finish). Thus the early versions of "A Wave" do not reveal the son's break with his father as the poem's covert confessional core. And these early versions are themselves already misrepresentative. The moral waste land at the beginning of "Landscape"—"a dumpscape / Of everybody's intentions, good and bad, preserved / By the intense dryness from the mutilating effects of history," displaying "all the famous sins of omission"—is no less allegorical, historical, and reflexive than "our landscape" (W 68) in the second stanza of "A Wave."

More noticeable than the absence of Tobias or the fish in "A Wave" is the lack of any single subject matter or narrative, such as the painting which organized "Self-Portrait in a Convex Mirror," the long poem "A Wave" most resembles. The ill-defined poem overwhelms its subjects, "sinking in the maelstrom of de-definition like spars" (W 84).[21] The elusive topic and transitional structural principle in "A Wave" is this flooding, the rupture of one discursive system by another. But how can the history of a revolution—political, intellectual, personal—be written if the very terms by which one could speak of the transformation have changed? Ashbery's figure for this rupture, apocalypse, crisis, breach, or revolution is the wave. In "A Wave" we pass repeatedly through three "phases" in turn: a wait or anticipatory prelude, a wave or crest (a problematic term since a crisis or revolution is characterized by historical discontinuity), and a wake or aftermath, each phase with its own characteristic atmosphere. Ashbery achieves an exhilarating novelty in "A Wave" by changing terms and scenes with every shift in phase. If we don't attend to the phases, we miss the tidal music.

A look at the first few stanzas of "A Wave" (W 68–69) shows how much variation the simple progression of prelude, crest, and aftermath can accommodate. The poem opens in the crest of a wave of pain brought on by a romantic breakup (or parental flare-up): "To pass through pain and not know it, / A car door slamming in the night. / To emerge on an invisible terrain." The infinitives and the disjointed lines resemble those of Dickinson, the American poet who first surveyed the invisible terrain of pain. In "To learn the Transport by the Pain—" for instance, three infinitives across eight lines defer the other side of the equation: "This is the Sovereign Anguish!" (#167). Ashbery considered the pain of transport in reading Stein and found a virtue in it: "The almost physical pain with which we strive to accompany the evolving thought of one of . . . Stein's characters is perhaps a counterpart of the painful continual projection of the individual into life. As in life, perseverance has its rewards—moments when we emerge suddenly on a high plateau with a view of the whole distance we have come."[22]

In "Landscape with Tobias and the Angel" the opening infinitive phrase was a grammatical subject; "To pass through pain and not know it," we are told, "is the important business." Proust's argument, that "voluntary memory, the memory of the intellect, . . . preserve[s] nothing of the past itself," here parallels Ashbery's.[23] In a mutual interview with Kenneth Koch in 1965, Ashbery had already associated the experience of pain with that of not knowing: "Getting back to my favorite theme, the idea of relief from pain has something to do with ambiguity. Ambiguity supposes an eventual resolution of itself, whereas certitude implies further ambiguity."[24] The term is of course new critical. In *Seven Types of Ambiguity* Empson points to the pleasure, not the pain, inherent in the various connotations of Shakespeare's "Bare ruined choirs": "there is a sort of ambiguity in not knowing which of them to hold most clearly in mind."[25] For Ashbery, what is significant is the dialectical historical dimension of ambiguity. He cited his 1965 remarks on pain at length in an interview conducted around the time he was at work on "A Wave," adding this clarification: "Things are in a continual state of motion and evolution, and if we come to a point where we say, with certitude, right here, this is the end of the universe, then of course we must deal with everything that goes on after that, whereas ambiguity seems to take further developments into account."[26] Ambiguities in "A Wave," such as whether you "pass through pain" or whether "It passes through you" (W 68), preserve open-endedness in a wake of not knowing.

After its opening infinitive, "A Wave" enters the wake of historical tenses, signaled by "emerge" and the punctuating "car door slamming." It thus coincides with Rimbaud's opening *Illumination,* "After the Flood": "A door slammed. On the village square the child swung his arms around and was understood by the weather vanes and the steeple cocks everywhere, under the pelting rain."[27] The waking phase spills into the second stanza where the deserted "saint" regrets "the luck of speaking out / A little too late" (W 68). At this moment the "waking" broadens into a three-tiered landscape (without angel or fish) reminiscent of Langland's *Piers Plowman* with its fair field full of folk, as Ashbery shifts to omniscient historical narration: "And our landscape came to be as it is today: / Partially out of focus, some of it too near, the middle distance / A haven of serenity and unreachable, with all kinds of nice / People and plants waking and stretching." This Dawn of Civilization has replaced the desolate morning after. But the peace of the homeland lasts only a stanzaic pause. The stanza's narrative close, "And they called it our home," sets the scene of the prelude—an uneasy house with its homebody waiting on the threshold: "no doorbell rang; / Yet each day of the week, once it had arrived, seemed the threshold / Of love and desperation again" (W 68).

This eroticized prelude, an interval with no interruptions ("no doorbell rang"), brings on the second crest of "A Wave"—not a returning or new lover but a new poem, a new discursive system:

And it could be that it was Tuesday, with dark, restless clouds
And puffs of white smoke against them, and below, the wet streets
That seem so permanent, and all of a sudden the scene changes:

278

It's another idea, a new conception, something submitted
A long time ago, that only now seems about to work
To destroy at last the ancient network
Of letters, diaries, ads for civilization.
(W 68)

Ashbery first submitted this idea fifteen years earlier in "Spring Day." In a quatrain beginning with a comic-strip outburst, "Wha—what happened?" (DDS 15), the poem hesitantly narrates the scene change:

A page turned; we were

Just now floundering in the wind of its colossal death.
And whether it is Thursday, or the day is stormy,
With thunder and rain, or the birds attack each other,
We have rolled into another dream.

The inauspicious birds of "Spring Day" (written in the changing times of 1967) are played in "A Wave" by "puffs of white smoke," and Thursday is replaced by Tuesday as another calm day before the cloudburst. The omnipresent "it," appearing ominously in two expletives ("And it could be that it was Tuesday"), soon comes to stand for the wave itself: "It passes through you, emerges on the other side" (W 68). In these revolutionary gaps, when one system is swamped by another, only narrative clichés are truthfully inadequate to the task: "and all of a sudden" (W 68). In "Syringa" the overwhelming loss of Eurydice is similarly chronicled: "Then one day, everything changed" (HBD 69). Whitman employed a related threadbare formula in "Out of the Cradle" to narrate the unthinkable breach: "Till of a sudden, / May-be kill'd, unknown to her mate, / One forenoon the she-bird crouch'd not on the nest, / Nor return'd that afternoon, nor the next, / Nor ever appear'd again" (389).

In Ashbery's poetry, a public or private crisis invariably results in a journey. In the aftermath of the revolutionary wave, the opening infinitives "To pass through" and "To emerge" reappear in tenses and in history. The new story or misrepresentative system has projected its conclusion onto "a distant city" (not the "two thriving desert cities") "with all / The possibilities shrouded in a narrative moratorium" (W 68). With the narrative once again under way, the poem's first pronoun appears, a generic and specular "you," and the wave (as of grain) becomes a temporal terrain: "as you mope and thrash your way through time." The third stanza ends without conclusion, in "a kind of tragic euphoria / In which your spirit sprouted. And which is justified in you" (W 69). The "tragic euphoria" of the aftermath arises from the fact that the crisis can neither be undone nor explained. As Ashbery put it in "Spring Day," "No use charging the barriers of that other: / It no longer exists" (DDS 15). This "new spirit" of the time is the perception of its inhabitants, "Imagining it as it is" (W 69), and they are its justification. Another feature of the aftermath is the implementation of the new system, often strategically masked as the old one. Ashbery seems to have Reagan's new administration (if not Nixon's old one) in mind at the opening of the fourth stanza, where he adapts Winston Churchill's adage ("business as usual"): "In the haunted house no quarter is given: in that respect / It's very much business as usual." "There would be more concerts / From now on," though the common ground between "a man and his wife" "Shrank and promoted a surreal intimacy" (W 69). Heterosexual marriage in this "new conception" remains the shrinking legal norm.

The rest of "A Wave" transforms itself fluidly from one phase to the next. I will focus on selected instances of each phase of "A Wave" in turn, beginning with its highest, most prominent crests in the eighteenth and nineteenth stanzas. The first of these narrates the irruption of the new poem: "But always and sometimes questioning the old modes / And the new wondering, the poem, growing up through the floor, / Standing tall in tubers, invading and smashing the ritual / Parlor, demands to be met on its own terms now" (W 79). This rupture, like that in "Self-Portrait" and "Down by the Station," raises questions about our ritual parlance. The new sprout grows "up through the floor" of its own accord, like Stevens's anonymous poetry in "The Creations of Sound": "We say ourselves in syllables that rise / From the floor, rising in speech we do not speak" (251). The progression of participles ("questioning," "growing," "standing," "invading," "smashing") and a gerund ("wondering") characterizes the wave as a work in progress. The interruptive new mode renews the fateful journey towards oneself. Merely stopping and wondering, like Frost in the "snowy evening" woods, "was not enough to save me from choosing / Myself now, from being the place I have to get to / Before nightfall" (W 79). As elsewhere in "A Wave," the path is broken by Dickinson, who charted the journey of "Experience," "Compelling Him to Choose Himself / His Preappointed Pain—" (#910; "Plan"). Choice itself entails a lifelong itinerary. The verse paragraph ends with the birth of another new spirit: "Being alone at the center of a moan that did not issue from me / And is pulling me back toward old forms of address / I know I have already lived through, but they are strong again, / And big to fill the exotic spaces that arguing left" (W 80). This crisis renews the "speaker's" affair with another lover or poem. As in Bishop's "In the Waiting Room," the labor pain awakens the ventriloquist of clichés to the once empty "forms of address," still the only ones available, that seemed smashed like china in the ritual parlor which the lover "arguing left." As at the end of "Down by the Station," the interruption reinvigorates the hollow, threadbare forms, "Confirming the new value the hollow core has again" (W 14).

Whatever its progeny (a new lover, a renewed affair, a renovated poetic style), this potency generates the compounded waves of the long nineteenth stanza (W 80–81). The sixty-three line verse paragraph, appearing some-what more than halfway through "A Wave," is in many ways its climax. It is structured, more neatly than most, around its coordinate grammatical and narrative conjunctions: "So all," "And as," "And what," and "And so." These ambiguous narrative or logical conclusions are characteristic of the aftermath or wake, as in the first wake of "A Wave": "So the luck of speak-ing out" (W 68). The stanza begins in the aftermath phase with a journey "from nowhere to nowhere" as a new generation of writers assumes its own "empty space in the endless continuum" (W 79): "So all the slightly more than young / Get moved up whether they like it or not, and only / The very old or the very young have any say in the matter." As Pierre Bour-dieu notes, the emergence of a new avant-garde displaces the entire cultural field of artists: "each of them moves a step down the temporal hierarchy which is at the same time a social hierarchy."[28] Ashbery's proximity to his own literary wake creates a kind of claustrophobic anxiety of being influen-tial: "A record of the many voices of the middle-young will be issued / And found to be surprisingly original. That can't concern us, / However, because now there isn't room enough" (W 80). In this spare economy, poets must share "room" and time with new poets.

This anxiety produces the first crest of the stanza, an overwhelming sen-tence spreading over twenty-seven ebbing and welling lines. There is "Not enough dimension" for a new mode,

Even just one word with a slightly different intonation
To cause it to stand out from the backing of neatly invented
Chronicles of things men have said and done, like an English horn,
And then to sigh, to faint back
Into all our imaginings, dark
And viewless as they are,
Windows painted over with black paint but
(W 80)

As this urgent argument proceeds, it forgets and thereby disproves the as-sertion that there is "Not enough dimension" to continue. Before they recover, the lines shrink to a Keatsian ("viewless wings of poesy") solipsistic dark in which "to say" is buried beneath the painful infinitive "to sigh." But the lines brighten and lengthen again, the vernal, virile spring "of love that at last oozes" returns, and faith returns that poetry makes something happen: "We can sufficiently imagine, so much is admitted, what / Might be going on out there" (W 80).

With the next sentence the "wave" is finally recognized and named: "The cimmerian moment in which all lives, all destinies / And incompleted destinies were swamped / As though by a giant wave that picks itself up / Out of a calm sea and retreats again into nowhere / Once its damage is done" (W 81). The tidal wave builds quietly with a maudlin inebriated scene: "And as the luckless describe love in glowing terms to strangers / In taverns," the sentimental irony enlivened by the reverberation of "lucky in love" and the reawakened imagery of "glowing terms." This survey of those in and out of love and time draws on Eliot's oceanic "Dry Salvages." "To apprehend / The point of intersection of the timeless / With time, is an occupation for the saint" but "For most of us, there is only the unattended / Moment, the moment in and out of time," like "music heard so deeply / That it is not heard at all, but you are the music / While the music lasts" (136). Eliot's saints and Ashbery's "small remnant" (W 81) seem blessed to remain in the eternal moment of love. Most of us, however, make do with what Ashbery calls "a few moments of music of such tact and weariness / That one awakens with a new sense of purpose" (W 72).

Unlike Eliot's momentary "shaft of sunlight" in which the Word is experienced, Ashbery's "cimmerian moment" illuminates nothing. All there is "to say about those series / Of infrequent pellucid moments" is that they surprised us, "Like a stranger on a snowmobile / But of which nothing can be known or written, only / That they passed this way" (W 81). "Cimmerian," which alludes to the legendary people dwelling in darkness on the edge of the underworld in Book IX of Homer's *Odyssey,* brings into play the *nekuia* episode (Odysseus's descent into the underworld to receive directions for his return home), an episode central—perhaps because it displaces the transcendental ascent with a Freudian descent—to the modernist epiphanic narrative (Williams, Eliot, Joyce, Pound). In the aftermath of Ashbery's postmodern cimmerian moment, the unilluminated poet is left with the question "And what to say. . . ?" Like a blind Tiresias without prophetic vision, the love poet in the wake knows only "That to be bound over / To love in the dark, like Psyche, will somehow / Fill the sheaves of pages with a spidery, Spencerian hand" (W 81). Psyche was "bound over" (kept as an indentured servant, held on bail) to Cupid without learning his identity; to see him was to lose him. Once the inevitable disclosure happens, and the cimmerian moment of love passes, the experience is written up as though automatically. Thus Ashbery passes over Edmund Spenser in favor of Pratt R. Spencer, an American calligrapher responsible for the slanting form of cursive handwriting. It is the hand writing, not the author, but the hand is moved by love.

Not only artists, Ashbery argues, are left in the dark about what they have produced. Everyone whose life is ruptured must pick up the pieces and start over without realizing what has transpired. In the stanza's final aftermath, a relatively short (eight-line) sentence, the waking survivors have forgotten their dreams: "And so it is the only way / That love determines us, and we look the same / To others when they happen in afterwards, and cannot even know / We have changed, so massive in our difference / We are" (W 81). After the wave hits, and one's system of life has changed, there is no way to measure the difference it has made; utter difference looks like no difference. Ashbery first delineated this argument in "The Skaters": "We step out into the street, not realizing that the street is different, / And so it shall be all our lives" (RM 57). "We" have changed beyond our own recognition. The narrative formula "And so," used in both "The Skaters" and "A Wave," accurately designates the aftermath about which nothing can be concluded. The only thing left is to resume "our inane rounds" (W 81). Dickinson narrates the wake of "great pain" from the inside, monotonously: "The Feet, mechanical, go round— / Of Ground, or Air, or Ought— / A Wooden way / Regardless grown" (#341). Ashbery's speaker, like the lay speakers of "The System" or "Litany," exclaims that we are "too dumb to profit from past / Mistakes—that's how different we are!" (W 81). Yet, as Ashbery knows, no other conclusion is available.

The wait or prelude is a phase of solitude characterized by stillness, quietness, and attentiveness. In this phase, the flux and surge which mark the waves of "A Wave," and which for many readers define the character of Ashbery's poetry, are hardly to be found. The wake tends to be set outside; it is public, practical, journeying, and oriented toward the past. The wait is set indoors; it is private, meditative, tense or resting, questioning, and future-oriented. In declaring the motto of Robert Schumann's closed circle, for instance, *"frei aber einsam"* (W 87), Ashbery looks back to "The Skaters": "'Frei aber Einsam' (Free but Alone) / Ought to be your motto" (RM 54), and reaffirms the continuity of private (communal) life. In the wait one resides anxiously under the shadow of interruption: "no doorbell rang" (W 68); "hours and days go by in silence and the phone / Never rings" (W 78–79); "When they finally come / With much laborious jangling of keys to unlock your cell" (W 86); and, in a brilliant parody of pastoral romance, "footfalls / Of the police approaching gingerly through the soft spring air"

(W 87). This phase is concentrated largely in the final six stanzas of "A Wave." With "the end of February, my cut-off date"[29] approaching, Ashbery may have insensibly drifted, in these final brief stanzas, into the anticipatory phase.

The wait in "A Wave" is also characterized by what may be termed systemic awareness. This awareness—the sense that an experience is structured and periodic—is marked by vocabulary such as "play" and "game" and by reflexive formations of active and passive verbs: "You thought you perceived a purpose in the game at the moment / Another player broke one of the rules; it seemed / . . . something in which you lose yourself / And are not lost" (W 71); "but as they come to see each other dimly / And for the first time, an internal romance / Of the situation rises" (W 83). Systemic awareness is one variety of what Ashbery in "The System" calls "latent happiness." From the lover's systemic perspective, all partners are equally attractive: "You / Might as well offer it to your neighbor, the first one you meet, or throw / It away entirely, as plan to unlock on such and such a date" (W 88). To be sure, there is a taste of sour grapes in the appreciation of the "internal romance / Of the situation," but this attentiveness at least keeps one in circulation, not waiting in vain for particular poems, times, lovers, or destinies.

But systemic awareness does not preclude wholesale regrets. Ashbery concludes one late, small stanza with an allegorical spectacle of days running out: "you see these / Days each with its disarming set of images and attitudes / Are beneficial perhaps but only after the last one / In every series has disappeared, down the road, forever, at night" (W 87). In the preceding stanza, Ashbery writes that he is not "the first person to confuse / Its solicitation with something like scorn" (W 87), thinking perhaps of Emerson in "Days," where he "hastily / Took a few herbs and apples, and the Day / Turned and departed silent. I, too late, / Under her solemn fillet saw the scorn" ("carpe diem").[30] With this growing awareness of time running out, the addressee becomes increasingly the system's putative Creator. Like "Litany," the final stanzas of "A Wave" take up the discourse of prayer. In the waiting room of the final stanza, the last ballooning "question that I asked and can't / Remember" rises out of sight, and the first-person questioner is left to himself, "the amazingly quiet room in which all my life has been spent" (W 89). Ashbery's periodic poem breaks off, at the end of February, where it began, with the break-up:

> And it is finally we who break it off,
> Speed the departing guest, lest any question remain
> Unasked, and thereby unanswered. Please, it almost

Seems to say, take me with you, I'm old enough. Exactly.
And so each of us has to remain alone, conscious of each other
Until the day when war absolves us of our differences. We'll
Stay in touch. So they have it, all the time. But all was strange.

In this wake, lover is divided from lover, poet from poem, and father from son, until history's grimly purgative wave "absolves us of our differences," or "sins." In the wake of estrangement "all was strange." After the wave hits, one feels numb and everything seems strange: "Not something so very strange, but then seeming ordinary / Is strange too" (W 77).[31] In Ashbery's sad last line, the "old forms of address" ("We'll / Stay in touch") no longer seem pregnant, "big to fill the exotic spaces that arguing left" (W 80). But the frighteningly dispirited mood or threadbare style with which he is determined to end "A Wave" cannot be the definitive conclusion. If not another stanza, another book will bring new life to these hollow forms.

# 11

## Conservation Measures

## *April Galleons*

By Ashbery's standards, *April Galleons* (1987) is a beautiful but conservative volume. It lacks a long poem—an expenditure of energy that defines most of his previous books. The volume is, moreover, neither conspicuously unified nor especially diversified in form; most of its lyrics are measured in free-verse lines and stanzas, contemporary poetry's path of least resistance. The volume thus cedes the experimental vanguard to the growing small press productions of the Language poets (it has in fact garnered less attention from poets and critics than two adventuresome books also published in 1987, both at Sun & Moon Press, Charles Bernstein's *The Sophist* and Lyn Hejinian's *My Life*). Though *April Galleons* does contain several compelling poems, it looks increasingly like a transitional volume between *A Wave* and *Flow Chart.*

Many of the poems in *April Galleons* concern themselves in one way or another with conservation—an inextricable network of remembering, redeeming, preserving, sheltering, and keeping hidden, as a few scattered passages show: "You hid it / So no one would find it / And now you can't remember where" (AG 25); "We've kept these old things / To practice on" (AG 46); "The quarries are closed now, / The terse, blue stone is no longer mined there" (AG 49); "He who comes to save says the single, / Enameled word that outlives us" (AG 34); "And I mean what shall be saved / Of us as we live aimed at some near but unattainable mark on the wall?" (AG 27); "The mad doctor is secure / In his thick-walled laboratory" (AG 55); "These wisps, I / Guess I'll save them for a while" (AG 7); "It's still too early to make concessions" (AG 23). Certain events in Ashbery's own history may have contributed to the collection's retrospective character. In 1985 he went back through thirty years of poetry to put together his *Selected Poems*. Also that year, he won a five-year MacArthur Fellowship, which, from the evidence of his output during that period, may have encouraged him to spend his time wisely. In January 1987 his mother died, and he collected a lifetime of manuscripts from his home in upstate New York and from his mother's home in Pultneyville, all of which were deposited in Houghton Library at Harvard. Increasingly recognized as an indispensable American poet, Ashbery thus found a permanent shelter for his life's work: "The monument / Didn't work out as planned, but we have been taken in" (AG 79).

It is interesting to see how Ashbery took in and arranged the poems for his latest collection. In the aftermath of "A Wave," finished in late February 1983, he seems to have written no poetry for nearly a year; the poems of *April Galleons* were written between the Februarys of 1984 and 1987, the bulk of them in 1986. Of the three preliminary title pages, two are handwritten on 14-inch legal-pad paper, the first entitled "BOOK," with the subheading "*In book.*" The titles are listed with page lengths following, and arranged under the headings "rev. and good but not placed," "pub. or placed in US," "pub. or placed in US and Eng," "pub or placed in Eng., Aust, or India," and "new." Beside three of the 21 poems in the first category, Ashbery wrote "NO 2/12" (1987). He kept all of the previously published poems, which swelled the volume to around one hundred pages. After admitting ten of eleven of his "new" poems into the volume, Ashbery rejected fifteen of the next seventeen—apparently not because they weren't as good as the first ten but simply because they came too late in the list. Like a belabored poem, Ashbery's table of contents had gone on long enough.

The poems are extensively rearranged in the next title list. Poems to be saved are marked with a check and their number, 53, is calculated. The typescript, labeled "Contents" as in the book, preserves the same number of poems (with "No Two Alike" and "Wet Are the Boards" added in handwriting), arranged roughly in final order. The exception is the opening sequence of ten poems.[1] Apparently concerned not to repeat his sometimes apprehensive openings, Ashbery made a list of words from these poems— "flower," "fish(erman)," "storm," "unique," "sea," "shore"—and made a note, "shift longer one to beginning." Thus the long-lined, two-page "Dreams of Adulthood" is moved up from seventh to fifth place, the suspicious "Becalmed on Strange Waters" is buried in position 33, and the campily sentimental "A Mood of Quiet Beauty" is replaced by the painterly, sentimental "Vetiver" as the opening poem. Both "Vetiver" (beginning "Ages passed slowly") and "April Galleons" feature the first capitalized letter of the alphabet, as did "A Mood." The volume thus regards itself as a new beginning rather than an approaching end, shadowed and tidal-waved.

*April Galleons* is in some ways defined by its framing poems. "Vetiver"

(AG 1; dated December 15, 1984) is an unassuming page-length poem in three stanzas of seven, twelve, and thirteen mid-length free-verse lines. The first announces the themes for the others to vary:

> Ages passed slowly, like a load of hay,
> As the flowers recited their lines
> And pike stirred at the bottom of the pond.
> The pen was cool to the touch.
> The staircase swept upward
> Through fragmented garlands, keeping the melancholy
> Already distilled in letters of the alphabet.

This opening reflexive fairy-tale setting recollects "Scheherazade," where "Fish live in the wells," "Day is almost reluctant to decline," and speaking "flowers outlined along the night / Alleys" (SP 9). But unlike the earlier more ambitious poem, "Vetiver" has neither heroine nor plot. Nevertheless, the landscape is charged with feeling. The opening pastoral misrepresentation varies some narrative convention such as "time passed slowly" or (preserving the plural and echoing "hay") "days passed slowly." "Ages" elongates the time to geological proportions while surreptitiously introducing the topic of age. In the middle stanza this topic again insinuates itself: "How many snakes and lizards shed their skins / For time to be passing on like this, / Sinking deeper in the sand." Here the misrepresentative reptilian particulars hide the death ("How many have died?") registered in the euphemism "passed on."

If mortal coils are lost in this narrative and lyric economy, their perfumed essence is saved. Vetiver, an East Indian grass with aromatic roots, is "distilled" in the first stanza in fragrant ("fragmented") perfumed "letters" (characters, epistles), Ashbery's implicit pun. The other, homotextual wordplay in "Vetiver" involves the masculine root and the spermal "tears" of "melancholy" and desire. As the Baudelairean perfume is squeezed out, the essence of the "situation" rises to the text's surface. The phallic imagery, beginning with the "pike" and "pen," is obvious enough, which makes the "catch in the voice" at the end of the second stanza of this piscatory pastoral all the more painful and fruitful: "a change is voiced, sharp / As a fishhook in the throat, and decorative tears flowed / Past us into a basin called infinity." The difficulty of mentioning "tears" is evident in "decorative," not a bad adjective for the erotic sentimentality of "Vetiver," pink with Ashbery's trademarked "color once known as 'ashes of roses.'"

The pen that "was cool to the touch" in the opening turns into something like a panpipe in the closing stanza's allegorical scene of instruction, as "someone examines his youth, / Finds it dry and hollow, porous to the touch." At this potentially sterile point, the narrative is interrupted by an unquoted appeal for salvation: "O keep me with you, unless the outdoors / Embraces both of us, unites us, unless," and so on for eight lines until the poem ends by returning to narrative discourse: "and the crying / In the leaves is saved, the last silver drops." The word we expect in this hyperbolic series is "until," as in Robert Burns's promise to love his rose "Till a' the seas gang dry." Ashbery's misrepresentative "unless" indicates the future anterior, where something might or might not be saved and remembered. In "Forgotten Sex," for instance, urban and personal history "Went untold, unless someone who was there once / Visited the old neighborhood" or "Unless children one day dig up the past, in the attic" (AG 17). The recollective "Vetiver" looks forward to saving its memories.

The final lines of "Vetiver," in which the Whitmanian leaves of grass are saved from "this bonfire," reorganize Stevens's powerfully repressed late poem, "The Course of a Particular," itself a commentary on John Donne's meditation "for whom the bell tolls." In Stevens's misrepresentative lyric (in the third rather than the first person), the "leaves cry . . . One holds off and merely hears the cry" (Stevens's ellipsis), as though they didn't cry for one. Though no man is an island, "though one says that one is part of everything" (367; "Donne says"), one is reluctant to join the other leaves in death. Unlike Stevens's inhuman solitude, Ashbery's community in "Vetiver" is dual ("both of us") and plural; as in "'They Dream Only of America'" (TCO 13), the fugitive lovers may hide from the policing "birdcatchers" and "fishermen" and hope to become "lost in the crowd" of burning leaves, "become part of the immense crowd / Around this bonfire, a situation / That has come to mean us to us." As in most of Ashbery's love poems, the homotextual "situation" of "Vetiver" is both personal and public; its secrets are kept from and for us.

In the privileged final position usually occupied by a long poem in Ashbery's books, the title poem "April Galleons" (dated April 29, 1986) becomes an ambitious envoy, which launches the volume into publication. The poem crosses the course of Baudelaire's "L'invitation au voyage" (especially the prose version) at several points, from the foreseen "pleasures / Of the great open sea" (AG 95) to the invitation to "Come / To look at us" (AG 96), and like Baudelaire's poem, its "Land of Cockaigne" is the poem itself.[2] Divided into two large verse paragraphs of twenty-three and twenty-seven lines, "April Galleons" measures the unbridgeable difference between "now" and "then," its two prominent temporal markers. Ashbery's time-ship is the sign, or the sign system of the poem, and its cargo is its original context and final realization. His argument in "April Galleons" proceeds by analogy. Signs, arriving after or before the fact, save by keeping to their signifying course; so too, belated poets preserve at least the possibility of the Golden Age in their time-bound, timeless poems.

"April Galleons" begins in the midst of things with a mismeasured sentence, too small for its line: "Something *was* burning. And besides," (AG 95). The poetry of the prosaic sentence lies in the specificity of its discourse. To read it properly, we need to supply its antecedent scene, in which someone thinks he smells something burning, perhaps tells someone else, and turns out to be right. Ashbery narrates the scene in the past of free indirect discourse, but the suspicion that nothing *is* burning or ardent is registered. As the sentence includes its situation, the burnt odor indicates its burning source, making it the kind of nonarbitrary causal sign C. S. Peirce called an index. "Besides" the reliable sign, the "discredited waltz / Was alive and reciting tales of the conquerors / And their lilies" ("singer was alive and well," "loves," "fleurs de lys"), like a golden-aged rhapsode. An earlier study of belatedness, "Business Personals," asked, "what are 'leftovers'?" (HBD 18). "April Galleons" begins with the same quandary, left in the questioning wake with depleted signifying supplies: "is all of life thus / A tepid housewarming? And where do the scraps / Of meaning come from?" If Baudelaire promises that "even the fare" will be "poetic," Ashbery is less sure of his provisions. The skeptical questions which launch "April Galleons" may be phrased as follows: perhaps the steaming main poetry courses have already been prepared and digested, and only cold scraps remain?

Rather than turning back to recapture the past, the prospective "April Galleons" faces forward, declaring "It was time to be off, in another / Direction, toward . . . / Names of cities that sounded as though they existed" (AG 95). Baudelaire asks whether his beloved reader shares "that nostalgia for the country which we do not know" (33). Like Baudelaire, and Proust after him, Ashbery has long interested himself in the paradoxical way names, like invitations, precede things. This poet is a namer not in the etymological, Emersonian sense, but in the magical, performative sense of calling a thing into being by inventing its name. The issue of names in poetry usually includes the name, or fame, of the poet. In "Dreams of Adulthood," for instance, the senior authorial speaker advises that "if one wants to become a diamond eventually it isn't too early / To begin thinking about it," and continues with a homotextually droll discourse on the proper name: "My name is Steve she said my name is Brian / My pretty baa-lambs each have names just like everything else upon earth, / Proper names, I mean. This way we are allowed to recognize species / From itinerant examples of them" (AG 6). This representative character is what proper, given names share with common names. But nothing of "Ashbery," for instance, would be saved in "John." In one surreally funny instance of oblivion, a landmark prominently featured in the unnamed Eliot's *The Waste Land* ends up, like Shelley's Ozymandias, ruling desert sands, "The Lake Havasu City of our dreams where London Bridge eyes the sands / Nervously, and vice versa" (AG 6). If "London Bridge" can wind up in Arizona, no mark is indelible. In "April Galleons," a soaring fourteen-line sentence beginning "I could see the scow" envisions an apocalyptic time when signs might be reunited with things. Pointers and signs proliferate in this sentence—the "scow / Like a nail file pointed at the pleasures," the "bird taking off," the "winged guitar." They augur a satisfying fulfillment: "and then, and only then, / Might the profit-taking of spring arrive" (AG 95; "prophet"). This "then" is revelatory, passing through "torn orange veils," and possibly fatal: the scow that "would stop for me" recalls the carriage of Death that "kindly stopped for" Dickinson (#712). The stanza is punctuated by a brief sentence, varying "Some Trees": "And all trees seemed to exist" (AG 95). In the fullness of time, the trees correspond to themselves.

"April Galleons" might have ended in this visionary fashion, but it wouldn't have sufficed; poetry may be composed for posterity, but it is written in the present. The second stanza resumes with darker possibilities, with previous signatures running in the downpouring text: "Tapestries stream initials of all the previous owners / To warn us into silence and waiting." Touchstones do begin to crop up in "April Galleons," but they are less a threat than an encouragement to face down oblivion. The skeptical reduction of publication to scattering, "It was all going / To be scattered anyway" (so why bother?), is not the last word. Signs, names, leaves, and poems may be "scattered," but perhaps, like the perfumed roots in "Vetiver," they conserve their essences, "as far from one's wish / As the root of the tree from the center of the earth / From which it nonetheless issued in time to / Inform us of happy blossoms" (AG 95). The vocabulary recalls the memorable close of Yeats's "Among School Children," which offers a parallel argument for conservative organic signs: "O chestnut tree, great rooted blossomer, / Are you the leaf, the blossom or the bole?" (217). As though to bolster his faith, Ashbery plucks a few notes on Stevens's blue guitar: "In intervals in the twilight notes from an / Untuned mandolin seem to co-exist with their / Question and the no less urgent reply" (AG 96). And his subsequent invitation borrows both from Cinderella and from Yeats's enchanting proem to *The Rose,* "To the Rose upon the Rood of Time": *"Come near, come near, come near—Ah, leave me still / A little space for the rose-breath to fill!"* (31). Today's poems are inviting: "Come / To look at us but not too near or its

291

familiarity / Will vanish in a thunderclap and the beggar-girl, / String-haired and incomprehensibly weeping, will / Be all that is left of the golden age, our / Golden age" (AG 96; "strangeness," "inconsolably").

As Cinderella's "golden [carri]age" became a pumpkin, so the poem when scrutinized might lose its ageless, golden-aged magic. Ashbery's assertion that postmodern poets have their own Golden Age recalls certain passages from "Litany": "*Isn't it normal for things to happen this way / During the Silver Age, which ours is?*" (AWK 31). The author of the mannerist "silver blur" of "Self-Portrait in a Convex Mirror" is no longer willing to be so defined. Even in "Litany" an "angel, / Goddess, whatever," soon announces the "Brass Age," with "magnificent / Clouds like overloaded schooners" (AWK 33). Ashbery, who chose one of John Constable's *Cloud Studies* for the cover of *April Galleons,* looks to the clouds' progeny (by way of Thomas Tusser's now proverbial rhyme, "Sweet April showers / Do spring May flowers"): "and no longer will the swarms / Issue forth at dawn to return in a rain of mild / Powder at night" (AG 96). The "mild" powder was "golden" in the typescript; the precious metal is saved by "swarms" of poets, associated with bees and honey. For the ordinary swarms of workers who head off in pursuit of an honest living every morning, the Golden Age "tales of colored cities" are patently escapist, "removing us from our boring and / Unsatisfactory honesty." Their heroes are "discredited" like the opening "waltz": "what were the / Directions the lepers were taking / To avoid these eyes, the old eyes of love" (AG 96). In Ashbery's split perspective, these eyes are those at once of the uninvited critics who would deny postmodern poets their Golden Age and of the old lovers. For "lepers," Ashbery first wrote "rabble" and then "pariahs." Like lovers plagued in the late 1980s, the poem and poet remain "untouchable."

Several poems in *April Galleons* save lines from anonymous ballads. The jaunty title "And Some Were Playing Cards, and Some Were Playing Dice" (AG 75), for instance, comes from the ballad "The 'Golden Vanity.'" Ballads and fairy tales, more than oral epics or archaic lyric, seem to represent for Ashbery the anonymous natural art of the Golden Age. In his recent and best pantoum, "Hotel Lautréamont," an inept expert admires the public authorship of the ballad: "Research has shown that ballads were produced by all of society / working as a team" (HL 14). In "Crazy Weather" (dated March 20, 1976) he drops his commas to praise balladic poetry as an unfettered verbal stream, which "had / A simple unconscious dignity we can never hope to / Approximate now except in narrow ravines nobody / Will inspect" (HBD 21). Though such praise sounds almost parodic, Ashbery treats the ballad as a reservoir of lyric energy. In "Forgotten Song" (dated May 15, 1984) Ashbery seems to generate his verse from forgotten sources.

The first couplet, an unusual stanza for Ashbery, splices together a mismatched pair of lines: "O Mary, go and call the cattle home / For I'm sick in my heart and fain would lie down" (AG 12). The second line, in anapestic tetrameter, ends the ballad "Lord Randal" in which the son explains to his mother that his own true love has poisoned him.[3] The first, pentameter line begins a Victorian-era art-ballad by Charles Kingsley, "The Sands of 'Dee," in which Mary is found drowned in the "cruel crawling foam," a phrase John Ruskin used to illustrate his "pathetic fallacy," appending his famous, clipped retort: "The foam is not cruel, neither does it crawl." Incorporated into Ashbery's poem, these forgotten songs, primary and (significantly) secondary, represent the life force, "the continual stirring / That we come to recognize as life" (AG 12), the unnameable "It." The balladic force manifests itself first as an orphan, a "bundle of pain / Left on my doorstep" ("joy"), possibly a savior or Nietzschean superman: "is it the new person, / / As yet indescribable, though existing here and there?" In the withered mismeasured sentences which end "Forgotten Song," the ballad is a kind of salve, represented by the italicized line from the ballad "The Unquiet Grave"[4]: "*The stalk is withered dry, my love, so will our hearts decay. / /* Unless we omitted something. And we did. It'll cure it. / It will have to. But I can't whisper that story yet" (AG 13). Somewhere along the line, the story goes, "it" got "omitted" from poetry. Envisioning a "then, and only then" (AG 95), Ashbery points toward an apocalypse, perhaps the ushering in of another Golden Age. But until then, the collaged fragments "will have to" do.

Ashbery follows the measures of oral poetry in "Finnish Rhapsody" (dated October 25, 1985), which, like "At North Farm" (W 1), uses the paraphrastic hemistichs of *The Kalevala*. This form, which Ashbery assigned to his poetry-writing class at Brooklyn College, was first used in English by Longfellow, whose not-long-forgotten "Song of Hiawatha" (1855) retains a distinctive American clunk: "By the shores of Gitche Gumee, / By the shining Big-Sea-Water, / Stood the wigwam of Nokomis, / Daughter of the Moon, Nokomis."[5] Ashbery's own paraphrases are hilariously varied: a long phrase qualifies a short one ("To be rescued, to be guided into a state of something like security"), or pretends to scientific precision ("Dusted with snow-white flour, glazed with farinaceous powder"), or translates ("Strong and severe punishment, *peine forte et dure*"), or defines ("Like Pierrot, like the white clown of chamber music"), or simply doubles the mystery ("Truncates the spadelike shadows, chops off the blades of darkness") (AG 14; "cuts the grass"). The rhetorical essence of poetry, saying one thing in terms of another, is here humbly preserved.

But Ashbery's paraphrases also juxtapose parallel lives. On the one hand, there is the nine-to-five crowd that seeks organization and financial security: "Many there are, a crowd exists at present, / For whom the daily forgetting, to whom the diurnal plunge / Truncates the spadelike shadows, chops off the blades of darkness, / To be rescued, to be guided into a state of something like security" (AG 14). On the other hand, there is a minority that recalls the natural, pre-capitalist rhythms: "And for these few, to this small group / Forgetting means remembering the ranks, oblivion is recalling the rows / Of flowers each autumn and spring; of blooms in the fall and early summer" (AG 14). The conservationist stops and smells the roses, and "Knows how short the day is" (AG 15). Whereas "April Galleons" confounds honey- and money-makers in a representative first person plural, Ashbery here detaches the sexually and textually alienated from the normative masses. These parallel lives, first chronicled in "The System," where an "other tradition" "developed parallel to the classic truths of daily life" (TP 55), were graphically represented in the parallel columns of "Litany." In "Finnish Rhapsody" the countercultural force looms a caesura away, as the rhapsode of the finish foresees ordinary language invaded by the linguistically outer spaces of poems:

> And it will be but half-strange, really be only semi-bizarre
> When the tall poems of the world, the towering earthbound poetic
>    utterances
> Invade the street of our dialect, penetrate the avenue of our patois,
> Bringing fresh power and new knowledge, transporting virgin might and
>    up-to-date enlightenment
> To this place of honest thirst, to this satisfyingly parched here and now.
> (AG 15)

Though he might wish it were otherwise, Ashbery cannot but smile at the "up-to-date" salvation postmodern poetry has to offer. At the same time, he cannot resist imagining the world absorbing his misrepresentative poems as they themselves "Suck up the common strength, absorb the everyday power / And afterwards live on, satisfied; persist, later to be a source of gratification, / But perhaps only to oneself, haply to one's sole identity" (AG 16). If they do not yet nourish humankind, these poems at least solace their misrepresentative author.

Ashbery parallels the "other tradition" with Reagan-era outcasts in "No Two Alike" (AG 35; dated September 19, 1984). As the November presidential primaries neared, a controversy arose over the voting rights of the increasing homeless population which had no "home address." In New

York it was decided in early September that those living in homeless shelters were eligible to vote (in Philadelphia the homeless could count benches as places of residence). This grim expedient drives the search for safety in "No Two Alike." Wryly titled after an advertising slogan appropriating American "individualism" for "homemade" consumer products, the misrepresentative poem concerns the vastly more influential misrepresentations of the media. Though Ashbery knows well that poetry can do nothing directly to alleviate the suffering of the homeless, he cannot but call attention to those left on the outside: "Those are people in the street, the ones you passed." "No Two Alike" is given what may be called, following Verlaine, an impaired stanzaic form: a series of sestets interrupted by a septet. It begins abruptly and haltingly with an apocalyptic play on "finish": "Wait—it has some kind of finish on it." Like an Ashbery poem, advertising's mercurial reproductions are noted for their "finish." But finishes soon wear off: "That / Patina got on it, and was what mattered for a while." Those too slow for rapid capitalist renovations are left without shelter, "propped against a wall, / Eating day-old bread. And then the world changed." The first sestet's last fairy-tale sentence, characteristic of Ashbery's wave-phase narratives, takes the perspective of its uncomprehending victims. The septet can only add, switching perspectives, that in this strict economy "we are calmer, and safer, for it." Ashbery struggles to imagine the unforeseeable global change, which happened "As though some big man had come in, and turned / And abruptly left in the few moments I was out." But the magnitude of the changes is unaccountable. Outside the media-marketed United States there must be some safe haven, some charitable "groves in England" where wealth is evenly distributed to the masses, "To the handy and the articulate, and bread left then / Won't be idle, part of a mass of frayed circumstance." The risk Ashbery takes with his misrepresentations may be measured by his encrypted phrases: "ministering to the needy," "the masses," and "idle hands," from Isaac Watts's severe proverb, "For Satan finds some mischief still / For idle hands to do." It is not only the homeless who may be "handy and articulate" but those dextrous "starving artists" who articulate their needs.

The final sestet interrupts these speculations with an intercessory prayer for oblivion:

Pray that in just one bubble the color
Will cover the whole surface sheen,
Polluting remembrance, the house where I was born.
And in that moment of curious rage an attic

Is pitched, a place to come after long love,
And dexterity after wearing these fingers out.
(AG 35)

With the strange marker after the stanza break, "in just one bubble," Ashbery encrypts the television announcer's promise to return "in just one moment" after the station's commercial break. In 1968, Ashbery recorded television's transformation into a dying "living color," as the set is shut off:
"Dotted rhythms of colors as they fade to the color, / A gray agate, translucent and firm, with nothing / Beyond its purifying reach. It's all there" (DDS
46). But here it's all about to burst, like a soap opera bubble. The end of
"No Two Alike" prays to repair the final rupture of "Down by the Station,"
with its "extraneous babble from the street" (W 14). But this new moment is
anti-cathartic, "Polluting remembrance." There is no cleansing in the city's
televisual "surface sheen." Yeats complained in "Adam's Curse" that the
poet's labors are seen as idle by the busy world, a far cry from the idleness
forced on the recently unemployed. Ashbery thus imagines himself with
some irony as "wearing his fingers to the bone" through life until he is at
last "worn out." All he can offer those out of work, who probably won't
read him anyway, is the temporary shelter of his poem, a textual "tent"
"pitched" in childhood's "attic." To ask anything more from the imagined
moment would indeed pollute remembrance.

In the next poem in *April Galleons,* "Amid Mounting Evidence" (dated
December 2, 1986), Ashbery again obliquely addresses contemporary affairs. The poem was written a week after President Reagan first disclosed,
"amid mounting evidence," the diversion of profits from the sale of arms to
Iran to the Nicaraguan Contras. With its breezy argumentation—Ashbery
wrote its 69 long lines (and longer sentences) in a single day without changing a word—the poem anticipates the long-winded harangues of *Flow
Chart.* Ashbery takes aim here at both Reagan and Lt. Col. Oliver North, a
fellow upstate New Yorker whose repeated invocation of the Fifth Amend-
ment before the Tower Commission was front-page news the day Ashbery
began his poem: "It's so easy to trudge and pretend to be a boy" (AG 37).
By the end of this tortuous sentence the speaker is "Complaining inaudibly
and in general installing / Oneself as a capital nuisance, never to be given
the time of day again." Reagan and North are of course easy and agreeable
targets, but from Ashbery's bifocal perspective the "capital nuisance" and
the poem's "Complaining" speaker are indistinguishable.

"Amid Mounting Evidence" begins from this same problematic point of
view. A paranoid speaker, who has been "reading about dinosaurs" (such as

Reagan), soon mounts his own conspiracy theory in an attempt to expose that plausibly deniable central radiating principle (AG 36):

> the world lies open
> To the radiation theory (tons of radiation, think of it,
> Reversing all normal procedures
> So that the pessimistic ball of wax begins
> To slide down the inclined plane again
> Bringing further concepts to their doom while encouraging
> The infinity of loose ends that
> Is taking over our government and threatening to become life as we know it!)

Rousselian onion-skin parentheses conceal layer on layer of deception. The circular rhetoric of center and circumference, cause and effects, whole ("ball of wax") and parts, inside and outside, upon which Ashbery constructed "Self-Portrait in a Convex Mirror," is now turned to parodic ends, as in the paranoid hyperbolic rhetoric of the breathless final line. Ashbery's political poetry is often concerned with our misrepresentations of events rather than with the "events themselves" (in this case, a congressionally assisted media fabrication).

The all-American public of "Amid Mounting Evidence" is invigorated by departures from the ordinary and spurred by an unshakable belief that some covert organization lies behind chaotic appearances: "The drilling / Of noon insects in high summer had to precede this or something / Else" (AG 37; "precedent," "president"). But the revolution, impeachment, or resignation that would follow such prospecting is not worth the loss of one's routine. "Amid Mounting Evidence" thus ends with an average public speaker celebrating ordinary life and clear sentences: "It seems / Shipshape now. Everything seems to be all right. / The storm, you see, told none of its secrets, / Gave nothing away" (AG 37). Neither the plausibly denying President nor the misrepresenting author have confessed anything. But what they keep in reserve also keeps the possibility of hidden order and meaning in life and in poetry as we now know it.

Ashbery considers the reading public's responses in the flagship of *April Galleons,* "The Ice Storm." The engaging four-page prose poem first appeared in Leland Hickman's groundbreaking poetry journal *Temblor* and next in a booklet with Ashbery photographed before a wooded pond on its tiny cover.[6] Midway through the unlineated wilds we are given the parable of the (p)rose:

Today I found a rose in full bloom in the wreck of the garden, all the living color and sentience but also the sententiousness drained out of it. What remained was like a small flower in the woods, too pale and sickly to notice. No, sickly isn't the right word, the thing was normal and healthy by its own standards, and thriving merrily along its allotted path toward death. Only we hold it up to some real and abject notion of what a living organism ought to be and paint it as a scarecrow that frightens birds away (presumably) but isn't able to frighten itself away. Oh, no, it's far too clever for that! But our flower, the one we saw, really had no need of us to justify its blooming where it did. So we ought to think about our own position on the path. Will it ever be anything more than that of pebble? I wonder. And they scratch, some of them feverishly, at whatever meaning it might be supposed to yield up, of course expiring as it does so. But our rose gains its distinction just by being stuck there. . . . What more do you want? it seemed to say. Leave me in this desert . . . (AG 92–93, Ashbery's final ellipsis)

This extravagance, reminiscent of "Thoreau's" ("the rose"), boils down to the flower's question: What authoritative sentiment or benefit do we expect to extract from the text at hand? "What I really want to know," Ashbery writes, miming the pragmatic American reader, "is how will this affect me, make me better in the future? Maybe make me a better conversationalist?" (AG 92). The author responds by considering the Archimedean displacement of the reading process, "the act of reading something, of being communicated to by an author and thus having one's ideas displaced like the water that pebbles placed by the stork's beak slowly force out of the beaker—*beaker?* do you suppose?" (AG 92). The author puts words into the mouth of his "speaker," who pours his purported ideas into our head. On its "far too clever" surface, "The Ice Storm," a transforming "I-storm," is a parable against parables, against ideal and abstract ("real and abject") notions, and against the probing of analytic delvers, "people" ("pebble") who murder to dissect.

The antecedent of Ashbery's parable is recoverable from the odd way he trails off: "Leave me in this desert . . ." The ellipsis encourages us to read "desert" as an adjective meaning "deserted," as in the most memorable couplet of Thomas Gray's "Elegy Written in a Country Churchyard": "Full many a flower is born to blush unseen, / And waste its sweetness on the desert air."[7] John Clare, for instance, passes unnamed (though he is named elsewhere, AG 34) in a collaged encyclopedia entry, seen as lost with the ice storms of yesteryear, "the pile of required reading such as obituary notices of the near-great—'He first gained employment as a schoolmaster in his native Northamptonshire. Of his legendary wit, no trace remains'" (AG 91). One of the many poems demonstrating the anonymous immortality of Gray's lines is Emerson's "The Rhodora," which seems to have grafted itself onto Ashbery's rose. Emerson finds his "fresh Rhodora" beside "the desert and the sluggish brook" and teaches his "rival of the rose" how to respond to "sages" who come seeking meaningful causes and purposes: "Tell them, dear, that if eyes were made for seeing, / Then Beauty is its own excuse for being" (412). But Emerson's own pose as one who, in the midst of Unitarian sages, simply whiles away the hours conferring with the flowers, is hardly less coy than the rhodora's in this song of assumed innocence. Ashbery's own self-reliant rose, which "really had no need of us to justify its blooming where it did," introduces a more frightening homiletics. What of our own unrooted, specular position, "positioned around to comment" on the rose, on our own "allotted path toward death"? What justifies *our* existence as Christmas "ornaments on a structure whose mass remains invisible or illegible" (AG 94)? "The Ice Storm" affords us no place to stop or start. Beginning, like a Garrison Keillor radio monologue, in the midst of things, it explains that an ice storm "isn't really a storm of course because unlike most storms it isn't one till it's over and people go outside and say will you look at that" (AG 91). Like an Ashbery poem, the storm will "emphasize a point that melts away as fast as another idea enters the chain of them in the conversation about earth and sky and woods and how you should be good to your parents and not cheat at cards" (AG 91). Not much to hold on to here.

The end of "The Ice Storm" is inviting but no more conclusive. The final paragraph begins with a dated journal entry, which announces itself as a purportedly private stream of consciousness: "October 28. Three more days till November. . . . I am being taken out into the country. Trees flash past. All is perhaps for the best then since I am going, and they are going with us, with us as we go. The past is only a pond. The present is a lake of grass. Between your two futures, yours and his, numbing twigs chart the pattern of lifeless chatter in shut-down night, starstruck the magnitudes that would make us theirs, too cold to matter to themselves, let us be off anywhere, to Alaska, to Arizona. I am fishing for compliments. The afternoon lasts forever" (AG 94). Like the end of *Flow Chart,* "The Ice Storm" dissolves into a traffic flow. Ashbery homotextually orients the confidential tag "between you and me," and explains, in suddenly obscure terms, that the icy Wordsworthian twigs chart the course for him and his confidant beyond his "starstruck" audience. Like "April Galleons," the prose poem invites us away, "to Alaska, to Arizona." Thoreau confided to his own pond that "Time is but the stream I go a-fishing in," adding "I cannot count one. I know not the first letter of the alphabet."[8] While the wish to begin again, to revisit the states in alphabetical order, will not save anyone from the future, at least it keeps possibilities from running out.

# 12

## Anybody's Autobiography
## *Flow Chart*

What does it profit me, then, O Lord, to whom my conscience confesses daily, confident more in the hope of your mercy than in its own innocence, what does it profit me, I ask, also to make known to men in your sight, through this book, not what I once was, but what I am now? I know what profit I gain by confessing my past, and this I have declared. But many people who know me, and others who do not know me but have heard of me or read my books, wish to hear what I am now, at this moment, as I set down my confessions.

—Saint Augustine, *Confessions,* Book X

What I'm doin' now is just like a regular worker. The only thing is listening to conversation, watching certain movements of people. Without thinkin', people reveal their innermost secrets and plots and everything."

—Anthony Ruggiero, Industrial Investigator,
in Studs Terkel, *Working*

In 1991 Ashbery overwhelmed his readers with a huge book-length poem in verse. Covering 216 oversized pages, *Flow Chart* dwarfed his earlier "long poems" and doubled the size of most of his previous books.[1] Though versified, *Flow Chart* is in many ways more prosaic than its prose predecessor, the midlife dialectic *Three Poems,* which seems by comparison relatively undiversified and abstract. *Flow Chart* contains more kinds of traditionally nonliterary language and consequently seems to encompass more extraliterary life; it has more life to look back on and less to look forward to. Like *Three Poems* a theodicy of an alternate destiny, *Flow Chart* is less conspicuously and consciously charted. Where *Three Poems* is a dialectical progression, *Flow Chart* is a retrospective ramble, wandering, seemingly without premeditation or embarrassment, from one vaguely defined scene or topic to the next. The two poems are characterized by different modes of discourse. *Three Poems* is dominated by written discourses (epistolary, meditative, sermonic, essayistic), while the prosaic verse of *Flow Chart* is largely rendered in American speech, much of which takes the form of what is known, paradoxically, as oral autobiography—written (or recorded) talk. Yet Ashbery's poem is at most the flow chart of an autobiography. As he said of the memories represented in "The Skaters," "I didn't want them to be specific ones that applied to me but only ones that anybody would use if they were thinking autobiographically; they were just to be forms of autobiography."[2] *Flow Chart* is anybody's autobiography, but nobody's in particular. But the peculiarity of its misrepresentations belongs only to its autobiographical author.

The flow chart, or project, of *Flow Chart* was proposed by someone else. In the fall of 1987 Trevor Winkfield, who eventually painted a waving-grained "flow chart" for the book cover, suggested to Ashbery that he write a one-hundred-page poem about his mother, who had died the previous January. Ashbery recalled thinking, "Say, that's something I haven't done before!" and hastened to add, "of course, it's not about my mother."[3] Like its subject, the generative form of *Flow Chart* is invisible. While the fifty-dizained design of "Fragment" is readily apparent, especially in the Black Sparrow edition, there is no way to determine from the Knopf edition of *Flow Chart* that the poem originated from a one-hundred-page, single-spaced typescript. Nevertheless, the buried form charts the poem's flow. The page limit which Ashbery accepted signifies wholeness ("one hundred per cent") and a proverbial fullness of years ("If I live to be a hundred"); no vital statistic, the magic number represents the immeasurable plenitude of a life and a life's work. Other autobiographical poems have watched their figures and marked their beginnings. Whitman, who rounded out his democratic life by dividing the final edition of "Song of Myself" into fifty-two sections, the number of weeks in a year, recorded his own years at the poem's birth: "I, now thirty-seven years old in perfect health begin" (188). Lyn Hejinian, who began her autobiographical prose poem, *My Life* (1987), at the age of 37, used a similarly invisible but verifiable form, 37 unnumbered sections (or chapters) of 37 sentences each (adding sections and sentences in a later edition, as Whitman "updated" or "aged" his own "Song" after the Civil War). Ashbery included his own age in *Flow Chart* by deciding, in advance, to finish his one hundred pages on July 28, 1988, the sixty-first anniversary of the day his mother gave birth to him. Starting on December 8, 1987, he wrote *Flow Chart* with his birthday (rather than, for instance, the day of his mother's death) as his destination and deadline, making almost daily entries and nearing the end ahead of schedule (he had finished

93 pages by the end of June 1988). He conscientiously recorded the dates of these typescript entries "for scholars to come" (he never intended to leave them in the poem); by 1987, most of his typescripts were already housed and being catalogued in Houghton Library, a fate that he was aware most likely awaited his latest work as well. The typescript of *Flow Chart* is unbroken, with no divisions other than stanza breaks. Ashbery added the numbered divisions later as "visual resting places for the reader" rather than "as breaks in the flow." Unlike the titled, discursive divisions of *Three Poems,* the six sections of *Flow Chart* (four in proof) operate simply as rest areas alongside the road.[4]

*Flow Chart* is channeled by the width as well as the length of its typewritten pages. Though the lines often stretch from one margin to the other, Ashbery never types over the right margin by more than a word. Thus one measurement of his meter here is the one hundred characters available to each line. Like the hundred-page length, this predetermined width is the poem's horizon. Some lines are conspicuously foreshortened. In one early stanza, following an underpunctuated sentence of nearly fourteen lines, Ashbery illustrates the definitive end of an unremarkable life: "And when the pitcher / is emptied of milk, it is not refilled, but washed and put away on a shelf" (FC 11). The first four-word line lies sadly unfulfilled. At the other extreme, the long lines, like the overall length of *Flow Chart,* represent (and will be experienced by many readers as) long life. This is an association of long standing in Ashbery's poetry. The line-measured "Sortes Vergilianae," for instance, begins with an unsubordinated, end-stopped word chain, written from the vantage point of a full life: "You have been living now for a long time and there is nothing you do not know." (DDS 74). More recently, "Unreleased Movie," a long-lined poem which along with "Dreams of Adulthood" (AG 6) may be seen as a blueprint for *Flow Chart,* unreels a psychoanalytic transcript of the traumatized speaker's schizophrenic development: "Let's start in the middle, as usual. Ever since I burnt my mouth / I talk two ways, first as reluctant explainer, then as someone offstage / In a dream, hushing those who might wake you from this dream, / Imperfectly got up as a lutanist." (AG 27; "talking out of both sides of his mouth"). For Ashbery as for Whitman, autobiographical discourse seems implicit in the lengthened line.

But the dominant measure of *Flow Chart,* for both the writer and the reader, is not the line but the sentence. Whereas the line sets the outside limit Ashbery periodically comes up against, the sentence, the reproduced oral utterance, is the rhythmic measure and medium he works within. He apparently began *Flow Chart* with an even more sentence-measured form in mind, breaking his first four stanzas, in the manner of Wordsworth's *Pre-*

*lude,* at the end of a sentence rather than a line. And he dispensed throughout with another visible cue of verse: *Flow Chart* is his first long poem since "Europe" to decapitalize the left margin (a procedure also adopted in his recent long title sequence, "And the Stars Were Shining") While it will be clear that Ashbery (as the right margins neared) attended to line endings and (as the carriage returned) to beginnings, the measures of his included middles are for the most part sentential.

The sentences of *Flow Chart,* though widely varied, differ significantly from the versified periods of Ashbery's earlier poems. They are orally and loosely structured rather than periodic, and dilated or diluted rather than condensed: "One wants, not to like, but to live in, the structure of things, and this is / the first great mistake, from which all the others, down to the tiniest / speck, bead of snot on a child's nose, proceed in brisk military fashion, encouraging / to some on a chilly afternoon in March" (FC 54; the sentence was written on March 4). We might expect the sentence to end at "mistake" or "proceed," and "proceed" to follow immediately after "others." Instead, Ashbery amplifies the sentence with Audenesque misrepresentative details, illustrating "others" with a sinful "speck" and extending the life line or column allegorically with a pun on a military "March." Modernist, new critical condensation has been displaced by rhetorical augmentation. While there are many short sentences in *Flow Chart,* of one or a few words, they seldom result from lyric concentration: "You see I wasn't going to be a good boy. / They just came. Took me." (FC 53). The third period punctuates an incomplete sentence but a complete utterance, dependent on the previous sentence for its elided subject. Unlike the linguistic fragments of *The Tennis Court Oath,* the discursive fragments of *Flow Chart* are perfectly incomplete.

As readers soon learn, *Flow Chart* is not an autobiography in any ordinary sense of the word. Its verse form already undercuts or qualifies its status as an autobiography. Forgetting that *Flow Chart* is a poem would be as naive as forgetting that *Remembrance of Things Past* is a novel, and more difficult. Moreover, as befits the misrepresentative poet, who expressed, after the publication of *Self-Portrait in a Convex Mirror,* little interest in self-portrayal—"My own autobiography has never interested me very much. Whenever I try to think about it, I seem to draw a complete blank"[5]—*Flow Chart* tells no chronological, personal story, buttressed by specifics of time, place, and event. A survey of proper names in *Flow Chart* reveals the misrepresentative contours of the poem. The personal names are popular and generic ("Babs," "Alf or Al," "Miss McGregor"), fictional and mythical ("Leda," "Santa," "God"), artistic and obscure ("Alvin and the chipmunks," "Kjerulf"), (in)famous ("Hitler," "Mary Stuart"), and algebraically variable ("A and B," "the names of heroes of boys' adventure novels"). Titles are both literary ("Queen Mab," "Lady-of-Shalott style") and popular ("'Why Girls Leave Home,' 'The Trial of Mary Dugan'" [1920s novels Ashbery hasn't read], *The Radiator Girls at Strapontin Lodge*" [invented; "strapontins" are retractable Paris metro seats]). Place names are, as usual, all over the map: "Mt. McKinley," "Siberia," "Shadowlawn," "Nuremberg in 1658." A fictional address helps introduce an equally fictional personage: "this is 901½ McKinstry / Place, and you are Judson L. Whittaker" (FC 61). What these names have in common is that they have little or nothing in particular to do with their autobiographer, whose life they are enlisted to chart. While the syllables of "Ashbery" may be scattered over the text, "John" appears twice, once in a noncommunication ("I called John but he couldn't come to the phone," FC 23) and once in a childhood attic record: "It was a kind of lumber / room, full of boxes filled with papers ('John's report cards') and branches / of artificial holly from Christmases past" (FC 114). These "report cards" are themselves flow charts, but the curator's voice, perhaps the mother's, knows him by his first name, not by the professional name under which his versified report card will be filed.

In his nonliterary autobiographical prose, by contrast, Ashbery is quite specific. In "A Reminiscence," written in the mid-1970s on Frank O'Hara, Ashbery begins with their beginning: "I first met Frank at a cocktail party at the Mandrake Book Shop in Cambridge in the spring of 1949."[6] In a reminiscent essay accompanying an exhibition of Jane Freilicher's work he employs a dramatic narrative: "After a considerable length of time the door was opened by a pretty and somewhat preoccupied dark-haired girl, who showed me to Kenneth's [Koch's] quarters on the second floor" (RS 239–40). His interviews offer personal descriptions: "My mother had been a biology teacher, and was rather shy and sort of a wallflower—pretty but a very retiring and timid woman. My father, on the other hand, was a sort of extrovert, interested in athletics, the outdoor life. . . ."[7] In a travel piece for *House & Garden* (in the anonymous third person), Ashbery waxes poetic over what he calls "one of the most beautiful train trips in America": "It isn't just the unpredictable river itself, now unexpectedly narrow, now suddenly opening out into broad wind-washed expanses like the Tappen Zee, elsewhere divided by islands or peninsulas which seem to have a private life of their own. . . . There is something harder to define: a sense of high adventure as the train detaches itself from the city and plunges due north into a land where place names like Rhinecliff, Tivoli, Wolf Hill Road, and—my favorite—Doodletown Road (nor must we forget Ichabod Crane Central

School) do nothing to discourage that sense."[8] While anyone may follow this commuter railway sentence, nobody can take the personal autobiographical line in *Flow Chart* since the ties were never laid.

And yet the poem does enter its own version of what Philippe Lejeune has termed the "autobiographical pact," a sometimes tacit and indirect agreement between writer and reader that the author (named on the title page), the narrator, and the protagonist are the same "person." While this "pact," as Lejeune later realized, simplifies issues of selfhood, authorship, audience, and form, it nevertheless describes the audience's expectations and perhaps the writer's obligations.[9] To learn about genre today, we would do well to consider how books are marketed. Autobiographies, for instance, are not grouped separately, and are usually shelved in the category where the author has made his or her "name"; Rousseau's *Confessions* is found in Philosophy, Wordsworth's *Prelude,* like Ashbery's *Flow Chart,* is located under Poetry, and Katharine Hepburn's *Me* is in Film. Differently than novels or poetry books, autobiographies point beyond themselves. To verify the autobiographical pact, for instance, Lejeune must consider the title page and the dust cover, which are aimed at potential buyers. Here we find the autobiographer's name and title, often including key words such as "autobiography," "memoir," or "life," and prefatory advertising statements, where the pact may be explicitly or implicitly affirmed. When, for instance, we read the words "What Did I Do? The Unauthorized Autobiography Larry Rivers with Arnold Weinstein," crayoned over a collage of a painting and early and later photographs, we expect an interview-oriented, witty, racy, first-person autobiography by the painter Larry Rivers (co-written with Weinstein) about his life and work—which is what we find.[10] It is equally illuminating, if not as reassuring, to look at the dust jacket of the clothbound edition of *Flow Chart,* where there appears a brief description of the poem (dropped from the paperback), drafted by Ashbery and revised anonymously at Knopf.[11] More lyrically complex and densely allusive than much of the poem it describes, the jacket copy will not meet literal "truth-in-packaging" standards. But this "authorized" (if not exactly "authored") description of *Flow Chart* is nonetheless an intriguing and valuable document. It begins (after a blurb from Harold Bloom attesting to Ashbery's canonical status) with a definition: "Webster's defines a 'flow chart' as 'a schematic diagram . . . showing the progress of materials through the various stages of a manufacturing process.' In this astounding book-length poem, John Ashbery deploys as the 'schematic diagram' for his latest creation nothing less than the entire poem itself. Vividly, and with superb art, he charts the internal ebb and flow of a life perceived—and perhaps even lived—through the somehow sacred act of self-reflection" (Ashbery's ellipsis). Unlike *Flow*

*Chart,* this third-person "poetic" description uses the author's full name while avoiding the word "autobiography" (used twice in the poem). Nevertheless, the definition and metaphorical elaboration of the title lead us to read "flow chart" as a synonym or metaphor for "autobiography," and consequently invite us to read the poem, in some way, autobiographically.

"Flow chart"—a technical, nonliterary term with which the "ordinary readers" Ashbery is always seeking may not be familiar (most reviewers provided a definition)—is one of Ashbery's most suggestive titles. A flow chart is a special kind of map which outlines a temporal, irreversible, repeatable process. As such, it nicely illustrates Ashbery's misrepresentative poetics. *Flow Chart* is a flow chart or schematic outline of an autobiography into which readers may process their own manufactured lives. The term "flow chart" is also familiar from computer programming. With *Flow Chart,* computer technology began to influence Ashbery's poetic production. The second draft of the poem was entered into the computer, and the title poem of his next book, "Hotel Lautréamont"—a pantoum, chosen to take advantage of the computer's copying function—was composed directly on the computer. At the level of composition, "flow" and "ch*art*" suggest different and differing tendencies, like the adverbs "Vividly, and with superb art." A "flow" represents a spontaneous passage of living matter and a "chart" its organized selective record; an autobiography charts a life's flow. We may think of the flow as the Hudson River, which flows past Ashbery's Manhattan apartment and his Hudson Valley home, and the chart as the railway line that follows its course, on which Ashbery commutes between city and town. Like a river, constantly present though unnamed in *Flow Chart,* "flow" promises at once a unity of origin and destination and a fluctuating Heraclitean difference: "we can't step into the same river twice, we are and we are not." The flow may also be interior, what the jacket calls "the internal ebb and flow of a life" and a Jamesian "quicksilver stream of consciousness." A "chart," on the other hand, originally meaning papyrus (as in "charter" or "card"), is both a representative outline and the outlining paper on which it is drawn. Unlike autobiographical charts, flow charts precede their flows; *Flow Chart* thus includes astrological and medical charts. The autobiographical pact is itself a kind of chart, representing all kinds of binding and nonbinding charters. One's autobiography is written in the stars, or in the files, if one only could read them.

But if "flow" and "chart" point in opposite directions, they are, like "content" and "form," practically inextricable. Thus in the jacket description the "chart" is the "entire poem itself," and the living "flow" is already self-reflective. The poem is a fluid chart and a Cartesian flow. Ashbery wrote *Flow Chart* very rapidly over the "course" of half a year, and left it largely unchanged. Though he revised a small number of words and phrases and dropped an occasional stanza, he added no lines or sentences to the poem until the typescript's final page. Thus Ashbery does make an autobiographical pact with himself and implicitly with us. *Flow Chart* is not the mimetic, autobiographical record of his entire life up to the time of writing, but the accurate, faithful transcript of over six months spent reflecting on his own and anybody's life and life story. *Flow Chart* is thus as autobiographical as Book X of St. Augustine's *Confessions;* it tells the story of "what I am now, at this moment, as I set down my confessions."[12] As Ashbery put it in an interview article for *New York,* which appeared soon after the book was published, *Flow Chart* is "a kind of continuum, a diary, even though it's not in the form of a diary. It's the result of what I had to say on certain days over a period of six months, during the course of thinking about my past, the weather outside. I free-associate and come up with all kinds of extra material that doesn't belong—but does."[13] Ashbery's psychoanalytic terminology, an oxymoron like "free verse," suggests the way in which *Flow Chart* tells the truth. By free-associating, the analysand allows an "uncensored" language to flow through his mind and mouth so that the analyst may record (and interpret) it. Obviously, *Flow Chart* is neither simply a diary (meant for his eyes only) nor a psychoanalytic transcript (meant for his analyst) but a poem (meant for us). But like a series of sessions in which Ashbery plays both analysand and uncritical analyst (until the analytical reader takes over), *Flow Chart* is a relatively undoctored flow. The transcript is "somehow sacred" in the sense that it is not to be desecrated.

The scriptural authenticity of *Flow Chart* derives from an expressive poetics. Ashbery's title recalls Wordsworth's early definition of poetry as the "spontaneous overflow of powerful feelings . . . recollected in tranquillity." In fact, the first day's walk and work of Wordsworth's autobiographical *Prelude* relies on the same enunciatory pact as *Flow Chart:* "Thus far, O Friend! did I," Wordsworth attests, looking back at his spirited opening, "Pour out that day my soul in measured strains, / Even in the very words which I have here / Recorded" as "poetic numbers came / Spontaneously" (I, 55–61). Thus Wordsworth makes his pact with an as yet unnamed Coleridge and himself. Unlike *The Prelude, Flow Chart* is not underpinned by a specific mimetic and chronological narrative. But Ashbery's poetics of performance is, like Wordsworth's, based on a "spontaneous" original impulse. As Ashbery put it soon after finishing "Self-Portrait," the postmodern poet tries to keep his work "as close as possible to the original impulse, . . . which somehow makes the poem, like the [action] painting, a kind of history of its own coming into being."[14] Ashbery's last phrase is not a bad description of his performative autobiography. This poetics is not limited to lyric or abstract expression. In the preface to *Division Street: America,* Studs Terkel notes that some feelings in his respondents "run deep . . . but time and the flow of words brought them to the surface."[15] According to the expressive pact, if the act of enunciation is true, the utterance may be trusted.

*Flow Chart* is autobiographical not only in its performance but in its schematic misrepresentations. The poem is composed of two overlapping modes of autobiographical discourse: anybody's talk and somebody's book. Everybody composes autobiographies all the time; not only remembering but narrating, interpreting, confessing, excusing, and justifying, to a co-worker, a (prospective) lover, a stranger, or to oneself, seem to be basic activities of contemporary American life—activities informed by the popularity of published oral histories, such as Terkel's, and the proliferation of sociological TV talk shows, such as *Oprah Winfrey,* where "ordinary people" rather than "stars" are the talking subjects. These prerecorded "live" autobiographies, self-delusions and excuses included, are compelling and even valuable to the degree that they are representative. As Ashbery puts it in *Flow Chart,* "Pick a channel, explore, document it— / please take *all* the evidence into account in your report, when you write it: / you'll find your story isn't so different from any honest man's, nor less / bizarre and compelling" (FC 43). Autobiography is stranger, and more representative, than fiction precisely when it is totally ordinary. People not already known by name may publish their autobiographies if they have witnessed some historical event or cultural movement (the "memoir"), or if they have an especially inspirational or scandalous story to tell, or if they are artful—a well-written memoir or autobiography may make a writer's name. But authors of autobiographies have often already made their names. A household name, as is well known, divides the public from the private I. As Katharine Hepburn puts it in *Me,* "Who am I? Well, I'm me—I'm what is called the power behind the throne. I am your—your character." In *Me* Hepburn both directs and plays her character.[16] Ashbery is a particular kind of somebody known as an "author"—in this sense a writer who has written and published, whose name is recognized, and who speaks in the first person to his or her implied plural audience about his or her work or profession—and one conspicuous type of autobiographical discourse in *Flow Chart* is delivered by an authorial persona. This kind of discourse, although necessarily fictional, is nevertheless not readily available to new writers without established audiences (Whitman is a notable exception). While Ashbery had occasionally adopted this discourse—in "Variations, Calypso and Fugue" (1969), for example, he simulates autobiographical verse ("I voyaged to Paris at the age of ten / And met many prominent literary men," DDS 25), and in "Introduction" (1982), written after he had achieved wide recognition, he lampoons the poetics of privileged experience ("To be a writer and write things / You must have experiences you can write about. / Just living won't do," W 34)—nothing in his earlier poetry matches the sustained authorial discourse of *Flow Chart*.

In his all-purpose autobiography Ashbery conflates authorial with misrepresentative autobiographical discourse and ranges widely among pronouns. Many autobiographical passages in *Flow Chart* aren't in the first person and several autobiographical descriptions involve no pronouns at all: "On this site / exactly ten years ago stood an oblong wooden toll booth" (FC 45). The deictic "this" brings the discussion around to the posthumous telecommunication of the poem. Ashbery occasionally adopts the third person singular, which distances the autobiographer from his subject, the budding writer. Sometimes it is novelistic, "A decade later he stumbled or became confused" (FC 26), and sometimes it views the subject with a distorting public eye: "I thought he was only farting around" (FC 15); "Interestingly, he hadn't done all the things he said he had" (FC 46). But if the author of *Flow Chart* had done everything his poem says, he would have left no room for his readers.

For anybody's autobiography, Ashbery foregoes the singular first person for the inclusive plural. The opening pages, with their religious atmosphere, feature a congregational "we": "And the horoscopes flung back / all we had meant to keep there: *our* meaning, for us, yet / how different the sense when another speaks it!" (FC 4; "horoscopes" was "charts" in typescript). As the encrypted pun "an author" implies, "we" represents us readers. But how representative is the experience of these readers? "In every work of genius," Emerson wrote, "we recognize our own rejected thoughts: they come back to us with a certain alienated majesty" (259; "flung back").[17] This experience of alienating recognition is particularly significant for future writers, since it validates their unpublished thoughts. Proust's rendition appears more expectedly in the slightly ironic first person: "if I happened to find in one of his [Bergotte's] books something which had already occurred to my own mind, my heart would swell as though some deity had, in his infinite bounty, restored it to me, had pronounced it to be beautiful and right" (I, 103). The reader who most identifies with Emerson's "we" is "another" author-to-be, but readers of *Flow Chart* will often have the strange sensation of having heard, and used, its words before.

*Flow Chart* will sometimes turn aside to address "you," whom the jacket terms "an unnamed 'significant other.'" One early passage turns the conversation toward him, varying the autobiographical cliché "Enough about me, what about you": "More of him another time but now you" the voice croons, "oh my / friend that knew me before I knew you, and when you came to me / knew it was forever, *here* there would be no break" (FC 7).

Ashbery's name for this intimate reader, "oh my / friend," recalls Wordsworth's Coleridge, but "you" never becomes a poet. As with Stein's *Autobiography of Alice B. Toklas,* the differences between biography and autobiography, like those between self and other, are blurred when one's partner is the joint subject. This particular "you" is one to whom Ashbery may speak most freely and securely about matters concerning them both, and who provides evidence of his life away from his books. When "success came," the friend's friend recalls, "we were off drinking in some restaurant, / too absorbed, too eternally, expectantly happy to be there or care" (FC 8). Readers don't need to know the name of the restaurant to recognize these extra-literary affairs.

Elsewhere, Ashbery makes a specular "you" representative, recalling for us how "an old guy comes up to you and tells you, reading your mind, what a magnificent / job you've done, chipping away at the noble experiment, and then, abruptly, / you change your plans, backtrack" until "you suddenly / see yourself as others see you, and it's not such a pretty sight either" (FC 124). The present tense of oral narration gives this historical "you" a general significance, and certainly people will recognize in anybody's autobiography the chapter entitled "Recognition." Yet the details of this story, signaled by the echo of *Some Trees,* which begins "We see us as we truly behave," also recall Ashbery's own story: his selection by Auden for the Yale Younger Poets' Series and subsequent turn away from that successful style to the fragments of *The Tennis Court Oath:* "And when we have succeeded, not know what to do with it / except break it into shards that get more ravishing as you keep pounding them. See, / I am now responsible though I didn't make it" (FC 124). The first person singular ends by taking charge of the story while denying responsibility for his collaged fragments.

The first persons in *Flow Chart* seem unlimited. An early instance is made representative through citational italics: *"Did I say that? Can this be me?"* (FC 10). One uses the first question in an argument to deny responsibility for one's own words, the second to query one's identity in an old photograph. Both questions illustrate the Emersonian "alienated majesty" of everyday words and images. Roland Barthes, in a captioned commentary to a pair of photographs, also protests (with his philosophical other countering): *"'But I never looked like that!'—How do you know? What is the 'you' you might or might not look like?"*[18] Sometimes "I" speaks for its bewildering poem, a terminal like New York's Grand Central: "I see I am as ever / a terminus of sorts, that is, lots of people arrive in me and switch directions but no one / moves on any farther" (FC 127). And at times the first person faces his readers from his book: "Yet I see you are uncertain where to locate me: / here I am. And I've done more thinking about you than you perhaps realize, / yes, a sight more than you've done about *me*. Which reminds me: / when are we going to get together? I mean really—not just for a / drink and a smoke, but *really*" (FC 27)—a hilariously contemporary rendition of Whitman's amorous proposals in "Song of Myself," "Missing me one place search another, / I stop somewhere waiting for you" (247), and "Crossing Brooklyn Ferry," "And you that shall cross from shore to shore years hence are more to me, and more in my meditations, than you might suppose" (308). In one straight line, the authorial persona responds to an interviewer's question about his sex life: "Girls, I don't know, there were a lot of them but no special one" (FC 92). In another, he directs a novelistic stream of consciousness, sounding (with its homotextual pun on "bent") less like Joyce than O'Hara: "I can see my reflection just fine in this bent / piece of aluminum. My hair, today, is beautifully combed. I am on a roll, I guess, and two / medicine men are coming to tea, and their letters of recommendation have already been mailed" (FC 45). This parodied authorial persona, preening in his convex mirror, is a narcissistic public figure courted by scholars and poets (not merely his "friend" or "reader") whom he may enhance through his own institutional standing. Early in *Flow Chart,* authorial popularity is accepted with surreal humility: "the world's colored paths all lead / to my mouth, and I drop, humbled, eating from the red-clay floor" (FC 6). This strange, erotically charged passage, typed at the end of the day and at the "floor" of the page, is structured on the anonymous proverb that Emerson made famous: "If a man can write a better book, preach a better sermon, or make a better mousetrap than his neighbor, though he builds his house in the woods the world will make a beaten path to his door." In Ashbery's misrepresentation, "mouse" resonates in the persona's "mouth" and "door" in "floor." And "I" now occupies the inventor's position. Briefly unrepresentative, the author reduces himself to an impoverished unworthiness.

The authorial persona and his audience are introduced at the outset of *Flow Chart:*

> Still in the published city but not yet
> overtaken by a new form of despair, I ask
> the diagram: is it the foretaste of pain
> it might easily be? Or an emptiness
> so sudden it leaves the girders
> whanging in the absence of wind,
> the sky milk-blue and astringent?
> (FC 3)

Like his forecast readers, the author writing these lines knows he has a long poem ahead of him but doesn't know whether it will be worth the effort. He therefore consults his schematic "diagram" for *Flow Chart*—what in "Self-Portrait" he called "The diagram still sketched on the wind, / Chosen, meant for me" (SP 82)—as if it were an astrological chart or a muse. Yet the sudden maternal absence includes God's overarching Plan among the charts to be questioned. Like "A Wave," *Flow Chart* begins in the waking, questioning phase of the aftermath, shading into the waiting, foreboding phase of the prelude, marked by "Still." The metaphysical pun is familiar from Eliot's *Four Quartets:* "Only by the form, the pattern, / Can words or music reach / The stillness, as a Chinese jar still / Moves perpetually in its stillness" (121). Ashbery's visible form or chart for the design above the flow is the "girders / of space," as he first called them, which, whether he knew it then or not, came to signify the bridge, the structure with which *Flow Chart* closes. At the beginning of what is now part III, the narrator observes, "A bridge erects itself into the sky, all trumpets and twisted steel" (FC 84), and forecasts its noiseless downfall, as in a long-shot film of a dynamited bridge: "And when these immense structures go down, no one hears: / a puff of smoke is emitted, a flash, and then it's gone, leaving behind a feeling that something happened there once, / like wind tearing at the current, but no memory and no crying either: it's just / another unit of space reduced to its components. An empty salute" (FC 85). Like an official recognition before one passes, the past is raised and then dropped.

Readers are indirectly introduced into *Flow Chart* with the wonderful misrepresentation, "I ask." The question subordinates the first line, which sounds at first like a diary entry, and initiates an uncertain new discursive form, neither quite the narrative past "I asked" nor exactly the dramatic, apostrophic present "I ask you" ("is this, I ask you, a mute entreaty. . . ?" FC 13). The present tense is best read as a speech act, "I hereby ask," with us as public witnesses of its performance, recalling Whitman's "I celebrate myself, and sing myself" (188). But Ashbery's performative, less confident and more confidential, is an appeal for singing directions.

In this regard too *Flow Chart* resembles *The Prelude,* its most prominent book-length forerunner.[19] Wordsworth questions the "gentle breeze," not strong enough to be directive, about his own future and poetic direction: "Or shall a twig or any floating thing / Upon the river point me out my course?" (I, 31–32). "From yon city's walls set free" (I, 7), and freed as well from financial cares, Wordsworth speaks from the open country, unmarked by civilization and poetry, asking for no more from the future than liberty: "Enough that I am free, for months to come / May dedicate myself to chosen tasks" (I, 33–34). Ashbery's place of work has long been "in the published city," where he is still "in the public eye" (the crypt phrase), New York, whose famed initials surface in "not yet" and whose name nearly appears in "new form." But his freedom to dedicate himself to his chosen poetic task is, like Wordsworth's, conditioned upon his financial situation. Nervous about the possibility of losing his job at *Newsweek,* under new editorship in 1985, he was temporarily freed from financial foreboding by a MacArthur Foundation grant. Financially liberated for the first time in his life, Ashbery recalled, "I spent five years recovering from a lifetime of drudgery."[20]

The hastily added "but not yet" has a darker, implicitly autobiographical resonance. One representative ending for the phrase would be "finished." Autobiographies are necessarily unfinished since their subjects are "*To be continued*" (FC 6). Beginning an autobiography, not to mention finishing one, is an unnerving act, tantamount to writing one's last will and testament. Hence autobiographies typically resist closure. Ronald Reagan's autobiography, which appeared a year before *Flow Chart,* concludes with an airborne farewell party aboard Air Force One, returning Ron and Nancy to private life: "There were warm handshakes, tearful embraces, and lots of picture-taking. Finally, champagne was poured and glasses were raised. 'Mission accomplished, Mr. President,' someone called out, 'mission accomplished.' Not yet, I thought to myself, not yet."[21] Roland Barthes's experimental autobiography ends similarly, in a handwritten "afterword" (one synonym for autobiography) entitled "And afterward?" ("Et après?"): "—What to write now? Can you still write anything?—One writes with one's desire, and I am not at the end of desiring."[22] In Ashbery's case, the proleptic "not yet" also signifies "not yet begun." There is a discursive parallel (again, not a literary source) in the proem to Whitman's *Calamus,* "In Paths Untrodden": "Clear to me now standards not yet publish'd, clear to me that my soul, / That the soul of the man I speak for rejoices in comrades" (268). Whitman uses "publish'd," made public, to indicate publicly exhibited as opposed to concealed signs of love. As Wordsworth has "escaped" from the city, Whitman in his own uncharted territory has "Escaped from the life that exhibits itself, / From all the standards hitherto publish'd" (268). But Ashbery's new publication will "not yet" publicize his life.

While "not yet" ending or beginning, autobiographies are preoccupied with origins and destinations. Autobiographies combine two narratives, the journeys of life and of memory. As Eliot put it at the end of "Little Gidding," the destination of the autobiographical way "Will be to arrive where we started / And know the place for the first time" (145). An autobiography is a homecoming or a family reunion, with the uninvited knowledge of death: "a truly grand homecoming: lifers off the sauce, raccoons that dodge, cheese / and pastry for everybody, canons praised, until the knife came / and sat on the chopping block" (FC 92). These journeys proceed in opposite directions, away from (or with) each other's destination: "and the farther one proceeded from one's destination / the closer it seemed and in fact was" (FC 116). The subject of autobiography appears at birth (his family name preceding him) in the maternal home; then, after "choosing" (being determined by) various distinguishing paths along life's way, he reaches his proper destination, the proper name's "immortal" significance: "our destiny: our fate and death / as one" (FC 158). The autobiographer goes in reverse. Starting from her destined name on the book cover, she seeks her beginnings, and determines those forks along the way where the subject might have got off the destined course. Both journeys, of course, may be less discovered than invented, though their constructed rightness often seems like a destined discovery: "Later the sources / became clear, as in a picture" (FC 210). Unlike biography, autobiography stresses the autobiographer's journey of revelatory invention, and often subordinates the lived chronology to the narrative of remembering. As Lyn Hejinian argues near the beginning of *My Life,* a historically accurate autobiography would omit the autobiographer: "What follows a strict chronology has no memory."[23] The autobiographical enterprise is essentially fictional; the subject is its author's character. The autobiographer constructs the bridge the subject crosses, and builds the house where he is born. The autobiographical plot is the revelation of and substitute for destiny.

The author who placed the circular line "Destiny guides the water-pilot, and it is destiny" (ST 9) on the first page of his first book has developed a postmodern suspicion of recoverable origins: "What we are to each other," for instance, has "no discernible root, no raison d'être, or else flowing / backward into an origin like the primordial soup it's so easy to pin / anything on, like a carnation to one's lapel" (FC 10; "label"). To pin something on someone means to accuse him or her of a crime. The postmodern poet neither confesses nor denies the sexual orientation of his journey: "but how / can I deny my true origin and nature even if it's going to get me into a lot of / trouble later?" (FC 29). But is one's way chosen or determined and does it matter? Like Augustine, Milton, and the Ashbery of *Three Poems,* the author of *Flow Chart* raises the question of predetermination: "But if one's destiny is enclosed in one's brain, or brain pan, how about free will / and predestination, to say nothing of self-determination?" (FC 129). This latest "upstart rephrasing" of the question opposes freedom not to God's but to the government's will as an individual's right to privacy or a people's right to democracy. As we shall see at the end of this chapter, the philosophical question has political and ethical dimensions.

In Ashbery's argument destiny, while it limits freedom, even the freedom to reach one's destination, creates desire. At the end of his writing session on June 29, Ashbery stops his refrain "We have seen" just short of home: "We have seen the house of the leader, / a little farther off. And the numbered apples on his trees" (FC 198; "father"). This viewed destination recalls Eden and the Father's apple orchards. Ashbery begins his next day's work with a concise negative thesis: "It can never be anything but symbolic" (FC 198). He then considers two symbolic and unreachable destinations: home and the reader. After a "scientific" model of ideal communication, and an Ammons-like argument for a centralized, interconnected, "internetted" universe, "the best model anyone has thought up / so far" (FC 199), Ashbery doubles his autobiographical speaker back toward home: "Still, / the doubling impulse that draws me toward it like some insane sexual attraction can / not be realized here" (FC 200). Really, not symbolically, going home again would collapse the distance and difference between cause and effect, origin and destination, and writer and reader: "For that to take shape one would have to be able to conceive a linear / space independent of laws in which blunted gestures toward communication could advance or recede / without actually moving from the spot to which they are rooted; in other words destiny could / happen all the time, vanish or repeat itself ad infinitum, and no one would be affected, one's / real interests being points that define us, the line, which is dimensionless and without desire" (FC 200). This vision of an alternate universe seems both confusing (what is the syntax of the last line?) and confused (points, not lines, are "dimensionless"). But the general line of argument is contained in the crypt word for "desire": "end." For God, there is no distance or difference between a gesture and its realization, cause and effect, beginning and end. But this heavenly "world without end," as the "Gloria Patri" in *The Book of Common Prayer* terms it, leaves no room for "desire." Human desire would be "a hunger for nothing, desire desiring itself, / play organized according to theology with a cut-off date" (FC 200), an empty birthday present. In *Flow Chart,* Ashbery plays instead according to the rules of teleology without reaching an ending, only the end of room.

Ashbery makes destiny a formal matter in the sole exception to his rule of freely channeled verse, a double sestina predetermined by the end-words of Swinburne's "The Complaint of Lisa," which Ashbery transposed directly into his poem. With twelve twelve-line stanzas and a sestet coda, this largest of finite fixed forms is indeed "hitherto unsuspected" (FC 185; "unprecedented"). The sestina is an elegant permutation (there are 23 others) interlacing the first three with the last three inverted end-words (positioned 6 1 5 2 4 3 in the second stanza), resulting in six sestets with the end-words in each of six positions, which couple, tail to head, between stanzas. An analogous double sestina, interlacing the first six with the last six end-words (positioned 12 *1* 11 *2* 10 *3* 9 4 8 *5* 7 *6* in the second stanza) has yet to be written. Sidney's "Ye goat-herd gods," commonly listed as a double sestina, merely runs through the sestina permutation twice, appending a single tercet coda to its twelve sestets. In "The Complaint of Lisa" Swinburne employs six rhyming pairs of end-words across twelve dodecazains and a sestet coda—reusing them, however, whenever it was convenient ("day," for instance, appears in the seventh position five times). But the strong-willed poem benefits from breaking the rules.

Ashbery, the postmodern poet of latent destiny, did not consult the Boccaccio tale (*Decameron,* 10.7) on which Swinburne's "Complaint" is based (imagine Joyce or Eliot not investigating the story of Tristan and Isolde).[24] By choosing to know only the transmuted form of Lisa's complaint, he transcribes the double sestina into a twelve-tone serial composition through which undertones of the original story pass unrecognized and changed. Boccaccio's tale illustrates the magnanimity of the nobility. Lisa is an apothecary's daughter who falls in love with King Peter of Aragon, the reigning monarch, after seeing him joust. Languishing unto death, she enlists a (male) singer to compose her complaint and sing it to the king, who (though married) is moved to call himself her "knight" and to arrange a prosperous marriage for her, thereby endearing himself to the populace. In Swinburne's hands, Boccaccio's ballad becomes a deathbed meditation on the survival of love after death: "For in that living world without a sun / Thy vision will lay hold upon me dead, / And meet and mock me, and mar my peace in death."[25] The deathbed lament resonates darkly in Ashbery's plague-era complaint: "when many were dead / who were thought to be living" (FC 187). But Ashbery struggles against the end marked out by Boccaccio's plot and Swinburne's end-words; while all of Swinburne's stanzas are end-stopped, eight of Ashbery's are enjambed. If it cannot be eluded, destiny may be overrun.

The somber sestina is in some ways falsely advertised by its hilarious introductory address, which begins with a Terkel-style worker complaining to his own "Lisa": "A girl named Christine asked me why I have so much trouble at the office. / It's just that I don't enjoy taking orders from my inferiors" (FC 184). This writer with a "superiority complex" has a sexually active fantasy life—"Sleeping while the navigator / is poised, adrift, and sucking each other's dicks"—reminiscent of the voyage section of "The Skaters." But private fantasies vanish into thin air: "you need an audience / for them to reach the third dimension" of a "volume." The need for an audience brings out the authorial persona, who pitches his upcoming sestina: "The expression will be just right, for it will be adjusted / to the demands of the form" (FC 185). It will be thoroughly postmodern, with only "a few beautiful archaisms" such as "'complaint'" (FC 185), which in the event, as we might expect, appears only cryptically in "those to whom thou goest never grumble" (FC 190). With its end-words jockeying for position, the double sestina cyclist promises he will leave his "breathless readers on the sidelines," like those waiting "to see the cross-country bicycle riders come zipping through / in their yellow or silver liveries, and it's all over so fast you're not sure / you even saw it" (FC 185; "writers"). The announcer sees the sestinist warming up in the rhyming ring: "The gate / to the corral is open, and he's in there now" (FC 186; "chorale"). Parading and parodying his "hitherto unsuspected" double sestina as a breathtaking circus trick, Ashbery announces his laps.

Mildly humorous (unlike this prelude or the zany sestina "Farm Implements"), marginally self-reflexive and loosely narrative (unlike "The Painter"), and oblivious of its reading audience, the untitled double sestina recalls the opening pages of *Flow Chart*. The sestina form is itself autobiographically significant; Ashbery's best known sestina, "The Painter" (ST 54; 1948), is also his earliest collected poem. One way of keeping an eye on the thoroughbred writer is to follow a single end-word through its paces. Among Swinburne's matched pairs—breath, death; her, sunflower; way, day; sun, done; dead, bed; me, thee—the most autobiographically important is "me," appropriately in the objective, desired case. In Swinburne's and now in Ashbery's "Complaint," the end-word couples two stanzas. And as elsewhere in Ashbery, "me" includes "thee," the overhearing reader, as Whitmanian addressee: "I pass it to thee / as generations of aspiring lovers and writers before me have done. / Look, this is what was done to me, written on me. Take it from me" (FC 191). What those writing "on Ashbery," penciling their marginalia on his pages, take from him is his sullied page, and, as the saying "Take it from me" suggests, the authorized guarantee of his experience. In the eleventh stanza "me" is his own destination, "It seemed that all had been destined for me / all along" (FC 192), and in the third it is anybody's goal of individuality: "Therefore we all ought to concentrate on being more 'me'" (FC 187). But such self-centered behavior is easily criticized as a socially blind self-indulgence. The traveler is careful to note that in charting his future, "I purposely refrained from consulting *me,* / / the *culte du moi* being a dead thing, a shambles. That's what led to me" (FC 186–87). A French contemporary of Swinburne's, Maurice Barrès, wrote a series of autobiographical and ideological novels collectively entitled *Le culte du moi.* The phrase has become a label for (unhealthy) self-absorption. But in an obituary essay on Frank O'Hara, Ashbery had used the term affirmatively to describe his friend's poetics of liberation: "It is not surprising that critics have found him self-indulgent: his *culte du moi* is overpowering."[26] When he was subsequently attacked by Louis Simpson, Ashbery countered that "All poetry is against war and in favor of life, or else it isn't poetry, and it stops being poetry when it is forced into the mold of a particular program."[27] Like O'Hara's before him, Ashbery's politics begins with "me": "My politics shouldn't matter. It's my finger / that should—it's here I'll take my stand" (FC 155). But that misrepresentative topic covers a great deal of territory.

The life-affirming protest of the double sestina lies with its end-word "breath," which nostalgically recalls and denies its final position: "We used to laugh; with every breath / we'd take, some new funny thing would point a moral and adorn the day" (FC 191). The pentameter line segment ending on "day" (the double sestina, with "sun" and "sunflower" among its end-words, was timed to be written during the summer solstice) varies the famous couplet from Samuel Johnson's autobiographical study, "The Vanity of Human Wishes," concerning the ignominious end of Sweden's Charles XII: "He left the name at which the world grew pale, / To point a moral and adorn a tale."[28] For Ashbery, the happy coincidences of everyday life adorn anybody's tale, famous or anonymous.

The end-words are recollected in the sestet coda (FC 193):

> The story that she told me simmers in me still, though she is dead
> these several months, lying as on a bed. The things we used to do, I to thee,
> thou to me, matter still, but the sun points the way inexorably to death,
> though it be but his, not our way. Funny the way the sun
> can bring you around to her. And as you pause for breath,
> remember it, now that it is done, and seeds flare in the sunflower.

It is clear from the typescript (see figure) that Ashbery began his poem by typing Swinburne's end-words down the page, as a kind of outline or flow chart, and then wrote out to meet them, as if to keep a fated appointment. In the coda, he neglected to include "day" among the end-words and used "sun" twice (by design or by accident—perhaps misreading Swinburne's "To fly all *day* from *sun*'s birth to sun's *death*"). Ashbery modified his destiny by punctuating the end-words as he reached them, sometimes underscoring them or putting them in quotes. Significantly, he punctuated his final end-word first with a period and then with a comma, adding "as" to subordinate the last phrase to the next paragraph's disjointed main clause "and left it that way." As published, the coda ends with a period. Why would Ashbery not have "left it that way," opening his "sunflower" and sestina with a final

as generations of aspiring lovers and writers before me have      done.
Look, this is what was done to me, what was written on me. Take it from    me."
She stood up and began to do a little dance, then as abruptly stopped, noting the sun

had passed its zenith, and was waiting to be relieved by a replacement-    sun .
In all our lives I still continue to try to make headway, and though to     her
what I do never makes much sense, I do it anyway, for       thee .
Scratching around one is sure to uncover bits of the ancient      way;
meanwhile I am reasonably well-fed, clothed and happy and spend nights in a   bed
that seems beautiful to me. We used to laugh, with every      breath
we'd take, some new funny thing would point a moral and adorn the     day
until at last the earth lay baking in the heat, and the      sunflower
had the last laugh. "Be strong, you that are now past your prime! When you are   dead
we'll talk again and see how you understand this thing men call     death
that is in reality but a shadow of what God has       done
to others, to the sun and to       me."

I awoke, yet I dreamed still. It seemed that all had been destined for     me
all along, and as I had travelled in fear, and alone, always the sun    ~~sun~~
travelled with me. At night one sleeps in fear of wetting the      bed
but he makes amends for that by pointing to our eventual      death
as a teacher would point with a wand to the solution of a problem on a blackboard.   His way
is as inscrutable as a fox's. He brings to full bloom the cornflower and the    sunflower,
then lets them slip into oblivion. Why? If I knew the answer, I wouldst tell    thee,
but since thou sufferest much, I'll vouchsafe that the way of the      dead
is as a lightness to our dreaming, a sense of gaiety, of irresponsability. She in   her *longing*
realizes much, and would tell it to us, but the       breath
is gone. Still, there'll come a time and not too far off when all we have    done
returns to charm us: we can go back, taste, repeat it any      day

So, for the moment, although tomorrow is our       day,
the sun shines through the meshes. You can have       me
for anything I am, or want to be, and I'll replace you with me, introduce you to the   sun.
When summer calls, and people wish they only had a      way
the nights are too thick, and days have barely begun to be spoiled, I'll riddle     thee
about what we heard before we came here, how much is already     done .
The moral of the story however is that the ubiquitous      sunflower
knows the secret and cares. At a door on its hinges, so he in his     bed
turns and turns, and in his turning unlocks the rusted padlock of     death
that flies apart and at once I am shriven. Take me in, teach me     her
ways, but above all don't leave me for       dead:
I live, though I draw only a little       breath .

The story that she told    me   simmers in me still, though she is    dead
these several months, lying as on a   bed . The things we used to do, I to
thou to me, matter still, but the    sun points the way inexorably to     thee
though it be but his, not our    way . Funny the way the      death ,
can bring you around to ~~her~~    her   And as you pause for      sun
remember it, now that it is    done, and seeds flare in the     breath
                             sunflower , 6/23

and left it that way, and then it kind of got shelved. It was a missing increment,
but as long as no one realized it was missing, calm prevailed. When they did, it was well
on the way to being a back number of itself. So while people cared, and some even wept,
it was realized that this was a classic, even a generic, case, and soon
they called attention to other aspects of the affair. No one ever explained how a trained
competitor of long standing would just bar itself from the care that way, there being no

Double sestina, *Flow Chart*

comma? In the coda, the writer recalls his maternal subject, "dead / these several months" and addresses his significant other, "thee." And in his ending, his reproductive "seeds" "flare" like their solar generator. The sestina coda has traditionally functioned as an envoy, a message from (mortal) sender to addressee. Thus Swinburne's Lisa, implicitly acknowledging her lyricist (and his precursor in Boccaccio), "addresses" her song to her beloved: "Song, speak for me who am dumb as are the dead." Like his gay precursor, Ashbery leaves not children but poems in his name for readers to come; what they reproduce is up to them.

The closing frame begins with a chilling grammatical fragment, a publication history without an authorial subject: "And left it that way, and then it kind of got shelved". The neutered pronoun dominates this lifeless paragraph: "it was with no love / or self-pity in its heart that it betook itself then down the few stone steps leading / to the crypt" (FC 193–94; "b[et]ook"). No longer "he," the unintentional subject becomes and joins "it," his corpus. But Ashbery backs away from this epitaph to refigure his poem as an enfolding cloud: "A hound-shaped fragment of cloud rises / abruptly to the impressive center of the heavens only to fold itself / behind itself and fade into the distance even as it advances / bearing news of the channel coast. That is the archetypal kind of development / we're interested in here at the window girls move past continually" (FC 194; cf. Francis Thompson's title, "The Hound of Heaven"). The elliptical syntax recollects Lisa and recapulates the sestina's opening line: "We're interested in the language, that you call breath" (FC 186). It is as though the fragment were about to dissipate into "mere fragments" without letting us witness the ending, since "to find out what that is, / we should be forced to relinquish this vantage point, so / deeply fought for, hardly won" (FC 194). In "No Way of Knowing," the nearest forerunner to this passage, the skeptical speaker complains that the "sheeted fragments" of the writer's "body" of work are "difficult to read correctly since there is / No common vantage point, no point of view / Like the 'I' in a novel" (SP 56). But in the densely encrypted last words of part V of *Flow Chart,* the autobiographer, who has "fought hard" for his "deeply felt" misrepresentative central position, struggles to hold it, though conceding the struggler may remain "hardly known."

In the narrative of return, the autobiographer's destination is a repository of images known as home, whose embodiment and ultimate source is the mother.[29] Mothers figure more prominently in autobiographies than fathers, whose paternal name (male) autobiographers may be trying to make their own (significantly, Hejinian's *My Life* begins with an early memory of her father). St. Augustine's mother figures prominently in his conversion narrative. Like Ashbery, Proust and (recently) Derrida began autobiographical works soon after the deaths of their mothers. Barthes places himself in his mother's arms in a photograph at the beginning of his autobiography, and Russell Baker ends *Growing Up* with himself and his sister visiting their mother in a nursing home: "'Russell,' I said. 'Russell and Mimi.' She glared at me the way I had so often seen her glare at a dolt. 'Never heard of them,' she said, and fell asleep"[30]—restoring her famous author son to a healthy, representative anonymity. Helen Lawrence Ashbery, whose maiden name is the autobiographer's middle name, goes unnamed in Ashbery's poem. But a maternal voice and disturbing image occasionally visit the poem: "Eleanor's here too. You remember Eleanor. So, nice and easy, / until it becomes something like grub, or a slug, something shapeless and horrible / you can talk back to" (FC 181). To "return home, to / our roots" (FC 22), as Ashbery has argued, is an impossible and unwanted goal. But it too makes occasional appearances, sometimes in a distorting nostalgic mist: "mightn't we return / to the old cabin, just for a glimpse of the driveway?" (FC 61). Home is a portable interior; memory itself, secure or not, is the storehouse to be inventoried and explored. The site may be visited, but all that remains is a haunted frame: "Inside the place reeked of mildew and decay though it looked pretty tidy / considering no one had set foot there for twenty years. A newspaper, still dangling / precariously from the rim of the mail slot, hadn't aged. There was a coffeepot, still warm, / on the stove" (FC 112). Time passes still here, decaying but "still" warm.

Mother and home are linked in the narrative, associative flow of an early sequence of stanzas. One small stanza begins with the mother's passing on: "So my old mother became a niche in time" (FC 30). Like the authors of the proverb "a stitch in time saves nine" and the idiom "in the nick of time," the mother here finds her anonymous niche. Her passing is followed by a eulogizing toast: "let's hear it for those who never won anything, whose time came and went / . . . , and they were never cheated on and never / lied, without telling anyone the truth" (FC 30). Her funeral is glancingly narrated. Like mourners, "bananas stand around stiffly" and the absent "standard bearers" stand in for pall bearers. The rising star from Pultneyville may escape the same anonymous fate by leaving home: "Pottsville is too small for a man of your caliber. Full many a flower / is born to blush unseen, and waste its fragrance on the arctic air / outside the Shady Octopus saloon, and then some" (FC 30). Gray's "Elegy," misquoted here, laments the unlettered and uncommemorated poor but ends with Gray's own epitaph. Whoever else they mourn, poets (like the rest of us) have their own names in mind.

After Pottsville is abandoned, the contents of home are auctioned off: "If all is going to be reorganized, the charming irregularities of the days / ahead may as well go too" (FC 31). As Ashbery knows, "auction" is etymologically related to "author": "The inventory of the silent auction / doesn't promise much: one chewed cactus, an air mattress, / a verbatim report. Sandals. The massive transcriptions with which / he took unforgivable liberties" (FC 6–7; "Scandals"). An autobiography is a "reorganized" "inventory" of a life, with which sexual and factual "liberties" have been taken. The auctioneer wonders who will assume his office after he's gone: "Who's going to take care of the association headquarters / and, likelier still, revert with us to the narrow-gauge railroad track that steals / through the yellow viburnum and buried cinders as though to point the finger of guilt / at the very beginning, the origin that is still a baby" (FC 31)? The return trip down these humble girders leads to the author's name fragmented in the "buried cinders." And as the passage makes clear, being named also means being charged. The autobiographical journey to the buried evidence is akin to returning to the scene of the crime. The following stanza lists the uninventoried items: "stiletto heels / and rubber miniskirts," "carloads of whatever," and "juleps / on porches" (FC 32). But the inventory soon changes into a "choice / of purgations": "electrocution for the theft / of a needle; simple tears for aggravated manslaughter" and so on. The nightmarish list sends the author off to check his holdings: "I started to awake, then thought better of it, then rushed to the phone to call / my broker, but it was too late," and "the bank closed its doors and the market suspended operations" (FC 32). Northrop Frye famously described literary valuation as a stock market in which the "reputations of poets boom and crash in an imaginary stock exchange."[31] Whether "Ashbery" is bought or sold, the name is at risk.

The dream or memory bank of images leads in the next paragraph to immortal infamy: "they managed to save Hitler's brain before it destroyed the world / with *zuppa inglese*" (FC 32). The 1963 thriller movie, *They Saved Hitler's Brain,* survives here as a flimsy monument and a ghastly idea of immortality. The autobiographer imagines the unearthing of his own corrupt origins: "Only long after your death / will the life you so busily led be imputed to the cornerstone of rot that was / the secret, driving force in it" (FC 32–33; "root"). The homotextual "rot," "something everyone at the time found to be OK," may be inherently "flawed" but, the accused adds, "it was flaws that produced the dazzling quicksilver sheen that attracted / so many to it for so long." The effect of autobiographical causation, if any, will be demonstrated in the marketplace: "Do you think there's some connection between this and that which happened before? / Perhaps not. Perhaps there is none, but the Patagonians will like it, all 499, 500 of 'em." The figures will authenticate the work. In the next stanza, "the subject of these / negotiations" is introduced but never appears: "To this day no one knows the shape or heft of the thing" (FC 34). The next tercet stanza brings on the unremembered parents: "So, 'marrying little with less,' *meliora probant, deteriora / sequuntur,* they footdrag in oblivion" (FC 34; "sanction the better way, follow the worse").[32] And the last in this series presents the obligatory paternal namesake: "My biological father thought enough of it to see that I was posited" (FC 34). The speaker then yields the first person to the father, whose oral history imputes their separation to a misrepresentative cause: "It was all because I told him he should change his shirt. He got mad / and went out and I didn't see him again for thirty years," long before which all was forgiven: "I / reminded him of the shirt thing and he just laughed" (FC 34; "change his ways"). Only in autobiography can opposite ends meet. All that returns is "that feeling / of emptiness" (FC 35) with which *Flow Chart* began, but it is an empty chart that must be filled.

Between their interchangeable origins and destinations, autobiographies narrate a journey of parting ways, each one an intermediate ending and new beginning. The word "way," an end-word in the double sestina and the last word in *Flow Chart,* is a key word in Ashbery's "career / (if it can be called that—'progress' is a better word, implying a development / but not necessarily a resolution at the end)" (FC 85). Choosing one's own way, somehow different from all the others, is like defining one's proper name. The most popular and concise narrative of autobiographical selection is Frost's "The Road Not Taken": "Two roads diverged in a wood, and I— / I took the one less traveled by, / And that has made all the difference" (131). As the subject chooses his direction, the autobiographer decides which of his innumerable winding paths were crossroads. Frost knows well that parting ways are constructed "ages hence" (131): "Ends and beginnings—there are no such things. / There are only middles" (145). Nevertheless, the individuating fork is one of autobiography's necessary fictions.

The fork in the road is a doubling mirror, reflecting what one was in what one might have been. Eliot's autobiographical sequence, *Four Quartets,* begins at Frostian crossroads: "What might have been and what has been / Point to one end, which is always present. / Footfalls echo in the memory / Down the passage which we did not take," which nevertheless leads "Into our first world" (117–118). Autobiography represents the illusory but seductive chance of starting over; its alternate route is the way of foreknowledge, gained after the fact: "the wind serves only to remind one of other possible / beginnings and an end, if one were likely to pass this way again" (FC 28). Frost is similarly tempted: "Yet knowing how way leads on to way, / I doubted if I should ever come back" (131). But simply reflecting on one's (mis)fortune puts the black cat back in one's way. "I" wouldn't be here, Ashbery writes, "if something not of my own construing, / something I rejected, hadn't interposed a feline quickness and fur just before the fatal /

gradient, and I stepped back and stared, and in that moment saw myself on a visit to myself, / with quite a few me's on a road receding sharply into a distance" (FC 144–45). The forking paths toward alternate lives in these jolly corners, rose gardens, and yellow woods are endless, but the nominal end justifies the tortuous means. After uncovering "John's report cards" among the "branches," the autobiographer lapses into regrets: "And I thought of all my lost days and how much more I could have done with them, / if I had known what I was doing. But does one ever? Perhaps it's best / this way," he concludes, but still imagines another "me" in the glass fork: "But what if there were other, / adjacent worlds, at one's very elbow, and one had had the sense to ignore one's / simulacrum and actually wade into the enveloping mirror, the shroud / of a caress, and so end up imbued with common sense but on a slightly higher level." But the narcissistic traveler stops short: "*but who would read that!*" (FC 114–15). The mirror's maternal "shroud / of a caress" terrifyingly ages the "shield of a greeting" (SP 82) of "Self-Portrait in a Convex Mirror," the "crossover" poem that made Ashbery's name with a signature polished style from which he subsequently turned away. A flawless career of flawless poems would have been unrepresentative. We all make mistakes.

The river forkings in *Flow Chart* are the covert, alternate routes of sexual and textual experimentation: "no one was wiser for knowing the way we had grown, / almost unconsciously, into a cube of grace that was to be / a permanent shelter" (FC 5; "gone"). Ashbery's permanent residence in the state of grace will be his homemade cubic volumes. But there is more than one experimental way: "How would it be if I said it this way, / or would so-and-so's way be better, easy on the adjectives?" (FC 81). Charles Olson ("so-and-so's") inveighed against modifiers in his famous manifesto "Projective Verse," included in *The New American Poetry,* where the New York School was first collected: "And when the line has, is, a deadness, is it not a heart which has gone lazy, is it not, suddenly, slow things, similes, say, adjectives, or such, that we are bored by?"[33] Unqualified or not, poetry is a tangled way: "just the idea that they want to sing leads to a fork in the path" (FC 97).

Writers have both advanced and sunk their causes by figuring their ways as experimental. Like the scientist (the self-serving likeness goes), the experimental poet advances knowledge and serves society through his or her tireless pursuit of truth. As Ashbery's autobiographer hilariously warns, experimental poetry isn't easy going: "But I'll tell you one thing: it wasn't easy. Mornings, I'd be at the library / while it was still dark outside, straining my eyes over useless newsprint" (FC 94). On the other hand, the experimentalist tampers with the laws of nature, like a B-movie mad scientist. In one passage, an island hermit, like those in the films *The Island of Lost Souls* and

*King of the Zombies,* is politely interrogated by his "guests": "Miss Winslow was just telling us about your island / and its cormorants and the—er— other problems. How do the natives feel / about what you're doing?" (FC 45). The homophobic dimensions of this interrogation are clear enough; experimentation is best kept quiet. Autobiographers experiment with themselves, objectively observing and transcribing their own behavior. Thus the experimentalist shares his observations of the author of the detective collage "Europe": "Once I even saw him reading a detective novel upside down. / I was too upset to include *that* in my report, as you may imagine" (FC 169). In this contagious environment, the autobiographer is no more stable than his subject on the other side of the one-way mirror.

The divergence of the homosexual from the heterosexual way of life is often represented in *Flow Chart* as an original fork or crossroads, as at the beginning of part II: "But how trivial the music. All this. Yet it is where part of the gender first starts to / emerge and become a blur" (FC 41). In this parting, paved by an etymological pun on "trivial" (*trivium* : crossroads), homosexual disorientation blurs gender difference. These trivial departures are sometimes personified. In one scene, an anonymous "gentleman" leaves his name: "after the gentleman had gone, leaving me his card, I stood in the hall / for a long time" (FC 126), facing "explosions of choices before one is ready / to choose" (FC 127). In another, the choice seems out of his hands: "It was decided to proceed another way / while I was out of the room" (FC 51). Another messenger, one "Herr Schmidt,"[34] magically transforms his "toad and pupil" into a prince: "I was won over instantly, from that day / never thought forward, looked backward, rain / or shine, from that anointed moment / I first kissed a king in you" (FC 52).

Frost's road not taken is also "the one less traveled by," which "has made all the difference" (131) not only between himself and what he might have been, but between himself and his readers. The popularity of the poem shows that most readers believe they too have taken the "less traveled" way toward their own names. Nostalgia for the road not taken may hide an anxiety about avoiding the more trampled way: "But at times such as / these late ones, a moaning in copper beeches is heard, of regret, / not for what happened, or even for what could conceivably have happened, but / for what never happened and which therefore exists, as dark / and transparent as a dream" (FC 12), a ghostly nightmarish dreamboat, "all dressed up with no place to go, that an axe / menaces off and on, throughout eternity" (FC 12). Those who have made their name are thought to have "no regrets," but they have them anyway. Ashbery, who remembers learning "the word *regret,* for instance, when he was in kindergarten,"[35] suffers the nightmare of anonymity. The winding passage continues into italics: "yes, '*And I in greater depths than he,'* I suppose, / yet it doesn't help deliver one back either to the after all sane and helpful blank square / one is always setting out from" (FC 13; "drawing a blank," "back to square one"). This unattributed (mis)-quotation, along with another in the same passage "(*'when such a destin'd wretch / as I, wash'd headlong from on board'*)" (FC 12), is rescued from "The Castaway" by William Cowper (from whom Ashbery earlier borrowed the allegorical title "The Task," DDS 13), a nightmarish true story of a man washed overboard and slowly drowning within view of his storm-tossed shipmates. But what sinks the relatively unknown Cowper in "deeper gulfs than he" is the unspoken fear of his own obliteration. "No poet wept him; but the page / Of narrative sincere, / That tells his name, his worth, his age, / Is wet with Anson's tear. / And tears by bards or heroes shed / Alike immortalize the dead."[36] Significantly, Cowper records the name of the ship's recording captain but not of the castaway, since he does not himself "dream, / Descanting on his fate, / To give the melancholy theme / A more enduring date." Death by water is a fate feared by poets because watery graves have no markers. Ashbery's paragraph ends on dry, remarkable land, "desert valleys / where one's feet take one," "broken tracts" resolving into a trail in the last word, "materializes" (FC 13). Those remembered make their own way.

But if "Stellification / Is for the few" (HBD 71), "what about the rest, / star-gazers in their midst, who make up the electorate?" (FC 77). While Ashbery was writing the story of his name, the United States electorate was following the 1988 campaign for the Democratic and Republican presidential nominations. Ashbery incorporates the national campaign as an allegory of selection (voting), nomination (naming), election (salvation), and representation, paralleling his own progress with campaign developments. On the evening of January 26, Vice President (and as yet unannounced presidential candidate) George Bush got into a shouting match with CBS anchor Dan Rather over Bush's contention that he was "out of the loop" on the arms-for-hostages dealings with Iran. The next day, Ashbery reported that "Care was off and running, ... / ... and no one was going to take issue, dispute the power vacuum / that was walking around shaking hands, acting for all the world like a candidate" (FC 21). Two days after the block of primaries known as Super Tuesday, one of Ashbery's electorate admits "I, too, voted for it" (FC 64). On the day of the New York primary, Ashbery began a paragraph with an Orwellian allegory: "Soon all the animals acclaimed the victor" (FC 120). And in the wake of the Democratic National Convention ("When the convention finally assembles," FC 69), which placed Governor Michael Dukakis's name on the ballot, the people speak, "We're going to stay. We've elected to" (FC 211), and a candidate reports: "And he says to me, I'll vote for you" (FC 214). For writers, election means canonization. With face-saving hyperbole, the poet looks forward to his own election, "a promotion / out of the ranks of futility into the narrow furrows of bliss and total sublimity" (FC 15). With the canon opening up and breaking down in the late 1980s, Ashbery's author sallies forth to defend the reading list, prophesying "there'll be such a scare / in the curriculum as only the oldest ones will want to get out, the others / impeded or impeached by the books they have a right to read / in this our own time" (FC 47). Being a canonical poet isn't what it used to be, but books, even by contemporaries, deserve to keep circulating.

Ashbery first takes up the question of election in a long passage (FC 36–40) written in mid-February during the New Hampshire primary, the first of the 1988 campaign. Selecting the massive electorate as his subject, Ashbery typed from one edge of the page to the other, virtually eliminating the margins. He begins with a brief dismissive conclusion: "It's the lunatic frequency this time" (FC 36). In his *Autobiography,* Franklin Delano Roosevelt remarked that there was a "lunatic fringe in all reform movements." The "fringe" in Ashbery's uninfringed verse paragraph is not "marginalized" experimental poets but their underrepresented, unelected electorate. Locating them "on the outskirts of some / city or suburb," the canvasser demands: "were *they* included in the survey, and, / if so, who are they? Shooting-gallery ducks waiting to be flattened, probably" (FC 36), afloat but not for long. History as most know it relates the stories of the few. Only for "a few can life resonate with / anything like serious implications. So many were hung out to dry, or, more accurately, to rot. / And these marginalia—what other word is there for them?—are the substance of the text, / by not being allowed to fit in" (FC 37). Like crypt words and phrases drawn from everyday discourse, which retain what Ashbery called "a marginal existence,"[37] these people are history's missing subjects. But elections, the broadcast speaker continues, give the unselected a voice and choice: "Everybody must vote. Everybody's vote must be accepted into the / tilting radio tower" (FC 38). Ashbery also understands voting as the personal matter of selecting a partner. In American terms, the heterosexual marital contract consecrates a more perfect union: "And if the parents of both parties pronounce it / a suitable match, why there you are, another union has been consecrated" (FC 37). For others in the memorable margins there is a different denouement: "that we should untie / gently, like a knotted shoelace" (FC 37; "unite"). The card-carrying representative also gets to be counted: "I can just stand up like everybody else and lay my cards on the table: look, / it says so, it's all here, written in this book" (FC 39). Even unmarried poets have a full hand to show.

Being elected a representative poet carries certain responsibilities. At one point, the author bills himself as the public's flow chart, "its infrastructure / and the only one who will bring it to the edge of a cross-section of the people's imaginings" (FC 137). And in a bumbling stump speech, the candidate thinks out loud about his worthiness for public office: "But I didn't know but what if I / didn't hang around a little longer the thrust / would be vouchsafed to *me* this time and of course as its public / repository I would use it to further the interests of all men and women, / not just some" (FC 165; "the public trust"). The poet's autobiography must also be representative. Benjamin Franklin recalled that, having "emerg'd from the Poverty & Obscurity in which I was born & bred, to a State of Affluence & some Degree of Reputation in the World," he decided that his "conducing Means" of achievement were so successful that "Posterity may like to know, as they may find some of them suitable to their own Situations, & therefore fit to be imitated."[38] Laboring on "something like / my autobiography," Ashbery's autobiographer has similar expectations: "maybe if I reduced it / all sufficiently, somebody would find it worth his while, i.e., exemplary" (FC 135). Thus, at the end of the "lunatic fringe" passage, the author pitches his Whitmanian catalogue as good for what ails anybody: "you can browse through this catalog and, who knows, perhaps come up with a solution that will apply / to your complicated case" (FC 40).

But election also has its perks, as the author confesses: "I am relieved of manifold responsibilities, / am allowed to delegate authority" (FC 39). Not the least of these is financial, as well as historical, security: "I mean we're talking / debts canceled, a link to the future, daybreak" (FC 204). For the weary elect, the future is finally taken care of. The postmodern poet, an information-age oxymoron, may then be indicted for failing in his representative duty, for belonging to an "elite minority" (FC 24). At one point Ashbery, who has represented as much plain talk and script in his poetry as any American poet, stages an unwinnable confrontation between an elitist author and a populist critic. The "weary sap" charges, wildly, that Ashbery's trademark "personal-pronoun lapses may indeed have contributed to augmenting the hardship / silently resented among the working classes" (FC 150). The "cozy" esthete reflects in character that "you / couldn't really begin with a proletarian, accustomed as they are to backbreaking / toil and so (you'd like to think) don't feel it that much. Besides they never read Henry James' novels. / Just for the sake of argument let's say I've never done an honest day's work / in my life" (FC 150). The parenthetical lowering of the ironic mask reveals how uncomfortable Ashbery is even parodying this pampered part. The middle-class poet, who has doubtless endured as many honest days' work as the average leftist critic and whose reading (and viewing) is hardly confined to the classics, quickly adopts another role, that of the toiling experimenter who spends his life improving the human condition through a "graduated series of studies" (FC 150). As with Franklin and his tempest-tossed kites, the practical results of experimental verse are difficult to measure, but "We can see the effects now in devices we use in everyday life without thinking of them, / in traces of the slightly altered climate and the disproportionately enormous effect it has had / on geography, roads and productivity" (FC 151). The drama lurches haphazardly from the doomsday revolutionary poet calling all hands of the ship of state on deck (*"Arise, / ye unchained millions"* FC 152) to the shipwrecked proletarian masses ("'And the fault of whose buns / ran it aground in Norwalk. . . ?'") to the esthete ("I find appealing the quality of danger / inherent in thunder," FC 153). Working through this page's and day's (May 23) labor, readers come to appreciate his effort: "I'm good at working under pressure, / *as indeed we all must be*" (FC 153). If Ashbery's poetry has not benefited the people he has so assiduously studied and incorporated, it is hard work nevertheless.

The argument between the author and his readers sometimes turns bitter. At one point, the author decides to rise above his envious reviewers: "It was time to climb up, to pull the ladder up, having construed pith in the latest verbal / assaults from onlookers who wished to be crowned too" (FC 156). At another, those who accuse him of merely "playing mind-games" come in for a blistering counterattack: "My reply, then as always, was that ignorance / of the law, far from being no excuse, is the law, and we'll see who rakes in / the chips come Judgment Day" (FC 123). Why such hostility from the usually congenial nominee toward his relatively anonymous judges? And what kind of "excuse" or "law" is "ignorance of the law"? These and related questions are not easily answered, but they are crucial to understanding the social contract of *Flow Chart*. Rereading his poem, Ashbery was surprised at how many times the phrase "ignorance of the law" appeared.[39] He had adopted the phrase in 1981 for the title of an unpublished poem, which includes the reflection that "Usually reliable sources have / Stained the anonymity of the law and still it empties / Everywhere" ("strained the credulity"). These unnamed "reliable sources," so often quoted by journalists, misrepresent the anonymous speaker, seeking to keep his secret stain from leaking. The seventeenth-century historian and politician John Selden argued that "Ignorance of the law excuses no man; not that all men know the law, but because 'tis an excuse every man will plead, and no man can tell how to refute him." Ashbery will nevertheless base his defense of poesy in *Flow Chart* on this inadmissible excuse, which he praises elsewhere as "that noblest, since most artless, of defenses" (FC 69).

Ashbery's defense protects the legitimacy of his poem: "the legal filigrane that penetrates every / page of the mouldering sheaf down to the last one" (FC 20; *le filigrane:* "watermark"). *Flow Chart* is drenched in legal discourse, employing nearly every stage of the judicial flow chart: surveillance, apprehension, indictment, defense, judgment, punishment, and (sometimes) escape. From the poem's testimony, readers can piece together any number of scenarios: "policemen stopped cars and it was getting to be spring" (FC 29); "with decreased services and an increased / number of spot-checks" (FC 9–10); "singles them out / by pointing so that some symbol of their shame never / goes away" (FC 24); "the governor's trick to trip you up, / make you confess what he already knew" (FC 161); "expecting nothing in return but the verdict" (FC 136); "wheel on the guillotine" (FC 25); "You see, we have escaped. But one always goes back voluntarily / before the next roll-call" (FC 82)—so that the trial of identification may begin again.

Chief among the laws broken in *Flow Chart* is the autobiographical pact. Implicit in Lejeune's equation of the autobiographer with his or her subject is the assumption that one promises to tell the whole truth of one's life and to judge (and "sentence") it accordingly. The autobiographer assumes innumerable critical roles: scientific observer, (psycho)analyst, lover, confidant, priest, God, parent, judge, policeman, spy, detective, consumer, and so on. If the author tells the truth, the verdict will always be "inexcusable. (That word.)" (FC 136). The autobiographer did it. Autobiography closes the vicious life cycle of cause and effect; the autobiographer is responsible for the life which is responsible for him or her. One confesses oneself the author of, and claims responsibility for, one's "life," both the past and its record. The author need not be caught to feel guilty. The flow chart of destiny, for instance, is itself a life sentence. As Walter Benjamin put it, "Law condemns, not to punishment but to guilt. Fate is the guilty context of the living."[40] In contemporary American poetry, confession has taken the form of freely versed (uncoerced and unsolicited) confessional poetry, a form that grew rapidly in the 1960s along with the popular psychoanalytic activities of encounter groups and sensitivity sessions. The notorious illegibility of Ashbery's poetry, resulting partly from his refusal to confess his personal life, is only heightened in this purportedly autobiographical poem.

Once one's life is published—exhibited and confessed—and enters the public domain, the reader, amateur or professional ("I will show you fear in a handful of specialists," FC 201; cf. Eliot's "handful of dust"), assumes the investigative position: "We're not authentic crime-busters, / only pals of the accused from school. When he wrote those / seemingly contradictory rules, he never dreamed we'd end up / following them, and him, into the oblivion he decreed for us" (FC 138–39). Paul de Man remarked on the transfer of judicial responsibilities to the reader: "the reader becomes the judge, the policing power in charge of verifying the *authenticity* of the signature and the consistency of the signer's behavior."[41] If the investigation is rewarding, readers may add the author's name to their "most wanted" list, which sounds in his ears too much like a schoolroom or prison "roll-call / that went on so many centuries to the accompaniment of battle-axes and cats-o'-nine-tails" (FC 68). Lists in *Flow Chart,* as in *The Vermont Notebook,* are inevitably associated with lists of charges and suspects. For the poet of the McCarthy era, being named is a desired but terrifying prospect: "Marry, save that alibi / for your autobiography. Serve me fresh drink, I'll drink on't. / They were getting closer to your name in the list; now, / nothing will remove that stain" (FC 181).

Autobiographical confessions are often indignant. Autobiographers have long resisted the idea that anyone except their Author should hear their confession. Augustine confesses only to God and to sympathetic "brothers . . . who rejoice for me in their hearts when they find good in me, and grieve for me when they find sin."[42] Rousseau challenges his eavesdropping readers: "Let them groan at my depravities and blush for my misdeeds. But let each one of them reveal his heart at the foot of Thy throne with equal sincerity, and may any man who dares, say 'I was a better man than he.'"[43] An indifference toward readers is implicit in the expressive poetics of *Flow Chart.* Among the poetic "materials" passing through the poem, the jacket lists "overheard dialogues with self, soul, and an unnamed 'significant other.'" Ashbery's curious qualifier (only oneself can "overhear" one's interior dialogue) recalls John Stuart Mill's value-laden distinction: "Eloquence is *heard,* poetry is *overheard.* Eloquence supposes an audience; the peculiarity of poetry appears to us to lie in the poet's utter unconsciousness of a listener. Poetry is feeling confessing itself to itself, in moments of solitude."[44] Poetry, that is, makes no confession to its readers. The expressive fiction of pretending to ignore one's readers is meant of course to persuade them that what they overhear is more "authentic" than "staged." But all the same, the audience is excluded from the cast.

Ashbery's disregard for the reader is underscored by the jacket's echo of Yeats's title, "A Dialogue of Self and Soul" (1928). After publishing his own autobiography, Yeats mounts a stern apology which dismisses critical distortion: "That defiling and disfigured shape / The mirror of malicious eyes / Casts upon his eyes until at last / He thinks that shape must be his shape?"

The autobiographer overrules their judgments: "I am content to follow to its source / Every event in action or in thought; / Measure the lot; forgive myself the lot!" Like Coleridge's ancient mariner, Yeats's shriven Self is "blest" with a final song of innocence: "We must laugh and we must sing, / We are blest by everything, / Everything we look upon is blest" (236). As only God can bless Augustine, and only Coleridge excuse Wordsworth, only Yeats can acquit himself.

Ashbery defends his poetry in *Flow Chart* against the law or publishing contract of autobiographical confession with "a sense of gaiety, of irresponsibility" (FC 192). Though he doubtless claims his royalties, awards, and honoraria, the author nevertheless denies responsibility for his life in his life. In an ethical sense, the autobiographer accepts and lives according to his "shameful" origin: "and always in a locker downstairs was this pocket / mirror with *the* thumbprint on it, a source of shame, but how / can I deny my true origin and nature even if it's going to get me into a lot of / trouble later?" (FC 29). The incriminating evidence of one's homosexual thumb and its homotextual print cannot simply be ignored. But if we take this question not only in a rhetorical and ethical but in a real and practical sense, the answer is that Ashbery denies his "thumbprint" by writing irresponsibly, without regard for the judgments of his over-reading public. He accepts his thumbprint but refuses to judge it as a "source of shame." Ashbery practices his irresponsibility through a willful ignorance of the autobiographical pact, writing *Flow Chart* by ignoring not only his audience but the facts and evidence, the paper trail, of his own writing life. Dismissing his internal industrial investigator, he writes without inspecting or scientifically testing his own word flow for purity or consistency. The autobiographer might have distilled his past for us, "drop by drop, from what I remembered, having / kept close watch over what went in," but "this would in some way have falsified / everything" (FC 135). Accordingly, Ashbery commits and pleads ignorance of the law. He barely monitors his output, catching his writing self in the expressive act.

Ignorance of the law follows the *via negativa* of latent happiness laid down in "The System." Ashbery's readers are asked to go and do likewise, reading with the flow: "Our words are interpreted left / and right as they become speech, and so it is possible at the end that a judgment may be / formed, and yet the intrepid / listener does no such thing, hypnotized by his reflection" (FC 87). The reader's narcissistic identification approximates the writer's trance, and either side of the image may excuse the other's subjected behavior. Instead of a series of confessions, *Flow Chart* is constructed irresponsibly out of excuses: "In time all excuses merge in an arch / whose keystone overlooks heaven" (FC 59). It springs from a Hawthornian original excuse: "An excuse / like a birthmark arose and flowered" (FC 166). We all make excuses, especially writers, and Ashbery often represents excuses in representative terms: "I was depressed when I wrote that. Don't read it. Still, if you must, take / note of certain exemptions in the / fourth paragraph where I was high" (FC 60). Ashbery can always claim that he "wasn't himself," as though claiming a tax exemption on his income flow chart.

Ashbery files his claim amid a tangle of legal and political questions of responsibility debated in the later 1980s. Probably the central legal principle behind *Flow Chart* is "the right of privacy." At one point, his interior interlocutor imagines being confronted by a would-be inner circle of readers familiar with his personal life: "Friends—you know the feeling— / are going to insist on knowing whose story it is. Better tell them. But wait— / you can't relate something and then connect it to some specific person. No job / says you ought to" (FC 46; "you know the kind," "Nobody"). No contracted "job" or pact will persuade this consciousness to violate another's or even his own privacy or anonymity with specifics. The right to privacy is a matter of public policy, and in *Flow Chart* it is associated with a publicized private affair: the Iran-Contra scandal. As it happens, Ashbery first learned the term "flow chart" from watching the Iran-Contra hearings on television, where the organizational, informational, and material flow of the National Security Council, a "secret government" within the U.S. government, was charted on enlarged placards for a national audience. The secret exchange of arms for hidden hostages, Oliver North's shredding of paper and deletion of computer documents, his unapologetic testimony, and the "plausible deniability" of President Reagan's responsibility are all misrepresented in *Flow Chart*. At one point, for instance, autobiographical records are deleted: "And it turned out that the inquiry was silenced, / deliberately erased from the file" (FC 42). Deniable evidence may be erased or hidden: "It was, in effect, highly unusual, / though no more so than circumstantial evidence or grass being covered up" (FC 100).

The right of privacy and the Iran-Contra affair both pass though the first paragraph of 1988, which concludes harshly: "Don't / excuse yourself, nothing could" (FC 16). In the middle of the passage, in one of his first appearances, the author figure reneges on what his audience considers his duty: "Mine's isn't the option to / show you how to escape or comfort you unduly" (FC 15; "duty"). Ashbery's ungrammatical rendition of some such disclaimer as "It isn't up to me" distortedly echoes Tennyson's popular newspaper poem, "The Charge of the Light Brigade": "Their's not to make reply, / Their's not to reason why, / Their's but to do and die."[45] Though Ashbery elsewhere extols the escapist and optimistic merits of his poetry, the speaker here refuses to do his duty by God and his reader. The news-print background opens the paragraph:

Latest reports show that the government
still controls everything but that the location of the blond captive
has been pinpointed thanks to urgent needling from the backwoods
    constituency
and the population in general is alive and well. But can we dwell
on any of it? Our privacy ends where the clouds' begins, just here, just at
this bit of anonymity on the seashore. And we have the right
to be confirmed
(FC 14)

The daily news stories behind this poetry also need to be "pinpointed." During the mid-1980s, while hostages were being held secretly in Lebanon, the United States goverment maintained to their insistent "backwoods" friends and relatives that no counterterrorist raids were possible because the hostages couldn't be precisely located. In the relational system of *Flow Chart,* the "blond hostage" misrepresents both an erotically identified insig-nificant other and the autobiographical subject, whose story still eludes the autobiographer and his reading public. The difference between captors and liberators is blurred. The subject's freedom within captivity raises the politi-cized legal question of his right to privacy. Oliver Wendell Holmes Jr. once illustrated the utilitarian limits of this right in everyday American: "My right to swing my arms ends where your nose begins." In the first draft of Ash-bery's misquotation, "Our privacy" was "Our right to privacy." Though "the right" is now delayed to the end of the next line, the embattled prin-ciple remains. In postmodern American law, it has been invoked most often to protect the sexual privacy of consenting adults. In *Griswold vs. Connecti-cut* (1965) it was called upon to prevent the banning of contraceptives, in *Roe vs. Wade* (1973) to protect the right to abortion. But in *Bowers vs. Hard-wick* (July 1986) the Supreme Court ruled 5 to 4 that the Constitution does not protect sexual relations between consenting homosexual adults. The Georgia sodomy case, as it is called, signaled a new activist incursion into individual rights by the Supreme Court, threatened further in 1987 by the possible confirmation of another conservative judge (cf. "the right / to be confirmed"; Robert Bork had recently been denied confirmation). In Reagan's 1980s, consenting homosexuals became hostages in their own bed-rooms. In *Flow Chart,* the right to privacy of the subject ends with its publi-cation and at its nameless text: "just here, just at / this bit of anonymity on the seashore." It is not factual but textual specifics that the author shares with his anonymous readers.

The subject in *Flow Chart* is held under surveillance, first by the autobiographer and next by (generations of) scrutinizing readers. The fugitive makes his own terms of surrender in the last paragraph of part III: "If, indeed, I am findable under the lens / of this disinterested red-haired scientist, and if he is willing to exchange me for / a hostage, why then I will go, no question of it" (FC 99). When the Iran-Contra scandal broke in November 1986, the Reagan administration denied trading arms for hostages, something against governmental policy. But in the privacy of one's thoughts and home, exchanges for open arms secretly transpire. Textual relations between writer and reader are necessarily consensual: "We / have no way of forcing others to cooperate except by vaguely acquiescing / to their most intimate desires and pretending we don't know what it's all about, what / we are doing" (FC 99). The assumed innocence of Ashbery's spontaneous poetics is one of his poem's most seductive features. Within a few lines, however, the relational subject shifts into the surveillant position: "while still enrolled in a course at a local community college I happened / once to overhear a conversation between two boys in the next row of lockers, and it / sounded, well, suspicious. I thought I should tell somebody something, and ran out, / but the office was closed, although it was only a little after four, and a tremendous / black bruise stood up in the sky" (FC 99). The right to swing one's arms ends where another's black "eye with a trembling eyelid" (FC 99) begins. In this terrifically foreshortened narrative, the "suspicious" exchange is violently curtailed. In the late 1980s incidents of "gay bashing" were on the rise; the homotextual poem may place its author at risk.

In this hostile autobiographical system, one constantly denies one's own accusations. The origin of irresponsibility is allegorized at the beginning of part III:

That was the first time you washed your hands,
and how monumental it seems now. Those days the wind blew only from
   one quarter;
one was forced to make snap judgments, though the norms unfolded
   naturally enough,
constructing themselves, and it wasn't until you found yourself inside a
   huge pen
or panopticon that you realized the story had disappeared like water into
   desert sand,
although it still continued.
(FC 84)

This confession of a representative masturbatory experience is no less allegorical than Wordsworth's boat-stealing episode in *The Prelude:* "She was an elfin pinnace; lustily / I dipped my oars into the silent lake" (I, 401–2; "penis"). In "Those days," the autobiographer recalls, experimentation was automatically condemned, as behavioral rules or flow charts of normal behavior grew "naturally enough" as though anonymously "constructing themselves"—no matter, as Ashbery had written in the first draft, "how wrong ~~all wrong~~ / many have since revealed themselves to be." Since there is "O so much God to police everything" (FC 35; "O[nly]"), one must police one's own behavior. The word "panopticon" was coined by Jeremy Bentham for his model circular prison with central-windowed cells in which prisoners wouldn't know when, or whether, they were observed, and would have to monitor their own behavior. Ashbery is familiar with Foucault's discussion of the regimen of self-surveillance in relation to Bentham's panopticon.[46] In the autobiographer's case, the suspect behavior is textual. As we know, the norms require that the guilt-crazed Lady Macbeth reveal the blood on her hands. But instead, like Pontius Pilate, the autobiographer "washes his hands" of "snap judgments," no matter how popularly demanded. The life may be condemned but not by his writing hand.

Perhaps the most detailed map in *Flow Chart* of the unsettled boundaries between the policed precincts and the badlands, the real and the dream worlds, and the right of privacy and the limits of irresponsibility, is found in part V (FC 174–80). The long verbal torrent, inspired or "inspirited" by Thomas Lovell Beddoes, "abrade[s] and swamp[s] its levees" (FC 5), as the frequent runover lines reveal, pausing only for interlinear sentence breaks. The previous paragraph ends with a wishful journey toward a seductive "blond warehouse" ("whorehouse"). But in the real world, "the police are everywhere" and tacitly apprehend: "you apologize profusely, like the ridiculous twit you are. / Where is it written that men must go out in the afternoon without a hat?" (FC 174). The frustration behind this excessive confession to an unwritten misrepresentative law is perhaps evidenced by Ashbery's excision of 22 lines before and 35 lines after the final question, nearly two days' work. These implicit regulations conjure up an equal and opposite dream of a sensuous landscape. Its "curvaceous rocks" lead to a "proposed bifurcating," "enabling all creatures to become something different" (FC 175; "be themselves"). These "mountainscapes" (FC 176) escape responsibility for their shifting surveys: "Waves, like weather currents on the map, / drift and coagulate above us," "absolving the map of all responsibility to present itself, / to be read as a guide" (FC 175). The fluent chart overhead cleanses its surveyor of guilt. We cannot fault the map's maker for leading us astray; *Flow Chart* is only a misguided guide for living.

This mountain hike in the dream world abruptly descends into the "real world" (FC 174) of "the Reagan / administration," which "insists we cannot go to heaven without drinking caustic soda on the floor / of Death Valley as long as others pay their rent and have somewhere to go without thinking" (FC 175–76). Ashbery's acid commentary here contrasts his dream world with the reel world of the chief executive, former host and pitchman of the early TV series *Death Valley Days,* sponsored by Twenty Mule Team Borax (from boric acid), a commercial cleanser which absolved one's soiled laundry. In the death valley days of the Reagan administration, the autobiographical dream and goal of home is compromised by the growing numbers of homeless, who have nowhere to go to escape observation.

But even those able to "pay their rent" cannot purchase their privacy. Another issue related to the right of privacy and freedom of speech, which was debated while Ashbery was writing his covert autobiography, was pornography. In January 1988 the U.S. Department of Justice, then headed by Attorney General Edwin Meese (who would be forced to resign in July, as Ashbery finished *Flow Chart*), ruled that pornographic material, in bookstores or homes, could be seized under the interstate racketeering law. It was a "family values" issue the Republicans hoped to exploit in the primaries. The courts, in this instance, did not follow the politicians. A state court overturned the conviction of Douglas Oakes, who had been convicted for taking photos of his teenaged stepdaughter with her consent. In *Flow Chart,* a confession, paraphrasing former U.S. Secretary of State Dean Rusk's plot summary of the Cuban missile crisis, is extorted and disavowed at once: "What would we have said? / That we confronted the monster eyeball to eyeball and blinked first. . .?" But the defense rests on the testimony of two homemakers, each of whom refuses help: "It's all right, I / like doing the housework naked and can see nothing wrong with it, / nor do I feel ashamed of it. I'll be all right when the government goes away"; "Oh, I'll be all right, provided / you shut up and don't read too much into the dog's picture. After all, / the mutt said he wanted it taken, and in the backyard, so how was I to know / there'd be hell to pay for even this seeming indulgence?" (FC 176). Both defendants deny reponsibility for their acts, the second by pleading consensual privacy, the first simply by refusing to be "ashamed." *Ash*bery thus rejects the guilt encrypted in his name.

Another indictment, italicized and indented, is voiced by Beddoes: "*But there were dreams to sell, ill didst thou buy*" (FC 177). One of Ashbery's favorite "unknown" poets, "Thomas L." (FC 178) was the subject of one of his 1989 Norton Lectures, written while he revised *Flow Chart.* The Beddoes poem Ashbery quotes from here and elsewhere in this passage, "Dream-Pedlary," is a remorseful lament over a life badly spent. In these haunted stanzas, Beddoes wonders "If there were dreams to sell, / What would you buy?" and wishes finally to "Raise my loved longlost boy / To lead me to his joy." But the reality is that Beddoes will only get his wish, if at all, when he "Fall[s] like a rose-leaf down" into the afterlife.[47] Ashbery noted that this poem has been cited as "evidence" for Beddoes's homosexuality. In this ghostly movement of *Flow Chart,* he first considers the "author," "with a number of books / to his credit" (FC 177), as a dream-peddler or auctioneer with his autobiographical inventory of present and missing topics: "not the man walking, the woman sitting on the toilet, the tuba-player unscrewing the mouthpiece / of his instrument and blowing into it, not the azaleas blooming in tubs; but the three policemen and the man / scratching his groin" (FC 177). Why couldn't the police have been struck from the list? The autobiographical peddler might have bought and sold other topics, such as the "tall houses," each with "its family," "to whom a truce was offered," or the surrounding "dark forests," "whose emptiness you could have peopled / merely by taking them up, in conversation" (FC 177–78). These missing or underrepresented topics coalesce into ghostly "longlost" subjects—both "strangers" "caterwauling" at night (FC 179) and the poem's maternal subject, "'out of hell's murky haze, heaven's blue hall'" (FC 178; from "Dream-Pedlary"): "so then they *do* rise up, and it can be one hell of a sight, / especially for those unaccustomed to it. I prefer to sit here and 'rest' my eyes" (FC 179; "Helen"). For those accustomed to the romantic tropes of voice, echo, irony, and spirit, "Ashbery's" final sentence, with its dead metaphor for dreaming borrowed from his mother's idiom, may still surprise with a renovated power.

In the severe poetic justice of this narrative, the ghost implies a murderer. The following antically parodic paragraph, located somewhere between a Dickens mystery and one of Beddoes's own ghoulish verse dramas, pounces on its suspect, who demands to confront his accusers: "I find you here too. I have found you out. You seem / convinced the killer is one of us. Why? Did a drowned virgin / tell you that, or Tim the ostler, or the one-eyed hay-baler / with a hook for a hand?" (FC 180). Or was it a self-incriminating autobiographical "letter" (FC 180)? In any case, the suspect turns on his interrogators, demanding they search his volume for evidence, and refusing to confess. "You know not one minnesinger has ever / reneged on a pledge. Until today, that is," he concedes; "I'll wager you / no one leaves the room, and that the tool chest be empty! Go on! Try it! ... / ... That's my last offer. Chain me to the iron bedstead / and electrocute me, so help me, that's all you're going to get out of me" (FC 180–81). Ashbery's treasure map leads to no buried treasure: "Now that the killer is caught / you can return the map to Mr. Isbark" (FC 181; Ashbery misremembered the name Isbrand from Beddoes's *Death's Jest Book*). As confessional evidence, the map itself is worthless.

Ashbery wrote the final paragraph of *Flow Chart* on the anniversary of his birth (the date is on the typescript). Lee Iacocca's autobiography, *Iacocca,* ends with a color photo bearing the caption "Mom goes back to Ellis Island 63 years later." [48] Ashbery's poem, anybody's success story, ends similarly by finding its way back to maternal and national births. Like "The Skaters" and "A Wave," *Flow Chart* winds down into smaller stanzas and shorter lines, until this last, relatively longer paragraph, which sums everything up with an abstracted genealogy: "The multiplication of everything ran on years back, she said, / until two scraps had been assembled" (FC 215). These genetic scraps of information survive the "great conflict" in the posthumous, cryptographic form of an "evergreen / canopy" which "became an anagram of itself": a family tree, a funeral bier, another treasure map ("telling us much / about how gold was hidden"), and a haunted storybook, from which ancestral "spirits . . . came forth, irritated, / from their resting place and pulled the magic latch-string, and the door flew open / and there were the wolf and Red Riding Hood in bed together, except that the wolf / was really Grandma. Whew! What a relief! They don't write them that way anymore" (FC 216). This fluid plot outline relates the (grand)mother's mysterious conception. But the secret volume—book, womb, tomb—needs a cover: "let's put a roof on the thing before it sidles." This anxious close is followed by a Dantesque excuse: "I'm more someone else, taking dictation / from on high, in a purgatory of words, but I think I shall be the same person when I get up / to leave." Ashbery's first person names Fate as the author of his "life" but reaffirms belief in his properly named identity. In his final exculpation, in the spectators' plural, Ashbery imagines his project as a drive-in movie projection:

> Every film is an abidance. We are
> merely agents, so
> that if something wants to improve on us, that's fine, but we are always the
> last
> to find out about it, and live up to that image of ourselves as it gets
> projected on trees and vine-coated walls and vapors in the night sky: a
> distant
> noise of celebration, forever off-limits. By evening the traffic has begun
> again in earnest, color-coded. It's open: the bridge, that way.

Ashbery avoids Dante's famous final "stelle," but stellar births are audible in the Independence Day fireworks, the best popular illustration of Dante's roseate cosmology. Halfway along in *Flow Chart,* at the end of part III, the stellified list is more distinctly visible: "And as we congregate this way, the actual lists of heaven seem roseate / anew" (FC 102). Writing on his birth-day, Ashbery had ended *Flow Chart* happily, with "a distant / noise of cele-bration, I suppose. So we should be glad, and so, ~~truly~~ I think, we are" (FC draft 100). The revised ending, penned onto his computer printout in April 1990, will "improve" on the old "formulas" (FC 216) by routing a color-coded (red rear and white front lights) traffic flow over a bridge. The re-vised, halting sentence excels by performing, rather than encoding, its open ending, as the poet who offers directions becomes himself a chart across the river. Ashbery may be the destined secret agent projected on the drive-in movie screen, but it's our own composite image which stars.

# Appendix

# The Building of "A Wave"

*And the underpainting is starting to show through.*

Soon after finishing "A Wave," Ashbery articulated his poetics of revision: "I like the idea of being as close to the original thought or voice as possible and not to falsify it by editing."[1] When working not with a "thought or voice" but with pages of written text, Ashbery keeps to the original by keeping new writing to a minimum. Rather than changing the fabric of his text by rewriting or interpolating phrases and lines, Ashbery revises from the outside by cutting and restitching—scrapping what doesn't work and leaving the reconnected pieces relatively intact. When this method fails, he starts over with a new original performance. Thus Ashbery can revise heavily and still keep close to an, if not the, original. To show how he produces a long poem, I present the first two drafts of "A Wave" through its first two stanzas.

There are six versions, six sets of revisions, of "A Wave." The first version, "Landscape with Tobias and the Angel" (begun November 28, 1982), was abandoned after two and a half pages. The second, "Long Periods of Silence" (begun January 1983), marks a new beginning, preserving intact from the first version only the line "To pass through pain and not know it." This nineteen-page typescript runs to the end of the poem as we know it but contains a great deal of eventually discarded material, especially in the first two pages. In the third version, "A Wave," Ashbery revised "Long Periods" by cutting and reconnecting stanzas (so that the first four stanzas begin "To pass through pain and not know it," "In the end he was simply caught out," "He was allowed to materialize elsewhere," and "And so the luck of speaking out"), and by making more stanza breaks. This revision contains as much bracketed and canceled as unedited poetry, and is abandoned after six pages. The fourth version of "A Wave" is the second full-length typescript, containing all the published stanzas (as well as two others which Ashbery later cut). It becomes the final original for the last two versions, which contain relatively minor changes.

The fifth typescript creates a textual problem since its changes were for some reason not incorporated into the final text of "A Wave." The text was apparently misplaced, and Ashbery made his last handwritten revisions on a sixth typescript (a copy of the fifth without the changes). I discussed these last versions with Ashbery in the spring of 1989, and asked him to choose between the changes he made in the fifth and sixth typescripts. Ashbery authorized the following changes, which should supersede the versions that appear in the Viking edition of "A Wave" (the published phrase is followed by its replacement): "confounding with" "confounding me in" (W 70); "Still, it is better" "Still, it's better" (W 70); "I moved on" "I worked through" (W 71); "then, gentle, anxious," "then, anxious," (W 71); "briskly back and forth" "briskly here and there," (W 75); "So the voluminous past" "The voluminous past" (W 78); "our fortunes" "our fortune" (W 78); "Actually was, and certain greetings will remain totally forgotten, / As water forgets a dam once it's over it. But at this moment" "Actually was. But at this moment" (W 78); "isn't space enough," "isn't room enough," (W 80); "will be to go away" "will be to leave" (W 81); "And then it's just" "Then it's just" (W 85).

I have marked cancellations like ~~this~~, I have italicized Ashbery's handwritten (and occasionally typed) additions and revisions, and I have enclosed in braces circled words and phrases, apparently considered for revision. I have retained Ashbery's misspellings, since they indicate his performative momentum.

## Landscape with Tobias and the Angel

And already the clouds are becoming less salmon-hued
And it may be useful, too, that as the world grows more
And more sophisticated with each passing year, the desert
Too becomes more stratified: a dumpscape
Of everybody's intentions, good and bad, preserved
By the intense dryness from the mutilating effects of history:

{Here they are}, all the famous sins of omission
Like bone-white cities under the never-vary8ng pallor of the sun,
*with* The mistakes in spelling, the ~~peculiarities~~ *idiosyncracies* of
    handwriting ~~still~~ *suddenly*

Perfect and individual as a snowflake, as though life stood still
For once, while preparing to belt out "None but the Lonely Heart"
Before a small and undistinguished audience. Not, perish the
   thought,
To yield up one iota of its uniqueness, the puzzling oddity
*That quality* We'll never ~~begin to succeed in~~ *begin to* truly
   understanding. Only

To become the mirror for once
As though one were to pass through a peach orchard and read
In the ~~shielded~~ *shaded* gazes of men the truth about oneself,
Plain because unspoken, and in that seeming
Rebuff of sun and disinterested ~~since~~ pure *burst of* {blue} sky,
In blinding whitewashed walls, know at last how one is
\# When circumscribed, and emer~~ged~~ cleansed and unharmed.
To pass through pain and not know it,
Through time conscious only of clockfaces of all sizes
And ~~descriptions~~ *styles* is the important business and the one
~~No one will~~ *Nobody* ever tell*s* you about. You've got to experience it,
And when it's over draw no conclusions about it,
*Or* ~~Else~~ the business is lost, a story
Like many another, that happened on a gray day
And seemed a little less strange than the fiction truth is supposed be:
A clean dump, again, of transparent and discarded though perfectly
   viable concepts
The book of millstones in which one reads the profit
The*at* loss has somehow been, and *then* discards for other fictions,
Shapely or not. ~~That part has been nice too.~~ And once tropical
   doodads         *11/28*
Have been visited on the landscape, what is there left to do?
Leave it, of course, but like a hostess
Giving the dining room a ~~final~~ *last* onceover before the guests arrive,
Since we can o only ~~was~~ well as is expected of us, only
Sometimes a little more, and that embellishes us certainly
When it happens, but each of us is to perform
Only to the ~~l~~generally accepted level of our capabaility*s*;
"No better than e should be," though the pejorative ring there
Is meant too: none of us, it now appears, is going to get off
With a slightly less onerous burden, and when
It all comes together, as it will, congratulate ourselves with the way

The sky has been shaping up while we took little or no notice of
    it.        *11/29*


But why cut off the flow when it's half-stammered anyway *to begin*
    *with?*
Fountain over which magpies drift, {faintly "biblical"} linecut
Meant {only} to remind us that last things shall be first,
That the entomologist ~~p~~places them that way anyway
Lest drift result, the sands, *the deep* channels abrade
The narrow way which was never meant to contain them.
W~~j~~hy notice the mangoes? The tired sawtoothed ~~pine~~ *palm* leaves
Overhanging half the world~~?~~, if it isn't going to matter,
Finally? And the answer


Is always in the folds of a letter,
In spidery handwriting shaken out like thread:
"It was thus for you, and not keeping to the trail,
Or reading it in a novel, or visiting a picture gallery
Where the pictures are ~~kept~~ *sequestered* behind a rail, at a safe
    distance,
Would have brought you sooner rather than later to those
Lachrymose adventures which must involve us all at the end:
Only be still, and bear witness.
Ir is the ~~knoledge~~ *wisdom* that ~~d~~comes from hunger, from gaps in
    reasoning,
From the sand shifting over the stone step that ~~informs~~ *instructs* as it
    bleed~~s~~,
Though house-arrest is not to be embraced, *nay,* nor
    considered."    *12/1*


And when the novel is read, and closed quickly,
The conversation clearly over, though you expected to learn more,
Still it is onl6 whiteness, and leading from that
Up into shade, that offers any promise, a break
In the small, regular flow of knowledge:
How once it seemed to be caving in on itself, a suitably
Deranged blue that dayOr dull plum tufts signifying
In the near distance, only that further interruptions were possible,
Indeed probable, indeed breaking ~~all~~ *up* around you
Already, a sea of spears and ~~frayed~~ *tired* shouting.
It's then that the two ~~small~~ figures in mid-foreground

Assume whatever importance is theirs and shamble
Off toward the middle-di~~x~~stance, the dog already there,
Having already spotted something and forgotten it~~, immediately~~.
And the underpainting is starting to show through.

Even less rhapsodically, when school was out,
You pretended to be someplace and then were, were that place,
A gaggle of comings and goings, wasted gestures
That another's hand could draw together, impose
A kind of unity on, the kind found in geography books,
History and plays. And when that person had conferred
Lightness and a setting, and withdrew,
The kind of life erupted that lives in deep wells,
The silence of someone coming, and the wind
Blew through the fragrant walls and polished them and they were no
    more,
Burnished fragments, secret jokes
From another political climate
And all of this has no meaning today, and could not,
Given the way things happen, laugh at themselves and disappear
Quickly the corner *some corner (?)* of something. It wasn't wise
To repeat it in the clear format of today
Yet nothing has happened, here or elsewhere,
Only the ringing true, the snapping shut of a rhyme
And then ~~blue~~ distance, the most sparkling emptiness imaginable.

He caught an enormous fish:
Actually, as the man who didn't look like an angel would say later,
It almost caught him, materializing
Like a dense puff of smoke a few feet aboce the water,
And then they roasted it, saving the part~~ws~~ that would be used
    later--
The liver to purge the poor devil Ax~~a~~smodeus (so much in love,
So totally ~~unable to~~ incapable of doing anything about it);
The gall to dispel his father's blindness,
The whitish cataracts blown away by the first drops, leaving him
    speechless
In the little enclosed yard, so familiar now again)
And turned in for the night that hissed with secrets,
Sorcery, commands, for so the night had grown to be,
A tissue of dreams erected one upon the other

Like a ladder scanning the sky. And if not much was to be made of it
Now, Tobias was only a little the wiser. What of this journey?
Why always some crude device, like the talents left on deposit
In distant Ecbatana, ~~and~~ or something equally implausible
And suddenly the journey is real, an pllacing one foot
In front of the next has gone on some time now:
What a way to imbibe one's sense of wholeness, of self
But of course that only happens when it'x over,
When you look back and not so much see the looped distance
As inspire it, to be something it never could have been without you.
Father would have appreciated that, he had so much practical sense.
And when

*In the end he was caught out*


*Long Periods of Silence*

To pass through pain and not know ~~o~~it,
*A* ~~C~~ar door slamming in the night,
To emerge on an invisible terrain.

The weather's ~~a "silly old thing"~~ *but*
~~She knows one thing though,~~
~~How to handle time as it's blowns through~~ *up,*
~~Through the enormous rents~~ that let everything through:
The whole year, mountains with their dependencies,
The trouble that was today and is yesterday.
~~How~~
~~About the mounts?~~
~~They are holding.~~
~~Buy I must xsay~~
~~*But*~~ This ~~keeping ajar's an uneven or a terrifying thing.~~
The bird's eye view
~~Was~~ pencilled in lightly:
Graphit3e waves that are scenes of things to come.
~~No t anks.~~
~~The awkwqrdness stinks.~~
[There is *[a]* ~~tremendous~~ chiming and clashing as the old year
   ends.*]?*

~~*The woman*~~ ~~Miss T.~~ ~~thinks it's like a snowball~~
~~Only she can't remember why.~~ A collectedness--
Why "the old year"? It seems newer as
It prepares to passnout. *of sight* ~~On the way~~
~~Bedouins and their children are massed,~~
~~Always out of some~~ *~~our~~* ~~book~~


You can't escape it be-
Cause you're more in it t*h*e more you get outside.
Breathing~~, you think,~~ the pure air*]*
Of cisterns and golf courses,
Rich, melancholy places,
We stand at the juncture of time as it forks
And carries a little of us to either side.
~~Some~~
~~Folks~~
~~Imagine their reflection on the roiled eddies: "Oh~~
~~That was my salad days.~~
~~Oh never mind."~~
~~In a year you'll be too young to care.~~
~~And the year~~
~~Anointsall of us with faint taboos, histrionic~~
~~Maun derings~~ *~~Pronouncements~~* ~~ffrom the stables~~
~~Wher at least it's cleaner but what about~~
~~Poush seats, the surrounding of anew job.~~
~~Junk it. We'll see.~~
And in the outlying rind of rime
The sun actually sparkles
~~There are those who'll take~~ *~~up~~* ~~a new fate~~
~~And dress it up with spangles so it actually looks old~~
~~Or too mature.~~ And then it's down
W~~o~~ith polite syllables again.
Across the square it's fainter but
~~Refreshed,~~ the sort of thing that only steals up on you gradually
If you are grateful
And can tell the difference between one unit and another.
It's thesde that are building.
A flourish.
And another one behind it. / A rainbow
And not something that might jump out at one

And then you know by its having made the familiar sound again
When ~~the~~ pressure is applied to the place.

Then, on New Years Day, the sunlight, pale and attractive,
Ministers once more to the burnt and broken
Ends of living, the discontinued places, and we have the feeling
Of having emerged from somewhere with the brilliantly simple
    solution
To ~~a nagging~~ *an old* question. You wonder once again why
Hazy sunlight isn't recognized ~~more~~, for the discordant,
stronger modes of thought wear away more
When examined closely, and besides the fudged
Edge has a brittle strength of its own, a never-to-be-refuted,
Strident, admirable selfiwhness of its own
Pluswhich it takes things around their own contours,
Wraps {them} around, though you can't see it all, with a final
Posited assurance of their well-being and yours.
Sure, it's only temporary, bu~~r~~*t* what isn't?
~~And~~ meanwhile the dappled
Surface of the river almost shyly
~~Approaches your own gaze~~, asks you out to play
In the most unassyming manner possible, and for a time,
[You think,] things have gone well,
As well as possible under the circumstances,
Under the rain of this specific time and place that sooner
Or later cuts everything down to size, its own,
And the smallness is dissipi~~t~~ated everywhere. But that ~~sotyr~~ *story* is
    its own,
Not in your own flesh, not in your body where you could tell it,
But aimless, seemingly, out over fields and locks of canals,
Places where you have to pay to stand, and others that are fenced off
And not ~~supposed~~ to be *thought of as being* there.

*Begin here?*

In the end he was simply caught out.
After so many long periods of silence
The new rhythm of dropping ashes on the carpet
And coming to the point couldn't help but attract
Some attention, thoug even in the first days this wasn't much,
Something could have been done, but finall~~t~~y
It started to turn into a dialogue
Between the silence and himself. Then, shaking one's head

Violently against tracks in the air soon
Became suspect, but there was still time to escape, and far from
Dragging his feet, he became literally inert,
Rooted to the spot where his conversation took off, and nothing
Could have induced him to leave the arena of these exchanges; it was
     like
That old line about "The boy stood on the burning deck,
Eating peanust by the peck." In the end though
Neighbors had informed on him, and soon the whole town knew,
He was allowed to materialize elsewhere on the main trail
Between two thriving desert cities, beholden
To silence as well as to the breaking of it,
Tilted perpetually forward
Like the figurehead of a ship that blown sand files down
To knife-edge sharpness, thriving on sensory deprivation,
The happies*t* and most inteeligent being in the whole kingdom.
And so the luck of speaking out
A little too late came to be worshiped in various guises:
A mute actor, a future saint intoxicated with the idea of martyrdom,
And our landscape came to be as it is today:
Partially out of focus, some of it too near, the middle distance
A haven of serenity and unreachable, with all kinds of cute
People and plants waking and stretching, calling
Attention to themselves with every artifice of which the human
Genre is capable. And they called it our home. /
And as what is named must soon be elaborated,
The art of how everything is connected up to everything else
Soon comes to stand in for the living objects,
A central mass that subsumes, and living now on a curve
More sheer than the one originally taken into account,
The family is scattered in all directions.

# Notes

## Introduction

1. John Koethe, "An Interview with John Ashbery," *SubStance* 37–38 (1983): 183.

2. A. Poulin, Jr., "John Ashbery," *The Michigan Quarterly Review* 20.3 (1981): 250–51.

3. For a treatment of the synecdochic trope "representative" as "the 'basic' figure of speech," see Kenneth Burke, *The Philosophy of Literary Form,* 3rd ed. (Berkeley: California UP, 1973) 25–33.

4. Walt Whitman, *Complete Poetry and Collected Prose,* ed. Justin Kaplan (New York: Library of America, 1982) 5. All citations of Whitman's poetry and prose are from this edition, cited hereafter in the text.

5. André Bleikasten, "Entretien avec John Ashbery," *La Quinzaine littéraire* 16–28 Feb. 1993: 7 (my translation of Ashbery's French).

6. John Ashbery, "John Ashbery," *A Controversy of Poets: An Anthology of Contemporary American Poetry,* ed. Paris Leary and Robert Kelly (New York: Doubleday, 1965) 523.

7. Wallace Stevens, *The Palm at the End of the Mind: Selected Poems and a Play,* ed. Holly Stevens (New York: Vintage, 1972) 250, 251. All citations of Stevens's poems are from this edition, cited hereafter in the text.

8. Cleanth Brooks, *The Well Wrought Urn: Studies in the Structure of Poetry* (New York: Harcourt, Brace Jovanovich, 1975) 203. For a discussion of Ashbery's undoing of new critical precepts see Vernon Shetley, *After the Death of Poetry: Poet and Audience in Contemporary America* (Durham: Duke UP, 1993) 103–33.

9. Emily Dickinson, *The Complete Poems of Emily Dickinson,* ed. Thomas H. Johnson (Boston: Little, Brown, 1960) 506. All citations of Dickinson's poetry are from this edition, with Johnson's numbers given in the text.

10. John Ashbery, "The Poetic Medium of W. H. Auden," senior thesis, Harvard College, 1949, 10.

11. W. H. Auden, *The English Auden: Poems, Essays, and Dramatic Writings: 1927–1939,* ed. Edward Mendelson (New York: Random House, 1977) 7. All citations of Auden's earlier poetry are from this edition, abbreviated hereafter in the text as EA.

12. W. H. Auden, *Collected Poems,* ed. Edward Mendelson (New York: Random House, 1976) 313. All citations from Auden's later poetry are from this edition, abbreviated hereafter in the text as CP.

13. David Remnick, unpublished draft of interview, 1979, 3. The interview was published in *Nassau Literary Review* (Spring 1980): 54–64. Unless otherwise indicated, all my citations of Ashbery's unpublished material are from John Ashbery manuscripts, AM6, by permission of The Houghton Library, Harvard University.

14. John Ashbery, "Three Novels of Henry Green," Columbia University, 1950, 5, 7–8; the master's thesis was directed by William York Tyndall and devoted a chapter each to *Living, Party Going,* and *Concluding.*

15. John Ashbery, "The Impossible," rev. of Gertrude Stein, *Stanzas in Meditation, Poetry* 90.4 (July 1957): 251.

16. Poulin 245.

17. Conversation, February 1993.

18. For related discussions, see Thomas E. Yingling, "Homosexuality and the Matter of Style," *Hart Crane and the Homosexual Text: New Thresholds, New Anatomies* (Chicago: Chicago UP, 1990) 24–56; Eve Kosofsky Sedgwick, *Epistemology of the Closet* (Berkeley: California UP, 1990) 67–91; D. A. Miller, *Bringing Out Roland Barthes* (Berkeley: California UP, 1992).

19. See John D'Emilio, *Sexual Politics, Sexual Communities: The Making of a Homosexual Minority in the United States, 1940–1970* (Chicago: Chicago UP, 1983) 40–53.

20. Richard Kostelanetz, "How to be a difficult poet," *New York Times Magazine* 23 May 1976: 20.

21. Quoted in Brad Gooch, *City Poet: The Life and Times of Frank O'Hara* (New York: Knopf, 1993) 190.

22. Ashbery remembers seeing Huston's bowdlerized film a year or two after it appeared. Conversation, February 1993.

23. Richard Jackson, "The Imminence of a Revelation (John Ashbery)," *Acts of Mind: Conversations with Contemporary Poets* (University, Ala: Alabama UP, 1983) 70. Crypt words are by no means limited to Ashbery, or to other contemporary or surrealist poets. My discussion will remind some readers of Michael Riffaterre's "hypogram" and "matrix." But this strictly semantic model would rule out sonic and visual, literal cryptography. Cryptography is a more encompassing and prevalent phenomenon. For related discussions of the impact of unwritten words and phrases, see Michael Riffaterre, *Semiotics of Poetry* (Bloomington: Indiana UP, 1978) 1–23; Jean Starobinsky, *Words upon Words: The Anagrams of Ferdinand de Saussure,* trans. Olivia Emmet (New Haven: Yale UP, 1979); John Hollander, *The Figure of Echo: A Mode of Allusion in Milton and After* (Berkeley: California UP, 1981) 141–42; Nicolas Abraham and Maria Torok, *The Wolf Man's Magic Word,* trans. Nicholas Rand (Minneapolis: Minnesota UP, 1986); Garrett Stewart, *Reading Voices: Literature and the Phonotext* (Berkeley: California UP, 1990); Jonathan Culler, ed., *On Puns* (Oxford: Blackwell, 1988).

24. Patrick Kéchichian, "Quelqu'un que vous avez déjà vu," rev. of John Ashbery, *Quelqu'un que vous avez déjà vu* (selected poems), trans. Pierre Martory and Anne Talvez, *Le Monde* 5 Feb. 1993: 23 (my translation).

25. Conversation, Fall 1986.

26. John Ashbery, "On Raymond Roussel," introduction, Raymond Roussel, *How I Wrote Certain of My Books,* trans. Trevor Winkfield and Kenneth Koch (New York: Sun Books, 1975) 53. See Rayner Heppenstall, *Raymond Roussel: A Critical Study* (Berkeley:

California UP, 1967) 41. As Heppenstall notes, Hugo's phrase "*vin de l'*espérance" contains the French pronunciation of "Handel."

27. John Ashbery, "In Darkest Language" (1967), second introduction, Raymond Roussel, *How I Wrote Certain of My Books* 64.

28. Michel Foucault, *Death and the Labyrinth: The World of Raymond Roussel,* trans. Charles Ruas (New York: Doubleday, 1986) 33–34.

29. Marjorie Perloff, *The Poetics of Indeterminacy: Rimbaud to Cage* (1981; Chicago: Northwestern UP, 1983) 254.

30. David Lehman, "A Conversation with John Ashbery," unpublished interview, 17 October 1977: 6.

31. This system resembles the actantial model of narrative developed by Algirdas Greimas, with its sender, helper, subject, object, opponent, and receiver, and Roman Jakobson's model of literary reception, with its addresser, context, message, contact, code, and addressee. See Algirdas Julien Greimas, *Structural Semantics: An Attempt at a Method,* trans. Daniele McDowell, Ronald Schleifer, and Alan Velie (Lincoln: Nebraska UP, 1983); Roman Jakobson, "Linguistics and Poetics," *Language in Literature* (Cambridge: Harvard UP, 1987) 62–94.

32. *The Kalevala: or Poems of the Kaleva District,* trans. Francis Peabody Magoun, Jr. (Cambridge: Harvard UP, 1963). Ashbery read this edition.

33. Quoted in David Lehman, "John Ashbery: The Pleasures of Poetry," *The New York Times Magazine* 16 Dec. 1984: 84.

34. Lehman 84.

35. Lehman 84. See Helen Vendler, *The Music of What Happens: Poems, Poets, Critics* (Cambridge: Harvard UP, 1988) 252–54: "Ashbery has said that this is the messenger of love, not death, but perhaps one can call him Fate, of whom we always think with mixed feelings" (253).

36. "The Wanderer," *Anglo-Saxon Poetry,* trans. and ed. S. A. J. Bradley (London: Dent, 1982) 323.

37. See Geoff Ward's discussion of *The Vermont Notebook* in his lively book, *Statutes of Liberty: The New York School of Poets* (New York: St. Martin's, 1993) 85–86.

38. Ross Labrie, "John Ashbery: An Interview with Ross Labrie," *American Poetry Review* 13.3 (May-June 1984): 33.

39. Sue Gangel, "John Ashbery," *American Poetry Observed: Poets on Their Work,* ed. Joe David Bellamy (Urbana: Illinois UP, 1988) 15. Only the typescripts of *The Vermont Notebook* seem to have been preserved.

40. Conversation, February 1993.

41. Gangel 16.

42. Gertrude Stein suggested a similar poetics of anal ex-pression in one cryptographic entry of *Tender Buttons:* "A brown which is not liquid not more so is relaxed and yet there is a change, a news is pressing" (cf. "anus"). Gertrude Stein, *Selected Writings of Gertrude Stein,* ed. Carl Van Vechten (New York: Vintage, 1972) 473.

43. The article, which Ashbery clipped from the *Sodus Record,* contains no by-line or date.

44. John Murphy, "John Ashbery: An Interview with John Murphy," *Poetry Review* 75.2 (August 1985): 23.

## 1. *Some Trees*

1. One possible exception, "Hotel Dauphin" (ST 52), which Ashbery remembers being a seedy West Side hotel, draws more from Joseph Cornell's boxes than from Manhattan's.

2. For a valuable discussion of Ashbery's "Canzone" and "Pantoum," see Joseph M. Conte, *Unending Design: The Forms of Postmodern Poetry* (Ithaca: Cornell UP, 1991) 178–85.

3. Laura (Riding) Jackson, *The Poems of Laura Riding* (1938; New York: Persea Books, 1980) 38. All citations of Riding's poetry are from this edition, cited hereafter in the text.

4. Kostelanetz 20. One week later, in "The Pied Piper" (dated 1/8/52), Ashbery appears to acknowledge Cage's hypnotic influence: "for his love was strongest / Who never loved them at all, and his notes / Most civil, laughing not to return" (ST 69).

5. Ashbery remembers first hearing the word "gay" as "homosexual" at Harvard in 1946. Conversation, February 1993. But "Poem" (1944), discussed below, seems already to employ this meaning. Its origin is obscure; Stein's "Miss Furr and Miss Skeene" (1922), for instance, seems to resonate this modern meaning: "They were regular in being gay, they learned little things that are things in being gay, they learned many little things that are things in being gay," Stein, *Selected Writings* 566.

6. John Ashbery, "A Sermon: Amos 8:11–14," *Harvard Advocate* 130.1 (April 1947): 12.

7. Dinitia Smith, "Poem Alone," *New York* 20 May 1991: 50.

8. John Ashbery, *Turandot and Other Poems* (New York: Tibor De Nagy Gallery, 1953). The book includes four drawings by Jane Freilicher. All the poems in *Turandot* except "White" and the short operatic drama "Turandot" were included in *Some Trees.*

9. Harold Bloom, "The Charity of the Hard Moments," *John Ashbery,* ed. Harold Bloom (New York: Chelsea House, 1985) 50.

10. Frank O'Hara, "Rare Modern," *Poetry* 89.5 (February 1957): 313.

11. From Boris Pasternak, "Safe Conduct," trans. Beatrice Scott, *Safe Conduct* (1931; New York: New Directions, 1949) 147.

12. Andrew Marvell, *The Poems and Letters of Andrew Marvell,* ed. H. M. Margoliouth, rev. Pierre Legouis, 3rd ed., vol. 1 (Oxford: Clarendon, 1971) 40–41. All citations of Marvell's poetry are from this edition, cited hereafter in the text.

13. Gertrude Stein, *Selected Writings* 462. See David Bergman's intriguing essay, "Choosing Our Fathers: Gender and Identity in Whitman, Ashbery, and Richard Howard," *Gaiety Transfigured: Gay Self-Representation in American Literature* (Madison: Wisconsin UP, 1991) 44–63.

14. When asked what she admired about Ashbery's poetry, the painterly poet Barbara Guest remarked, "he doesn't make any mistakes." Conversation, January 6, 1993.

15. Lynn Keller, *Re-making it new: Contemporary American poetry and the modernist tradition* (New York: Cambridge UP, 1987) 22; David Shapiro, *John Ashbery: An Introduction to the Poetry* (New York: Columbia UP, 1979) 47; Leslie Wolf, "The Brushstroke's Integrity: The Poetry of John Ashbery and the Art of Painting," *Beyond Amazement: New Essays on John Ashbery,* ed. David Lehman (Ithaca: Cornell UP, 1980) 224–27.

16. John Ashbery, rev. of *The Complete Poems* [*New York Times Book Review* 1 June 1969] *Elizabeth Bishop and Her Art,* ed. Lloyd Schwartz and Sybil P. Estess (Ann Arbor: Michigan UP, 1983) 203.

17. Robert Browning, *Browning: Poetical Works, 1833–1864,* ed. Ian Jack (London: Oxford UP, 1970) 675. All citations of Browning's poetry are from this edition, cited hereafter in the text.

18. Gangel 17–18.

19. See Shapiro 50; Bloom, "Charity" 2–3; Keller 19–20.

20. Louis Osti, "The Craft of John Ashbery," *Confrontation* 9.3 (1974): 88. This interview will be cited hereafter as Osti.

21. Labrie 30.

22. Aeschylus, *The Oresteia,* trans. Gilbert Murray (London: Allen & Unwin, 1928) 162.

23. Guillaume Apollinaire, *Alcools,* trans. Anne Greet (Berkeley: California UP, 1965) 7.

24. W. K. Wimsatt, *The Verbal Icon* (Lexington, Kentucky UP, 1967) 5.

25. David Kalstone, *Becoming a Poet: Elizabeth Bishop with Marianne Moore and Robert Lowell,* ed. Robert Hemenway (New York: Farrar, Straus, and Giroux, 1989) 18.

26. Hart Crane, *The Poems of Hart Crane,* ed. Marc Simon (New York: Liveright, 1986) 43. All citations of Crane's poetry are from this edition, cited hereafter in the text.

27. Elizabeth Bishop, *The Complete Poems: 1927–1979* (New York: Farrar, Straus, and Giroux, 1983) 14. All citations of Bishop's poetry are from this edition, cited hereafter in the text. Bishop's "The Moose," finished in 1972 a few months after the death of Marianne Moore, may likewise be read as an elegy for her friend, whose name she encrypts in her title (along with a play on "Muse").

28. Wallace Stevens, *Letters of Wallace Stevens,* ed. Holly Stevens (New York: Knopf, 1977) 678.

29. W. H. Auden, foreword, *Some Trees* (New Haven: Yale UP, 1956) 13–15.

30. Ashbery thinks he remembers writing "And You Know" after "The Instruction Manual," which he remembers writing in June 1955, after he returned from Mexico. The typescript date may concern penciled revisions.

31. Perloff, *Indeterminacy* 263–65.

32. Gangel 18.

33. Conversation, February 1990.

34. Raymond Roussel, "The View," trans. Antony Melville, *Raymond Roussel: Selections from Certain of his Books* (London: Atlas Press, 1991) 229, 231.

35. I am using Ashbery's unpublished contemporary translation, rather than his later version published in *The Random House Book of Twentieth-Century French Poetry,* ed. Paul Auster (New York: Random House, 1982) 45.

36. Gangel 18.

37. Ashbery, *Bishop* 204.

38. Charles Baudelaire, *Les Fleurs du Mal,* trans. Richard Howard (Boston: Godine, 1982) 151–52. The importance of Baudelaire's voyages for Ashbery's has been cogently demonstrated by Alan Williamson, *Introspection and Contemporary Poetry* (Cambridge: Harvard UP, 1984) 128–31.

39. Marcel Proust, *Remembrance of Things Past,* trans. C. K. Scott Moncrieff and Terence Kilmartin, vol. 1 (New York: Random House, 1982) 420.

40. James Schuyler, *The Home Book* (Calais, Vt.: Z Press, 1977) 75.

41. Ashbery, *Bishop* 204.

## 2. *The Tennis Court Oath*

1. Bloom, "Charity" 52.

2. Bruce Andrews, "Misrepresentation," *In the American Tree,* ed. Ron Silliman (Orono, Maine: National Poetry Foundation, 1986) 524.

3. Conversation, Chicago, December 1990.

4. Ron Silliman, *What* (Great Barrington, MA: The Figures, 1988) 111.

5. Poulin 245.

6. John Ashbery, "Antonin Artaud," *Portfolio & Art News Annual* 2 (1960): 167–68.

7. Marjorie Perloff, "'Fragments of a Buried Life': John Ashbery's Dream Songs," *Beyond Amazement* 78. For an early, engaging discussion of "Leaving the Atocha Station," see Paul Carroll, "If Only He Had Left From the Finland Station," *The Poem in Its Skin* (Chicago: Follett, 1968) 6–26.

8. The most disjunctive poems of *The Tennis Court Oath,* written after Ashbery's return to Paris in the winter of 1958, coincided with the Algerian revolt and the attendant uncertainties which brought down the Fourth Republic and returned Charles de Gaulle to power.

9. Irving Sandler, "The Club," *Artforum* 4.1 (Sept. 1965): 27–31. Quoted in Marjorie Perloff, *Frank O'Hara: Poet Among Painters* (New York: George Braziller, 1977) 59.

10. John Ashbery, lecture, "Poetry Now," National Book Awards Symposium, New York City, March 5, 1968.

11. "Winter," *Locus Solus* 1 (Winter 1961): 66–75. The poem was selected by James Schuyler.

12. Kéchichian 23; Ashbery, "Poetry Now."

13. James Schuyler, letter to Ashbery, 3 September 1960.

14. Kéchichian 23, 34.

15. Labrie 30.

16. Quoted in David Kermani, *John Ashbery: A Comprehensive Bibliography* (New York: Garland, 1976) 23–25. I am enormously indebted to Kermani's scrupulous scholarship. A second bibliography, extending beyond 1975, is projected.

17. John Ashbery and James Schuyler, *A Nest of Ninnies* (Calais, Vt.: Z Press, 1975) 9.

18. Carl Little, "An Interview with James Schuyler," *Talisman* 9 (1992): 178.

19. In 1953, Ashbery, Koch, and O'Hara wrote the first act of another drama, *Play,* and wrote a second act shortly before O'Hara's fatal accident. See Kenward Elmslie's journal *ZZZ* (1974): 107–22. Ashbery remembers writing one speech from Act I, for "Roger," 108–9.

20. *Locus Solus* 2 (Summer 1961): 196, 157.

21. *Locus Solus* 2: 62, 65.

22. *Locus Solus* 2: 69.

23. John Ashbery, "A Note on Pierre Reverdy"; "Reverdy en Amérique," *Mercure de France* 344.1181 (Jan. 1962): 111 (my translation).

24. Roland Barthes, "L'effet de réel," *Communications* 11 (1968): 84–89.

25. Pierre Reverdy, "The Invasion," *Evergreen Review,* 4.11 (Jan. / Feb. 1960): 24. Ashbery's translations are available in Pierre Reverdy, *Selected Poems,* ed. Mary Ann Caws (Newcastle upon Tyne: Bloodaxe, 1991).

26. Ashbery, "A Note on Pierre Reverdy."

27. Ashbery, "The Impossible," 250.

28. Gertrude Stein, *The Yale Gertrude Stein,* ed. Richard Kostelanetz (New Haven: Yale UP, 1980) 369.

29. Wallace Stevens, *The Collected Poems of Wallace Stevens* (New York: Knopf, 1954) 352.

30. Frank O'Hara, letter to Ashbery, 9 March 1962.

31. A. Hamilton Gibbs, *Soundings: A Novel* (Boston: Little, Brown, 1925) 84. Ashbery collaged passages from *Soundings* into "Idaho" in this order: 137–38, 84, 144, 192–93, 256–58.

32. Ashbery's resounding of Gibbs's train whistle echoes the blast, "aigu et prolongé," which begins Alain Robbe-Grillet's *Le Voyeur,* the title of which was modified from Roussel's *La Vue,* which had inspired Robbe-Grillet's novel. See Alain Robbe-Grillet, *Le Voyeur* (Paris: Èditions de Minuit, 1955) 9. Ashbery had read *Le Voyeur* before writing "Idaho."

33. Only the idea of a typewriter is necessarily for painterly punctuality. In "Three Madrigals," written in 1958 and published a decade later, Ashbery painstakingly hand-lettered ten pages of polyphonic verse including one line of purely instrumental notation: """"**** * :: :::::.:;,:::., ... ,. / : / .:-* *Three Madrigals* (New York: Poet's Press, 1968) 10.

34. Osti 94.

35. Ashbery saw Rauschenberg's early collage work and the first exhibit of Jasper Johns's paintings in New York during the winter of 1957–58. While an undergraduate, Ashbery himself did an Ernst-like collage with Fred Amory for an issue of *The Harvard Advocate* (Nov. 1948).

36. Quoted in Fred Moramarco, "John Ashbery and Frank O'Hara: The Painterly Poets," *Journal of Modern Literature* 5.3 (Sept. 1976): 454.

37. Osti 94.

38. Piotr Sommer, "An Interview in Warsaw," *Code of Signals: Recent Writings in Poetics,* ed. Michael Palmer (Berkeley: North Atlantic Books, 1983) 301–2.

39. *John Ashbery and Kenneth Koch (A Conversation)* (Tucson, Ariz.: Interview Press, 1965) 10.

40. Frank O'Hara, letter to Ashbery, 7 January 1960.

41. O'Hara, letter to Ashbery, 1 February 1961.

42. O'Hara, letter to Ashbery, 14 July 1960.

43. Frank O'Hara, *The Collected Poems of Frank O'Hara,* ed. Donald Allen (New York: Knopf, 1971) 380. All citations of O'Hara's poetry are from this edition, cited hereafter in the text.

44. Kermani 76.

45. Roussel, *Selections* 11–65.

46. Osti 92.

47. William Le Queux, *Beryl of the Biplane* (London: Pearson, 1917) 97. Thanks are due to Ashbery for the loan of this book.

48. After he wrote "Europe," Ashbery constructed a puzzle-poem, "The Secret of the Old Mill," by gridding 7 pages into 36 squares and parcelling Franklin W. Dixon's Hardy Boy novel by this title among them.

49. John Tranter, "An Interview with John Ashbery," *Scripsi* 4.1 (July 1986): 97.

50. Peter Stitt, "The Art of Poetry XXXIII: John Ashbery," *The Paris Review* 90 (Winter 1983): 58.

51. Perloff, *Indeterminacy* 269–70. See also Jonathan Culler, *Structuralist Poetics* (Ithaca: Cornell UP, 1975) 169–70.

52. Conversation, April 1990.

53. Ezra Pound, *Personæ: The Shorter Poems,* ed. Lea Baechler and A. Walton Litz (1971; New York: New Directions, 1990) 134.

54. Bloom, "Charity" 52.

55. The homotextual dimensions of Ovid's myth of Tiresias, who changes sex after witnessing two snakes copulate, merit further study.

56. James Schuyler, *Collected Poems* (New York: Farrar, Straus, Giroux, 1993) 11.

57. John Ashbery, "Schubert's Unfinished" and David Schubert, "Kind Valentine," *David Schubert: Works and Days, Quarterly Review of Literature* 24 (1983): 308, 4.

58. Barbara Guest, "His Jungle," *Locus Solus* 3–4: 210.

59. While in France, Ashbery wrote that he was reading *Harmonium,* "which I find disappointing except for 'To the One of Fictive Music.'" Letter to Fairfield Porter, 15 May 1956.

60. Michel Foucault, *The History of Sexuality,* Vol. 1: *An Introduction,* trans. Robert Hurley (New York: Random House, 1978) 22.

## 3. *Rivers and Mountains*

1. *Locus Solus* 2: 166–68.

2. "Rivers and Mountains" was actually inspired by an exhibition of Korean paintings at Musée Cernuschi in Paris. See Ashbery's "Korean opulence at Paris museums (from Han period to 19th century)," *The New York Herald Tribune, European Edition* 13 Dec. 1961: 5.

3. John Ashbery, "Second Presentation of Elizabeth Bishop," *World Literature Today* 51 (Winter 1977): 8.

4. See especially Robert von Hallberg, *American Poetry and Culture, 1945–1980* (Cambridge: Harvard UP, 1985).

5. Janet Bloom and Robert Losada, "Craft Interview with John Ashbery," *The Craft of Poetry: Interviews from the New York Quarterly,* ed. William Packard (New York: Doubleday, 1974) 123.

6. See Sigmund Freud, *Civilization and Its Discontents,* trans. Joan Riviere (New York: Doubleday, 1958) 2, 52.

7. Ashbery has confirmed that the period after "you see" in line 24 is a misprint.

8. Bonnie Costello, "John Ashbery and the Idea of the Reader," *Contemporary Literature* 23.4 (1982): 496.

9. Kostelanetz 24.

10. Hart Crane, "General Aims and Theories," *The Complete Poems and Selected Letters and Prose of Hart Crane,* ed. Brom Weber (New York: Doubleday, 1966) 221.

11. Leary 523.

12. William Wordsworth, *William Wordsworth: The Poems,* ed. John O. Hayden, vol. 1 (New Haven: Yale UP, 1977) 360. All citations of Wordsworth's shorter poems are from this edition, cited hereafter in the text.

13. I discuss these units of poetic measurement more fully in "The Music of Construction: Measure and Polyphony in Ashbery and Bernstein," *The Tribe of John: John Ashbery and Contemporary Poetry,* ed. Susan Schultz (University, Ala.: Alabama UP, 1995).

14. In the congruent narrative of Ashbery's life, the "other / Authority" (either the setting sun or the passing moon) would be Ashbery's father from whose funeral Ashbery had recently returned.

15. Bloom, "Charity" 56.

16. Henry James, *European Writers and The Prefaces,* ed. Leon Edel (New York: Library of America, 1984) 1250.

17. Conversation, May 1991. The notebook hasn't survived.

18. Bloom and Losada 113.

19. Bloom and Losada 123.

20. Quoted in Kermani 81.

21. William Wordsworth, *The Prelude: 1799, 1805, 1850,* ed. Jonathan Wordsworth, M. H. Abrams, and Stephen Gill (New York: Norton, 1979) 52. All citations of the 1805 *Prelude* are from this edition, cited hereafter in the text.

22. Elizabeth Bishop, letter to Ashbery, 27 April 1976.

23. Interview with Bill Berkson, 1969. Quoted in Kermani 80–81.

24. [Many Hands], *Three Hundred Things A Bright Boy Can Do* (London: Sampson Low, Marston & Co, 1911) 380.

25. *Three Hundred Things* 384–85. In the manual the experiment was labeled "The Well of Fire."

26. The "Storm-fiend" was a constant companion of the popular Victorian sea balladeer William McGonagall: "Then every man struggled manfully to gain the shore, / While the storm fiend did loudly laugh and roar." William McGonagall, *Last Poetic Gems* (London: Duckworth, 1968) 43.

27. Apollinaire, *Alcools* 7.

## 4. *The Double Dream of Spring*

1. Louis Simpson, "Dead Horses and Live Issues," *The Nation* 24 April 1967: 521.

2. John Ashbery, letter to *The Nation* 8 May 1967: 578; 29 May 1967: 674, 692.

3. Ashbery, "The Impossible" 250.

4. The phrases "urban development" and "Descending scale" were used in the first typescript of "Decoy."

5. Remnick 62.

6. In an important study of Ashbery's construction of "Farm Implements" which reproduces the Popeye comic strip, Helen Vendler includes a submerged nursery rhyme: "On a misty, moisty morning, when cloudy was the weather / I met an old man, all dressed in leather." "Ashbery and Popeye," *The Marks in the Fields: Essays on the Uses of Manuscripts,* ed. Rodney G. Dennis with Elizabeth Falsey (Cambridge: The Houghton Library, 1992) 163.

7. Murphy 25.

8. See *Preferences* ed. Richard Howard (New York: Viking, 1974); Kermani 88.

9. Thomas Traherne, *Poems, Centuries and Three Thanksgivings,* ed. Anne Ridler (London: Oxford UP, 1966) 92.

10. Remnick 62.

11. I. A. Richards, *Principles of Literary Criticism* (New York: Harcourt Brace Jovanovich, 1925) 203–5.

12. See Ella Wheeler Wilcox, *Poems of Power* (London: Gay and Hancock, 1903) 18–19. This volume went through 21 reprintings before the war.

13. Conversation, April 1991. Roy Rockwood, *The City Beyond the Clouds, Or, Cap-*

*tured by the Red Dwarfs* (New York: Cupples & Leon, 1925) 28. The first chapter is included among Ashbery's papers at Houghton Library.

14. Bloom and Losada 125–26. See also Peter Baker, *Obdurate Brilliance: Exteriority and the Modern Long Poem* (Gainesville: U of Florida P, 1991) 135–49.

15. Koethe 184.

16. John Ashbery, "Straight Lines Over Rough Terrain," *New York Times Book Review* 26 Nov. 1967: 1, 42; Marianne Moore, *The Complete Poems of Marianne Moore* (1967; New York: Viking, 1981) 91. All citations of Moore's poetry are from this edition, cited hereafter in the text.

17. Maurice Scève, *Délie,* ed. Françoise Charpentier (Paris: Gallimard, 1984) 132. All citations of *Délie* are from this edition, with dizain number noted in the text; translations are mine.

18. Bloom and Losada 127.

19. The first number refers to the stanza, the second to the page of *The Double Dream of Spring.*

20. Conversation, April 1990.

21. Ashbery recalled that his mother first discovered his homosexuality in June 1945 from "a letter left lying around" (conversation, April 1991).

22. Bloom, "Charity" 67–68. For a valuable deconstructive commentary on "Fragment," see Charles Berger, "Vision in the Form of a Task: *The Double Dream of Spring,*" *Beyond Amazement* 190–208.

23. Williamson 117.

24. George Herbert, *The English Poems of George Herbert,* ed. C. A. Patrides (London: Dent, 1974) 181.

## 5. *Three Poems*

1. Poulin 254.

2. Bloom and Losada 126.

3. "The New Spirit," begun in November 1969 and mostly written between January and April 1970, was published in *The Paris Review* (Fall 1970); "The System," written between January and March 1971, was published in *The Paris Review* (Winter 1972); "The Recital," written in April 1971, appeared both in *The Poetry Review* (Winter 1971–72) and, significantly, in *Fiction* (Spring 1972). E. P. Dutton, which had published *The Double Dream of Spring,* turned down *Three Poems,* freeing Ashbery to publish it with Viking Press.

4. Charles Bernstein, "Of Time and the Line," *Rough Trades* (Los Angeles: Sun & Moon, 1991) 42–43.

5. Sommer 301; Labrie 31.

6. Sommer 302.

7. Marjorie Perloff, *Poetic License: Essays on Modernist and Postmodernist Lyric* (Evanston: Northwestern UP, 1990) 281.

8. Osti 90. Stephen Fredman has opted for the term "poet's prose" in order to capture the revisionary peculiarity of American twentieth-century "prose poetry." For an exemplary discussion of *Three Poems,* see *Poet's Prose: The Crisis in American Verse,* 2nd ed. (Cambridge: Cambridge UP, 1990) 101–35.

9. Bloom and Losada 126.

10. Conversation, November 1989.

11. Bloom and Losada 126.

12. Conversation, November 1989.

13. John Clare, *John Clare,* ed. Eric Robinson and David Powell (Oxford: Oxford UP, 1984) 470. Clare resisted conventional spelling and punctuation.

14. Poulin 253.

15. Charles Baudelaire, *Œuvres complètes,* ed. Claude Pichois, vol. 1 (Paris: Gallimard, 1975) 291 (my translation).

16. Arthur Rimbaud, *Œuvres complètes,* ed. Antoine Adam (Paris: Gallimard, 1972) 134 (my translation).

17. Kostelanetz 26.

18. Giorgio de Chirico, from *Hebdomeros,* trans. John Ashbery, *Art and Literature* 4 (1965): 13.

19. Stitt 38.

20. Labrie 31.

21. Stitt 55.

22. See Shapiro *Ashbery* 133–75; Perloff, *Indeterminacy,* 270–74 and *Poetic License* 276–84; Margueritte S. Murphy, *A Tradition of Subversion: The Prose Poem in English from Wilde to Ashbery* (Amherst: U of Massachusetts Press, 1992) 168–98.

23. Abraham Lincoln, *Selected Speeches and Writings,* ed. Don E. Fehrenbacher (New York: Library of America, 1992) 450. For an influential discussion of postmodern pastiche, see Fredric Jameson, *Postmodernism, or, The Cultural Logic of Late Capitalism* (Durham: Duke UP, 1991) 16–19.

24. The first paragraph, unindented in the text of *Three Poems,* is indented in the typescript. I suspect this is an error.

25. Conversation, April 1991.

26. Bloom and Losada 131–32.

27. Sommer 304. For a related discussion, see W. H. Auden's 1964 essay, "The Protestant Mystics," *Forewords and Afterwords,* ed. Edward Mendelson (New York: Random House, 1973) 49–78.

28. Bloom and Losada 114.

29. Conversation, November 1989.

30. Conversation, November 1989.

31. Conversation, November 1989.

32. Bloom and Losada 123–24.

33. John Keats, letter to Richard Woodhouse, 27 October 1818, *The Letters of John Keats: 1814–1821,* ed. Hyder Edward Rollins, vol. 1 (Cambridge: Harvard UP, 1958) 387.

34. Koethe 180. In 1939, when Ashbery was twelve, his brother died at nine of leukemia.

35. Ashbery's analyst suggested he read Aldous Huxley's anthology *The Perennial Philosophy,* through which he was introduced to "this really extraordinary book," Traherne's *Centuries of Meditation,* whose discourses on love are an important discursive model for "The System" in particular (Sommer 303).

36. Traherne 245–46.

37. Bloom and Losada 126.

38. Conversation, November 1989.

39. T.S. Eliot, *The Complete Poems and Plays: 1909–1950* (New York: Harcourt Brace

Jovanovich, 1971) 50. All citations of Eliot's poetry are from this edition, cited hereafter in the text. In Ashbery's draft, the other lover appeared as "she," making her transatlantic voyage: "She supposed that he would get over it when he was feeling better, and meanwhile there were tons of things to get done. . . ."

40. De Chirico, from *Hebdemeros* 34; conversation, October 1988.

41. Conversation, October 1988.

42. Conversation, November 1989.

43. Langston Hughes, *Selected Poems* (New York: Random House, 1959) 268.

44. Dante Alighieri, *The Divine Comedy,* trans. Charles S. Singleton, vol. 1 (Princeton: Princeton UP, 1977) 160. All citations from Dante's *Divine Comedy* are from this edition, here in my translation. See also Perloff, *Indeterminacy* 255–63.

45. Remarking in a 1965 interview that "Andy Warhol gets more publicity than any other single living American artist," Frank O'Hara affirms that the avant-garde has lost both its invisibility and its struggle: "There is no underground and there is certainly no embattlement. . . . Which is a *change* . . . from the general idea . . . that all avant-garde art has to be attacking the bourgeoisie." Frank O'Hara, *Standing Still and Walking in New York,* ed. Donald Allen (San Francisco: Grey Fox Press, 1983) 8–9. On the absorption of avant-garde techniques by "mass mediated culture," see Andreas Huyssen, *After The Great Divide: Modernism, Mass Culture, Postmodernism* (Bloomington: Indiana UP, 1986) 3–15.

46. Conversation, November 1989.

47. Raymond Roussel, *La Vue* (Paris: Jean-Jacques Pauvert, 1963) 73 (my translation).

48. Sigmund Freud, *Beyond the Pleasure Principle,* trans. James Strachey (New York: Norton, 1961) 4.

49. Keats, *Letters,* 185.


## 6. Self-Portrait in a Convex Mirror

1. Conversation, December 1989.

2. Marvell, *Poems* 94, 97.

3. Giorgio de Chirico, "On Silence," trans. John Ashbery, *Big Sky* 9 (1975): 3–5. A revised translation appears in *Hebdomeros* (Cambridge: Exact Change, 1992) 224–31.

4. For an extensive close reading, see Roger Gilbert, *Walks in the World: Representation and Experience in Modern American Poetry* (Princeton: Princeton UP, 1991) 233–51.

5. Jackson 73.

6. Stein, *Selected Writings* 461.

7. Gerard Manley Hopkins, *Gerard Manley Hopkins,* ed. Catherine Phillips (Oxford: Oxford UP, 1986) 129.

8. Conversation, February 1993.

9. Robert Frost, *Complete Poems* (New York: Holt, 1949) 467. All citations of Frost's poetry are from this edition, cited hereafter in the text.

10. Esther Quinn, *The Quest of Seth* (Chicago: Chicago UP, 1962).

11. Compare Quinn's plot summary: "The eldest prince begs the dying king to be allowed to fetch the water of life, hoping thereby to win his father's favor and kingdom. He meets a dwarf, is discourteous, and is caught in a ravine. The second prince meets the same fate. The youngest, however, is courteous to the dwarf and, after many adventures, is aided by him in drawing the water of life from a spring. Before returning to the

king, he rescues his brothers, who proceed to steal the water of life. The two oldest succeed in restoring the king, though after further adventures the youngest is returned to favor and marries the princess" (19). See also John Ruskin's fairy tale, "The King of the Golden River."

12. *The Oxford Book of Light Verse,* ed. W. H. Auden (Oxford: Oxford UP, 1938) 287–88. For two fine antithetical readings of Ashbery's poem, see James E. B. Breslin, *From Modern to Contemporary: American Poetry, 1945–1965* (Chicago: Chicago UP, 1984) 262–65; Karen Mills-Courts, *Poetry as Epitaph: Representation and Poetic Language* (Baton Rouge: Louisiana State UP, 1990) 272–78.

13. J. L. Austin, *How to do things with Words,* ed. J. O. Urmson and Marina Sbisà, 2nd ed. (1962; Cambridge: Harvard UP, 1975) 22. See also Jacques Derrida, "Signature Event Context," *Margins of Philosophy,* trans. Alan Bass (Chicago: Chicago UP, 1982) 307–30.

14. Conversation, May 1991. The opening in question was that of *Flow Chart,* "Still in the unpublished city but not yet" (FC 3).

15. For an extensive discussion, see Charles Altieri, *Self and Sensibility in Contemporary American Poetry* (New York: Cambridge UP, 1984) 137–45.

16. Conversation, Spring 1992.

17. Tranter 94. Ashbery's most examined poem has received a number of detailed discussions. I am most indebted to the following: Harold Bloom, "The Breaking of Form," *John Ashbery* 115–26; Anita Sokolsky, "'A Commission That Never Materialized,'" *John Ashbery* 233–250; David Kalstone, *Five Temperaments* (New York: Oxford UP, 1977) 176–85; Altieri, *Sensibility* 150–60; Andrew Ross, *The Failure of Modernism: Symptoms of American Poetry* (New York: Columbia UP, 1986) 163–65; Richard Stamelman, "Critical Reflections: Poetry and Art Criticism in Ashbery's 'Self-Portrait in a Convex Mirror,'" *New Literary History* 15 (1983): 607–29; Lee Edelman, "The Pose of Imposture: Ashbery's 'Self-Portrait in a Convex Mirror,'" *Twentieth Century Literature* 32.1 (Spring 1986): 95–113.

18. Sydney Freedberg, *Parmigianino: His Works in Painting* (Cambridge: Harvard UP, 1950). The first draft of "Self-Portrait" incorporated this bibliographical information.

19. John Ashbery, rev. of Richard Bogart, *Art News* 67.1 (Mar. 1968): 11; rev. of Neil Welliver, *Art News* 68.1 (Mar. 1969): 71; "Cornell: the cube root of dreams," *Art News* 64.4 (Summer 1967): 56. Ashbery's review of Cornell also appears in RS 13–18.

20. Freedberg 127. See John Ashbery, foreword, *Joseph Cornell's Theater of the Mind: Selected Diaries, Letters, and Files,* ed. Mary Ann Caws (New York: Thames and Hudson, 1993) 9–12.

21. See Freedberg 3–8, 127.

22. John Milton, *Complete Poems and Major Prose,* ed. Merritt Y. Hughes (New York: Macmillan, 1957) 216. All citations of Milton's poetry are from this edition, cited hereafter in the text.

23. Sir Philip Sidney, *A Defence of Poetry,* ed. J. A. Van Dorsten (Oxford: Oxford UP, 1971) 25.

24. Freedberg 21.

25. Ralph Waldo Emerson, *Essays and Lectures,* ed. Joel Porte (New York: Library of America, 1983) 404. All citations of Emerson's prose are from this edition, cited hereafter in the text.

26. Freedberg 14.

27. John Ashbery, "Brooms and Prisms," *Art News* 65.1 (Mar. 1966): 83.

28. Sigmund Freud, *General Psychological Theory: Papers on Metapsychology,* ed. Philip Rieff (New York: Macmillan, 1963) 69. On the heterosexual bias of Freud's concept of narcissism, see Yingling 48–50.

29. One of Hoffmann's characters, Erasmus in "A New Year's Eve Adventure," meets a courtesan in Italy who takes his reflection as a pledge of his love. See *The Best Tales of Hoffmann,* ed. E. F. Bleiler (New York: Dover, 1967) 122.

30. John Ashbery, "Proust and His Times in Paris Exhibition," *The New York Herald-Tribune, European Edition* 8 June 1965: 5.

31. Freud, *Theory* 71; Jacques Lacan, *Écrits: A Selection,* trans. Alan Sheridan (New York: Norton, 1977) 4.

32. Giorgio Vasari, *Lives of the Most Eminent Painters, Sculptors, and Architects,* trans. Mrs. Jonathan Foster, vol. 3 (London: George Bell and Sons, 1874) 361.

33. Mahler composed his ninth symphony while living in New York; Roger Reynolds's setting of Ashbery's "Self-Portrait," *Whispers Out Of Time,* is based in part upon a distortion of Mahler's phrase.

34. One person informing Ashbery's composite portrait of Parmigianino appears to be Frank O'Hara, whose familiar name inevitably echoes in "Francesco." One passage, for instance, calls up a mirror image of erotic and enunciative latency: "Once it seemed so perfect—gloss on the fine / Freckled skin, lips moistened as though about to part / Releasing speech" (SP 82). The freckled skin recalls O'Hara's (Parmigianino's painted face is clear), and "Frank" is almost audible in "Freckled."

35. John Ashbery, "Growing Up Surreal," *Art News* 67.3 (May 1968): 41.

36. Ashbery had not read Walter Benjamin's essay "The Work of Art in the Age of Mechanical Reproduction" but knew of Benjamin's use of "aura" as an art object's historical authenticity. Ashbery was thinking of the "aura" in sixties parlance as an individual's vibes (conversation, Fall 1991). See Walter Benjamin, *Illuminations,* ed. Hannah Arendt, trans. Harry Zohn (New York: Schocken, 1968) 217–252.

37. Jackson 75.

38. Robert Lowell, *Day by Day* (New York: Farrar, Straus, Giroux, 1977) 127.

## 7. *Houseboat Days*

1. On the "position of 'pure' writer or artist," see Pierre Bourdieu, *The Field of Cultural Production,* ed. Randal Johnson (New York: Columbia UP, 1993) 62–63.

2. Labrie 31.

3. Compare George Gascoigne, "The Divorce of a Lover": "Divorce me nowe good death, from love and lingring life, / That one hat bene my concubine, that other was my wife," *English Sixteenth-Century Verse: An Anthology,* ed. Richard S. Sylvester (New York: Norton, 1984) 250.

4. Stitt 54.

5. For an illuminating extended analysis of "Houseboat Days" see Mary Kinzie, "Irreference," *The Cure of Poetry in an Age of Prose: Moral Essays on the Poet's Calling* (Chicago: Chicago UP, 1993) 230–46.

6. *National Geographic Magazine:* 56 (October 1929): 437ff.

7. Walter Pater, *Plato and Platonism: A Series of Lectures* (1893; London: Macmillan, 1901) 103–4.

8. George Gordon, Lord Byron, *Byron,* ed. Jerome J. McGann (Oxford: Oxford UP, 1986) 199.

9. Pater 120.

10. Pater 106–7.

11. Pater 115.

12. Remnick, unpublished interview 17.

13. Franz Kafka, *The Complete Stories,* ed. Nahum N. Glatzer (New York: Schocken, 1976) 53.

14. These casements may be related to the fact that Ashbery began wearing glasses around this time.

15. For another likely source of Ashbery's "bottle-imp" (first called "ludion"), see Roussel, *Locus Solus,* trans. Rupert Copeland Cunningham (New York: Riverrun, 1983) 51–92.

16. Harold Bloom, "Measuring the Canon: John Ashbery's *Wet Casements* and *Tapestry,*" *Agon: Towards a Theory of Revisionism* (New York: Oxford UP, 1982) 283. See also David Bromwich, "John Ashbery," *Raritan* 4 (Spring 1986): 54–57.

17. *The Oxford Book of Ballads,* ed. Arthur Quiller-Couch (Oxford: Clarendon Press, 1910) 138–40.

18. I include a list of fugitive or obscure references, which Ashbery helped me compile: "La Celestina" (a sixteenth-century play by Fernando de Rojas), "'I Thought about You'" (Billie Holiday song), *Amadigi di Gaula* (Handel opera), "Rumford's Baking Powder" (Rumford Baking Powder), "Speedy / Gonzales" (cartoon character), Helen Topping Miller (novelist, wrote *Let Me Die Tuesday*), "greige, deckle-edged / Stock" (a combination of gray and beige, rough-cut hand-made paper), "That mean old" (cf. cartoon character Tweety-Bird: "Dat mean old puddy-tat"), "me mug's" (cockney, also Popeye's lingo), "Fudd's" (Elmer Fudd, slow-witted foil of Daffy Duck and Bugs Bunny), "Gadsden Purchase" (U.S. southwest land bought from Mexico in 1853), "cover" (envelope bearing collectable stamp and postal markings), "happy-go-nutty" (cartoon title), "jacqueries" (peasant revolts), "Up / The lazy river . . ." (popular song by the Mills Brothers), *"carte du Tendre"* (allegorical map of the country of love, first used by Madeleine de Scudéry in *Clélie, histoire romaine,* 1654), "algolagnic" (sado-masochistic), *"nuits blanches"* (sleepless nights), "Princesse de Clèves" (title character of a 1678 narrative by Marie-Madeleine de Lafayette), "Tamigi" ("Thames," Italian), "the Wallets" (family in the comic strip "Gasoline Alley"), "Ollie / Of the Movies" (another comic strip), *"châlets de nécessité"* (roadside toilets), "Tophet, that / . . . return" (Hell, cf. *Hamlet,* III.i: "The undiscovered country, from whose bourne / No traveller returns"), "borborygmic" (belching), "pecky acajou" (a worm-eaten finish that adds value to mahogany), "creative evolution" (philosophical concept of Henri Bergson), "Aglavaine . . . Sélysette" (title characters of Maeterlinck play), "New Brutalism" (architectural school), "garance" (dark red pigment from the bush; character in Marcel Carne's film *Les Enfants du Paradis,* "Aureng-Zebe" (title character of Dryden's tragedy), "earnest" (advance payment to seal a contract).

19. Stitt 45.

20. Ashbery, rec. 16 May 1976, Lamont Library, Harvard University.

21. Conversation, April 1990.

22. Stephen Vincent Benét, *Selected Poetry and Prose,* ed. Basil Davenport (New York: Rinehart, 1960) 3–4.

23. On "Pyrography," see Perloff, *Indeterminacy* 275–79. For an admirable discussion of the romantic poetics of Ashbery's later poetry, see Helen Vendler, "John Ashbery, Louise Glück," *Music* 224–61.

24. Lehman, "Pleasures" 89.

25. In its first rendition, "Sonatina," the poem contained a 22-line fourth stanza.

26. When I asked Ashbery whether this poem was based on an actual death, he said he made up the situation (conversation, November 1989).

27. The best discussion of this elegiac myth of poetry is found in Peter M. Sacks, *The English Elegy: Studies in the Genre from Spenser to Yeats* (Baltimore: Johns Hopkins UP, 1985) 1–37. For a fascinating discussion of Elliott Carter's setting of "Syringa," see Lawrence Kramer, *Music and Poetry: The Nineteenth Century and After* (Berkeley: California, 1984) 203–21.

28. William Butler Yeats, *The Collected Poems of W. B. Yeats,* ed. Richard J. Finneran (New York: Macmillan, 1989) 214. All citations of Yeats's poetry are from this edition, cited hereafter in the text.

29. This challenge from Apollo originates in Callimachus (*Aetia,* I), a famous passage adapted by Virgil in his sixth eclogue.

30. Ashbery explained the title in a 1976 reading: "in some newspapers before the personals and after the classified ads there is a sort of gray area of business personals, which are really not very personal, people who have guitars for sale and things like that. I was wondering about the way in which they were personal, which caused me to begin writing this poem. The first line is a reference not to Sylvia Plath but to a painting by de Chirico." Rec. 16 May 1976, Lamont Library, Harvard University.

31. Labrie 31.

32. "The Nut-Brown Maid," *The Oxford Book of Ballads* 295–307. All citations of "The Nut-Brown Maid" are from this edition, which Ashbery used. For comparison purposes, I will also note the stanza numbers of Ashbery's "Fantasia."

33. "The Perfect Orange," *Harvard Advocate* 130.3 (21 May 1947): 7.

34. Since part of the poem is in prose, the lineation is relative to the published edition. I have counted the prose lines from the Viking edition of *Houseboat Days.*

35. Conversation, November 1991.

36. The line appearing in the first edition, "falling back to the vase again like a fountain. Responsible" (HBD 83), is a misprint.

37. Jackson 74.

38. See Douglas Crase, *Beyond Amazement* 58; Shapiro 10; Calvin Bedient, *Parnassus: Poetry in Review* 6.1 (1977): 163.

39. Rec. 9 Nov. 1978, Lamont Library, Harvard University.

40. Rec. 9 Nov. 1978, Lamont Library, Harvard University.

41. Roland Barthes, *Image—Music—Text,* ed. and trans. Stephen Heath (New York: Farrar, Straus, Giroux, 1977) 142–48; Michel Foucault, *Language, Counter-memory, Practice,* ed. Donald F. Bouchard, trans. Donald F. Bouchard and Sherry Simon (Ithaca: Cornell UP, 1977) 113–38.

42. Barthes 147.

43. Foucault 127.

44. Barthes 142.

45. Foucault 124–125.

46. Rec. 9 Nov. 1978, Lamont Library, Harvard University.

## 8. *As We Know*

1. In an essay on Saenredam, Roland Barthes was struck by his interiors: "Never has nothingness been so bland, so self-confident, so bland in its self-confidence." See "The World Become Thing," trans. Stanley Geist, *Art and Literature* 3 (1964): 148. "The Skaters" appeared in the same issue of *Art and Literature,* which Ashbery helped edit.

2. Jackson 74–75.

3. Ashbery performed part of "Litany" in Cincinnati in 1978 with the poet Ann Lauterbach and later recorded the poem with her.

4. For a liberating cross-columnar discussion of "Litany," see Perloff, *Indeterminacy* 279–87.

5. Stitt 50.

6. The reader should note that Ashbery's columns, after revision and printing, are no longer aligned as he wrote them. Two stanzas ending with "sky" (AWK 7), now half a page apart, ended simultaneously in Ashbery's original typescript.

7. Tranter 100.

8. *The Tennis Court Oath* contains a short double-columned poem, "To The Same Degree" (TCO 86), which also served as a formal diagram for "Litany."

9. Ashbery is a practicing Episcopalian. For his use of the Litany service in "Litany," see Mutlu Konuk Blasing, *American Poetry: The Rhetoric of Its Forms* (New Haven: Yale UP, 1987) 208–9.

10. Conversation, Feb. 1993.

11. In a marginal note beside the peculiar line break, appearing in the typescript as "*accept- / ed*" (AWK 67), Ashbery wrote, "2 lines—no cap. in '-ed'" At some point the printers must have undone Ashbery's sole exception to the rule of capitalized margins in "Litany."

12. Stitt 50.

13. Harold Bloom, "Transumption: Towards a Diachronic Rhetoric (Blanks, Leaves, Cries)," in *The Breaking of the Vessels* (Chicago: Chicago UP, 1982), 78. Regrettably, Bloom omits Dickinson from his essay.

14. Jackson 71. Derrida, a friend of the Yale school, is familiar with Ashbery's poetry. He attended the book party for *As We Know* at Gotham Book Mart, in fact, which Ashbery felt was "quite a coup" (conversation, Spring 1991). Though Derrida has never written on Ashbery, his son, Pierre Alféri, has translated "Self-Portrait in a Convex Mirror" into French.

15. Jacques Derrida, *Writing and Difference,* trans. Alan Bass (Chicago: Chicago UP, 1978) 292.

16. Jacques Derrida, *Glas,* trans. John P. Leavey and Richard Rand (Lincoln: Nebraska UP, 1986) 1.

17. This lyric was written before the AIDS virus was discovered.

18. Auden, *Forewords* 69–70.

19. Giacomo Leopardi, *Selected Prose and Poetry,* trans. Iris Origo and John Heath-Stubbs (New York: New American Library, 1966) 48.

20. Gangel 14.

21. Stitt 46–47.

22. Harold Bloom, Paul de Man, Jacques Derrida, Geoffrey Hartman, and J. Hillis Miller, *Deconstruction and Criticism* (New York: Continuum, 1979).

23. Interview with John Ashbery, *Morning Sentinel* (Skowhegan, Maine) 3 August 1970: 6.

24. John Keats, *The Poems of John Keats,* ed. Jack Stillinger (Cambridge: Harvard UP, 1978) 88–89. All citations of Keats's poetry are from this edition, cited hereafter in the text.

25. William James, *The Principles of Psychology* (Cambridge: Harvard UP, 1983) 238.

26. Most of the surviving typescripts of *As We Know* are dated. Poems dated "summer 1978" were identified as such at a reading at Harvard University, 9 Nov. 1978. Page numbers of poems are followed by their dates (month/day/year): 71 (8/31/78), 72 (sum. 78), 73 (sum. 78), 74 (6/20/78), 78 (sum. 78), 80 (sum. 78), 82 (sum. 78), 83 (originally "Seeing Is Believing," sum. 78), 85 (sum. 78), 86 (6/16/78), 87 (6/18/78), 88 (6/21/78), 89 (6/27/78), 90 (6/28/78), 91 (7/8/78), 92 (6/12/78), 93–96 (6/6/78), 97 (sum. 78), 99 (sum. 78), 100 (sum. 78), 102 (8/2/77, before "Litany"), 106 (6/2/78), 108 (7/20/78), 110 (1/16/78), 111 (8/22/78), 112 (9/11/78), 113 (9/13/78).

27. *Ploughshares* 4.1 (1977): 60–70.

28. Rec. 9 Nov. 1978, Lamont Library, Harvard University.

29. Remnick 61.

30. Remnick 60.

31. Conversation, Feb. 1993.

32. John Ashbery, "A Prisoner of His Own Fame?" *Newsweek* 23 May 1983: 72.

33. Reverdy, *Selected Poems* 99.

34. Bloom, *Agon* 274.

35. John Donne, *Selected Prose,* ed. Helen Gardner and Timothy Healy (Oxford: Clarendon, 1967) 101.

36. See two fine readings Perloff, *Poetic License:* 277–80, and Charles Altieri, "Ashbery as Love-Poet," *Verse* 8 (Spring 1991): 11–13.

37. Rec. 9 Nov. 1978, Lamont Library, Harvard University.


## 9. *Shadow Train*

1. Conversation, Spring 1990.

2. Koethe 184.

3. Following in chronological order are the dates of composition for the poems from *Shadow Train,* with page numbers in parentheses: 3/10 (41); 3/14 (40); 3/17 (42); 3/20 (43); 3/21 (44); 3/24 (46); 3/28 (33); 3/26 (10); 3/3 (47); 3/31 (6); 5/2 (49); 5/4 (11); 5/6 (12); 5/7 (1); 5/11 (45); 6/22 (8); 6/23 (13); 6/26 (4); 7/5 (14); 7/11 (15); 7/12 (16); 7/15 (17); 7/17 (18); 7/26 (48); 7/29 (3); 7/30 (19); 8/2 (20); 8/5 (21); 8/7 (7); 8/8 (39); 8/9 (22); 8/13 (23); 8/23 (24); 8/27 (25); 8/28 (26); 8/29 (27); 9/10 (28); 9/12 (32); 9/13 (29); 9/21 (31); 9/22 (34); 9/24 (30); 9/25 (35); 9/26 (36); 9/27 (37); 9/28 (5); 10/1 (38); 10/2 (2); 10/3 (9); 10/6 (50).

4. Jackson 75.

5. Compare Barbara Herrnstein Smith's notion of "terminal modification" in *Poetic Closure: A Study of How Poems End* (Chicago: Chicago UP, 1968) 53.

6. Jackson, 75–76.

7. John Ashbery, "Capital Gains," *New York* 3 Sept. 1979: 56.

8. John Ashbery, "Decoration Days," *New York* 2 July 1979: 51.

9. Koethe 182.

10. Giorgio de Chirico, "Mystery and Creation," *Theories of Modern Art,* ed. Herschel B. Chipp (Berkeley: California UP, 1971) 402.

11. John Ashbery, "Metaphysical Overtones," *New York* 11 Feb. 1980: 73.

12. Brooks, "The Language of Paradox," *Urn* 3–21.

13. The fable first appeared in the Latin of Odo of Sherrington; William Langland translated the moral fable in *Piers Plowman.* Though Ashbery has not read the later work, he is familiar with the fable.

14. Labrie 33.

15. Labrie 33. The actual heroine, in a series of mystery novels from the fifties and sixties by Marcia Miller, was Donna Parker. The name of Ashbery's heroine probably reworded the well-known writing utensil, the Parker Pen.


## 10. *A Wave*

1. *From the Country of Eight Islands: An Anthology of Japanese Poetry,* ed. and trans. Hiroaki Sato and Burton Watson (New York: Anchor, 1981). On the significance of the number 37, see Auden's foreword to *Some Trees:* "if an ambitious young poet dreams of the number 37, it may take him considerable reflection before he remembers that Shakespeare wrote thirty-seven plays" (13).

2. Sato 290.

3. Ben Jonson, *Ben Jonson's Plays and Masques,* ed. Robert M. Adams (New York: Norton, 1979) 357.

4. Roussel, *Locus Solus* 25.

5. Gangel 13–14.

6. John Ashbery, "Two For The Road," *New York* 28 July 1980: 53.

7. Jackson 72.

8. John Ashbery, "On Winter's Traces," *New York* 24 March 1980: 58.

9. Stitt 54.

10. Aristotle, *Aristotle's Theory of Poetry and Fine Art . . . in The Poetics,* trans. S. H. Butcher (New York: Dover, 1951) 23.

11. Vendler, *Music* 255.

12. Jorge Luis Borges, "The Wall and the Books," *Other Inquisitions,* trans. Ruth L. C. Simms (Austin: Texas UP, 1964) 3.

13. Borges 4.

14. Jackson 70.

15. Jackson 70; Borges 4.

16. Walter Pater, *Selected Writings of Walter Pater,* ed. Harold Bloom (New York: New American Library, 1974) 61.

17. Sommer 307. See Jonathan Monroe, "Idiom and Cliché in T. S. Eliot and John Ashbery," *Contemporary Literature* 31.1 (1989): 17–36.

18. John Ashbery, "Baroque Is Back," *New York* 11 August 1980: 54–55. See appendix for early drafts. "Landscape with Tobias and the Angel" was not filed with the drafts of "A Wave," but Ashbery agreed that it was the first version of the poem when I showed it to him.

19. Ashbery recalls naming "A Wave" after an ominous sign he saw on the Oregon coast at Oswego: "Caution: A Wave Can Wash You Over The Coast in A Calm Sea." Compare "a giant wave that picks itself up / Out of a calm sea" (W 81).

20. Lehman, "Pleasures" 86.

21. See Harold Rosenberg: "Painting, sculpture, drama, music, have been undergoing

a process of de-definition. . . . No one can say with assurance what a work of art is—or, more important, what is not a work of art." *The De-definition of Art* (Chicago: Chicago UP, 1972) 12.

22. Ashbery, "The Impossible" 252.

23. Proust, *Remembrance of Things Past* vol. 1, 47.

24. Ashbery and Koch 13.

25. William Empson, *Seven Types of Ambiguity,* 2nd ed. (1947; New York: New Directions, 1966) 3.

26. Stitt 46.

27. Rimbaud 213.

28. Bourdieu 60.

29. Lehman, "Pleasures" 86.

30. Ralph Waldo Emerson, *Selections from Ralph Waldo Emerson,* ed. Stephen E. Whicher (Boston: Houghton Mifflin, 1957) 451. All citations of Emerson's poetry are from this edition, cited hereafter in the text.

31. Ashbery's systemic awareness of ordinary things as ordinary owes to Bishop: "It is this continually renewed sense of discovering the strangeness, the unreality of our reality at the very moment of becoming conscious of it *as* reality, that is the great subject for Elizabeth Bishop." See Ashbery, "Second Presentation" 10.

## 11. *April Galleons*

1. The initial ten titles are given with their final position in parentheses: "A Mood of Quiet Beauty" (6), "Becalmed on Strange Waters" (33), "Riddle Me" (2), "Morning Jitters" (3), "Vetiver" (1), "A Snowball in Hell" (4), "Dreams of Adulthood" (5), "When half the time . . ." (7), "Finnish Rhapsody" (10), "Forgotten Sex" (11).

2. Charles Baudelaire, *Twenty Prose Poems,* trans. Michael Hamburger (San Francisco: City Lights, 1988) 33.

3. *The Oxford Book of Ballads* 292.

4. *The Oxford Book of Ballads* 140.

5. Henry Wadsworth Longfellow, *The Song of Hiawatha,* ed. Daniel Aaron (London: Dent, 1992) 20.

6. *Temblor: Contemporary Poets* (Spring 1987): 3–4; *The Ice Storm* (Madras & New York: Hanuman Books, 1987). I reviewed *April Galleons* in *Temblor* 7 (Spring 1988): 172–77.

7. Thomas Gray, *Gray and Collins: Poetical Works,* ed. Austin Lane Poole (London: Oxford UP, 1937) 87.

8. Henry David Thoreau, *A Week, Walden. . . ,* ed. Robert F. Sayre (New York: Library of America, 1985) 400.

## 12. *Flow Chart*

1. Ashbery had even toyed with the idea of combining *Flow Chart* with a group of short poems, which were gathered separately and published only a year later as *Hotel Lautréamont.* Conversation, April 1989.

2. Bloom and Losada 123.

3. Conversation, May 1991. Typescript page 33 is missing from *Flow Chart.* When I showed the gap (between "other mooted toys" and "or motion at a stranger," FC 66) to

Ashbery, he confirmed that a page must have been accidentally left out of the poem when it was transcribed into the computer. I have reproduced the missing text below, with italicized words representing handwritten revisions:

so long away from us it barely became time to think and they had fallen away;
whispering in the organ loft, after you had begun to tell it and now, nothing

could ever interrupt you. You were an impossible storm from space
bearing down on us and each individual's name was clearly marked on the serpent's

whitish flank. Oh not we too, and how did we too come to be in here?
So pleasant and eager were the first ~~foot~~steps

and even later in a rare descending moment
there was some strict mood that sustained you. Later, after all had been truly lost

for a long time, fragments of the monument's original intention surfaced,
were cleaned off, polished, and thought a wonder. Only on alternate days,

though, was the artifact then visible for the mind, a substance one partook of
until the next rot shut it down. Oh there were

brilliant chasms for the attention available even then. But as the slope flattened out
the higher we grew, in time a contentious stratum *like chalk*

came to soak up the forest of all we knew. We knew we were living there, but moving on
to a widest horizon where collective destinies sank like motes, and even the tonic

future was hollow, because suggestible; where dramas were played out as though on
a carpet
and were nothing the clear-eyed ever saw. Eventually, then, destiny comes to seem a
frank,

level extension of oneself, while nothing in the blue-green noon gleam casts a
shadow.
Later, the fits and starts are predictable, rude

awakenings redden every eye, but it's OK ~~because~~ *since* colloquial: remember how
grand was that
vernacular, how suited to living in. But now, look, the needle has plummeted

into something once again; there are barest chances for holding out
and another repulsive dream of a kitchen with handlebars offered to the grip

and an appendix that writes itself: "all was put away here, once, but as often,
men came to disturb the mounds, ~~thus~~ gravely insulting the local deities,

who, empowered thus, ~~wrecked~~ *wrought* their vengeance on all the land, out of proportion to the gravity
of the offence as it seemed then, yet this too was part of the plan:

nobody ever said it was going to be equable. What we did know was that it would
be gentle
in its unfolding, only ruthless after that, and that one's notion of "civilization," i.e.,

373

what we think we've got coming to us, would be rudely transformed, not shattered,
into a desolate plain whose unblinking design brings us low, parallel

to the lives of plants and insects we had never wondered about.
And lo, this makes you a caring member of your species. You can't see

any more, but that's all right; you are locked up in the original cipher
to be told as you are if an occasion ever arises, unless, trampled by demons, you
   return

to the condition of dust floating not disagreeably in middle airs where, at least,
you can never be separated from what drowned you some twenty days previously

4. Conversation, May 1991.

5. Gangel 10.

6. John Ashbery, "A Reminiscence," *Homage to Frank O'Hara,* ed. Bill Berkson and Joe LeSueur (1978; Bolinas, Cal.: Big Sky Books, 1988) 20.

7. Labrie 29.

8. John Ashbery, "Tales of the Hudson River Valley," *House & Garden* April 1992: 160–61.

9. Philippe Lejeune, *On Autobiography,* ed. Paul John Eakin, trans. Katherine Leary (Minneapolis: Minnesota UP, 1989) 3–30, 119–37.

10. Larry Rivers, *What Did I Do?* (New York: Harper Collins, 1992).

11. Conversation, May 1991.

12. Saint Augustine, *Confessions,* trans. R. S. Pine-Coffin (New York: Penguin, 1961) 209.

13. Smith 48. Not coincidentally, Smith's article contains the most detailed biographical summary of Ashbery's life yet published.

14. Osti 88–89.

15. Studs Terkel, *Division Street: America* (New York: Pantheon Books, 1967) xxiii.

16. Katharine Hepburn, *Me: Stories of My Life* (New York: Ballantine, 1991) 1–2.

17. Emerson's sentiment may have a particular resonance for Ashbery. When Ashbery was at Deerfield Academy, another student sent in two of his poems, "Poem" ("Though we seek always the known absolute") and "Lost Cove," under the assumed name, "Joel Michael Symington," to *Poetry,* and they were accepted. Ashbery recalls that "when I sent them the same poems a few months later the editors there naturally assumed that I was the plagiarist" (Stitt 33). Ashbery's first major poetry publication was thus under another name; he has never published either poem under his own.

18. Roland Barthes, *Roland Barthes by Roland Barthes,* trans. Richard Howard (New York: Farrar, Straus and Giroux, 1977), 36.

19. See Marjorie Perloff, "The Forest of Agony and Pleasure," *New York Times Book Review* 16 June 1991: 12; Mutlu Konuk Blasing, "The American Sublime, c. 1992: What Clothes Does One Wear?", *Michigan Quarterly Review* 31.3 (1992): 425–31.

20. Smith 52.

21. Ronald Reagan, *Ronald Reagan: An American Life* (New York: Simon and Schuster, 1990) 726.

22. Barthes, *Barthes* 188. I have altered Howard's translation somewhat to emphasize the discursive echoes.

23. Lyn Hejinian, *My Life* (1980; Los Angeles: Sun & Moon, 1987) 13.

24. Ashbery's serendipitous antischolasticism is evident elsewhere in *Flow Chart.* The

phrase *"and roam at will, timeless"* (FC 53) varies Richard Sieburth's translation of Friedrich Hölderlin's "Tinian" rather than Hölderlin's German. See Friedrich Hölderlin, *Hymns and Fragments,* trans. Richard Sieburth (Princeton: Princeton UP, 1984) 181.

25. Algernon Charles Swinburne, *The Complete Works,* ed. Sir Edmund Gosse and Thomas Wise, vol. 3 (London: Heinemann, 1925) 37.

26. As quoted in *The Nation* 8 May 1967: 578.

27. Letter to *The Nation* 29 May 1967: 692. For a fuller account, see my chapter on *The Double Dream of Spring.*

28. Samuel Johnson, *Poems,* ed. E. L. McAdam, Jr. (New Haven: Yale UP, 1964) 102. Ashbery used another line from Johnson's "Vanity," "Where then shall Hope and Fear their objects find?," to begin "An Additional Poem" (TCO 44).

29. See Michel Beaujour, "The Places of the Return," in his *Poetics of the Literary Self-Portrait,* trans. Yara Milos (1980; New York: New York UP, 1991) 139–63.

30. Russell Baker, *Growing Up* (New York: New American Library, 1983) 278.

31. Northrop Frye, *Anatomy of Criticism: Four Essays* (Princeton: Princeton UP, 1957) 18.

32. See Ovid, *Metamorphoses* (7.20–21). Ashbery quotes Ovid's Latin tag the ordinary reader's way, from Roget's Thesaurus.

33. Charles Olson, "Projective Verse," *The New American Poetry: 1945–1960,* ed. Donald M. Allen (New York: Grove Press, 1960) 390.

34. Stephen Yenser reminds me of "Herr Jakob Schmidt" in Kurt Weill's opera *Mahagonny,* written by Brecht.

35. Smith 52.

36. William Cowper, *Poetical Works,* ed. H. S. Milford, 4th ed. (London: Oxford UP, 1971) 432.

37. Jackson 70.

38. Benjamin Franklin, *The Autobiography* (New York: Library of America, 1990) 3.

39. Conversation, May 1991.

40. Walter Benjamin, "Fate and Character," *Reflections: Essays, Aphorisms, Autobiographical Writings,* ed. Peter Demetz, trans. Edmund Jephcott (New York: Harcourt Brace Jovanovich, 1979) 309.

41. Paul de Man, "Autobiography As De-Facement," *The Rhetoric of Romanticism* (New York: Columbia UP, 1984), 71.

42. Augustine 209.

43. Jean-Jacques Rousseau, *The Confessions,* trans. J. M. Cohen (New York: Penguin, 1953) 17.

44. John Stuart Mill, "What Is Poetry?" *Essays on Poetry,* ed. F. P. Sharpless (Columbia: South Carolina UP, 1976) 12.

45. Alfred Lord Tennyson, *Tennyson: A Selected Edition,* ed. Christopher Ricks (Berkeley: California UP, 1989) 509.

46. See Michel Foucault, *Discipline and Punish: The Birth of the Prison,* trans. Alan Sheridan (New York: Vintage, 1979) 195–228.

47. Thomas Lovell Beddoes, *The Works of Thomas Lovell Beddoes,* ed. H. W. Donner (London: Oxford UP, 1935) 111.

48. Lee Iacocca, *Iacocca: An Autobiography* (New York: Bantam, 1984) 366.

## Appendix

1. Stitt 53.

# Index

381